ON THE BEATEN TRACK
A HISTORY OF
STANSTED MOUNTFITCHET

Peter Sanders

© 2016 Peter Sanders

ISBN 978-0-9955544-0-5

All rights reserved.
No part of this publication may be reproduced in any form without
the prior permission of Peter Sanders.

Published by the Stansted Mountfitchet Local History Society 2016

To the members of the
Stansted Mountfitchet Local History Society
in thanks for their encouragement, help and inspiration

CONTENTS

Acknowledgements vii
Preface viii
List of maps ix
List of illustrations ix
Abbreviations xii

PART I	INTRODUCTION	
Chapter 1	Stansted Mountfitchet	3
Chapter 2	Sources	13

PART II	FROM PREHISTORY TO THE MIDDLE AGES	
Chapter 3	Stansted before the Normans: the archaeological record	21
Chapter 4	The Domesday Book and the Montfichets	31
Chapter 5	Plague and the Peasants' Revolt	39

PART III	FROM THE REFORMATION TO THE NAPOLEONIC WARS	
Chapter 6	The Reformation	47
Chapter 7	Sir Thomas Myddelton	53
Chapter 8	The Civil War	61
Chapter 9	The aftermath of the Civil War	71
Chapter 10	The Heaths	77
Chapter 11	Population, growth and prosperity	81
Chapter 12	The Quarter Sessions and crime	93
Chapter 13	The church courts and morality	97
Chapter 14	The parish vestry and poverty	101
Chapter 15	The wars with France	111

PART IV	FROM THE NAPOLEONIC WARS TO WORLD WAR I	
Chapter 16	The farm labourers' 'riot' of 1834	117
Chapter 17	The new Poor Law	123
Chapter 18	Arson, the 'revolt of the field' and emigration	129
Chapter 19	Friendly societies, clubs and almshouses	137
Chapter 20	'Such a prosperous village'	145

Chapter 21	'A number of rich gentlemen': the Fuller-Maitlands 157
Chapter 22	More 'rich gentlemen' 165
Chapter 23	The elections of 1830 and 1831 177
Chapter 24	Radical Stansted 181
Chapter 25	The Boer War. 187
Chapter 26	Not so radical Stansted 191
Chapter 27	The churches: the Independent scandal of 1822 195
Chapter 28	The churches: Anglican and Nonconformist, high and low 201
Chapter 29	The schools 213
Chapter 30	From education to entertainment. 223
Chapter 31	Sport 235
Chapter 32	Crime 243

PART V:	MODERN TIMES
Chapter 33	The First World War 251
Chapter 34	Between the wars: the decline of the gentry, politics and economic depression. 263
Chapter 35	Between the wars: local government. 275
Chapter 36	Between the wars: religious and social 279
Chapter 37	The Second World War 293
Epilogue	Stansted since 1945 307
Appendix	Stansted Airport. 313

Sources 319

Index. 327

ACKNOWLEDGEMENTS

The Stansted Mountfitchet Local History Society was formed in 1987. As well as being a great success in its declared aim to stimulate interest in local history, it has been one of the friendliest and most enjoyable societies to which I have belonged. This book, which would not have been written without the support and encouragement of its members, is dedicated to them.

I am particularly grateful to Jenny Allaway for allowing me to use her excellent thesis on the Gilbeys, the Golds and the Blyths; to Roger Barrett for sharing with me his research on the Fuller-Maitlands; to Paul Embleton and Ken McDonald for their help with the illustrations; to Richard Gibson and John Morgan for information about their finds as metal detectorists; to Frances and Toby Lyons for making available documents and maps relating to Bentfield Bury manor and the Goslings; to Ralph Phillips for his work on the railway, the Methodist Church and the Croasdailes; to Roger Plumb for drawing to my attention the documents relating to the funeral of Sir Thomas Myddelton; and to Patrick Streeter for information about the Blyths and their various doings in Africa. I have also been helped by the work of historians in the villages around, in particular by Jacky Cooper at Clavering and Anthony Tuck and his fellow researchers at Newport. At all the libraries and archives I have used the staff have given every help possible, but I mention especially the staff of the Essex Record Office in Chelmsford, Zofia Everett of the Saffron Walden branch of that office, and Martyn Everett of the Victorian Studies Centre in Saffron Walden.

I am grateful to those institutions and persons who have given their permission to reproduce images in their collections and whose names are given under the List of Illustrations below. I owe a special debt of gratitude, however, to Louise Barker, Lesley Lister and Tim Sanders for their permission to use the photographs collected by their father, Irving Sanders.

Nick Crawley's artwork and design have been invaluable, and I am grateful to those whose financial support has made this publication possible, namely Roger Barrett, Alan Dean, Paul Embleton, Toby and Frances Lyons, Ray Rogers, Geoffrey Sell, the Stansted Mountfitchet Baron's Association, the Stort Valley Rotary Club, the Uttlesford District Council and James and Daphne Wallace-Jarvis.

PREFACE

I began this book for the simple reason that there was no written history of Stansted and the need for such a history was widely felt. As I went on I quickly realised that the whole concept of a parish history was problematic. What should be included, what excluded? I came to the obvious conclusion that it all depended on what sort of history the author was trying to write.

I have adopted two broad principles. First, while trying to write an account that is coherent and comprehensive, I have concentrated on those aspects of the village's history that I have found interesting or important, whether as narratives or analyses of change, and I have not hesitated to explore them in detail in the hope, and indeed the belief, that others too will find them interesting or important. This of course is a matter of subjective judgement, but it is a subjective judgement that has been informed by talks and discussions in the Local History Society over a period of almost 30 years. Secondly, and not unrelatedly, I have tried to place what was happening in the parish in a wider context. Throughout their history the people of Stansted have been involved in developments and disputes reaching far beyond their parochial community, and what was happening in the parish cannot be understood in isolation.

In the particular case of Stansted, however, the historian has to cross the parish boundary in almost a literal sense. The name Stansted is firmly linked in the public mind with Stansted Airport. The WW2 American airbase on the site fell largely within the parish of Stansted, but the new airport has taken in not just the old airbase, but also an extensive area of the neighbouring parish of Takeley. The airport terminal itself falls within Takeley.

For this reason the archaeological investigation that was carried out before the airport was expanded to its present size covered parts of both Stansted and Takeley. Since most of the findings pre-dated the establishment of parishes and parish boundaries it makes sense to look at all of them, even if some of them lay outside the present parish of Stansted. Similarly it makes sense to look at the history of Stansted Airport as a whole rather than to attempt the impossible task of examining only that part of it which falls within Stansted. It should be borne in mind, however, that these parts of the book - the archaeological findings related to the airport and the history of the airport - belong as much to Takeley as to Stansted.

I have stopped my main narrative at 1945, covering the last 70 years in a brief epilogue. To have dealt with this period on the same scale as previous periods would have made a long book dauntingly longer. The only exception to this is an account of the development of the airport – a major theme that I could not possibly have ignored. I hope, however, that this book will be an inspiration for other studies and in this way become the start of a living and growing history.

LIST OF MAPS

1. Stansted Mountfitchet in 1777. 3
2. Stansted Mountfitchet in its wider setting today. 4
3. Stansted Mountfitchet today: the parish. 5
4. Stansted Mountfitchet today: the centre of the parish. 6
5. Roman roads. 25
6. Part of Bentfield Green Farm in 1804. 84
7. Bentfield Mill Farm in 1815. 85
8. The American airbase in WW2. 302

LIST OF ILLUSTRATIONS

Except where otherwise indicated photographs, including postcards, have been supplied by members of the Stansted Mountfitchet Local History Society. ISC is Irving Sanders's Collection. The graph of Stansted's population (28) was prepared by the author with help from Nick Crawley.

1. Lower Street. 7
2. Chapel Hill, looking westwards. 7
3. Chapel Hill, looking eastwards. 8
4. Burton End. 8
5. Village sign. 9
6. The Cambridge Road. 9
7. Joseph Green. *Anon (n.d.), Joseph Joshua Green. A Life Sketch.* 15
8. Irving Sanders. *ISC.* 16
9. John Wilkins. *Wilkins (1892), The Autobiography of an English Gamekeeper.* 16
10. Red tessellated floor, c.300 AD. *By courtesy of the Saffron Walden Museum.* 21
11. Iron Age settlement. *Brooks and Bedwin (1989), Archaeology at the Airport. By courtesy of the Essex County Council.* 24
12. Onyx ring-stone of Diomedes carrying off the Palladium from Troy. *Brooks and Bedwin (1989), Archaeology at the Airport. By courtesy of the Essex County Council.* 25
13. Aerial view of the castle. *By courtesy of Alan Goldsmith.* 34
14. Interior of St Mary's Church. 36
15. St Mary's south doorway. 37
16. St Mary's north doorway. 37
17. Effigy of Roger de Lancaster. *By courtesy of Graham Field, Medieval Combat Society.* 40
18. Brass commemorating Robert de Bokkyngg. *By courtesy of Graham Field, Medieval Combat Society.* 40
19. Wayside chapel. *ISC.* 43
20. Sir Thomas Myddelton. *By courtesy of the Guildhall Art Gallery.* 53

21	Sir Thomas Myddelton's monument in St. Mary's Church.	57
22	Stansted Hall c.1770. *Muilman (1770), New and Complete History of Essex.*	57
23	Hester Salusbury's monument in St. Mary's Church.	58
24	Part of the list of vicars in St. Mary's Church.	67
25	The Independent Chapel on Chapel Hill, erected in 1698. *By courtesy of the Essex Record Office.*	73
26	The Friends Meeting House, erected in 1703. *ISC.*	74
27	St. Mary's Church, 1756. *By courtesy of the Essex Record Office.*	79
28	Graph of Stansted's population.	81
29	The barn at Bentfield Bury farm.	82
30	The windmill.	83
31	The Bell. *Harper (1904), The Newmarket, Bury, Thetford and Cromer Road.*	89
32	The Three Colts.	90
33	The White Bear. *Harper (1904), The Newmarket, Bury, Thetford and Cromer Road.*	90
34	The Rose and Crown.	91
35	The old workhouse. *By courtesy of the Essex Record Office.*	107
36	Notice of District Ploughing Match, 1834. *By courtesy of the Saffron Walden Museum.*	120
37	'The Home of the Rick-Burner'. *John Leech, Punch 1844.*	130
38	The Order of Ancient Shepherds outside the Barley Mow, c.1900. *ISC.*	138
39	Procession in Lower Street led by Ethelbert Goodchild, 1919. *ISC.*	139
40	The Fuller Almshouses, c.1913.	143
41	The Central Hall, c.1908.	145
42	Stansted railway station, 1916.	147
43	The visitors at the pumping station, 1907. *ISC.*	152
44	Ebenezer Fuller-Maitland. *Percy Noble (1905), Park Place: a history.*	158
45	Stansted House, c.1920.	159
46	The Recreation Ground, 1916.	159
47	Stansted Hall, now the Arthur Findlay College. *By courtesy of the Spiritualists' National Union.*	160
48	The second William Fuller-Maitland.	161
49	Walter Gilbey. *Illustrated London News, 21 December 1889.*	165
50	Henry Parry Gilbey. *Bishop's Stortford and District Local History Society.*	165
51	Hargrave House.	165
52	Blythwood House.	166
53	The Prince of Wales at Blythwood Dairy, 1892. *ISC.*	168
54	Charles Gold, 1895. *HEO, 17 July 1895.*	169
55	St. John's Church.	170
56	Green's Stores, 1840. *ISC.*	171
57	Green's Stores after renovation in 1877/78. *ISC.*	171
58	Herbert Gardner. *Sketch by Spy in Vanity Fair, 1886.*	182
59	The Independents' New Meeting House, Silver Street, later the Sunday Schoolroom, 1917. *ISC.*	200

60	The Primitive Methodist Church.	201
61	Daniel Davies. *By courtesy of the Stansted Free Church.*	203
62	Eustace Long. *By courtesy of the Stansted Free Church.*	203
63	Arthur Cook. *By courtesy of the Stansted Free Church.*	203
64	The Stansted Free Church.	204
65	Thomas Luard. *By courtesy of St. Mary's Church.*	205
66	St. Mary's Church.	205
67	Alexander McKinney. *By courtesy of St. Mary's Church.*	206
68	George Valentine. *By courtesy of St. Mary's Church.*	209
69	George Oakshott. *By courtesy of St. Mary's Church.*	210
70	Augustus Manley Winter. *By courtesy of St. Mary's Church.*	210
71	British School infants, c.1905.	221
72	Golden Jubilee committee, 1887. *ISC.*	230
73	Diamond Jubilee committee, 1897. *ISC.*	231
74	Stansted's football team, 1897. *ISC.*	237
75	Stansted's cricket team. *ISC.*	240
76	WW1 volunteers in Lower Street. *ISC.*	252
77	The parish fire engine.	256
78	Soldiers billeted in the village in WW1 with Mrs. Dixon and her family.	259
79	Bentfield Hucks.	260
80	Arthur Findlay. *By courtesy of the Spiritualists' National Union.*	264
81	Gertrude Findlay. *By courtesy of the Spiritualists' National Union.*	264
82	Ethelbert Goodchild. *By courtesy of St. Mary's Church.*	279
83	Arthur Turberville. *By courtesy of St. Mary's Church.*	280
84	John Barrow. *By courtesy of St. Mary's Church.*	281
85	Marian Annetta Godefroy. *By courtesy of St. Mary's Church.*	281
86	Arthur Davies. *By courtesy of the Stansted Free Church.*	282
87	Sydney Pay. *By courtesy of the Stansted Free Church.*	282
88	Illingworth Jagger. *By courtesy of the Stansted Free Church.*	282
89	American airbase during WW2. *By courtesy of Stansted Airport.*	303
90	St. Theresa's Roman Catholic Church.	310
91	Forest Hall School. *By courtesy of Forest Hall School.*	311

ABBREVIATIONS

BL	British Library
CC	*Chelmsford Chronicle*
DNB	*Dictionary of National Biography*
EC	*Essex Chronicle*
ECC	*Essex County Chronicle*
ERO	Essex Record Office
FA	Framework Archaeology
HEO	*Herts and Essex Observer*
ISC	Irving Sanders's Collection
LMA	London Metropolitan Archives
NA	National Archives
SMLHS	Stansted Mountfitchet Local History Society
SMPM	*Stansted Mountfitchet Parish Magazine*
TEAS	*Transactions of the Essex Archaeological Society*
VCH	Victoria County History

PART I
INTRODUCTION

1: STANSTED MOUNTFITCHET

The Essex village of Stansted Mountfitchet, or Stansted as it is commonly known, lies about three miles north of the Hertfordshire town of Bishop's Stortford. According to the old milestone in the centre of the village it is 31 miles from London to the south and 23 miles from Cambridge to the north. With more than 4,000 acres it is one of the largest parishes in Essex. The landscape is varied and attractive, the rises and falls on the flinty chalk and gravels in the west giving way to flatter land on the boulder clay in the east. It was probably the flints that gave Stansted its Anglo-Saxon name, 'stony place'. The River Stort, no more than a stream at this stage, forms part of the parish's western boundary, while Stansted Brook, its tributary, runs from north to south through the centre. Today, with the exception of Stansted Airport, which has been built on the boulder clay, the parish consists mainly of good arable land.

Although it is generally referred to as a village, Stansted had its origins in four settlements and was often described in that way. They were the Street, low-lying and liable to be flooded by Stansted Brook; the Chapel, higher up to the west, named after a wayside chapel at the crossroads where the fountain now stands; Bentfield

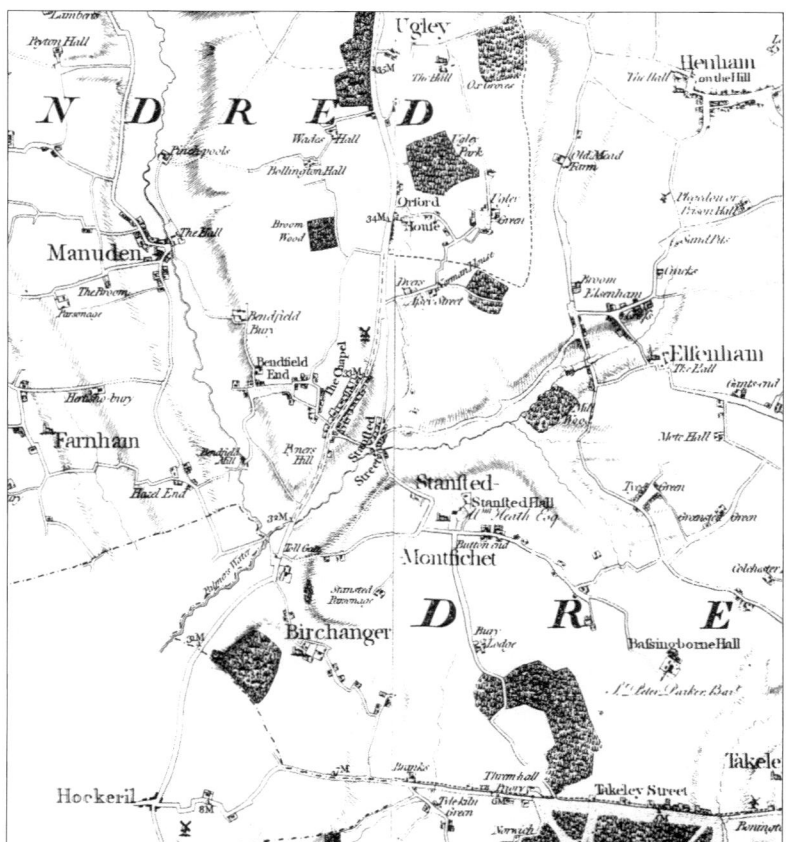

Map 1. Stansted Mountfitchet (Stansted Montfichet on the map). From Chapman and André's map of Essex, 1777. The four settlements of the Street, Burton End (Button End), Bentfield End (Bendfield End) and the Chapel are all shown. Stansted Hall is between the words Stansted and Montfichet.

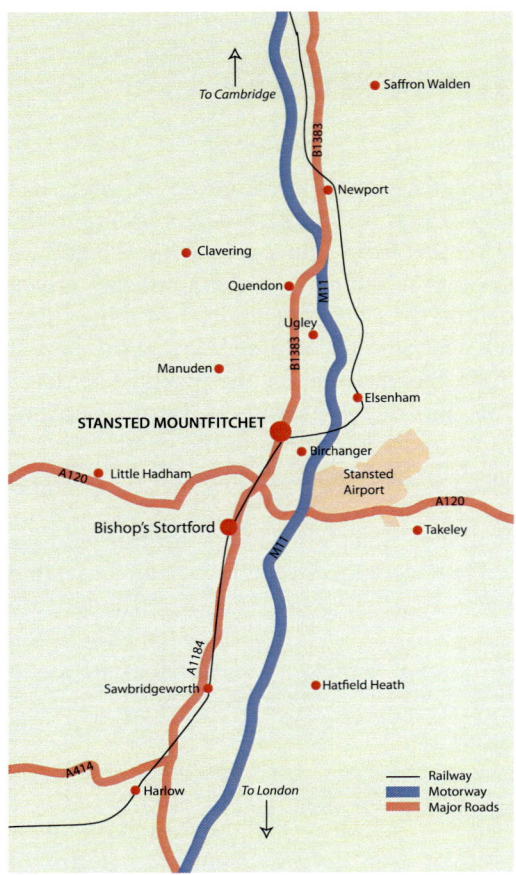

Map 2. Stansted Mountfitchet in its wider setting today.

End, further to the west; and Burton End to the south east. These four settlements were separated by fields, woods and orchards, some of which are still recalled in the names of the housing developments which have replaced them, such as Greenfields and Woodfields on either side of Chapel Hill. The present Stansted Hall, which was built by the Fuller-Maitlands in the Victorian period, is now a spiritualist college. It stands in its park on a hill between the Street and Burton End, and close to it is the church of St. Mary the Virgin. Because St. Mary's was so far from the main body of the population a second church, a chapel of ease, St. John's, was built on Chapel Hill and opened in 1889.

For much of Stansted's history there were two main manors in the parish, Stansted to the east and Bentfield Bury to the west. Both manors were usually held by the same family – at first the great Norman barons, the Gernons and the Montfichets, and then, after a period in which Stansted was divided, by the de Veres, the Earls of Oxford. In the seventeenth century came the Myddeltons and in the eighteenth the Heaths, both of whom had made their fortune in trade. In the nineteenth century Stansted was purchased by the Fuller-Maitlands, who also owned property elsewhere in Essex and had land in Buckinghamshire and Breconshire, while Bentfield Bury was purchased by the Goslings, a banking family, whose local base was in the neighbouring parish of Farnham. There was a third manor, Thremhall Priory, which was smaller, and which became part of the land of the Houblons, another banking family, who lived nearby at Great Hallingbury. By common consent in the nineteenth century it was the Fuller-Maitlands who were looked on as the squires of the village.

Today, as you approach the village from the south, on the old A11, now the B1383, you are confronted by a bristling array of signs and directions. The most striking is the village sign, the cartoon-like portrait of a mediaeval knight in full armour with a large shield bearing the device of three white chevrons on a red background. Above the portrait are the words Magna Carta and the date 1215.[1] The knight is Richard de Montfichet, whose family gave the village the second part of its name, and Magna Carta makes its unexpected appearance because Richard was one of the 25 barons who were chosen in 1215 to ensure

1: STANSTED MOUNTFITCHET

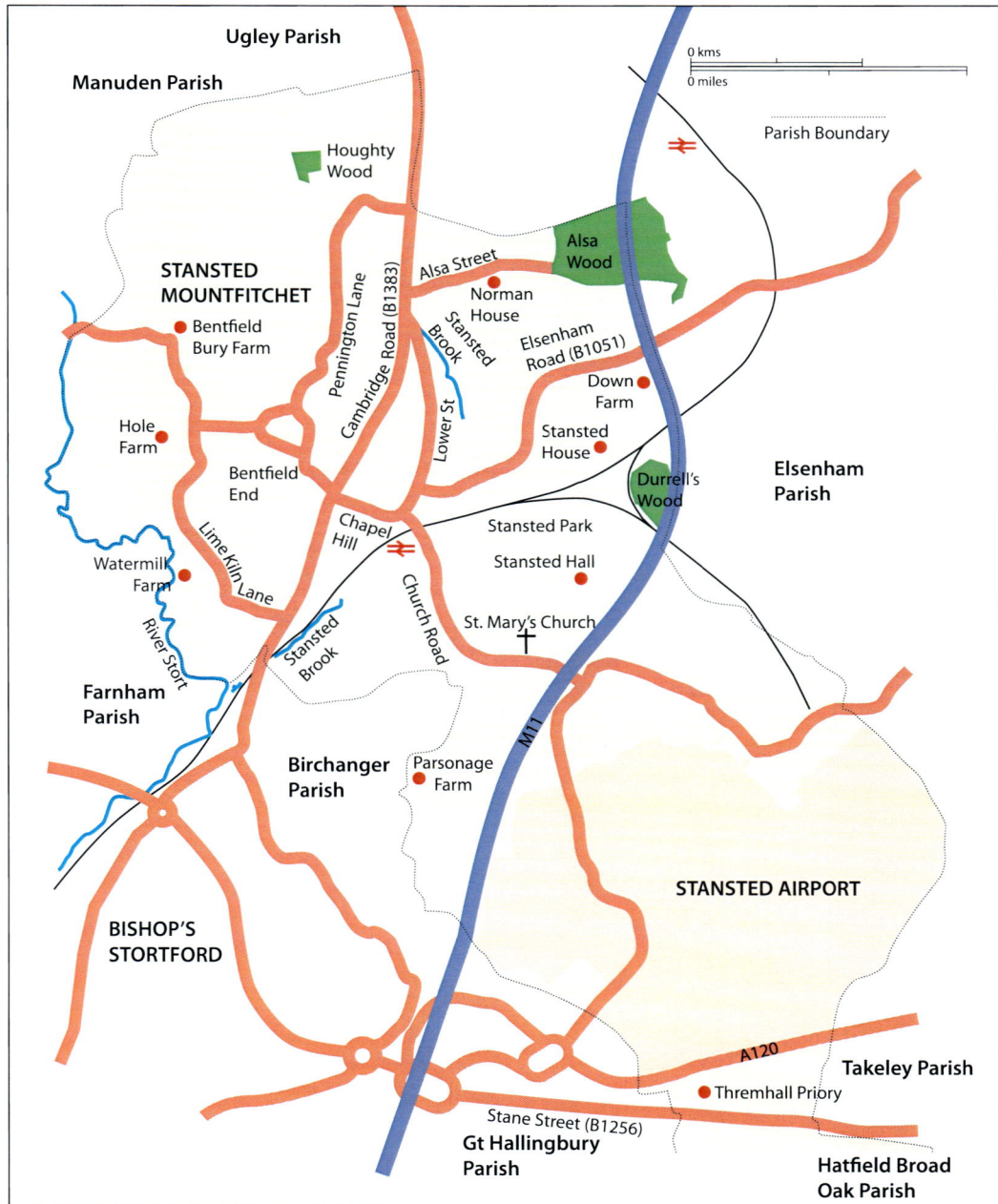

Map 3. The parish of Stansted Mountfitchet today.

that King John observed the terms of that historic document.

Another sign points you towards 'Mountfitchet Castle 1066', a bold title that probably raises too many expectations because the castle was probably built somewhat later than

1: STANSTED MOUNTFITCHET

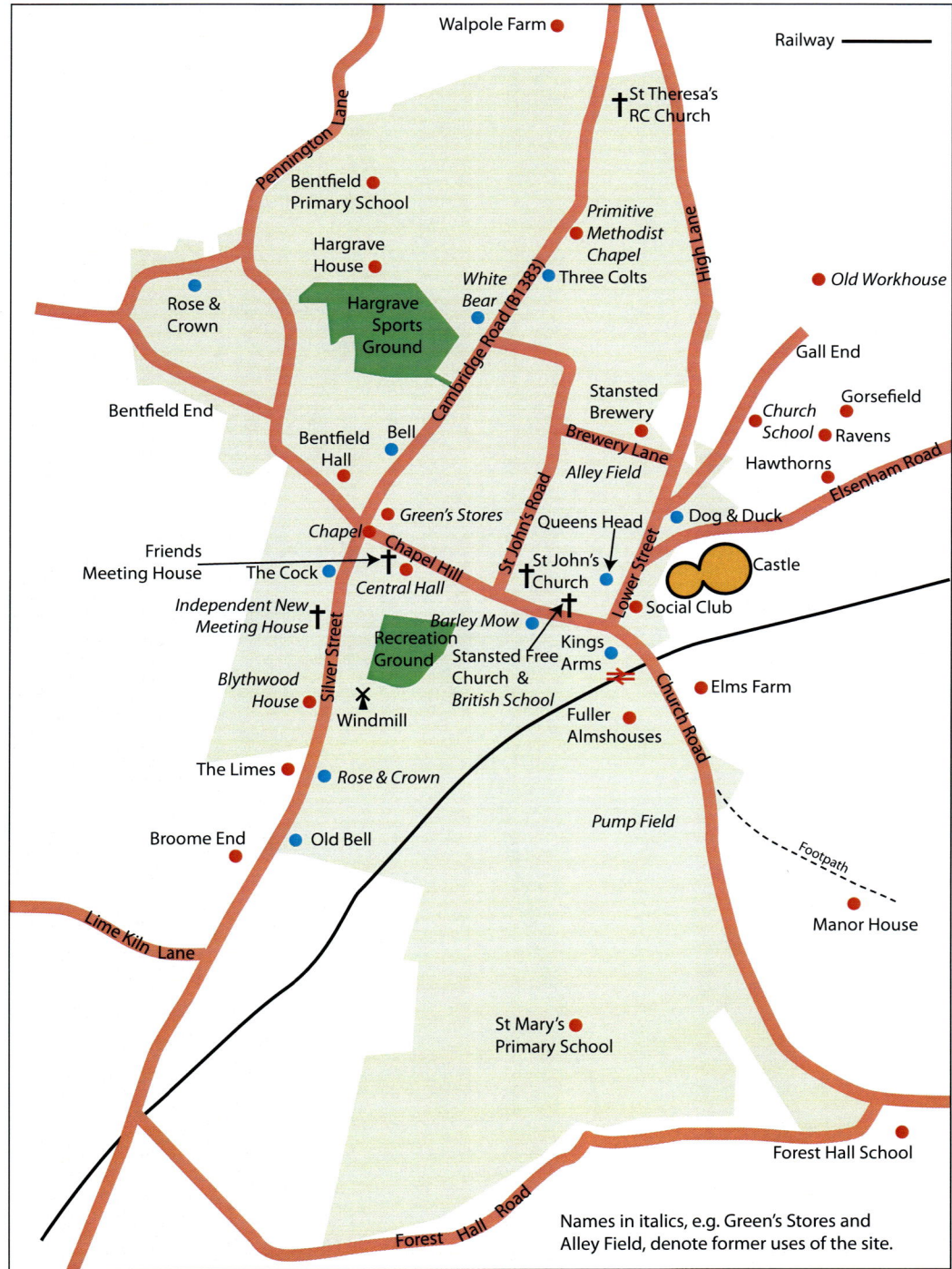

Map 4. The core of the village today.

1: STANSTED MOUNTFITCHET

1. Lower Street in the 1960s.

1066 and it was subsequently destroyed by King John. All that remains of it are two mounds of earth and a block of flinty stonework sticking up like a last decaying tooth. A local entrepreneur, however, has transformed this unpromising site into a successful tourist attraction. A 'Norman village' has been constructed inside a wooden palisade, where you can see Richard de Montfichet seated with his guests in his hall and hear him tell of his struggles with King John, where you can watch the village craftsmen plying their trades, and where you can feed deer, sheep, goats and chickens as they roam over the mounds. In the Edwardian period the Castle Hills, as they were known, were used as part of a golf course.

2. Chapel Hill in the 1950s, looking upwards and westwards from Lower Street.

1: STANSTED MOUNTFITCHET

3. Chapel Hill looking downwards and eastwards, c.1915. The slope opposite is part of the grounds of Stansted Hall.

4. Burton End c.1908. This view is much the same today, but Stansted Airport now lies beyond the cottages and the M11 in a cutting behind the trees.

1: STANSTED MOUNTFITCHET

5. Village sign in the south, on the B1383, showing the second Richard de Montfichet in full armour.

As you approach the village on the same road from the north another sign directs you to Stansted Airport. With a throughput in 2015 of 22.6 million passenger movements, this is London's third airport, Heathrow and Gatwick being the first two. Over the past 50 years proposals and plans have been made to extend it beyond its existing runway to become as large as Heathrow or even larger, a development that has been fiercely resisted, so far successfully, by most of the local population.

In one important way, however, the airport's development is consistent with Stansted's history, for the village has always stood on major lines of travel and communication. The Roman road of Stane Street ran along its southern boundary, where Thremhall Priory was established later. In the reign of Charles II the Great Newmarket Road, as it was then called, was improved and developed, since the King insisted on travelling quickly and comfortably between his palaces in London and his stables in Newmarket. Going north it ran close to Saffron Walden, with a branch leading off to Cambridge on the way, and it was also one of the routes between London and Norwich. Going south it ran through Hockerill, which was part of Bishop's Stortford. Too important for parish administration, it was made a turnpike road in 1744 and soon became one of the finest roads in the country.[2] It is now known as the Cambridge Road, the B1383. In 1845 came the railway, served by the station called Stansted at first, in spite of pressure from

6. The Cambridge Road c.1913.

the local historian, Joseph Green, to have it renamed as Stansted Mountfitchet - a change that came about at last in 1990 to avoid confusion with the station at the airport. The M11 was extended northwards to Stump Cross in 1979, relieving traffic on the Cambridge Road but cutting a wide and noisy swathe through Alsa Wood and the fields towards the east. Finally came the airport, developed on the site of an American airbase in WW2.

Its situation on these lines of travel and communication and its proximity to London made Stansted less isolated and more prosperous than many other rural communities. In or around 1340 the Prior and Canons of Thremhall Priory asked for more funds, partly because of the expense involved in having to give hospitality to so many travellers on Stane Street.[3] Four centuries later inns flourished along the Great Newmarket Road, and the villagers would gawp at the gentry's finery when they stopped to take refreshment on their way to the Newmarket races. In 1781 the traveller George Byng observed how, at the humblest level, the turnpike roads in general had 'imported London manners' into the country, so that even the milkmaids had 'the dress and looks of Strand misses'.[4] In the latter part of the 19th century, during the agricultural depression, while many of the villages around went into decline, Stansted's population went up from 1,719 in 1851 to 2,208 in 1901, an increase that was mainly due to its position on the railway. It was convenient for travelling to London, and during this period it was commonly described in the local press as a thriving and flourishing village.

There were other ways in which the people of Stansted were exposed to the winds of the wider world. Each week they might go to the market town of Bishop's Stortford, where their farmers could sell their wheat and barley and where, after 1769, they could purchase goods brought up the Stort Navigation from London, such as coal, which up to this time had to be carted in and only the well-to-do could afford it, and slate, which came to replace the local tiles and thatch. Those villagers who went to school would be given at least an elementary understanding and knowledge of life beyond the parish boundaries, and at church they were indoctrinated in the Christian religion and buffeted from time to time by the shocks of religious change. Men from Stansted fought in the retinues of their manorial lords, for Parliament in the Civil War, and for their country in the wars against France, in the Boer War and in two World Wars. Throughout the nineteenth and twentieth centuries there has been emigration abroad, mainly to America and Australia.

Stansted's elites moved in wider circles. Robert Gernon, the first Norman lord of Stansted, had taken part in William the Conqueror's invasion and was rewarded with extensive landholdings, mainly in the east of the country. His successors, the Montfichets, played a leading part in the councils of the nation, helping to curb King John but being punished for this by the destruction of their castle. The Myddeltons, the manorial lords in the 17th century, had made their money in trade and were prominent Parliamentarians in the Civil War. The Heaths, who took over from the Myddeltons in the 18th century, were closely associated with the East India Company. The Fuller-Maitlands, who took over from the Heaths, helped to found a strong Liberal tradition in the area - at the turn of the 19th and 20th centuries Stansted was known as 'radical Stansted' - an undertaking in which they were supported by the Gilbeys, the Golds and the Blyths, the wealthy wine merchants who had settled in the village and nearby. One of the Fuller-Maitlands was a pioneering collector of early Italian art and his paintings now form an important part of the holdings of the National Gallery, while one of the Blyths supported ground-breaking research into tuberculosis and was elevated to the peerage.

Stansted became the most populous village in this part of Essex, and it was therefore able to sustain institutions and initiatives that were beyond the reach of smaller communities. Indeed it developed certain features that were usually associated with towns – an economy that was diversified beyond agriculture and related trades, for example, and, in the Victorian period, the establishment of a Literary Institution and a magistrates' court. But it was still more commonly called a village and in terms of population alone it always fell short of Bishop's Stortford or Saffron Walden.

It is impossible to capture the entire history of an entire community in a single sweep. Loyalties were engaged at several different levels. For many villagers for most of the time it was the local community that above all absorbed their energies and engaged their interests. They were aware of more distant horizons, but the foreground was dominated by the manor and then the parish, by the squire and the vicar, the churchwardens and the overseers of the poor. For many practical purposes neighbourly obligations were defined by the manor and the parish. The supreme expression of this was the working of the old Poor Law, under which the parish conducted itself in much the same way as a state today, even to the extent of exercising its own immigration control, making sure that no newcomer was allowed to settle if he or she seemed likely to become a burden on the rates.

County allegiance also played a part. Although its trading and business links were mainly with Bishop's Stortford and therefore with Hertfordshire, for purposes of administration, and in particular for elections and the administration of justice, Stansted looked more to Saffron Walden and Essex. Sentiment ran high. When the new Poor Law was passed in 1834 Stansted and nine other Essex parishes were made part of the Bishop's Stortford Union, but when in 1888, and again in 1904, it was proposed that they should therefore be transferred from Essex to Hertfordshire this provoked an outcry and the boundary remained unchanged.

The dominant overall impression, however, is not one of narrow parochialism, still less of rural somnolence and lethargy, but of lively engagement with the wider world, whether economically, socially, religiously or politically. One of the strongest appeals of Stansted's history derives from the part which its people played, not just in their local community, but in the wider communities of the church, the county and the country, and from the ways in which wider developments and events influenced their actions and changed their lives. Stansted was the least parochial of rural parishes. Unlike many of the villages around it was very much on the beaten track.

---

[1] More correctly the chevrons should have been gold against a red background.

[2] Bishop's Stortford and District Local History Society (1973: 56).

[3] ERO, D/DWv/T16, Prior and Canons of Thremhall Priory to Earl of Oxford; Edwards (1958: 16).

[4] Andrews (1954: 33).

2: SOURCES

The extent to which any local history can be written obviously depends on what evidence is available - for the earliest periods, what the pattern of the countryside can tell us and what material evidence has been unearthed by the archaeologists, and for the later periods, additionally, what records have survived the depredations of time and what we can learn from oral tradition.

Stansted is embedded in what Oliver Rackham called Ancient Countryside, which he defined as 'districts whose fields, woods, roads, etc. date predominantly from before A.D. 1700',[1] as distinct from the 'Planned Countryside' of enclosure, the land of straight roads and rectangular fields. So Stansted is in the countryside of hamlets, great barns and ancient woods, of hollow ways and winding footpaths lined by hedgerows centuries old.[2] Apart from the Roman road of Stane Street and the M11 there is hardly a straight road or footpath in the parish. And this 'ancient countryside' is studded with ancient buildings: Uttlesford, of which Stansted forms a part, is one of only two local authority districts in the country with more than 2,000 listed buildings dating from before 1700. In Stansted itself there are 129 listed buildings. In the absence of local stone most of them are timber-framed or built of brick, with roofs that are thatched or tiled.

Our knowledge of the area in the early periods of human settlement is strikingly uneven. In the 1980s and 1990s BAA (formerly the British Airports Authority) was obliged to commission archaeological work in the fields, woods and lanes that it would soon be obliterating for the extension of its airport. The results were surprisingly rich and varied and led to a substantial revision of our beliefs about early settlements on the boulder clay in the east. As yet, however, we know very little about the settlements on the gravels and the chalk in the west.

For later periods, on the whole, we are lucky, though there is one disastrous gap in our evidence. The records of Stansted, the largest manor in the parish, were kept by solicitors, Bird and Bird, at their offices in Grays Inn in London. When the Inn was destroyed by bombing in 1941 a vital part of Stansted's history went up in the flames, 'destroyed by enemy action'. The records of the other two manors are for the most part safely housed in the Essex Record Office in Chelmsford, but the Bentfield Bury records go back only to 1649, and the records of Thremhall Priory, which begin in 1357, are limited in the information they can give us, since this was the smallest manor. For the mediaeval period, therefore, the period for which manorial records are most useful, we have little evidence at the local level. There are of course other records for this period, such as the Domesday Book and the Subsidy Rolls, and Robert Gernon, the Montfichets and the de Veres played their parts on the wider stage. But any history of mediaeval Stansted is bound to be thin.

For the post-mediaeval period our evidence is encouragingly detailed. The parish records that survive are varied and extensive. The registers of baptisms, marriages and burials date from 1558, when Queen Elizabeth I came to the throne, the vestry minutes from 1642, and the accounts of the overseers of the poor from 1744, when proper records were first required. There are some rate books dating from 1750, and some militia records from the Revolutionary and Napoleonic Wars. The most remarkable survivals are the vicar's tithe books, which begin in 1682 and end in 1818. They record the small tithes given to the vicar, and so we have a detailed account for over a hundred years of the fruit and vegetables that were grown and the animals that were kept.

But there have been losses over time at the parish level too. In 1939 and 1941-4 Frank Reader, the assistant priest, wrote several series of articles in the parish magazine about documents that had been 'discovered in the Parish Chest at St. Mary's', among them a 'large quantity' of the churchwardens' accounts, arranged in bundles, from 1700 to 1836. After the war the contents of the chest were handed over to the Essex Record Office, but by then many of the documents mentioned by Reader had been lost: in particular, only two thin files of the churchwardens' records had survived. Perhaps the lost documents will reappear, but in the meantime we are thrown back on the information in the magazine.

At the village level there are also the records of the Independent Church, which tell of the dramatic conflict which tore it apart in 1822, and of later conflicts as well, and from 1860 onwards we have the minutely detailed log books of St. Mary's School.

There are occasional references to Stansted in early newspapers, notably the *Chelmsford Chronicle*,[3] and this trickle of evidence turns into a flood after 1861 with the founding of the *Herts and Essex Observer*, published in Bishop's Stortford. The affairs of Stansted, being the largest village close to Stortford, appear regularly and prominently and often at great length.

At the county level there are extensive records, the most important being those of the Quarter Sessions, including court judgements, poll books, and hearth tax and land tax assessments. From these we can tell which way the people of Stansted voted in elections, how many hearths they had in their houses in the late 17th century, and how much land they occupied. There are also extensive ecclesiastical records, some of them formerly in the Bishop of London's archives in the Guildhall Library, now in the London Metropolitan Archives. Stansted's parishioners make many appearances in the records of the diocesan courts, and also, from 1500 onwards, in the records of their wills. There are many other sources which Stansted shares with the rest of the country, notably the census records.

All these sources are of the type, or types, that one might expect to find for any parish. But for Stansted there are four further collections of evidence gathered over the years by people who have taken an interest in the history of the parish - by Joseph Green, who died in 1921; by Irving Sanders, who died in 1984; by members of the Stansted Mountfitchet Local History Society, who in the 1980s conducted interviews with the older inhabitants of the village; and finally by Glyn Warwick, who collected evidence about the men from Stansted who died or were wounded in the two world wars.

Joseph Joshua Green was born in Stansted in 1854, the second son of Joshua and Elizabeth Green. Joshua and his friend, James Marsh, were the owners of Stansted's largest shop, Green and Marsh, which became known as Joshua Green & Company after Marsh's death in 1871 and was said to sell 'everything from a pin to an elephant'. It had been founded in 1687, and when it was 200 years old Joseph dutifully wrote its history.

2: SOURCES

The Greens were Quakers, and Joseph held fast to the Quaker tradition. From his childhood, according to a brief biography published by the Quakers, 'Veneration and reverence were among his notable characteristics'. Educated at home, and later at Ackworth School and then Sidcot School, he developed a passion for making collections - fossils, birds' feathers, stamps, coins, and then early printed versions of the Bible and autographs. As expected, he went into the family business, but he was never entirely happy in the work, and in 1891, because of failing health, he gave up the world of commerce and he and his family left Stansted and moved to Hampstead Heath. In 1921, after several more moves, he died at Hastings at the age of 67.[4]

Green made a study of Quaker history, and wrote many articles for Quaker publications. For our purposes, however, what is most important is that while at Stansted he amassed a large collection of papers about the parish, some of it previously kept by his father. These papers have been placed in the Essex Record Office, originally in 40 boxes, and they are described in the ERO catalogue as 'Notes, transcripts and newspaper cuttings relating to the history of Stansted Mountfitchet and to social activities and trade in that parish from about 1850 to 1893, collected by Joshua and Joseph J. Green, grocers and provision merchants'. They make up an extraordinary range of material - genealogies of the leading families in the parish, posters and handbills advertising missionary meetings and property sales, notes and correspondence about the church bells and the parish boundaries, the Liberal Party and the Literary Institution, the pest house, the police, the postal service, the pound and the pump - and so we might go on. As well as this material in the ERO a few of Green's papers may be found in Friends House in London.

7. Joseph Green.

Green never wrote a history of Stansted, and he was generally referred to as an antiquarian and collector rather than a historian. Among his papers, however, there is the beginning, just nine pages, of what he called his autobiography, but what was turning out to be a lively and well written account of Stansted and its inhabitants. It begins with a description of the village, and then gives some account of the gentry of the parish. On the final page Green wrote: 'Before dismissing our account of the Fuller-Maitlands, mention must be made of some of their retainers. Amongst ...' That is the last word of Green's 'autobiography'. It is a great loss to Stansted's history that he did not go on.[5]

On the day that Joseph Green died, on 24 October 1921, Irving Sanders was born. Irving too came from a long-established Stansted family. Until his retirement in 1979 he worked as a surveyor draughtsman for British Rail, but he was also a parish councillor for many years, standing as an independent and serving for some time as chairman. In the best Victorian tradition he entertained social gatherings with 'humorous songs and monologues'.

Irving, like Joshua Green, compiled a collection of documents about Stansted, in part overlapping with Green's, but for the most part covering a later period, and also many valuable photographs of the village. He took an interest in the same subjects, such as the genealogies of the leading families, sales of property and the Literary Institution, and in other topics such as the railway, the Recreation Ground (which his own house fronted), the celebration of royal events and the Stansted Central Hall Company Limited. This collection, now kept by his family, adds substantially to our evidence, particularly for the 20th century. Irving was only 62 when he died in 1984. Perhaps he had been hoping to write a history of the village, but in the event his only publication of this nature was a brief ten pages produced for the parish in the 1950s.

8. Irving Sanders.

Neither Joshua Green nor Irving Sanders recorded much in the way of oral tradition. Green noted down the recollections of one old inhabitant in 1891, again, like his autobiography, a lively account of the village, making us regret that he did not do more work of this sort. In Irving Sanders's papers there are the boyhood reminiscences of a certain 'BWL', who appears to have been born around 1890. For the 20th century, however, this deficiency has been partly made up by members of the Stansted Mountfitchet Local History Society, who in the late 1980s recorded, either in notes or on tape, and sometimes at considerable length, about 40 of the older inhabitants, whose information in some cases went back to the Victorian period.[6] At the same time Glyn Warwick gathered material, including reminiscences and family letters, about the men who died or were wounded in the two world wars. In 2008 this was published as a book, *They Sleep in Heroes' Graves*.

Finally there is John Wilkins's *Autobiography of an English Gamekeeper*. Wilkins came to Stansted as a young man in 1843 to work as a gamekeeper for William Fuller-Maitland, and his reminiscences were published in 1892. They were edited by Arthur Byng and Stephen Stephens, who claimed that while the smooth style was theirs the rough substance was Wilkins's - or, to use their metaphor, while the writing was that of Jacob the words were those of Esau.[7] They also claimed that Wilkins was 'the first of his profession to publish genuine reminiscences'. Though heavily biased and boastful, this autobiography provides a valuable insight into the dark and murky world of Stansted's poachers.

9. John Wilkins.

1 Rackham (1986: 416).
2 Rackham (1989: 13).
3 The *Chelmsford Chronicle* was established in 1764. On 25 July 1884 it became the *Essex County Chronicle,* and on 2 January 1920 the *Essex Chronicle.*
4 Anon. (n.d.)
5 ISC, 'The autobiography of a Quaker Antiquary 1854-1911 by Joseph J Green'.
6 At the time of writing a further series of interviews is being conducted.
7 Wilkins (1976: Preface).

PART II

FROM PREHISTORY TO THE MIDDLE AGES

3: STANSTED BEFORE THE NORMANS: THE ARCHAEOLOGICAL RECORD

There is a striking contrast between the archaeology of the west of the parish and the archaeology of the east, between the area that has not been examined, except patchily by local amateurs, and the area now occupied by Stansted Airport which was thoroughly surveyed by professional archaeologists before that development was allowed to take place. It is a contrast that coincides roughly with the chalks and gravels in the west and the boulder clay in the east.

What the archaeological record reveals in the eastern part of Stansted, and in the adjacent part of what became the parish of Takeley, is a progression from hunting and gathering to the domestication of animals and arable farming, with more and more woodland being cleared until the Saxon period, when for some reason, perhaps plague, settlements were abandoned and woodland reasserted itself. Such evidence as we have from the western part of Stansted appears to confirm these findings.

Towards the end of the Saxon period the population began to recover, and it was the Saxons who developed the more nucleated settlements, with the open field system, that formed the basis of the mediaeval parish. By the time of the Norman invasion, as we know from the Domesday Book, the population of what became the parish of Stansted had increased to about 200, and it was organised into manors which, by and large, the Normans took over as their own units of administration.

The chapter that follows is an account of how these conclusions came to be established, first, from discoveries made and information collated by Joseph Green, the Victorian village historian; secondly from the findings of the professional archaeologists at Stansted Airport; and thirdly from the more recent work of two metal detectorists.

In 1887, when St. Mary's Church was being restored, a plain red tessellated

10. Red tessellated floor, probably from a Romano-British house, c.300 AD. Found under the floor of St. Mary's Church during the restoration of 1887. Now in the Saffron Walden Museum.

pavement, thought to be Roman, was found two or three feet below the surface in the nave. This prompted Joseph Green to speculate that it had been the floor of a temple and that the site had therefore been used, on and off, for 'services for the living and the dead' for nearly 2,000 years, but it is more likely that it was the floor of a Roman house.[1] Four years later, in 1891, Green found Roman remains in the churchyard and wrote two long letters to the *Herts and Essex Observer*, the first to announce these recent finds and the second to put on record everything that had come to light over the previous 20 years.

Green's discoveries in the churchyard were made entirely by chance, as he informed the *Observer's* readers in the first of these letters. He had been examining some of the floral offerings on the graves in Stansted churchyard, he wrote, when his eye fell on what he immediately identified as the remains of a Roman pan or saucer. Looking around he found that 'the whole churchyard simply teemed with Roman remains', which he described in some detail, such as fragments of urns and of 'unmistakeable Roman combed tiles, both in straight and wavy patterns'. The builder responsible for renovating the church handed him a piece of Roman pottery which he had found within the church walls. Green also mentioned some 'fine Roman urns' which had been discovered at Burton End some years before, together with another 'very fine one' which had been built, 'curiously enough', into the old Stansted Hall, which had been pulled down in 1812. Taking all this into account, together with Stansted's position by the Roman road of Stane Street, Green surmised that local Roman settlement had been considerable. He was confirmed in this because of the quantity of Roman remains in his possession, many of which he had discovered in another part of the parish during the previous 20 years.[2]

These he described in his next letter to the *Observer*. There was a circular horse shoe found in the road opposite Wood House or nearby, then in the possession of a local builder, and there were several coins that were now in Green's collection, one of which he had purchased from the local blacksmith while another had been handed over the counter at one of the village shops. He had also found fragments of Roman pottery in the gravel pit by the Castle Hills and in a rubbish heap in a field near his home at Tayspill House. Finally, in an excavation made for gravel and chalk, near Lime Kiln Lane, he had found many remains that he described in detail, among them a considerable portion of a red glazed Samian bowl with the potter's mark at the centre; a piece of glass with prismatic colours, which he was told was Durobrivian ware; thousands of pieces of black ware, many with a beautiful glazed surface, belonging to vessels of a great variety of shapes and sizes; and also many tiles, nails and oyster shells. What seemed most significant to him was that he found not a single complete piece, but everything in a fragmentary state, which led him to believe that this was a Roman rubbish heap, a conclusion in which he was supported by a Roman expert at Colchester.

Green took the opportunity of this second letter to tell the *Observer's* readers that he had found yet further Roman remains in St. Mary's churchyard, and he reported his 'impression ... that the Norman window discovered over the chancel arch in 1887 was composed of tiles which were originally of Roman origin ... on one of which the impression of a dog's foot was conspicuous'.[3]

Such were Green's findings. A hundred years later two major surveys were conducted by professional archaeologists on land that was about to become part of the airport. The first of these surveys lasted from 1985 to 1991, and was carried out by the Stansted Project, headed by Howard Brooks as director, under the auspices of the Essex County Council. Its findings were recorded in an interim and attractive booklet by Brooks and Bedwin, *Archaeology at the Airport* (1989), and then, more fully, by Havis and Brooks in *Excavations at Stansted Airport 1986-91* (2004). The second survey was carried out by Framework Archaeology (FA) between 1999 and 2005, and its findings were published in 2008 in a comprehensive and well illustrated report, *From hunter gatherers to huntsmen: a history of the Stansted landscape*.

The significance of the Stansted Project's excavations was recognised from the outset, since the airport was situated on the boulder clay plateau of north-west Essex where there had been little opportunity for archaeological investigation before on a large scale. This significance was dramatically enhanced by 'the huge and unexpected number' of sites that were discovered, and this was confirmed by Framework Archaeology's later excavations.[4]

In the New Stone Age (4,500-2,000 BC), the boulder clay plateau was covered by woodland, and for this period the Stansted Project found no trace of settlement, only the broken end of a polished flint axe and a number of waste flakes. The team concluded that in that period 'there can only have been minimal impact on the woodland ... perhaps the occasional hunting foray, or journeys to gather plants available only in woodland, with little or no forest clearance'.[5] Then, for the Early Bronze Age (2,000-1,500 BC), the only finds made by the Stansted Project were three arrowheads, which probably reflected hunting trips into the woodland. For these periods Framework Archaeology also found no trace of any permanent settlement, but surmised that there might have been a sparse population, sporadic and opportunist, grazing animals and occasionally farming.[6]

For the Middle Bronze Age (1,500-1,000 BC) the Stansted Project again found no trace of settlement, but for the Late Bronze Age (1,000-700 BC) it discovered a structure 16 feet by 9 feet which might well have been residential. What mainly caught the team's attention, however, were two parallel shallow ditches, almost certainly a droveway, indicating that the local community was largely dependent on stock for its livelihood, rather than crops. They concluded that these people were 'pioneers in beginning the lengthy process of clearing the woodland', but because only one site was found the team concluded that the penetration of the woodland at this time was still limited.[7]

Framework Archaeology, following on from the Stansted Project, found several settlements dating onwards from the Middle Bronze Age, and they agreed with the Project that, while arable farming on the heavy boulder clay was still beyond the capabilities of these settlers, new opportunities were now being opened up by the domestication of animals, in particular sheep and cattle.[8]

For the first 300 or 400 years of the Iron Age (700 BC – 43 AD) there was still little to show, but in the Middle Iron Age occupation increased 'dramatically'.[9] Three settlements were identified by the Stansted Project, including one with a roundhouse that was about 50 feet in diameter.

In the late Iron Age the Stansted area lay in the border zone between two major Celtic groups, the Catuvellauni to the west, with their capital at Wheathampstead, and the Trinovantes to the east, with their capital at Camulodunon (the fort of Camulos, the Celtic war-god), the modern Colchester, with the River Stort possibly forming the boundary between them.[10] Some

3: STANSTED BEFORE THE NORMANS: THE ARCHAEOLOGICAL RECORD

say that the Trinovantes' capital was at Braughing, and that it was moved to Camulodunon only in 20-15 BC. Either way, the people in this area were probably Trinovantes. Close by, near the present village of Great Hallingbury, was the great Iron Age fort of Wallbury, occupying about 31 acres. This dated from about 400 BC, and was probably one of a line of Iron Age forts built by the Trinovantes to guard their western flank against the Catuvellauni.[11] Since there was constant friction between the two groups, and since Stansted was close to the border, the people in this area might well have led an unsettled existence, a possibility that is strengthened by the archaeological evidence.

It was in this period that what Brooks and Bedwin described as the 'Jewel in Stansted's Crown'[12] was built, an Iron Age settlement consisting of some round houses surrounding a central building, all enclosed by a deep ditch surmounted by earthen banks which, if they were made from the earth removed from the ditch, were perhaps about six feet high. It was first established in 75 BC, grew until 25 BC, and then, after a quiet period, was settled again in 40-60 AD.

The round buildings were probably domestic housing, though some might have been animal enclosures and others industrial, but what intrigued the Stansted Project team was the square structure in the centre of the settlement. Because of its position it must have been a building of some importance. It was small, 15 feet by 15 feet, and so it could not have been a chief's house or a village meeting place. In the gully around the building there were many bones but very little pottery, which suggested that the building was not domestic in function, and there were two pits near the building in which objects appeared to have been dropped for ritual or religious purposes. Among them were some brooches and, most striking of all, a beautiful onyx ring-stone that might have been placed there by a Roman soldier as an offering to a resident deity. It was engraved with a scene from the Trojan War, the Greek warrior Diomedes stealing away from the Trojan camp with the Palladium, the figure of Pallas Athene which was believed by the Trojans to give them protection. For all

11. 'The Jewel in Stansted's Crown'. Reconstruction of an Iron Age settlement on the site of Stansted Airport. The small building in the centre was almost certainly a shrine.

3: STANSTED BEFORE THE NORMANS: THE ARCHAEOLOGICAL RECORD

12. Onyx ring-stone of Diomedes carrying off the Palladium from Troy. Found near the building believed to be a shrine shown in illustration 11, it was perhaps an offering by a Roman soldier to a resident deity.

these reasons the team concluded that the little square building must have been a shrine. Next to one of the round houses in this settlement 51 potin coins were found, the regular currency of the area at this time, potin being an alloy of bronze. These were the currency of the area until the Romans introduced their own minted and regulated coinage after the conquest in AD 43.

The walls and ditch testify to the need for protection, and at first perhaps this was due to no more than the normal tension with the Catuvellauni. But this tension was now being aggravated by the intervention of the Romans. Julius Caesar's invasion in 55 BC had been ineffective, but shortly afterwards the Catuvellauni had attacked the Trinovantes and murdered their king, whose son, Mandubracius, had fled to Rome to ask for help. In 54 BC Caesar came back, this time with a stronger force. He successfully stormed the Catuvellauni's capital, but when they agreed to pay a yearly tribute he accepted their formal surrender and withdrew.

After the Romans had gone the Trinovantes renewed their struggle with the Catuvellauni, but with disastrous results, and for a long period the Catuvellauni king, Cunobelin (Shakespeare's Cymbeline), occupied their capital at Camulodunon. He died in 40 AD, and three years later the Emperor Claudius decided to win some glory for himself by invading Britain with a strong and well equipped force under Aulus Plautius. Overthrowing the two sons of Cunobelin, Caratacus and Togodumnus, the Romans occupied Colchester, Latinizing the name to Camulodunum, established their magnificent capital there, and set up a system of forts throughout the conquered territory. It is possible that they built Stane Street at this time.

In AD 60 the Romans' harsh treatment of their new subjects provoked a revolt among the Iceni of Norfolk, led by their queen Boudicca, who were joined by the Trinovantes. The governor, Suetonius Paulinus, was away, leading a campaign in

Map 5. Main Roman roads and settlements in the Stansted area.

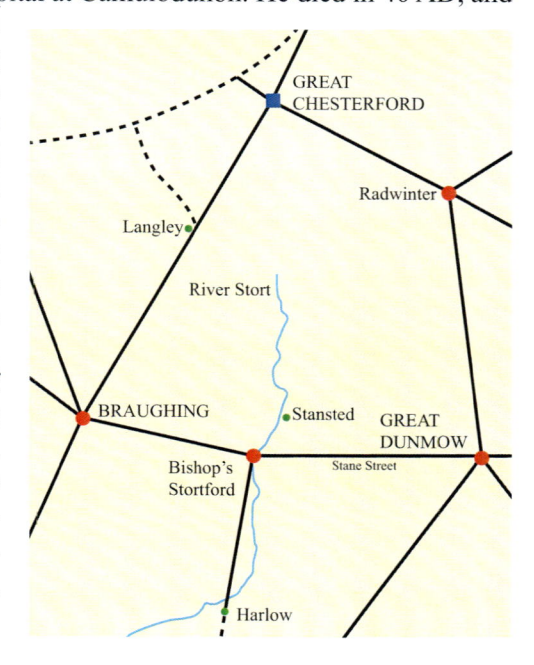

25

Wales, and without any opposition from the legions the rebels captured Camulodunum and burnt it to the ground. They then swept down on Londinium (London) and Verulamium (Saint Albans) and destroyed those settlements too. The governor and his legions turned back and in a battle somewhere between Towcester and Atherstone inflicted a terrible defeat on the rebels.

If our people in the little Iron Age settlement were in fact Trinovantes they might well have taken part in the revolt, and if so they would probably have suffered in the backlash. It seems more than just a coincidence that the settlement unearthed by the Stansted Project came to an end around 60 AD. Although sporadic raids continued the Romans took steps to ensure that there was no further revolt on the same scale: the people around Stansted would have noted that several new forts were established at this time, including one at Great Chesterford.[13]

Going back to the archaeological record, it is clear that the growth in settlement continued, so that by the end of the Roman period (43-410 AD) virtually all the area later occupied by the airport was opened up to farming, the only exception being the extreme north-east, where the heavier soils had still not been subdued. This farming was a very profitable business, as was demonstrated by the opulence of two burials uncovered by the Stansted Project.

The first was a box burial, so called because the remains of the cremated person were placed in a wooden box, which was buried together with several vessels containing food and drink for the journey into the next life, and perhaps a few personal items of clothing or ornament. Among the remains were a fine jug and an expensive dinner service of eight red plates of Samian ware, one of them made by Sacroticus, which means that it was made in the area of Lyons around 140 AD. The second burial, probably a woman's, was close by, and here there were two glass vessels, a small rectangular bronze mirror, hob nails from a pair of sandals, five red vessels, and a perfume container melted in the heat of the fire.

Although these burials reflect the wealth of the people who no doubt owned the land no contemporary dwellings with mosaic floors and stone walls were discovered nearby. Perhaps these people lived in wooden structures, or else their settlements were just outside the airport landtake area. The team thought that a site at Bury Lodge Lane, about 500 yards to the north, was the most likely place. Roman pottery and tiles were found there, including a hypocaust tile, but no villa. Or perhaps, a speculation which the team did not entertain, the settlement was near the site of Stansted church, where the red tessellated floor had been found below the church and Joseph Green had found the churchyard 'teeming' with Roman remains.

Framework Archaeology, like the Stansted Project, took the view that with the introduction of improved techniques and more suitable crops during the Roman period there was a significant intensification in the clearing of woodland, mainly for arable farming.[14] Three settlements were excavated, all processing large quantities of cereal grain, and on at least one site animals were apparently butchered for market.

Green's chance discoveries in the west of the parish, the part not covered by the archaeologists, suggest that there was substantial Roman settlement there, much more than on the boulder clay, and it is clear from the archaeological record as a whole, from the findings of the professionals as well as those of Green, that the whole area formed part of a rich and distinctive Romano-British culture. Stane Street, linking the area with

Camulodunum to the east and Verulamium to the west, must have been a great stimulus to the local economy.

On the whole the Roman period was a time of peace and prosperity. But the great Empire was coming under threat from peoples beyond its borders, and the province of Britannia fell increasingly under the control of the Angles, Saxons and others. Whether they came as invaders or peaceful settlers is disputed, but at Stansted the Romano-British settlements identified by Framework Archaeology were abandoned in the second half of the 4th century, and in 410 the legions were finally withdrawn in order to defend the heartlands of the Empire. By that time there was already a substantial Saxon population in what is now the county of Essex, and Stansted, as we can now begin to call it, became part of the Kingdom of the East Saxons.

The Saxon period lasted from about 400 to 1066 AD. There were constant shifts in the balance of power, but from about 700 onwards there were seven main kingdoms, Northumbria, Mercia, East Anglia, Wessex, Essex (the kingdom of the East Saxons), Kent and Sussex. At times Essex was subject to Mercia, Wessex or Kent, and at times it took in London, Middlesex and even Kent, but the present county of Essex was always at its core. Some of its kings were Christians, others remained pagans or reverted to paganism. By the end of the Saxon era, however, England was united in a single kingdom and the Christian church was firmly established.

For ecclesiastical purposes the whole of Essex fell within the diocese of London, a reflection of the time when London was part of the kingdom, and perhaps there was a church in Stansted, but if so no trace of it has been discovered. Although the system of parishes was beginning to be established it was not fully in place until late in the twelfth century, and at the time of the Norman Conquest the most important local unit was still the manor. There were two manors in what became the parish of Stansted, and in the Domesday Book they were recorded as Stansted and Bentfield, which, to avoid confusion, will be referred to by its later name of Bentfield Bury.

In the Anglo-Saxon dispensation the whole country was divided into Hundreds. The meaning of this term is still the subject of debate: perhaps each Hundred had to provide 100 men under arms, or perhaps it was an area that was sufficient to support 100 households. Originally, it seems, both Stansted and Bentfield Bury fell in the Hundred of Uttlesford, but at some point, perhaps to satisfy the ambitions of a local thegn, six parishes were taken out of Uttlesford to form the Half Hundred of Clavering, and one of these six was Bentfield Bury. So the parish of Stansted was divided not just into two manors but into two Hundreds as well.

At this point, to find out what was happening in Stansted, we have to turn back to the archaeologists, and again this means concentrating on the area in the east that was carefully surveyed before the airport could be extended.

After all the evidence of activity in the Roman period there was a dearth of evidence for what the Stansted Project called the Saxon period. In fact there was only one site to show that anyone was living in the area at that time, a single pit with 6th/7th century pottery. The team speculated on why this was so. Was the area in fact deserted, or was it more difficult to find Saxon remains? Although they believed it was a combination of the two, they concluded that there was in fact a much lower level of activity in Saxon times, and that we should imagine old Roman farming estates falling into disrepair and settlements shrinking. One possible cause was plague.[15] These findings were confirmed by Framework Archaeology's excavations. The decline, they wrote, was 'severe'. Old Romano-British landholdings rarely survived in identifiable form, and many fields were once again taken over by woods.[16] It was only in the late Saxon period that the woodland started to be cleared again as the population began to recover.[17]

Since Framework Archaeology completed their dig in 2005 the only work that has been done has been carried out by two very able detectorists. They have used field walking and metal detectors, and have also examined cropmarks revealed by aerial photography. They have reported their finds to the appropriate authorities, among them the Saffron Walden Museum and in one case the British Museum.

For the most part what they have found has been what one might expect, such as axes, arrow heads and scrapers from the New Stone Age, awls and a fragment of a mirror from the Bronze Age, brooches from the Iron Age, buckles, coins, an oil lamp hanger and a stylus from the Roman period, and a few objects from the Saxon period, such as coins and pottery and buckles. But there are three findings which add significantly to the record.

The first is as yet tentative: it appears that there was a line of Roman farmsteads, one of them probably a villa, about half a mile apart, overlooking the Stort from what is now the Stansted side of the river. This, if correct, would confirm the view of the Stansted Project and Framework Archaeology that the area was well populated in the Roman period.

The second, noted already, is the comparative paucity of finds from the Saxon period, which suggests that, perhaps because of plague, there was a sharp fall in population in these areas in the 5th and 6th centuries as well in the areas to the east that were covered by the professional archaeologists

The third, which is of more than local importance, is the discovery of four gold coins dating from the Iron Age, about 150 BC, which must have been imported from the Ambiani region of France, the Ambiani being a Belgic people speaking a Celtic language and living in the valley of the Somme. These coins bear the image of Apollo, a design derived from the Macedonian gold staters of Philip II, who reigned from 359 to 330 BC. On the reverse is a charioteer with a horse, and this too is Macedonian in origin, though the horse is depicted in the Celtic style. These finds belong to the earliest type of coin ever found in this country. Three are full staters and the fourth a quarter stater. Such coins have been found in other parts of south-east England and many more in France. The three full staters are well worn, and had clearly been in use for some time, but it has been suggested that they were not sent as currency, but as offerings and bullion, perhaps as payment for troops sent over to fight in the wars against the Romans. Who received them we do not know, nor do we know why they buried them, but their use suggests a well developed authority and organisation which might possibly, even at so early period, have been that of the Trinovantes. Until there has been proper archaeological excavation in the western part of the parish it will be impossible to place this remarkable find in its proper context.

1. Royal Commission on Historical Monuments (England) (1916: I.275). A tessellated floor indicates a site of some importance.
2. *HEO*, 11 July 1891.
3. *HEO*, 29 August 1891.
4. Brooks and Bedwin (1989: 2,3).
5. Brooks and Bedwin (1989: 5).
6. FA (2008: 23, 29).
7. Brooks and Bedwin (1989: 6-7).
8. FA (2008: 281).
9. Havis and Brooks (2004: 521).
10. Havis and Brooks (2004: 525).
11. Kemble (2001: 135).
12. Brooks and Bedwin (1989: 8). In this case the Stansted referred to is the airport and not the parish. In fact 'The Jewel in Stansted's Crown' now falls within the parish of Takeley.
13. Kemble (2001: 87,134); Ken Smith (1998:18). Another fort was established at Dunmow (Kemble 2001: 88). Maria Medlycott (talk to Saffron Walden Town Library Association, 13 June 2012) agrees that the fort at Great Chesterford was probably built in response to the revolt, but says that it was soon abandoned and superseded by the town because evidently the Romans found that they did not need such a strong defence.
14. FA (2008: 281).
15. Brooks and Bedwin (1989: 18). See also Timby and others (2007: Chapter 4, 'What happened to the Saxons?'), and John Hunter (2003: 7).
16. FA (2008: 281-2).
17. FA (2008: 197).

4: THE DOMESDAY BOOK AND THE MONTFICHETS

Hundred of Uttlesford

Robert holds Stansted in lordship, which a free man held in the time of King Edward as a manor…

Half Hundred of Clavering

Robert holds Bentfield [Bury] in lordship, which a free man held in the time of King Edward as a manor…

With these words in the Domesday Book, compiled in 1086 on the orders of William the Conqueror, the manors of Stansted and Bentfield Bury, which today make up most of the parish of Stansted Mountfitchet, appear for the first time in the written records.[1] So too does the first named landowner, a man called 'Robert'. Another man, a free man, had held Stansted in the time of Edward the Confessor, a man no longer important enough to name, just one of the many Saxon landowners swept aside by the triumphant Normans. Perhaps it was the same free man who had held Bentfield Bury.

Robert's full name was Robert Gernon, 'gernon' being the Norman French for 'moustache', and he was a baron who probably came from the area around Bayeux.[2] He had no doubt crossed the Channel with William the Conqueror and he had been well rewarded, for in all he held 44 manors in Essex and 47 in Cambridgeshire, Middlesex, Hertfordshire, Buckinghamshire, Suffolk, Norfolk and Herefordshire. Among his Essex manors were properties in what became the neighbouring parishes of Takeley, Farnham, Ugley and Manuden. This wide dispersal of properties was typical of the way in which William rewarded his supporters, and it has been suggested that he did this to make it difficult for them to organise a rebellion against him. Whether or not this is true, conflict between kings and barons was built into their relationship and was to have profound consequences for the lords of Stansted.

The information in Domesday is given separately for Stansted and Bentfield Bury. It is also given, not only for 1086, the year of Domesday's compilation, but for 1066, the year of the Conquest and the last year of the reign of Edward the Confessor.[3] In the account that follows the data for Stansted and Bentfield Bury are collated.

Domesday tells us that Robert held both Stansted and Bentfield Bury in lordship for 11 hides, six for Stansted and five for Bentfield Bury. 'In lordship', or 'in demesne' as it is sometimes translated, means that he held these manors as a tenant of the King on the usual terms of feudal tenure, and that he kept them for himself rather than letting them out to other tenants. Of his 44 manors in Essex he held 12 in his own hands. The assessment in hides was related to tax, a hide being based on the economic resources of the manor rather than a measure of land.

Then the great record deals with 'ploughs'. The term plough does not mean literally a plough, but the amount of land that could be ploughed in a year with a team of eight oxen, which was about 120 acres. There were 20 ploughs in all, six of them held in lordship and 14 held by homagers (a homager being a vassal who paid homage to Robert). The comparable figures for 1066 were 24 ploughs in all, seven held in lordship and 17 held by homagers.

There were 20 villeins (men who would normally expect to farm 30 acres), compared with 19 in 1066, 29 bordars (smallholders, of lower standing than villeins), compared with 6, and 22 serfs, or slaves, compared with 15. At both times there was a priest.

There was woodland enough for 1200 pigs, 36 acres of meadow, 30 head of cattle (nine in 1066), 150 sheep (220) 100 pigs (70) 24 goats (40), five horses (two) and five asses. There were two mills, i.e. watermills, since there were no windmills at that time. One was in Stansted and the other in Bentfield Bury.

As for the population as a whole, it is generally believed that, while the slaves and clergy should be counted as individuals, the figures for homagers, bordars and villeins stood for their households which were on average about 4 persons each. This would give a population of about 160 in Stansted and 100 in Bentfield Bury, a total of 260 in all, compared with a total of about 192 in 1066. The value of the manor had increased in Stansted from £8 to £11 and in Bentfield Bury from 100 shillings (£5) to £7. Such increases normally reflect an increase in the land under cultivation, and this may be associated with the striking increase in the number of bordars, or smallholders, from 6 to 29. The figures for woodland are high, for this was one of the most wooded parts of Essex.

The head of Robert Gernon's barony was at Hamme, about 25 miles to the south, the area later associated with West Ham and East Ham, and, apart from making sure that he exacted his rights and dues, he probably had little to do with Stansted. He was the Keeper of the Forest of Essex, but apart from this little is known about him, and by the reign of Henry I, perhaps earlier, his entire barony, including the manors of Stansted and Bentfield Bury, was in the hands of the Montfichet family. How this came about is not clear. Philip Morant, the eighteenth-century Essex historian, says that Robert had two sons, William and Robert the younger, that William inherited the barony, and that it was William, not his father, who built the castle by raising an artificial mound. Because of this, says Morant, he became known as William de monte fixo, which was Normanised into de Montfichet.[4] But the name Montfitchet goes back before this. Between Bayeux and St. Lô is the village of Montfiquet, which was once of great consequence and had a grand castle. Old Norman writers spelt the name Montfichet, the Norman-French 'c' being hard. Morant was evidently unaware of it, but this village was the home of the Montfichet family, and 'le sire de Montfichet' was mentioned by the poet Wace as having been present at the Battle of Hastings. Wace tells us that he was a Keeper of the Forest and that he served the Duke of Normandy as a steward in his household, a post which he held by hereditary right. He was 'a very noble and bold vassal', and though small in stature was 'very bold and valiant'. With the numerous fighting men he had brought with him he clashed with the English on the battlefield at Hastings, and there 'you would have heard commotion, shouting and a great crunching of lances'.[5]

4: THE DOMESDAY BOOK AND THE MONTFICHETS

This 'sire de Montfichet' may well be the same as the William de Montfichet who, as we know from other sources, was still in full possession of his Norman estates in the 1080s, and this William de Montfichet was probably the man who not only acquired the Gernon barony but was also the chatelain of one of the towers in London, which was given the name of Montfichet's Tower. It is possible that the name of Montfichet derived from an artificial mound in France, but it certainly was not the mound in Stansted.

Morant was probably right, however, when he stated that Gernon had two sons, William and Robert, and it is possible that this William was William de Montfichet. The Montfichets do not appear as such in the Domesday Book, but there was a William who was one of Robert's feudatories in Hertfordshire, holding 10 of his 13 manors there, and this might well have been the William de Montfichet who took over the barony of Gernon.[6] It may also be significant that the hereditary post of Keeper of the Forest of Essex, which had been held by Robert Gernon, was held by the Montfichets after him. But doubt remains, and Katharine Fry, who went through the records in great detail, concluded that 'Some tie, either of feudality or blood, seems to have united the names, but what that tie was ... remains unexplained'.[7]

William was succeeded by his son, also William, who died young and was succeeded by his son, again William. He too must have died young, for he was succeeded by his younger brother, Gilbert, who in turn was succeeded by Richard de Montfichet in 1186/7.[8]

The Montfichets, whether in Normandy or in England, were reckoned to be a family of great antiquity and consequence,[9] and they had strong connections with royalty. William – we do not know if it was the first or second William – was among the hunters in the New Forest in 1100 on the day when King William II, William Rufus, was killed by an arrow. A bier was made of branches on which flowers and ferns were placed, and William took off his grey mantle and spread it over the bier. The chronicler adds the curious detail that he had had it patched and mended only the day before, as if this made his gesture all the more generous.[10] In 1157 Gilbert, who was described as 'a gay courtier' in his young days, owed King Henry II two hundred marcs of silver for two hawks and two gyrfalcons – a large sum for the time. As the successive Keepers of the Forest of Essex the Montfichets must all have had constant dealings with the court.

It was the second William, Gilbert's father, who moved the head of his barony from Hamme to Stansted, a step of great importance for the village which must have set it apart from the villages around and added considerably to its population. It is also reported that to mark this change he built the castle at Stansted.[11] There might possibly have been some kind of castle before this, but if so it was no doubt William who developed it to its full extent and strength. Overlooking Stansted Brook, which was probably more of a barrier at that time, it was of motte and bailey construction. Its two mounds were surmounted by walls and surrounded by ramparts and a ditch, with a keep on the motte and a settlement of William's retainers within the bailey, where he perhaps maintained a priest. Linked to his castle was a park, a large fenced area of several hundred acres, used for the hunting of fallow deer, which the Normans had reintroduced to England. Such a park was a great status symbol, a mark of nobility, and this part of Essex abounded in them.

From the earliest years of Norman rule there were rumblings of that antagonism between the Montfichets and the monarchy that would later be caught up in the wars between the

13. The castle, c.1990, now a tourist attraction, with the motte below and the bailey above. The buildings are those of the modern 'Norman village'.

mighty barons and King John. I have already mentioned Montfichet's Tower in London. This was one of the castles that William the Conqueror and his successors had built, or allowed to be built, in the capital. The city had submitted unwillingly to the Normans, and William's first care was to erect fortifications that would keep it in obedience. The Tower of London is the best known of these, but in the west were two other strong castles, Baynard's castle which was under the Clare family, and Montfichet's Tower, which probably stood on Ludgate Hill. The dangers of allowing powerful barons to occupy fortified positions at the very heart of the kingdom had been implicit from the outset. Both William de Montfichet and Ralph Baynard had offended King William by running up their flags over the towers they commanded, and the King had given orders, which were promptly carried out, that they had to be replaced by his flag. It was a small incident, quickly resolved, but indicative of the underlying tensions in the King's relations with his barons.[12]

In the revolt of 1173-4, when three of Henry II's sons tried to overthrow him, the King, then in Normandy, was alarmed to hear from the Bishop of Winchester that Gilbert de Montfichet had strengthened his castle in London and was in league with the hostile Walter fitz Robert fitz Richard of Clare, the lord of Baynard's castle: 'God have mercy', Henry replied, 'and protect [the inhabitants] of my city of London'.[13] The revolt was suppressed, but 40 years later it was a different story.

The Montfichets were great supporters and benefactors of the church, being convinced that such generosity would work to the salvation of their souls and the souls of their ancestors and descendants. At Stansted St. Mary's Church was built in the early 1100s. Most of it has now been altered and Gothicised, and the main Norman features that survive are the font, the spacious chancel arch, and the two highly decorated doorways, one to the north and the other to the south. The position of the church, about half a mile south-east of the castle, is something of a mystery. Stansted Hall is close by, and it might be thought that this is yet another example of the lord of the manor having the church close to his own residence regardless of the inconvenience to the villagers. But at that time, as far as we know, the Montfichets were living in the castle and Stansted Hall had not yet been built, and it may be that the house followed the church rather than the other way around. Some years later, in a comparable benefaction in Normandy, Gilbert converted the chapel belonging to the castle of Montfichet into the parochial church, dedicating it to Thomas Becket; and in Stansted he or his son Richard established Thremhall Priory, fronting Stane Street, for monks of the Augustinian order.[14]

Richard, Gilbert's son and successor, joined King Richard I in his expedition to France in 1194, and in 1202 was Governor of the Castle of Hertford and Sheriff of Hertfordshire and Essex. According to the monks of Thremhall he went on pilgrimage to Rome, where he died in 1202.

Richard was succeeded by his son, also Richard, who was to play a big role in the troubles that were about to engulf the country. He was still a minor under guardianship when he succeeded his father, but as soon as he became of age he joined the barons who were in rebellion against King John. Among them were John de Lacey, the son of his former guardian, the Constable of Chester; two of his brothers-in-law, the Earl of Albemarle and Hugh de Playz; and his cousin, Richard de Clare (from the same family as those de Clares with whom his grandfather Gilbert was in alliance in 1173-4). He was exiled by John in 1213 and stripped of his Forestership of Essex, and at the same time Montfichet's Tower in London was dismantled. According to the monks of Thremhall Priory he went to Rome, and, 'being a person of extraordinary strength, he obtained much fame in the casting of a stone, no man being able to do the like. In memory whereof certain pillars of brass were set up to show the distance'. But while Richard was away in Rome all his castles were destroyed in the wars between the barons and the King, and among them was Stansted castle.[15]

When Richard returned he joined the struggle against John. He was present at Runnymede on 15 June 1215 when the King was compelled to agree to Magna Carta – he owned land close by[16] - and although he was so young he was one of the 25 barons chosen to make sure that the charter's provisions were observed. Six days later he was reinstated in his office of Keeper of the Forest of Essex, but when John repudiated the charter and civil war was renewed in October he was dismissed again. In the struggles that followed he gained a reputation for boldness and courage, and was described as one of the three most valiant knights in England, famous for 'his high prowesse and chivalrie'.[17] But he was more than just a fighter, for when the barons invoked the aid of the French King Richard was one of their two envoys, the other being Robert Fitz Walter. All of his lands were now seized by the King, and when the barons were defeated in the battle of Lincoln

14. Interior of St. Mary's Church, looking east towards the Norman chancel arch.

in 1217 he was taken prisoner. Henry III, however, was now King, though still a minor, and the Regent, the Earl of Pembroke, released Richard and restored his estates. He was also reinstated as Keeper of the Forest.

His relations with the King remained difficult, and in 1223 he attended the famous tournament at Blyth in Nottinghamshire, which was held in defiance of the express command of the young King and his advisers, who were nervous about such a gathering of discontented barons. The estates of those who took part were forfeited to the Crown, but were restored the following year, and Richard was soon playing his full part in public affairs again. He witnessed two of Henry III's reissues of Magna Carta, in 1225 and 1237, and from 1242 to 1246 he was Sheriff of Essex and Governor of Hertford Castle.

After the turbulence of his youth Richard's later years were relatively uneventful. Like his predecessors, he was a great benefactor to the church: he gave more land to Thremhall Priory and allowed the monks to use his park for grazing their cattle.[18] And in the records relating to nearby Hatfield Forest, which abutted onto Stansted's boundary at Stane Street, there are many entries relating to his actions as Forester – providing venison for the King, granting the right of estover (to cut wood), preventing unauthorised hunting, and responding to orders for timber, charcoal and other products of the forest.[19]

15. St. Mary's Church, the south doorway.   **16. St. Mary's Church, the north doorway.**

It seems likely that in the wars against King John he had called on the men of his numerous manors to serve in his following, and Stansted would have been among them. After the destruction of his castle, however, he probably spent less time in the village, though according to one source he had a fortified manor house built in the ruins and the manor court was held there until well into the sixteenth century.[20] He died in 1267, and he appears to have been buried in St. Paul's Cathedral, since the beautiful pall which was used at his funeral was kept there for many years.

His wife was Jacosa, a lady eminent for beauty, virtue and piety, 'but alas childless', wrote the author of the *Origo Baronum de Montfichet*.[21] Richard's three sisters had all died before him, and the barony was now divided and subdivided among their descendants.

The destruction of Stansted castle must have been a severe blow to the village, but the archaeological surveys suggest that throughout the 12th and 13th centuries, roughly the period of the Montfichets' lordship, there was a steady expansion of economic activity.[22] By this time the whole area was farmed, including the difficult and heavy clay soils in the north-east, and the population was probably about 450.[23] But this was to be the high point of Stansted's mediaeval prosperity. What lay in store for the whole of Europe were the calamities of the fourteenth century, and Stansted was not exempt.

1. The information required by William was collected at Winchester, corrected and abridged. The abridgement was not complete, and the material relating to Norfolk, Suffolk and Essex remained unabridged. The abridged material is the Domesday Book and the unabridged material the Little Domesday Book. It is more common, however, to refer simply to the Domesday Book.
2. For Robert Gernon and his successors in Stansted I have relied heavily on Katharine Fry (1873a). See also Katharine Fry (1888).
3. Domesday also records that attached to the manor of Bentfield Bury was '1 berewick [an outlying holding or farm, not part of the manor, but counted as part of it for tax purposes] which is called MANUDEN with one hide. Always 1 plough in lordship; 2 bordars (smallholders); Woodland, 10 pigs.' I have not included these figures in the account that follows.
4. Morant (1760-68: 576).
5. Wace (2002: 281).
6. Fry (1873a: 181). By way of supporting evidence Fry points out that among these 10 manors were Letchworth and Wallington, and that in the time of King Henry I William de Montfichet, together with Rohais, his wife, and William, their son, gave the church of Letchworth to the abbey of St. Albans.
7. Fry (1873a: 178).
8. It has been suggested – see Waters (1878: 187) - that Fry was wrong in stating that there were two Williams, and that in fact Gilbert immediately succeeded his father. For the date 1186/7, see Rob Brooks (2005: 11).
9. Fry (1873a: 179).
10. Fry (1873a: 181-2).
11. Morant (1760-68: 576); Fry (1873a: 183-4).
12. Fry (1873b: 265-6).
13. Stenton (1960: 183-4).
14. The records of several gifts of land to the Priory are preserved in the ERO, D/DWv T1 series. See also the transcription of D/DWv Tl/1 in T/Z 197/9.
15. Dugdale (1817-1830: VI:77). The quotation is a translation from the Latin of Dugdale's transcription of the *Origo Baronum de Montfichet*, which was written by the monks at Thremhall Priory. This is the version of events related by Katharine Fry, though she acknowledges that the monks are an unreliable source. Others believe that Stansted castle was destroyed in the wars between the King and the barons that followed Magna Carta, but there is no direct evidence of this.
16. Runnymede was on the south bank of the Thames and Richard was lord of the manor of Wyrardisbury on the north bank opposite.
17. Fry (1873a: 194).
18. Dugdale (1817-1830: VI. 77).
19. Rackham (1986: 51-2, 54, 72, 75).
20. Saffron Walden Library, Jack Sayers's manuscript, 'The Arms and History of the Manor Lords of Stansted Mountfitchet in the County of Essex 1066-1922', p. 31. See also Muilman, Vol. III (1770: 20) for a slightly different account.
21. Dugdale (1817-1830: VI. 77). Translated from the Latin of Dugdale's transcription.
22. Brooks and Bedwin (1989: 20).
23. There is no direct evidence of the population at this time, but in the parish of Littlebury, about nine miles to the north, it went up from about 230 at the time of Domesday to more than 400 at the time of a survey conducted in 1251. See Sanders and Williamson (2005: 26). A comparable increase at Stansted would have taken the population to about 450, though there must have been a drop when the castle was destroyed by King John.

5: PLAGUE AND THE PEASANTS' REVOLT

Up to this time, except for the transfer from Robert Gernon to the Montfichets, the ownership of the manors in Stansted was straightforward. Over the next two centuries it became fragmented and complex. The simplified account that follows is based mainly on that given by Philip Morant in his 18th-century *History and Antiquities of the County of Essex*.

After Richard de Montfichet's death in 1267 his Stansted estates were divided among the descendants of two of his three sisters – Margery, who was married to Hugh de Bolebec of Northumberland, and Philippa, who was married to Hugh de Playz. (The descendants of his other sister, Aveline, who married the Earl of Albemarle, inherited land elsewhere.) Bolebec acquired the manor of Stansted and de Playz acquired the manor of Bentfield Bury.

The Bolebec inheritance, the manor of Stansted, was subsequently divided among the four daughters of Hugh's great grandson, also Hugh. Two of the newly formed manors came into the possession of Robert Burnell, Bishop of Bath and Wells, and became known as the manor of Burnells; the other two came into the possession of Roger de Lancaster and may be referred to as Stansted Hall. Roger, who had married Philippa, the eldest of the four daughters, was described by Morant as 'a very considerable man in his time, and Baron of Kendal in Westmoreland'. He died in 1290 and Philippa in 1293, and they were succeeded by their son, John de Lancaster. John died in 1334, and after the death of his widow, Annora, Stansted Hall passed to the family of de Vere, Earls of Oxford, the greatest landowners in Essex, whose headquarters were at Castle Hedingham. The de Veres also came to acquire the manors of Burnells, Bentfield Bury and Thremhall Priory. So by the 15th century they owned the whole parish of Stansted, and it remained in their hands until 1582 when the profligate seventeenth Earl parted with it along with many other family estates.[1]

There was however one serious gap in the de Veres' ownership. In 1461 John de Vere, the twelfth Earl of Oxford, who was a leading champion of the Lancastrian cause, together with his eldest son Aubrey, was beheaded on Tower Hill by Edward IV for plotting rebellion. His estates were then forfeited to the Crown, and were only restored to the family in 1492 after Henry VII had become King.

The main points to note in Morant's account are, first, that it was only the largest manor, Stansted, that was fragmented, and not Bentfield Bury; second, that alongside these changes Thremhall Priory continued as a separate manor, the patronage passing to the de Veres and remaining in their hands until the suppression of the monasteries;[2] and third, that by the end of the process the whole of the parish of Stansted was back in the hands of one family again, the de Veres, the Earls of Oxford. Morant, writing in the 1760s, found it convenient to lay out his account under the headings of three manors – 'Stansted-Hall', 'Bendfield-bury' and 'The Priory of Thremhall'.

The de Veres maintained their headquarters at Castle Hedingham and never lived in Stansted, but the Lancasters seem to have been more closely connected. Towards the end of the thirteenth century Roger de Lancaster built the Lancaster Chapel on the north side of the chancel of St. Mary's, and he is probably the man who is commemorated in the effigy

5 : PLAGUE AND THE PEASANTS' REVOLT

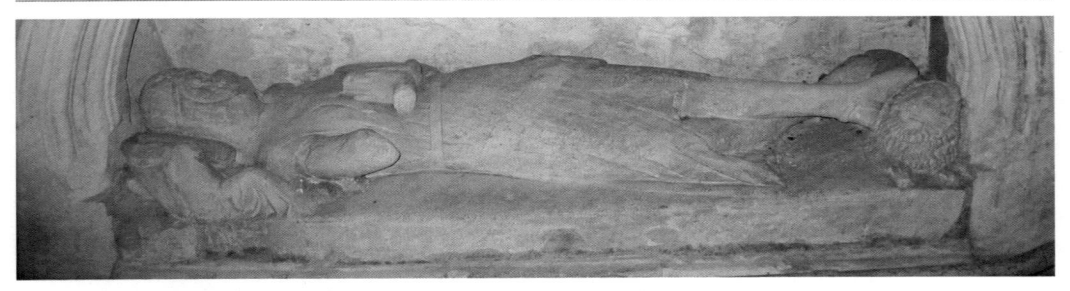

17. Effigy of Sir Roger de Lancaster in St. Mary's Church.

18. The brass in St. Mary's Church in memory of Robert de Bokkyngg. The Latin inscription: 'Here lies Robert of Bocking, the first Vicar of the Parish of Stansted Mountfitchet who died August 31st 1361'.

of a cross-legged knight in the north wall.[3] In the next generation, in 1305, John de Lancaster gave Thremhall Priory the advowson of Stansted church, i.e. the right to appoint the vicar.[4] In the chancel floor at St. Mary's is a brass to the memory of Roger de Bokkyngg, who died in 1361 and according to the Latin inscription was the first vicar of Stansted.

More important than the changes of ownership, however, were the profound economic and social changes that were taking place. Throughout the 13th century the population of England had continued to rise until it reached critical levels, and at times of bad harvests and high prices for corn there was high mortality among the poor. In 1294, for example, East Anglia was devastated by famine. Crops were destroyed by heavy rains and fungus, and there was a sixfold increase in the price of corn. There was another widespread famine in 1315-17 following a series of bad harvests and a sheep murrain, and in 1319 disease wiped out large numbers of cattle. Many smallholders abandoned their farms.

In 1327 we get a partial insight into the parish through the returns drawn up for the Lay Subsidy, the tax of one twentieth of moveable property imposed by Edward III to fund his wars against the Scots. Householders whose property was assessed at less than 10s. were not liable to pay, and it seems that they made up most of the population, since only 29 names were listed, 14 from the Stansted part of the parish and 15 from the Bentfield Bury part (but including for some reason the little hamlet of Pledgdon which was not in fact part of the parish). This joint figure of 29 taxpayers is higher than that of most of the surrounding villages, such as Ugley (10), Farnham (15), Manuden (23) and Elsenham (24) – though Takeley had 38 - but smaller than Walden (65), Thaxted (59) and Bishop's Stortford (56). There were great variations among those who were wealthy enough to be taxed, ranging from the two Lords of the Manor, John de Lancaster in Stansted and Margaret de Playz in Bentfield, who had to pay 12s.3d. and 7s. respectively, to Benedicto Burre, whose goods were assessed at the taxable minimum of 10s. and who had to pay only 6d. The total sum to be paid was 69s. 6d. Two names are of special interest to us – Robert le Parker, who was evidently responsible for the park attached to Stansted Hall, who had to pay 2s.7d., and Roger in the Hale, i.e. the Hole or Hollow, a name that is still preserved in Hole Farm, who also had to pay 2s.7d.[5]

In 1348-9 came the greatest of all the calamities of the fourteenth century, the Black Death, which was followed by four further outbreaks of plague during the second half of the century. In all, between 1300 and 1375 the population of England probably fell by about 40%.

As Framework Archaeology drily observed, 'Mass death had its compensations for the survivors'.[6] In the shortage of labour following the Black Death there was a swing in the balance of power from the landowners to the tenants, many of whom, though often with a struggle, commuted their labour obligations into money payments and became copyholders. Labourers could command higher wages and many serfs were granted their freedom. There was an improvement in the diet of the poor and a substantial increase in the consumption of ale. The whole feudal structure was loosened. Reaction inevitably kicked in. In 1351 the Statute of Labourers was passed holding down wages to pre-plague levels and restricting the mobility of labour, and the manorial courts tried to ensure that this was enforced.

These changes were reflected in the survey which Framework Archaeology undertook in the south-eastern part of Stansted and the adjacent part of Takeley, a survey which they were able to supplement by a close examination of the manorial rolls of Thremhall Priory (from 1357 onwards) and some of the Takeley manors. What they found was that 'The shock to the agricultural economy often led to the shrinkage of cultivated areas and settlements, a retreat from marginal land, and the abandonment of direct exploitation of demesnes by manorial lords'.[7]

In 1356/7 tenants in Thremhall Priory were convicted under the Statute of Labourers of charging high wages and lost their holdings, and there were refusals to carry out labour services in 1368-72. The lord's pound was broken into and his hedges cut down, and there were similar disturbances in the manor of Warish Hall in Takeley. Some manors now found it difficult to find tenants to work the customary holdings. In the last decade of the century Maud de Vere, who held the lands as dower, allowed three bond tenements to fall down for want of repair – clearly they were not occupied.[8]

It was not only the poor who were discontented, but men who had risen in the world and were determined not to be pulled down again. The advisers and the officials of the young King Richard II were condemned as incompetent and corrupt, and matters came to a head when a regressive series of poll taxes was imposed to pay for the unpopular wars against the French. The first of these taxes was imposed in 1377 and the second in 1379, and when the third was imposed in 1381 a great wave of anger and discontent broke over the heads of the men who were sent to collect it. At Fobbing and Brentwood in Essex the villagers refused to pay and drove out the officials who tried to compel them. The revolt spread rapidly through the rest of Essex and Kent, and two great bodies of men advanced on London, where the gates were thrown open and many Londoners joined them. They did not demand the abolition of the monarchy, but envisaged a society in which all men were free and equal under the King. More specifically they demanded the abolition of the manorial lord's right to exact unpaid labour and the dismissal of the King's corrupt councillors. The story of how the revolt was put down, how King Richard made concessions and then withdrew them, how Wat Tyler was stabbed by the Mayor of London and later decapitated, all this is well known.

But how was Stansted affected? We know that manors were attacked and documents destroyed in several of the parishes nearby, such as Thaxted, Clavering and Debden, and that men from some of those parishes were brought before the courts and punished. At Bishop's Stortford the Bishop of London's gaol was broken open and the rebels interned there set free. All that is clear from the documentary evidence, whether in court proceedings or in later entries in the manorial records, and there is no mention of Stansted in any of them. The only manorial records for Stansted to survive from the fourteenth century are those of Thremhall Priory (1357-1373, and then from September 1382 onwards). Although these make no mention of the revolt, they appear to provide the clue for which we are looking. Throughout the county the insurgents destroyed manorial rolls, since these contained the records of their duties and obligations to the manor, and in many cases these rolls were begun again immediately or very soon after the revolt. As a result, as Ken Newton has demonstrated, 'The widespread nature of the Peasants' Revolt is disclosed not only by surviving documents, but by the significant number of manors whose rolls do not begin until late 1381 or 1382'[9] – and, he might have added, those manors whose rolls are interrupted but begin again in 1381 or 1382. The rolls for the manor of Great Dunmow, for example, begin in 1382, and also the rolls for the manor of Warish Hall at Takeley. At Saffron Walden, in the manor of Walden, the court rolls begin in December 1381. So the gap of nine years in the rolls of Thremhall Priory, from 1373 to September 1382, may well have been caused by the destruction wrought by the insurgents,[10] and we can legitimately imagine them bursting into the Priory, threatening the Prior's servants, seizing the rolls and setting fire to them. It is possible that the same happened at Stansted Hall and Bentfield Bury, but in the absence of their manorial records for the whole of this period we cannot know.

It may be thought that the Revolt was a failure. It did not achieve its stated aims, and manorial rule soon resumed its normal course. But it showed the nobles the depth of the peasants' dissatisfaction and hostility and their unexpected ability to wreak havoc, and in the long term it hastened the break-up of the feudal world. The shift from bond tenants (who owed labour service to the manor) to ordinary tenants (who paid rents) continued.

Again this is reflected in what was happening at Stansted. More prosperous peasants increased their land by leasing or buying the deserted holdings of their neighbours and by consolidating their strips in the open fields. They also leased portions of the demesne land from the lords of the manor. In Thremhall Priory in 1369 and 1388 tenants were taking over the lands of their dead cousins without authority and were taking up vacant holdings on 10 or 12 year leases. By the 15th century these surviving and successful tenant families formed what Framework Archaeology described as 'a peasant aristocracy'. One such family was the Parkers, the hereditary park-keepers of Stansted.[11]

From about 1430 to 1470 there was a severe agricultural depression, and in northern and central Essex rents fell to about half of the levels that had obtained before the Black Death. Most labour services due from the tenants were abandoned.[12] By the 15th century the direct management of most of the Stansted and Takeley manors had been given up, and it is known that the de Veres were leasing out the Stansted demesnes in 1442/3 and both the Stansted Hall and Bentfield Bury manors in 1488/89.

Throughout these troubled times the de Veres maintained their headquarters at Castle Hedingham and, as Earls of Oxford and therefore senior members of the nobility, were heavily involved in national affairs. Sir John de Vere, the seventh Earl, was a commander in the army of Edward III at Crecy and Poitiers; Robert de Vere, the ninth Earl, was a boyhood friend of Richard II and was at his side at Mile End to confront the rebellious peasants; and Richard de Vere, the eleventh Earl, fought under Henry V at Agincourt. It seems probable that, like the Montfichets before them, these great lords would have enlisted the men of Stansted in their military adventures.

But Stansted would not have been neglected, and not just for economic reasons. The de Veres would have held hunting parties in their park in Stansted, since this was the kind of display which was fitting for a great aristocratic family, and they not only extended the park to 429 acres but built a new hunting lodge.[13] They were also religious patrons. They were generous with their grants of land to Thremhall Priory,[14] and it must have been they who donated to St. Mary's what was later described as a 'vestment of purple velvet broydered with Colygraves and molletts [five-pointed stars]', since molletts were the well known badge of the de Veres and 'Colygraves' represented the 'calygreyhound' which was frequently mentioned in documents relating to the family.[15] At what became the crossroads, where the fountain now stands, they had a wayside chapel erected, described in 1492 as 'new built and not yet completed'. In that year John Alcock, Bishop of Ely, granted an indulgence of 40 days to those who should contribute to the support of John Parrot, Hermit, Keeper of the Chapel of Our Lady in the parish of 'Stanstede Mounfychet' or to the ornaments of it when finished.[16] So just as indulgences, that is reductions in the time sinners spent in purgatory, were granted by the Pope to those who gave money for the building of St. Peter's in Rome, the practice that aroused the wrath of Martin Luther and so helped to ignite the Reformation, so indulgences were granted by the Bishop of Ely to those who contributed to the support of John Parrot the hermit or the ornamentation of this little wayside chapel in Stansted.

19. The de Veres' wayside chapel, seen here being demolished in 1870.

All this was part of the established pattern of Catholic practice. But the religious ground was shifting. Already the country had been shaken by the Lollards, the followers of John Wycliffe, who attacked the worldliness and corruption of the church, mocked its veneration of relics and looked to the Scriptures for inspiration. At first they were tolerated, but both secular and religious authorities were disturbed when John Ball, a Lollard priest from Colchester, took a leading part in the Peasants' Revolt. His sermon to the insurgents is still well remembered:

When Adam delved and Eve span
Who was then the gentleman?

Although Wycliffe and other Lollard leaders opposed the revolt their movement was now seen as a threat to the established order. It is impossible to know how far the people of Stansted were affected, but we do know that in 1430 the vicar of the neighbouring parish of Manuden was burnt at the stake at Smithfield as a Lollard heretic.

In the following century the whole country was convulsed in the great religious upheaval that became known as the Reformation.

1. Morant (1760-68: 577-8).
2. Dugdale (1817-1830: VI. 75-6).
3. He died in 1291 and Pevsner says that the effigy is c.1300.
4. FA (2008: 194-5); Tricker (1992: 1). More correctly, the Priory would have presented its nominee to the Bishop for appointment, but in effect it was the Priory which determined the appointment. There are references to two rectors of Stansted before this: John de Malteby (1295 and 1303) and Thomas de Shymplynge (1331 and 1340). See Reader, 'Rectors of Stansted', *SMPM,* April 1943.
5. Ward (1983: 46, 48).
6. FA (2008: 223).
7. *Ibid.*
8. NA, Calendar of Inquisitions Miscellaneous 1392-99, no. 14.
9. Quoted in Wood (1982: 67).
10. The evidence for all this is helpfully collated and analysed by Wood (1982: 67-98).
11. FA (2008: 224).
12. FA (2008: 225).
13. FA (2008: 244, 258).
14. Dugdale (1817-1830: VI. 76).
15. J.H. Round (1923: 120).
16. Gibbons (1891: 415).

PART III

FROM THE REFORMATION TO THE NAPOLEONIC WARS

6: THE REFORMATION

The religious life of the de Veres' wayside chapel was short-lived, coming to an end with the abolition of such hermitages in the Reformation under Henry VIII,[1] and in 1536 Thremhall Priory was dissolved as part the general dissolution of the monasteries. Like many other religious houses in Essex it had fallen into decline. In or around 1340, when it had 12 canons and two seculars, the Prior and Canons had described it as a small and poor house,[2] and after that its fortunes plummeted so far that for many years there were fewer than the six inmates needed for the election of the Prior who therefore had to be appointed by the Bishop of London.[3] When it was finally dissolved its plate was 'of low quality', the household goods that were sold, mainly feather beds, blankets and sheets, raised only 23s., its Prior, Simon Spooner, was pensioned off with £10 a year, and the few remaining monks were either sent off to some other religious house or released from their vows and allowed to go out into the world.[4] The advowson of St. Mary's Church was passed to the de Veres as the lords of the manor. In some parishes the dissolution of the local monastery left a painful void in their social and religious life. It seems unlikely that this was so in Stansted. The whole property was granted for an annual rent of £26 10s. to John Cary and Joyce Walsingham, who were about to marry, the buildings were destroyed and a handsome manor house was erected on the site. By the time Philip Morant came to write his history of Essex in the 1760s the only fragment of the Priory that survived was a stone wall on the north side of the manor house garden.[5] More recently the bowl of a font was found buried in a flower bed of the modern house that now occupies the site.[6] Below ground, somewhere, some of the Montfichets are interred.

At around the same time St. Mary's Church underwent a transformation. The mediaeval glass in its windows was smashed, its wall paintings obliterated (remains of these were discovered during the restoration in 1888), and its carvings broken up.[7] One of the glories destroyed was almost certainly a resplendent rood loft, since we know that in 1518 two parishioners, Thomas Watson and Thomas Gyver, left money in their wills towards gilding it.[8]

It was not only the church fabric that was changed. Under Henry VIII no move was made to get rid of the rich vestments and plate with which many churches had been endowed over the years, but the continued use of these gave offence to those who wanted to bring the church back to simplicity and plainness, as well as holding out a tempting source of enrichment. In many parishes they were sold off and the proceeds were used for various purposes, some of them very worthy and creditable, such as the relief of the poor or the repair of the church, but in some places, as the King's Council was informed, 'great quantities of the said plate, jewels, bells and ornaments be embezzled by certain private men'. In 1552, in the reign of Edward VI, a revised Book of Common Prayer was issued ordering that the wearing of eucharistic vestments and copes should be discontinued, and in the same year commissioners were appointed to draw up inventories of all the goods, plate, jewels, bells and ornaments still remaining and to take them away, leaving only such chalices or cups and ornaments as they deemed to be 'requisite for the Divine Service'.

They were also to identify all those who had embezzled church goods and to cause these goods to be produced.

In due course four commissioners presented themselves at Stansted: Lord Rich, Sir George Norton, Sir Thomas Joslyn and Edmund Mordaunt. For some reason they summoned the curate of the parish, Roger Mapleton, rather than the vicar, together with the two churchwardens and other leading parishioners, and with them drew up an inventory of 'all Copes, vestments, plate, Juells, and other implements' belonging to the church.

They found that the parishioners had already sold a chalice for £4 10s., a cope and vestments of cloth of gold for £5, a silver pix for 40s., old latten for 12s. 6d., and wax for 10s. Some of this money had been bestowed on the church, but £5 was still in the hands of Thomas Joslyn[9] and 48s. 4d. in the hands of William Marshall. If these two men had been hoping to hold on to the money for themselves then here was a case of embezzlement, but there is no suggestion of this and more probably they were holding it in trust for the church.

Other goods had not been sold, but had been delivered into the hands and custody of one Thomas Sibbly, and they included seven vestments, white, scarlet, green and black, some of them richly embroidered or woven with gold, a chasuble of stout damask linen and a silver chalice, a copper cross, eight bells, a sanctus bell and two handbells. It has been suggested that cases such as this, in which goods were said to be delivered into the hands of a particular person, were 'nearly all cases of unlawful possession by purchase or otherwise',[10] and it is certainly difficult to understand why all these goods should have been delivered into Sibbly's hands. They were now, however, to be yielded up to help fill the royal coffers. All that was left for the 'ministration of the devyne Service' was a silver chalice, a cope of red damask, and the 'Communyon clothes and there Surplices'.[11]

All these changes – the closing of the wayside chapel, the destruction of windows and the obliteration of paintings in St. Mary's, the dissolution of Thremhall Priory and then the seizure of the fine vestments and plate from the church – were the outward and visible signs of a profound religious change. For as long as the people of Stansted could remember their beliefs and practices had been those of the Roman Catholic Church. Now they were being told that these beliefs were erroneous and these practices idolatrous, and they were to adopt instead the more severe tenets of the Protestant Church, headed no longer by the Pope but by the reigning monarch. For five years, 1553-8, under the reign of Henry's daughter Mary, the Catholic faith was reimposed, but under Elizabeth England became once again a Protestant country. Elizabeth did not go as far as some Protestants wanted, and in particular her prayer book was regarded as conceding too much to the Roman church, but after the wars against Catholic Spain and the Pope's excommunication of the Queen Protestantism became synonymous with patriotism and Papist a term of condemnation and abuse.

How did the people of Stansted respond to these changes? It was common practice to include a statement of religious faith in the preamble to a will, and these preambles, taken in some cases with the legacies which followed, often reflected, with varying degrees of clarity, Catholic or Protestant belief. Margaret Spufford suggests that 'Any will which mentions the Virgin, the saints, or the angels may be suspected of Catholic tendencies.

6: THE REFORMATION

Any which stresses salvation through Christ's death and passion alone, or the company of the elect, may be thought of as Protestant.'[12] In the surviving wills of Stansted's parishioners there are no references to individual saints, except St. Mary and (once) St. Gregory;[13] and the saints as a whole are usually covered by the phrase 'all the holy (or blessed) company of heaven'. There is no mention of angels. We may add, however, that any will that contains legacies for masses to be said for the soul of the deceased will be Catholic, whereas a will which contains legacies for a sermon to be given by a learned or godly preacher will almost certainly be Protestant, even Puritan. The normal practice was to date a will by how many years the reigning monarch had been on the throne, and in Protestant wills the monarch may be described as the head of the church.

It might be thought, therefore, that an examination of the wills drawn up in the parish would reveal whether the testators were clinging to their old Catholic beliefs or embracing the new doctrines of the Protestant faith. It is not however as simple as that. Wills were usually written for the testator, sometimes by a local scrivener or a minister of the church, and the preamble may reflect the advice and practice of the writer rather than the convictions of the testator. More important, there were the pressures of conformity – to write a Catholic preamble under a Catholic monarch or a Protestant preamble under a Protestant monarch. While many testators were no doubt men and women of genuine faith, others perhaps were merely going through the motions. A religious preamble, usually in a set formula, could be merely a matter of form.

All the Stansted wills that survive from the reigns of Henry VII and Henry VIII – at least until 1528, since we have no Henrician wills after that - are of course couched in pre-Reformation terms. William Skynner, for example, making his will in 1501, bequeathed his soul to almighty God, our lady Saint Mary and all the blessed company of heaven, and left 6s. 8d. for masses to be said for the souls of himself, his parents and his friends and for all Christian souls. Katherine Spooner, the sister-in-law of the last Prior, left several of her possessions to Thremhall Priory, among them a silver goblet, a featherbed and a great brass pot.

There are five wills from the reign of Edward VI (1547-1553), when the Reformation was in full spate. In only one of these, that of Elizabeth Welpston, is there any indication of the Roman faith: 'First I bequeath my Soul to Almighty God and Our Lady Saint Mary and all the blessed company of heaven.' Contrary to normal practice, she did not date her will by how many years the reigning monarch had been on the throne, but only by the year AD, which was 1552.[14] Three of the other four testators, Letice Pache, John Ilger and John Stonnerde, bequeathed their souls to the mercy of almighty God, with no mention of St. Mary, and they described Edward VI not only as defender of the faith but also as the supreme head on earth of the Church of England. The first will in the full Protestant style was that of Margaret Cannan in 1551: 'First I bequeath my soule to allmightie god' who through his son's 'most precious death and passion hath redeemed me and all mankind'. She too referred to Edward VI as 'defender of the faith and of the Church of England and also of Ireland on earth the supreme hedd'.[15]

Then come eight wills drawn up in the reign of Queen Mary (1553-1558), who was leading a strong reaction back to Catholicism. Five of them bear the imprint of the Catholic faith. John Sawell bequeathed his Soul 'unto the great mercy of Almighty God, our Lady

Saint Mary and all the blessed company of Heaven', and left 3s. 4d. to 'the poor people of Stansted to pray for my soul and all Christian souls'.[16] Thomas Browne, William Cooke, Thomas Crabbe and John Smyth also bequeathed their souls to almighty God and to all the holy (or blessed) company of heaven, and in the cases of Browne and Cooke to our lady Saint Mary as well.[17] Margaret Godfre, Thomas Crabbe and John Smyth gave no indication either way.[18]

In the 45 wills[19] drawn up during the reign of Queen Elizabeth (1558-1603) Catholic references almost disappear. No souls are bequeathed to Saint Mary and no money is left to pay for prayers for the dead. In only two are there references to 'the holy company of heaven'. Of the remaining 43, while 10 have no indication of either Protestant or Catholic leanings, 33 are clearly Protestant. These range from the brief and formal, such as that of the widow, Margaret Allyn, in 1581 – ' I do bequeathe my Soule unto all mighty God my creator and redeemer, by whose merytes I trust to be saved and by no other meanes'[20] – to the fervent outpourings of John and Margaret Thoroughgood.

John, a yeoman who drew up his will in 1584, besought God to be merciful unto him and to forgive the manifold transgressions of his sinful life, and to receive him into the fellowship of his church, trusting through Christ and Christ alone to have remission and forgiveness for all his sins. He then disposed of the goods which the Lord God had lent him in this life, and among his bequests was £20 ... to 'Mr. Rogers preacher', i.e. to the well known Puritan lecturer, Richard Rogers, who was then based at the nearby village of Wethersfield and had recently been suffering persecution.[21] Two years later John's widow Margaret entrusted her soul into the hands of almighty God her creator, who because of his love of mankind had restored the world through the death and bloodshedding of his only son. In the assurance of faith and in boldness of spirit she presented herself before the throne of his majesty stedfastly believing that by and through Christ her sins would be forgiven and she would be 'in the number of them who shall be partakers of that everlasting blessedness prepared for his children in his heavenlie kingdom'. She also gave 20 shillings for four sermons 'to be preached by some godlie preacher after my death....'[22] The importance attached to godly preaching was one of the hallmarks of the Puritans, and as Cambridge University poured out more Puritan divines they also placed a high value on learning. So Robert Helham, who drew up his will in 1579, left 20s. each to two 'godly learned preachers',[23] while Thomas Cooke in 1595 gave and bequeathed 20s. to 'a lernyd preacher to make a Sarmond at my burial'.[24]

From all this it would seem that, insofar as they indicated any Catholic or Protestant beliefs, the testators of Stansted, or their advisers, generally followed the government of the day: Protestant in the time of Edward VI, Catholic in the time of Mary, and Protestant again in the time of Elizabeth. There were also some individuals who were passionately committed to their religious beliefs and practices and who may confidently be identified as Puritans.

By the end of Elizabeth's reign Protestantism had become so closely identified with England and Catholicism with the country's enemies, especially Spain, that Anglicanism was the accepted norm: the Church of England was established in every sense of the word. The Stansted cases referred to in the church courts reveal no trace of adherence to the Catholic faith, and the same is true of most of the villages around.

In some parishes there were disputes about church belief and practice, in particular about the wearing of the surplice and the administration of holy communion – the authorities wanted it administered at the communion rail, the Puritans in the main body of the church. There is no evidence of any such disputes at Stansted, though, as we shall see when we consider Puritanism more generally, John Wilkinson, vicar from 1573 to 1591, scandalised some of his congregation by his gambling. Perhaps in the case of one 'Elliot' in 1588 we catch a bizarre expression of the Calvinist belief in predestination, for he said he could tell how many of the village should be saved (at the day of judgement) and, by implication, how many would go to hell – though he added modestly that he would need half an hour's notice.[25] There is no trace of Catholicism in the secular courts either, and in the 1620 census only one 'recusant' was listed, the squire's brother, William Myddelton, who had married a Catholic wife and settled in Flanders, though at the time of the census he was apparently living in Stansted.[26]

In 1582 the de Veres, short of cash because of the extravagances of the seventeenth Earl, disposed of their Stansted estate to John Southall, a Master Clothworker of London, and in 1584 Southall passed it on to his son-in-law, Edward Hubbard (the name is spelt in several ways, also Hubberd and Hubert), a wealthy Clerk in the Court of Chancery.[27] Edward came from the nearby village of Birchanger, and although as a Clerk in Chancery he must have spent much of his time in London he would have been more involved in the affairs of Stansted than the lordly de Veres. This was not always to good effect, however. In 1589 he was accused of detaining £100 which should have been 'employed towards the erecting of a free school at Stansted'.[28] He also became embroiled in a dispute with the vicar, Richard Laughlin, the two churchwardens and 31 other parishioners about the use of the Lancaster Chapel adjoining the chancel in St. Mary's. What gave rise to this dispute is not clear, but in 1593 the parties agreed that Hubbard and his heirs and assigns, being Lord or Lords of the manor of Stansted Mountfitchet, should have the exclusive use and enjoyment of the chapel for ever without the least interference from the parishioners of Stansted. In return Hubbard and his heirs would maintain and repair the said chapel at their own expense. But if Edward, or his heirs and assigns, 'goe aboute to pull downe the sayde Chappell or to sell awaye the lead' the churchwardens and parishioners could enter the Chapel and repossess it and they would have the right 'utterlye to expell remove and putt out' Edward Hubbard and his heirs and assigns.[29] Hubbard also gave them an annuity of 40s. a year to be derived from certain land to be used for the repair of the church.[30]

Two of Hubbard's daughters married sons of Roger Harlakenden of Colne Priory, Margaret marrying Richard the heir – about whom we shall hear more when we consider emigration to America.

Edward left the Stansted estate to his eldest son, Francis, who was not only, like his father, a clerk in the Court of Chancery, but an author and poet, winning royal favour and a knighthood with a work that claimed to demonstrate that King James was Elizabeth's rightful successor. He seems, however, to have fallen from favour, and in 1615 he sold his estate to Thomas Myddelton.

1. The building was not pulled down, and at some point it was turned into a blacksmith's shop.
2. ERO, D/DWv T16, Prior and Canons of Thremhall Priory to the Earl of Oxford.
3. Oxley (1965: 46, 283).
4. Oxley (1965: 110, 113). See also Fowler (1906: 280-1, 341-6).
5. Morant (1760-68: 579).
6. Internet: Communication from Heritage Conservation at Essex County Council.
7. Tricker (1992: 2).
8. ERO, D/ACR 2/71 and D/ACR 2/91.
9. It is possible that this reference to Thomas Joslyn is a mistake, since Sir Thomas Joslyn was one of the Commissioners. Or it may be that Thomas Joslyn is not the same man as Sir Thomas Joslyn.
10. King (1869: 209).
11. For a general account of these inventories, see King (1869: 197-215). For Stansted's inventory, see Chapman-Waller (1911: 96).
12. Quoted in Gyford (1999: 13).
13. There is a reference to the mass in the form prescribed by St. Gregory in Katherine Spooner's will of 1523: ERO, D/ACR 2/147.
14. ERO, D/ABW 39/123.
15. ERO, D/ABW 8/156.
16. ERO, D/ABW 33/272.
17. ERO, D/ABW 4/44. D/ABW 8/240, D/ABW 8/249 and D/ABW 34/25.
18. ERO, D/ABR 1/88, D/ABR 2/21.
19. There are also eight nuncupative wills (i.e. oral wills witnessed by at least two persons and dealing only with the distribution of personal property) in which there are no religious preambles.
20. ERO, D/ABW 2/34.
21. ERO, D/ABW 37/223.
22. ERO, D/ABW 37/230.
23. ERO, D/ABW 19/93.
24. ERO, D/ABW 10/51.
25. ERO, D/AZ 1/2, p. 102.
26. Thrush and Ferris (2010: 466), and the entry for Richard Myddleton in Lloyd, Davies and Davies (1959: 676).
27. This account, taken from Morant, is a simplified version of a protracted and complicated set of transactions in which the poet and playwright John Lyly was involved. Lyly was the Earl's secretary and steward. See Pearson (2005:81).
28. Emmison (1970: 90).
29. ERO, D/P 109/7/1.
30. *Acts of the Privy Council*, xvii, 410: quoted in F.G. Emmison (1970: 90). See also Probert (1930).

7: SIR THOMAS MYDDELTON

In rank, being gentry rather than nobility, Thomas Myddelton was not the equal of some of his predecessors, but in achievement he was second to none, save possibly the last Richard de Montfichet. By the time he bought his new estate he was about 65 years old. His father, Richard Myddelton, had been Governor of Denbigh castle in Wales, and Thomas was the fourth of his nine sons. The two eldest had died young and the third was probably living abroad by the time of Richard's death, and so Thomas was in effect his father's heir. He had been apprenticed to a London grocer, Ferdinando Poyntz, who had extensive dealings in the Netherlands, mainly in refined sugar, and by 1578 he had been Poyntz's factor at Flushing. In the words of the inscription on his tomb in the parish church,

20. Sir Thomas Myddelton.

> *He was sent as a merchant into foreign parts. He made himself well acquainted with countries and their languages, merchandise and manners. He performed the private mysteries of his profession (that of a merchant) as well as the public business of the kingdom under the auspices of Lord Walsingham (to whom he was intimately known) with great integrity and an uncommon prudence.*

In 1583, after completing his apprenticeship, he became a freeman of the Company of Grocers and acted as a factor to a group of London sugar bakers in Antwerp, and when this enterprise was ended by the Spanish siege in 1584/5 he moved to London and set up his own 'sugarhowse' in Mincing Lane.

His first wife, Hester, was the daughter of Richard Saltonstall, Governor of the Merchant Adventurers and, in 1597/8, Lord Mayor of London, whom Thomas joined in many commercial enterprises. In 1585 he moved to St. Mary Aldermanbury in Cripplegate, and between 1588 and 1596 he helped to finance many voyages, sometimes as treasurer of the voyage, sometimes victualling the ships of others, sometimes as a shareholder of the vessels. In these enterprises he often joined forces with Drake, Hawkins, Frobisher and Raleigh. He was a founder member of the East India Company and an adventurer in the Virginia Company. He also supported the New River Company, which was formed to realise the ambition of his younger brother, Hugh Myddelton, to bring a new water supply to London. In 1591/2 he and three others were appointed surveyors of the customs in all parts of England except London, an advancement which he owed largely to his connection with Walsingham. In 1603 he was knighted by King James, and in 1613/14, like his father-in-law before him, he became Lord Mayor of London. After that, by virtue of office, he became an alderman and was for many years the senior alderman or father of the city. He represented the City of London in the Parliaments of 1624-26.[1]

During this time his business interests had rapidly expanded. He exported cloth to Germany, importing haberdashery and dyestuffs in return, and he had also turned to other forms of investment, such as cattle fattening in Lincolnshire, copper works in Neath and a brass foundry in Lambeth. As with many wealthy merchants, his ready access to cash led to his undertaking the functions of a banker, and money-lending became a major activity. Courtiers offered jewels and plate by way of security, his neighbours in North Wales mortgaged their land. Partly through purchases, partly through the foreclosure of mortgages, he amassed a large estate in North Wales, centred on Chirk Castle, which he bought in 1595 for £4,800. His estates and banking business were said to be worth an astonishing £8,000 a year at his death.[2]

It was against this background that in 1615 he purchased his estate in Stansted. According to one authority he remained a Welsh magnate first, a London merchant second, and a member of the Essex gentry 'only a poor third'.[3] But he quickly put down roots in Stansted, where he began the erection of a new Stansted Hall, a grand house close to St. Mary's Church, and after his death in August 1631 at the age of 80 or 81 it was in the chancel of St. Mary's Church that he was buried and his magnificent tomb was erected.[4]

He had strong Puritan convictions. According to the inscription on his monument 'He was a man of the greatest virtue; devout to his God, faithful to his Prince, true to his country, courteous to his friends, respectful to all, the strictest defender of widows and orphans', and after all his affairs had been 'continually crowned with the desired success, he piously and calmly resigned his soul to heaven ... in earnest expectation of a better life than this'. His religious faith was again emphasised in some anonymous verses composed after his death, *The Muses Oblation*. He had no fear of death, said the poet, because his name was enrolled in the book of life.

> *True Christian faith endued his constant minde,*
> *And unto such the promise was asign'de.*
>
> *His faiths eye saw one hanging on a tree,*
> *By whose great power death seemed dead to be.*[5]

As mayor of London he had set beggars to work in the Bridewell, mounted an investigation of brothels and reduced the amount and strength of beer brewed within the metropolis. A report drawn up towards the end of his mayoralty had noted his endeavours 'to keep the Sabbath day holy, for which he hath been much maligned'.[6] In 1621 it had been recorded that 'Yt pleased the Right Worshipful Knight Sir Thomas Middleton to make a very religious speech and exhortation to the whole assemblie of the Misterie of the Grocerie of London'.[7] Towards the end of his life he and another Welshman, Alderman Rowland Heylin, had financed the publishing of the Welsh Bible in portable and therefore popular form. *The Muses Oblation,* no doubt referring to his protection of Puritan ministers and his support for their publications, tells us that

Hee to religious Pastors was a shield,
And unto them encouragement did yield ....

The preamble to Myddelton's will anticipated the wording of his monument and the *Oblation*: 'I commend my sole into ye hands of Almighty God my maker hoping and stedfastly believing to be saved and to have free remission of all my sinnes and to inherit everlasting life only by the merritts and passions of Jesus Christ my only Saviour and Redeemer'. But what his memorialist emphasised above all, and what his will reflected above all, was his generosity to his family. 'But what a support he was to his own relations: some he advanced to honour, all to riches.' To his family he was '(as it were) a deity'. Thomas, having been generous to them, was clearly revered by his relations.

He was also loyal to his friends, making provision in his will, for example, for the descendants of his first master, the grocer Ferdinando Poyntz.

He did esteeme the bond of friendship so,
As where he once laid hold he ne'er let goe.

He was not as radical in politics as in religion. In 1626 he helped to raise a forced loan for King Charles I, which was probably the reason why he was not re-elected as a Member of Parliament for the City of London.[8]

In all he was married four times. His first wife, Hester, died within a few years, having given birth to two sons, Richard, who died young, and Thomas, who inherited the Chirk Castle estate. He then married Elizabeth, the widow of John Olmested of Ingatestone in Essex, by whom he had two sons and two daughters – Henry, who died young, Timothy, who succeeded to the estate of Stansted, Hester, who married Henry Salusbury of Llewenny, Denbighshire, and Mary, who married Sir John Maynard, younger brother of the William who became the first Lord Maynard in 1620.[9] Third, he married Elizabeth, widow of Miles Hobart, clothworker of London, and fourth Anne, widow of Jacob Wittewronge, a London brewer of Huguenot origins, who survived him. Since she was a young woman and he an old man, this last marriage gave rise to a scurrilous song, 'Room for Cockolds, here comes my Lord Mayor'.

His funeral on 8 September 1631 was an occasion of great pomp and ceremony: in *The Muses Oblation* it was said to be attended 'with as much, or more Honor, Pompe, Cost and Magnificence, than any Knight, or Lord Maior of London, ever had to men's remembrances' - and the detailed accounts of it in the papers of his fourth wife and widow make it clear that, like all funerals of the

King's great subjects, it was conducted as a heraldic funeral controlled by the College of Arms.[10] According to Claire Gittings, 'The reason for [such funerals] was political; the death of a powerful subject weakened the social hierarchy and had to be compensated for by a display of aristocratic strength'.[11] So the people of Stansted were to be impressed by a grand demonstration of wealth and power, and it was also an occasion from which the poor would benefit from gifts of money, food and clothing.

The order of procession from the hall to the church, which was organised by heralds from the College of Arms, was set out in elaborate detail. First came two 'conductors', and then 'the poore in gownes', who proceeded two by two. Perhaps there were 80 of them, since they usually numbered the age of the deceased, which in this case was 80 or 81, and the accounts record the payment of £4 5s. for 'making and cutting 80 poore gownes'. They would have taken part in the procession to the church, but would have waited outside during the funeral service. Then came another two conductors, then two trumpeters with banners, and then Peter Myddelton, clearly a member of the family, bearing a guidon (a forked or pointed flag). A black-draped horse was led by a gentleman, followed by the menservants of the gentlemen, squires, knights and nobles, all of them in black cloaks. The standard with Sir Thomas's crest and motto was carried by one Benjamin Walden, who was followed by 'gents etc. in gowns', the 'minister & Doctors etc.', the preacher, and 'the Pennon [banner] of his owne armes borne by Mr. Rich: Midelton'. Behind them came four Heralds, and behind the Heralds came the embalmed corpse 'borne by 20 men in gownes'. On one side of it were members of the family carrying the four pennons of Sir Thomas's own arms impaled by those of his four wives. On the other side were men carrying the four pennons of the City of London, the Grocers, the Merchant Adventurers and the East India Company. Then came the chief mourner and four assistants, then Lord Maynard (the older brother of Sir Thomas's son-in-law), a gentleman usher, and the ladies, gentlewomen and other knights and gentlemen who had been invited to attend.

The church would have been draped in black, and after the funeral service and burial the procession would have returned to the hall where the guests were entertained to a sumptuous feast. There were three 'faires', or menus, the best, the second best, and the third for the parish, and the accounts list every item – 54 boiled pullets, 48 partridges and 144 wild pigeons, roast swan, roast pheasant, roast tongue and udder, roast heron, three fresh salmon, 12 lobsters, half a barrel of sturgeon, 30 quails, 120 larks, 36 rabbits, six geese, 400 eggs, 192 lb of butter, six lb of anchovies, six gallons of oysters, to mention just some. The 20 sheep and two bullocks, listed on a separate page, appear to have been provided for the second best 'faire' and the parish. There were over a hundred gallons of wine and other casks weighing 18½ hundredweight.

As well as the outlay for mourning clothes and the banquet there were the fees to be paid to the heralds, the painters and the trumpeters, and also to doctors and apothecaries for 'physick & ymbalmeing'. There was more expense on carriages to bring guests to and from London and on board and lodging for them before and

7: SIR THOMAS MYDDELTON

after the funeral. Eighteen guineas were 'given for a dole at church dore and to poore widows and other poore people at Stansted'.

Sir Thomas's monument in St. Mary's was as magnificent as his funeral. He is shown ruffed and recumbent, his hands clasped in prayer, encased in gilt-studded plate armour and with a red robe trimmed with fur, and he is watched over by four angels, two on either side, those nearer to him holding the long inscription, and surmounted by his coat of arms and those of the City of London and the Grocers Company. Behind two pairs of flanking black columns there are a sword and a helmet, a drum and spears, and the base is decorated with skulls. Here are two messages for those who come to admire: this was a great man, but, like all of us,

21. Sir Thomas Myddelton's monument in St. Mary's Church.

22. Stansted Hall c.1770.

subject to mortality. At the east end of the north aisle (though formerly in the chancel, and then the Lancaster chapel), is the strikingly beautiful tomb of Hester Salusbury, Sir Thomas's daughter, the work of Epiphanius Evesham. In 1608 she had married Henry Salusbury, the head of a powerful Welsh family whose ancestral home was at Lleweni in Denbighshire. Having had four children, she died in 1614, 17 years before her father, and a year before he bought the Stansted estate. Perhaps she was buried in advance and in anticipation of her father's purchase, but her husband was still alive and it seems strange that she should not have been buried at his home at Lleweni. Her dress is distinctive, the narrow bodice contrasting with the voluminous folds below, and she is wearing a lace collar and cuffs and, most striking of all, a high hat with a wreath of material twisted over the brim.

And here we come to a puzzle. Norman Scarfe in the Shell Guide poetically describes Hester as 'dressed and ready for heaven'. The more prosaic Nikolaus Pevsner merely refers to her 'wearing the fashionable high hat'. The latest church guide, however, written by Roy Tricker in 1992, says that 'This very slender lady is dressed in hunting costume' and 'Tradition has it that she was killed by a stag in

23. Hester Salusbury's monument in St. Mary's Church.

Stansted Park'.[12] The inscription says nothing about this, merely recording that she died on the 26th January 1614 (1615 by the later reckoning), and the first reference to the tradition mentioned in the church guide is in *Kelly's Directory* of 1882, 267 years after the alleged event.[13] Framework Archaeology also describe her, solely on the basis of the *Directory* and the Guide, as 'dressed in full hunting regalia' and refer again to the tradition that she was killed by a stag in Stansted Park.[14]

It seems most likely, however, that the story of Hester's being killed by a stag stems from the belief that the clothes she is wearing are a hunting costume. But in fact what she was wearing was normal dress for well-to-do women at that time. Muilman, writing in 1770, makes no mention of a hunting accident, but merely refers to her being 'dressed in the attire of the days she lived in'.[15] Just five miles to the north, in Clavering church, a brass on the south wall shows Joane Day, who died in 1593, dressed in a similar way, complete with hat, and at Holy Trinity Church in Littlebury, about nine miles to the north, there is a similar brass commemorating Anne Byrd, who died in 1624. Further afield, at Whitchurch church in Wales, a brass commemorating another branch of the Myddeltons shows the daughters all wearing hats and dressed in this style. It is very unlikely, therefore, that Hester was killed by a stag.

Regardless of how she met her death, however, care was taken to proclaim Hester's religious faith. A wall tablet shows the instruments of Christ's passion set out in heraldic form - his hands and feet with the imprints of the nails and a royal helmet with a crown of thorns. The inscription reads:

The passions w[hich] thou didst endure
Sweet Saviour for my sins
My soules salvation did procure
Though body rest herein.

---

1. Dodd (1961: 280).
2. Thrush and Ferris (2010: 467).
3. Stephenson (1976: 282).
4. In his will, dated 1630, he directed that he should be buried either at Chirk Castle or at Stansted.
5. Manuscript in Rothamsted Research.
6. Thrush and Ferris (2010: 467).
7. *DNB*; also Dodd (1961: 280).
8. Thrush and Ferris (2010: 468).
9. Sir John represented Essex in the Long Parliament. He was one of five members accused by Charles I of treason, and in a celebrated confrontation the House of Commons refused to hand them over to the King. Later he ran into trouble with the army because of his opposition to more radical policies.
10. For these records, see the Lawes-Wittewronge papers, D/ELw Z22/1-3, in the Hertfordshire Archives.
11. Gittings (1988: 166).
12. Tricker (1992: 10).
13. An earlier church guide, by G.W.D. Winkley, n.d., makes no mention of the hunting tradition. In the *SMPM*, May 1939, 'Notes on the Church and Parish of Stansted Mountfitchet', Frank Reader refers to the account of Hester's death in *Kelly's Directory* and says: 'We are, however, unable to find any evidence for this, and Kelly's are unable to trace their authority.'
14. FA (2008: 260, 282). The park was in decline at this time: parts of it had been leased out as meadows and pastures as early as 1585 and in the late 17th century the whole area was 'disparked'.
15. Muilman, Vol. III (1770: 32).

8: THE CIVIL WAR

The epitaph and ornamentation on Hester Salusbury's tomb remind us of her father's strong Puritan convictions, and it is not surprising that in the coming Civil War her brothers, Thomas and Timothy, were among the leaders of the Parliamentarians in North Wales and Essex respectively.

Old Sir Thomas's Puritanism sat comfortably with religious belief and practice in Essex. There was a long tradition of radical belief in the county, mainly in the cloth towns of the east, but also in and around Saffron Walden. In the fifteenth century Lollardy had been strong in the area, and in the reigns of Elizabeth and the early Stuarts Essex was reckoned to be the most Puritan county in the country, while across the border in Hertfordshire Bishop's Stortford was also strongly Puritan. The term has been defined in many ways. Originally it was a name that was used by the Puritans' enemies to denote a narrow and canting hypocrisy, and it was then taken on by themselves to denote piety and godliness. They were zealous Protestants, fiercely hostile to any church practices that suggested Roman Catholicism and intent on effecting a reformation of manners. They riled and infuriated those who were more tolerant and less demanding: they were, it was said, like a pitchfork to a dog, they were 'painful' (i.e. painstaking) and 'uncomfortable preachers'.[1]

They received little or no support from successive monarchs and archbishops. Elizabeth was unsympathetic. In 1584 great pressure was brought to bear on the clergy to subscribe to the Book of Common Prayer and the Thirty-Nine Articles, and at least 43 Essex ministers were suspended for refusing to comply.[2]

In the same year a group of Puritan ministers centred on Dedham, the so-called Dedham conference, undertook a survey of the Essex ministry. Based on information that must have been supplied by Puritans throughout the county, they claimed to demonstrate that fewer than one third of beneficed ministers were competent preachers of reputable morals, and that of the 'painful preachers' nearly half objected to some aspect of Anglican practice.[3] In support of these contentions they listed 162 'unpreaching' ministers, and among these were several who held their posts in parishes that were contiguous with Stansted - Mr. Lucking at Takeley, 'one that cannot preach the Word of God truly and soundly'; Mr. French at Birchanger, 'a very insufficient and careless minister, a gamester'; Mr. Batho at Elsenham, 'a very insufficient man, and cannot preach'; Mr. 'Jenewaie' at Manuden, another 'unpreaching' parson; and Mr. Darloe at Ugley, 'a common swearer, a proude careless man, a riotous man; he hath [been] absent from his benefice and preacheth not'.[4] They also listed 14 ministers 'of scandalous life', who were presumably even more reprehensible than those who were merely 'unpreaching', and among these was John Wilkinson of Stansted Mountfitchet, who was condemned as 'a gam[e]ster'.[5] (We would say 'gambler' today.) There were no doubt other complaints against him. When John Luddington, vicar of Great Sampford and Hempstead, was accused of holding Romish views, Wilkinson was one of four clerics who rose to his defence.[6] A contrasting list was added of 'the sufficient painful and carefull preachers and ministers in Essex' who had been molested and vexed.[7]

8: THE CIVIL WAR

Twenty-seven ministers who had been suspended sought protection from the Privy Council, and some Councillors were receptive and intervened. Among them was Walsingham, a great friend of the Puritans, who, it will be remembered, was a powerful sponsor for Thomas Myddelton.[8] Echoing the sentiments of the Dedham survey, they drew up a protest to the Archbishop of Canterbury in which, while defending the ministers who had been silenced, they attacked others who in their view were unfit for the work.[9] All the suspended ministers bar one were restored, but the respite was temporary. In the summer of 1586 40 were suspended again.

Following the Parliamentary elections of that year the Puritan ministers based on Dedham sought to exert pressure on the new Parliament by instigating more petitions from all over the county. Two of these were from the Hundreds of Uttlesford and Clavering, complaining of idleness and scandal among their ministers – no doubt John Wilkinson was one they had in mind - and lamenting the increase of 'atheists, papists and other heretics'.[10] No action resulted, and a further petition to Parliament prepared by the suspended ministers in Essex was also ineffective. The Puritans were in despair and their defeat seemed total, but in Essex they continued to enjoy the support of powerful patrons such as the Rich family at Leighs Priory, near Chelmsford – Robert Rich was made Earl of Warwick in 1618 – and the closely linked Barringtons of Hatfield Broad Oak.[11]

After Elizabeth's death the Puritans expected great things of James I, but they were quickly disillusioned, and under Charles I they came under renewed attack. At Stansted Hall the lord of the manor was now Sir Thomas Myddelton, and the vicar was Edward Rumbold, a Cambridge graduate and evidently a man of a very different character from John Wilkinson. In 1628 Thomas Hooker, a Puritan lecturer at Chelmsford, fell foul of the authorities and was forced to leave his ministry. When he went on preaching further action was taken against him, and in the following year a petition in his support was signed by 49 ministers. Edward Rumbold was one of them, and Sir Thomas Myddelton would surely have sympathised with him and supported his action.[12]

This is not the only evidence of Puritan sympathies at Stansted at this time. In the 1630s the famous Puritan lecturer, Daniel Rogers, led groups of devout Puritans 'gadding about' to hear other preachers, and his son, Samuel, also sought out Puritan divines. Stansted was among the places they frequented.[13] (It was Daniel's father, Richard, who had received a legacy of £20 from John Thoroughgood of Stansted in 1584.) In 1635 the churchwardens of Stansted were presented for allowing Mr. Lockie to preach and hold divine service in their church when he did not have a licence: it seems very likely that Lockie was a Puritan lecturer.[14]

In 1628 William Laud was appointed Bishop of London (with responsibility for Essex) and in 1633 Archbishop of Canterbury. He provoked and infuriated the Puritans, and others too, by insisting on practices that in their eyes were steeped in Roman Catholicism, such as wearing a surplice and administering holy communion at the altar rails and not in the main body of the church; and when they refused to comply he intensified his attacks on them, making full use of the Star Chamber and the High Commission to inflict savage punishments on their leaders. This persecution had two main effects.

8: THE CIVIL WAR

First, it provoked a great wave of emigration to America, which lasted throughout the 1630s. How many left from Stansted we do not know, but we have evidence relating to several individuals and there may have been others as well. In 1632 Thomas Sandford went out with his brother Robert and his uncle, Andrew Warner, and was later to become one of the founders of the town of Milford in Connecticut. Two other brothers, Andrew and Zachariah, also crossed the Atlantic, either then or later, and apart from Thomas they all settled in Hartford, Connecticut, where the family was later noted for all being Quakers.[15] There were other emigrants whose connection with Stansted was more tenuous. Roger Harlakenden, who went out in 1635, was the son of Margaret Harlakenden, née Margaret Hubbard, who had been brought up in Stansted and whose brother, Francis, was the squire who had sold the estate to Thomas Myddelton.[16] At a humbler level William Saville, a joiner from Saffron Walden, who emigrated in 1640, had his family roots in Stansted.[17]

Another man who thought of leaving his homeland at this time was Thomas Thurgood, who was just 19 years old and was probably a member of the same family as John and Margaret Thoroughgood whose Puritan wills were quoted in Chapter 6. In 1631 he was intending 'by God's providence shortly to depart this realm of England and to goe beyond the seas into some other forran contry', and considering the risks and uncertainties involved he decided to make his will – for 'the estate of man is transitory and passinge away like the flowere which this daye springeth and tomorrow vanisheth and withereth'. He commended his soul to almighty God, and he drew up a schedule of all his goods and chattels which he bequeathed to his brother Nicholas.[18] It would seem, however, that he never left Stansted, or if he did he had to return, for he was buried there in April 1632.

The second effect of Laud's persecution was to drive the Puritans from being a social and religious movement into a powerful force for revolution, and the resulting religious conflicts were at the heart of the great political and military struggle that built up between Charles I and Parliament. The King's marriage to a Roman Catholic princess disturbed and angered many of his subjects, and so did the increasingly arbitrary nature of his government backed up by his insistence on the divine right of Kings. In 1629 he dismissed Parliament and embarked on a period of personal rule that lasted 11 years. Without Parliamentary backing he had to raise cash himself and among the measures that he resorted to was the unpopular Ship Money, which in 1635 was extended from the coastal districts to the whole country. Essex was assessed for £8,000 for a ship to be ready at Portsmouth on 1 March 1636, and Stansted had to contribute £34 16s. 9d.[19] In due course most of this was paid, but the shortfall in Essex was greater than in any other county and the sheriff reported that every penny had to be forced from the people.[20] The collectors continued to enforce their demands, but in 1639 only £331 was collected.[21] The King's sale of monopolies enraged the emergent manufacturers and merchants, and the long period of economic hardship in the country, lasting through the 1620s and 1630s, was seen by the Puritans as God's judgement on the nation.

In 1637 Charles tried to force the Scottish version of the Book of Common Prayer on the Scottish Presbyterians. In response the Scots formed the Scottish National Covenant whose members swore to defend the Presbyterian faith. The Presbyterian Kirk did without the rule of bishops, being ruled by ministers and elders, and there was a full scale rebellion which lasted from November 1638 to June 1639 and resulted in a humiliating defeat for

8: THE CIVIL WAR

Charles. In 1640 he returned to the attack, raising trained bands in the southern counties. But the conscripted men became mutinous, refused to march northwards, and began tearing down what they regarded as symbols of popery in the churches, such as the communion rails. About 50 Essex churches were attacked. Stansted, already under Puritan control, is unlikely to have suffered, but it is known that there was trouble at nearby Radwinter and Saffron Walden. In the conflict that followed the Scots invaded England and Charles was forced to come to terms again.

Confronted by the rebellious Scots Charles was forced at last to recall Parliament to raise the money needed for his attempts to put them down. After the election of 1640, however, the Puritans dominated the House of Commons, and, while prevailing on Charles to abolish Ship Money, they refused to vote the necessary subsidies and overturned many of his policies. In the summer of 1642 Charles, determined to reverse these defeats, began to raise troops and there was a rapid descent into civil war.

While the King established his court at Oxford, Parliament continued to be based in London, and as the Royalist armies began to threaten the capital it rallied its forces, calling on its supporters throughout the country, but above all in Essex. The main Parliamentary army was led by Robert Devereux, the Earl of Essex (who in spite of his title was based outside the county), but the dominant man locally was Robert Rich, Earl of Warwick. The Royalists were not without support in the county, and when Parliament became unpopular later this was quick to reassert itself, but for the present Warwick's dynamic leadership strengthened the Parliamentary cause and most of the gentry, including Timothy Myddelton, supported him. Trained bands were raised and assembled at Thaxted and Dunmow,[22] and there can be little doubt, in view of Myddelton's sympathies, that Stansted would have been well represented.

The Royalist forces, though checked at Edgehill and Turnham Green, were still threatening. A reorganisation of the Parliamentary armies was needed, and for this purpose the counties were grouped into Associations. Essex, together with Cambridgeshire, Hertfordshire, Norfolk and Suffolk, was included in the Eastern Association, created in December 1642, with Huntingdonshire and Lincolnshire being added later. Led by the Earl of Manchester, but inspired by Oliver Cromwell, this was the most powerful and well organised of the Associations. It soon made its presence felt locally. In January 1643 meetings were held throughout Essex, and in April that year the Association sent orders to the constables in each parish to provide men, horses and arms. In north-west Essex they were ordered to report at Stansted, some on 3 May and others on 11 May. The constables' returns from Stansted have not survived, though we know that the parish had to contribute,[23] but it is clear from the returns of the surrounding parishes that the most common arrangement was for the better-off inhabitants, sometimes acting individually, sometimes in small groups, to pay and equip volunteers, who would be either foot soldiers or dragoons (light cavalrymen).

Some parishes responded well, but in others there was considerable reluctance. The constables for Takeley replied that although they had 'tacken greate paynes ... they that we would have are run a way out of our Toune', but if they were given a little time they hoped for more success: 'We deleuered four men at Dounmoue. We deleuered 2 solgers at Stansted.'[24] The constables at Elsenham were told to supply volunteers to appear at

8: THE CIVIL WAR

Stansted on 3 May, 'but we have not any volunteers, nor but one dragonere'.[25] It is possible that, because of Timothy Myddelton's strong commitment to the Parliamentary cause, the parishioners of Stansted were more forthcoming.

Throughout the war there were impassioned calls on the county to provide men, money, horses and arms, and Timothy, as a Deputy Lieutenant and therefore a key figure in the local military administration, was heavily involved in this activity. Essex as a whole rose to the challenge, but there were many local difficulties. Later in 1643 one of Timothy's neighbours, Sir Thomas Nightingale at Newport, complained to him, to his 'loveing frend' as he called him, that 'this small town [of Newport] shall find three nags with muskets and able riders. …. Besides, we are to find men well affected to the Parliament, but where we shall find them God in Heaven knows; for we do not.' He was hard put to it to make his own financial contribution to the war effort.[26] So too was Elizabeth Soame at Heydon, who wrote complaining to Sir Thomas Barrington, adding however 'Sir, I knoe Mr. Midelton will doe anything for me'.[27]

In 1644 we have direct evidence of Stansted's involvement in the war in the unusual form of a memorandum in the parish register. Timothy Myddelton's brother, Thomas, unlike the other great landowners in North Wales, had come out strongly for Parliament, and on 17 August 1644 30 Stansted parishioners, obviously with Timothy's encouragement, subscribed £21 6s. 8d. to help Thomas to bring North Wales under control. Timothy himself gave £10, Mark Downe, the 'minister', £2, and the rest sums varying between 2s. and £1 10s.

The way in which this first stage of the Civil War was fought out lies beyond the scope of a parish history. It was a massive upheaval, and it has been estimated that between 1641 and 1651 one man in five bore arms, a figure which might have been even higher in Essex.[28] Men from Stansted would certainly have taken part in the great battles of that time, and there is evidence that in 1645 one of them, John Mylburne, described as 'Tymothy Middleton's man', helped a certain Jeremiah May to arrest 'a cavilleer with his horse and armes'.[29] (May later fell on hard times and asked the authorities for a pension, which is why we know about this incident.) In 1645 the army of the Eastern Association was disbanded and replaced by the New Model Army, the Ironsides, and after the crushing Parliamentary victories of that year Charles took refuge among the Scots, who handed him over to Parliament. With this the first phase of the Civil War came to an end.

Throughout this time Timothy Myddelton was at the heart of the Parliamentary administration of Essex. From 1642 he was one of the Deputy Lieutenants of the county, by 1644 he was sheriff, and two years later he was one of the contractors appointed by Parliament to dispose of the bishops' lands 'for the service of the Commonwealth'. As well as being a member of the county committee for Essex he was also a committee member for the Eastern Association, the great driving force of the Parliamentary armies.[30] Between 1643 and 1645 he was appointed to at least six committees, four of them to raise men and money for the Parliamentary cause, one to carry out the Ordinance for the sequestration of notorious delinquents' estates, and one to carry out the provisions of the Act 'for the punishment of scandalous Clergymen and others'.[31]

So as well as being a key figure locally in the military administration Myddelton was an active agent in the Puritan reformation of society. It was in the early years of the war that most of the Puritan-driven sequestrations took place, i.e. the removal of ministers from their livings because they failed to live up to Puritan standards, and two of the men who were ejected, Samuel Southern of Manuden and Thomas Heard of Takeley, were in parishes that bordered on Stansted. Among his many offences Southern had 'persecuted his parishioners even to excommunication, for going to heare sermons at other churches on the Lord's day afternoons....' They were doubtless sermons by Puritan lecturers, and Stansted would have been among the churches where they were given.[32]

Richard Ward, the vicar of Stansted, was firmly on the side of Parliament, as we might expect from a man who had been presented to the living by Timothy Myddelton in 1640. Like so many Puritan divines he had graduated at Cambridge, and his doctrine was unremittingly Calvinist.[33] In November 1641 official approval was given for the publication of *The Pious Man's Practice in Parliament Time*, Ward's 'seasonable and necessary tractate concerning the presages, and causes of a common-wealth's ruine'. It was dedicated to, among others, 'his worthie, and much honoured Patrons, Sir Iohn Mainard Knight (together with his Religious and virtuous Lady) and Timothy Middleton, Esquire'. (Maynard was Myddelton's brother-in-law, and his religious and virtuous Lady was Myddelton's sister, Mary.)[34] At this stage Ward was merely warning the country of its parlous condition and urging it to turn to prayer, but in *The Anatomy of Warre*, published in 1642, he addressed more contentious issues. Was it ever lawful for subjects to take up arms against their Sovereign? His answer was yes, if the Prince had not observed his covenants and promises, and provided that the war had Parliamentary approval. And was it lawful to use military means? Again his answer was yes, since these were 'ordained by God ... if we use them in the feare of the Lord....'[35] He was even more forthright in *The Vindication of the Parliament, and their Proceedings*, which was also published in 1642. He urged his readers to stand by Parliament, for the King had fallen into the hands of 'evil counsellors'. The choice was between Popery and Protestantism, Slavery and Liberty, Estates or no Estates.[36] And he was just as outspoken in a pamphlet whose lengthy and innocuous-sounding title began 'Jehoshaphats going forth to battell with the wicked'. Just as Jehoshaphat had listened to the prophet of the Lord and mended his ways, so now should Charles mend his ways. Ward rejected the divine right of Kings and denied that the opposition were guilty of treason: far from it, they had been restraining tyranny. 'You [Charles] talk of peace, but who has stricken the first stroke and given the first blow?' Such no doubt were the sentiments which he conveyed to his parishioners from his pulpit in St. Mary's.

It would be surprising if a man of Ward's persuasion wore a surplice in church, and there is evidence which suggests that he did not. When an inventory of the church's goods was drawn up in 1644 it was noted that the surplice was in the hands of Gyles Buttalls, who might have been the parish clerk, which suggests that it was not being used by the vicar; and in 1659 the surplice was no longer there.[37]

Ward stayed as vicar until 1647, when his place was taken by Robert Abbot, but there is an unresolved question here. In 1644, among the people of Stansted who had contributed to the support of Sir Thomas Myddelton in North Wales, the 'minister' was Mark Downe, and not, as we might have expected, Richard Ward. Downe, who was a Cambridge graduate, had been a minister in the parish of St. Petrock's in Exeter until 1641, and went back to St. Petrock's in 1657. Perhaps for a spell in 1644 he stood in briefly for Richard

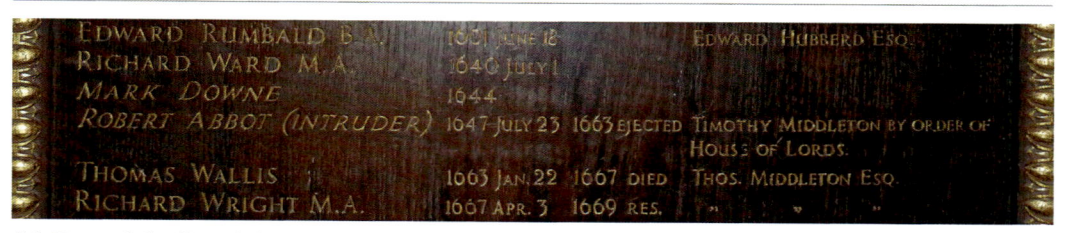

24. Part of the list of vicars in St. Mary's Church. This list was given to the church by Ormond Blyth in 1934, and was based on a previous list that had been framed and hung in the church. The original list was in place at least as early as 1931, when Arthur Turberville was vicar. Turberville was highly critical of the Puritans: see pages 280-1 below. Compiled almost 300 years after the Civil War, the list still reflects its animosities and conflicts. The date of Downe's appointment is given as 1644, there is no date for his departure and his name appears in italics. His inclusion in the list appears to be based solely on the reference to him in the list of men who gave money to support Thomas Myddelton in Wales – see page 65 above. The name of Robert Abbot is also italicised. The names of all the other vicars are in upright capitals. Abbot is described as an 'intruder', a word which would normally indicate a man who had taken the place of a sequestered Royalist (which Abbot certainly was not), and he was 'ejected' in 1663 when he refused to take the oath required by the Government of King Charles II under the Act of Uniformity. The most likely reason for the italics is that the compiler regarded the appointments of Downe and Abbot as irregular (SMPM, April 1931 and March 1935). Abbot was appointed in 1647 under an order of the House of Lords and on the presentation of Timothy Myddelton, who was patron of the living. Downe, I think, was not formally appointed at all.

Ward – this seems most likely, since Ward's name did not appear in the list of contributors - or perhaps he was a Puritan lecturer maintained by Timothy Myddelton. We know that he was of the Puritan persuasion. In a later history relating to Devon he was described as 'Mark Downe, of puritanical memory', and in 1662 he was ejected from St. Petrock's for refusing to take the oath under the Act of Uniformity.[38]

By the end of the first phase of the Civil War, although the Royalists had been defeated, opposition to the King was so badly divided that he hoped to take advantage of this to secure his return to power. Parliament was dominated by the Presbyterians and the New Model Army by more radical elements with strong political views, such as the Levellers and the Anabaptists. These divisions were so sharp that in 1648 the Army marched on London and purged Parliament of the members of whom it disapproved, and in debates among the soldiers at Saffron Walden, Dunmow and elsewhere there were demands for all adult men to have the vote, for Parliaments to be elected annually or biennially, and for religious tolerance for all except Catholics.[39] (Though tolerance had not been extended to Archbishop Laud, who had been executed in 1645.) No doubt the debates at Saffron Walden had reverberations in Stansted, but Timothy Myddelton stayed firmly within the Presbyterian mainstream. One of the measures introduced by Parliament had been a new system of Presbyterian administration whereby the church was to be ruled, not by bishops and priests, but by 'Classes' (presbyteries, singular 'Classis') of ministers and elders. Fourteen Classes were established in Essex, and one of them, the Clavering and Uttlesford Classis, included in its number two representatives from Stansted, Timothy Myddelton and William Vincent. Both were listed as elders and, in common with the arrangements in several other parishes in the Classis, no minister was appointed.[40]

Robert Abbot, it seems, took up the same moderate position as Myddelton. In December 1647, alarmed by the demands of the radicals, London ministers issued a Testimony 'against the Errors, Heresies and Blasphemies of these times, and the toleration of them', and this gave rise to similar testimonies, among them the Essex Testimony of 1648 which was signed by 127 ministers, including Robert Abbot.[41] Meanwhile Abbot continued to win official approval: in a survey of the clergy in 1650 he was listed as a preaching minister.[42]

By 1647 support for Parliament had weakened even in Essex: many objected to soldiers being quartered in their homes, taxes were high, and the county committees were regarded as oppressive. It was against this background that in November 1647 the King escaped from Hampton Court, where he had been kept under detention. He was trying to get a Scottish army to invade, whereupon there would be an uprising of his supporters in England. But the Royalists in Kent, led by Lord Goring, jumped the gun. Goring's regiments were defeated by Fairfax at Maidstone, but they then crossed the Thames into Essex and in June 1648 they captured as hostages ten members of the county committee, including Timothy Myddelton, who had been meeting in Chelmsford. Fairfax again beat the Royalists in the open field and when they took refuge in Colchester, taking their hostages with them, he laid siege to the town.

As soon as Goring had crossed the Thames Fairfax sent urgent instructions to the parish constables to send in men and arms. The only local warrants to survive are those to the constables at Thaxted – 'Heareof faill not', they were warned, 'as you will ancer the Contrari'[43] - but we also have an account of the expenses incurred by the parish of Messing at this time, and from these it is clear that the parish constables must have been employed full time during the siege organising supplies and collecting rates to meet the cost.[44] Two thousand men served in the county regiment of Essex and 2,400 in the county regiment of Suffolk. The Parliamentarian siege was effective: by the end of August Colchester had run out of provisions and the soldiers and the townspeople, and no doubt the hostages too, were reduced to eating cats, dogs and horses. The Royalists' hopes of a relieving force came to nothing, and when news came of Cromwell's victory over their regiments at Preston the garrison surrendered and Timothy Myddelton and his colleagues were released.[45] In every year following, on 27 August, they celebrated the day of their deliverance.[46]

The second phase of the war quickly came to an end, and Charles was beheaded on 30 January 1649. One of those who signed the death warrant was John Jones from Merioneth, a relative of the Myddeltons. Before the war he had come to London in the service of his wealthy kinsmen and is known in 1639 to have been staying with Timothy Myddelton in Stansted. During the war he served as a captain in the forces raised by the second Sir Thomas Myddelton in North Wales, and he later married Cromwell's sister and rose to some pre-eminence in the Protectorate.[47] But it seems very unlikely that the moderate Timothy would have supported the execution of the King. His links were with those conservative Parliamentarians generally known as Presbyterians, among whom were his brother-in-law, John Maynard, and his brother in Wales, Sir Thomas Myddelton. Timothy continued to hold office – he was the head of the Essex militia committee – but with increasing age and the ending of hostilities he was no doubt less active.[48]

1. Hunt (1983: 149).
2. Hunt (1983: 97), Davids (1863: 77-8).
3. For sources see Hunt (1983: 328, fn. 42).
4. Davids (1863: Appendix to Chapter IV).
5. Peel (1915: II.163); Harold Smith (n.d.: 10).
6. Emmison (1973: 297).
7. Davids (1863: 106).
8. Hunt (1983: 99). They are listed in Davids (1863: 79).
9. Davids (1863: 79).
10. DWL 31/B/I/143-5, 185-7. See also Hunt (1983: 100-1); Davids (1863: 83).
11. Hunt (1983: 104).
12. Davids (1863: 155); Hunt (1983: 256).
13. Webster (1997: 269), and Webster and Shipps (2004: xix, xxiii, 30 and 60.).
14. ERO, D/ACA 51, pp. 15, 18, and D/AZ 1/8, p. 35. In 1636 Gervase Lockey was referred to as the clerk 'nuper [recently] de Takeley (D/AZ 1/9, p. 172) and this may be the same man.
15. Thompson (1994: 136). See also the website on Sandford Family History. Zachariah was living in Braintree before he emigrated: Brownell (1957: 41).
16. Brownell (1957: 44); Hunt (1983:197).
17. Thompson (1994: 90).
18. ERO, D/ABW 51/231.
19. ERO, T/A 42/1, copied from originals in NA.
20. *VCH* ii.228.
21. Hunt (1983: 280).
22. Thompson (lecture given in 1999). See also Davids (1863: 201).
23. ERO, D/DBa/O18/1.
24. ERO, D/DBa/O18/31.
25. ERO, D/DBa/O18/26.
26. BL, Egerton MSS 2647, f. 251. See also Kingston (1897: 133).
27. BL, Egerton MSS, 2647, f. 367.
28. Thompson (lecture given in 1999).
29. ERO, Q/SBA 2/78.
30. Stephenson (1976: 283).
31. Bannard (1936: 101-5).
32. Davids (1863: 239-40, 249).
33. Richard Ward (1641: 56).
34. Richard Ward (1641).
35. Richard Ward (1642A).
36. Richard Ward (1643B). Other publications included *The explication and application of the sacred vow and covenant*, and *The Principal Duty of Parliament men*. See also Davids (1863: 473).
37. Reader, 'An Inventory of 1644', *SMPM*, August 1941.
38. Oliver and Jones (1828:36).
39. For the debates in Saffron Walden and the immediate consequences, see Everett (2007: 35-48).
40. Davids (1863: 286). Vincent added his signature to an inventory of the church's goods in 1644: Reader, 'An Inventory of 1644', *SMPM*, August 1941. Reader speculates that he might have been a churchwarden.
41. Davids (1863: 473).
42. *Ibid*.
43. ERO, D/DU 87/2, Thomas Morrell to the constables of Thaxted or either of them, 6 June 1648: see also D/DU 87/3, John Gyver to the constables of Thaxted, 23 June 1648. These two documents were discovered in a chimney in Thaxted.
44. ERO, T/Z 597/1.
45. Kingston (1897: 272).
46. Macfarlane (1976: 352).
47. National Library of Wales, Chirk Castle, E.5602, Humphrey Jones to … 13 September 1639; Dodd (1971: 47); entry for John Jones in the *Dictionary of Welsh Biography Online*.
48. Stephenson (1976: 284).

9: THE AFTERMATH OF THE CIVIL WAR

The Protectorate of Oliver Cromwell, established in 1653, soon lost whatever popularity it had enjoyed. It imposed heavy taxes and was effective in collecting them. Once again we hear a direct voice from Stansted, that of the blacksmith, John Milton. He seems to have had his forge on the main road between London and Newmarket - perhaps it was housed in the old chapel erected by the de Veres - since he was evidently in the habit of haranguing people as they passed by in coaches or on horseback. Information about him was bought to the justices by Richard Hubbert on 23 April 1655. Hubbert alleged 'that divers and sundry times he did hear [Milton] use divers wicked, seditious, and scandalous words and language to the disgrace of the Lord Protector [Cromwell] and present government, and to the promoting of new insurrections and rebellion, viz. that about Christmas last past, or a little before – between Michaelmas and Christmas – seeing divers in company passing upon the road, some in a coach and some on horse back, the said Milton used these words: "These are Parliament rogues and I am faine to work hard to get money with ye sweat of my browse to maintain such Parliam[en]t rogues."[1] We do not know what the outcome was, but in complaining about paying taxes to support the Protectorate John Milton was voicing a widespread discontent.

Timothy Myddelton died in 1655, to be succeeded by his son, Thomas. Like many others, Thomas carefully distanced himself from his family's Parliamentary past. His uncle in Wales, at Chirk Castle, changed sides so far as to become one of the leaders in an unsuccessful Royalist uprising in Cheshire in 1659. Thomas did not go as far as that, but in the prevailing uncertainty he withdrew from public affairs and then, in 1660, when it was clear that the future lay with the Royalists, he worked as a member of the Essex militia committee which, like its counterparts in other counties, helped to secure the smooth return of Charles II. David Stephenson sums up his role:

> *Thomas's timely readiness to facilitate the Restoration, with its promise of order in religion, and a world made safe for gentlemen against the subversion of sectaries and soldiers alike, laid the foundation for the family's continued prominence in Essex.*[2]

According to Morant he 'built the new part of Stansted-hall'.[3]

Thomas's son, another Thomas, who succeeded him in 1668, was more politically active and ambitious. Knighted in 1675, four years later he stood as a candidate in a fiercely contested county election. The great issue was whether or not Charles II would be succeeded by his Catholic brother James, Duke of York. There were those, the Exclusionists, who wanted to exclude all Catholics from the throne: their candidates were Colonel Henry Mildmay and John Lamotte Honeywood. On the other side were those who supported James, and their candidates were Sir Eliab Harvey and Sir Thomas Myddelton. As a rough generalisation the former were the 'country' party (the embryonic Whigs), the latter the party of the court (the embryonic Tories). It seems surprising that Myddelton should have supported James, and he and Harvey were crushingly defeated. How far were the voters from Stansted involved? When Myddelton rode into the county town of Chelmsford he was accompanied by 150 followers, and the poll book reveals that 15 men from Stansted voted. Of these 12 voted for Myddelton alone, two for Myddelton and Harvey, and one brave man, Edward Solmes, for the Exclusionists, Mildmay and Honeywood. Clearly loyalty to the squire, or fear of the squire, was a major factor in their choice and took precedence over any inclination they might have had to stand firm against the Catholic James.[4]

This was not the end of Myddleton's ambitions, however, for 11 days later he was returned for the borough of Harwich, being described as 'a very worthy gentleman' and being 'agreed upon by all parties'. He served his constituency well and was re-elected in 1681. Later, seeing which way the wind was blowing, he abandoned the future James II, not standing for election in 1685, but being returned again in 1689 when there was a strong reaction against James's rule. In December the same year he confirmed his loyalty to the newly enthroned William and Mary by lending £1,000 to the government.[5] He continued to serve in Parliament, being consistently Whig and pro-Orange, until two years before his death in 1702. The people of Stansted would have had little to do with all this, not being involved in the elections at Harwich, but the doings of their squire in London no doubt provided much local talk and interest.

Sir Thomas's son, also Thomas, inheriting an estate worth £1,500 per annum,[6] followed his father's Whig tradition. He married the daughter of the Whig Speaker, Sir Richard Onslow, and succeeded where his father had failed, being elected for the county in 1708 and representing it, with a gap of two years, until his death in 1715 at the age of 39. Just as the voters from Stansted had supported his father, so they supported him: of the 47 men who voted in 1710, for example, 43 supported their squire. The votes in the neighbouring parishes were more evenly spread.[7]

By the time of his death Thomas had built up a reputation as 'a Person well approved of for his Gravity and Wisdom',[8] but the family's political eminence was then extinguished, for he left no son. His brother Stephen briefly held the Stansted estate in trust for Thomas's five daughters, and in 1715 it was sold to Thomas Heath of Mile End.

With the exception of the dalliance with the Court party in 1679 the Myddeltons had been able to negotiate the rapids of the Civil War, the Commonwealth and the Stuart monarchy with great success. They had kept their property and continued to prosper. Not so the vicar, Robert Abbot. After all the turmoil and turbulence of the Civil War the government of the newly restored Charles II, the Cavalier Government, was determined to enforce adherence to approved religious belief and practice. In the Act of Uniformity of 1662 it was laid down that no one could hold office in the church unless he took an oath of adherence to the form of prayers, sacraments and doctrines set out in the Book of Common Prayer. Abbot refused to take the oath and was ejected from his living. Seventy other ministers in Essex took the same course, among them those at some of the parishes nearby, Arkesden, Chickney, Clavering, Little Hallingbury, Quendon and Thaxted, and so too did the minister at Bishop's Stortford. Two years later the Conventicle Act of 1664 forbade meetings for unauthorized worship of more than five people who were not members of the same household. Failure to attend Anglican worship was punishable by fines. The Church of England now officially embraced the whole community, and no other form of public worship was allowed – a total ban that was not relaxed until 1672, when the Royal Declaration of Indulgence allowed a certain number of non-Anglican chapels to be established and served by approved ministers.

Nonconformists remained vigorous under repression, and they later drew proudly on their experience at this time to foster their self-image as a courageous minority that was prepared to suffer persecution for its beliefs. In the 1676 census of religious adherence carried out by Bishop Compton, Stansted, which fell in the Newport deanery, reported that it had 20 Nonconformists, compared with 348 Conformists and no Papists, not a high number, but a higher proportion than in any of the other villages in the deanery except Arkesden and Little and Great Sampford.[9]

There were two main branches of Nonconformity in Stansted, the Independents (or the Congregationalists as they were later known) and the Quakers (otherwise known as the Friends). The Independents met in each other's houses, where they welcomed fellow worshippers from other villages nearby, and they in turn went to meetings in other villages.[10] On several occasions they were taken to court for failing to attend the Anglican

25. The Independent Chapel on Chapel Hill, 'Erected 1698'.

church, and in July 1684 eight of them, together with co-religionists from the area, were accused of being unlawfully assembled 'under cover of religious exercises'. In 1682/3, after the Royal Declaration of Indulgence, an Independent church was founded at Wood Hall in Arkesden: its 86 members were drawn from 24 parishes, and three of them, John Edridge and his wife and 'Sister Cannon', were from Stansted.[11] In 1689, after William and Mary came to the throne, the Toleration Act was passed, and in 1698 the Independents in Stansted established their first church in a converted barn towards the bottom of Chapel Hill. It is indicative of their strength that according to a return made in 1716 there were 350 'hearers' attached to the church, many of whom came from other villages, and they were proud to record that 35 of them were county electors and 11 were 'gentlemen'.[12] The rest would have been mainly shopkeepers and craftsmen and their families. During the Civil War there had been many free-spirited Christians who had threatened to turn the world upside down, but the Independents of the 18th century were respectable men and women of God, with more interest in preserving the social order than in overthrowing it.

The Independents were particularly strong in Essex,[13] and indeed in Stansted, but it was the Quakers whose religious convictions gave rise to the greatest conflict with the authorities. They not only held unlawful meetings, but refused to take oaths or to pay tithes. In particular they refused to swear an oath of allegiance to the King, which was required under the so-called Quaker Act of 1662, though there is no record of Stansted's Quakers being taken to court for this. In 1666 20 people were 'taken at a meeting' held at Stansted in the house of Thomas Leeds 'under pretence of serving God': as well as the leading Quakers from Stansted those taken included Quakers from the villages around, such as Ashdon, Rickling, Henham, Manuden and Quendon, and also from Bishop's Stortford.[14]

26. The Friends Meeting House, erected in 1703 and demolished in 1967.

9: THE AFTERMATH OF THE CIVIL WAR

They were not deterred, and in March 1672 George Thorne, Benjamin Stanwood, John Burnet, Thomas Leeds and their wives, all Quakers, were presented to the authorities for holding a meeting by the constables for Bentfield Hamlet,[15] and there were many prosecutions for failing to attend the Anglican church. In 1677 Thomas and Mary Leeds, with their three sons, William, Daniel and Thomas and their families, boldly struck out for religious freedom and emigrated to America, where they and their fellow Quakers built a meeting house on the east bank of the Delaware river where Burlington City now stands. In 1687, however, the Stansted community was strengthened by the arrival of John Day, who opened a shop that was to continue in business for over 250 years.

Like the Independents, the Quakers benefited from the Act of Toleration, and in 1703 they established their meeting house on what is now Chapel Hill. They were not all uncompromising. Their religious principles ruled out the payment of tithes, but John Day, perhaps inadvertently, hit upon a way of keeping out of trouble and yet maintaining a good conscience. In 1691 John Reynolds became vicar at St. Mary's, and for four years Day refused to pay a penny in tithes. In November 1694, Reynolds noted, 'I ... sent to John Day's the Quaker for 6 quires of writing paper which came to 3 shillings and for 2 pounds of candles which came to 1 shilling, in all it came to 4 shillings which I did not pay him for, because he owes me as much for Tyths at ye rate of 1 shilling a year for four years last past.' In this way Day not only avoided prosecution but could also satisfy his Quaker friends that he had not compromised his principles. At this time, however, he was the only Quaker who was recorded as not paying his tithes.[16] John Burnet, by contrast, was recorded as paying, though sometimes late and not always in full.

Two other leading Quakers were John and Mary Farmer, though their connection with Stansted was short-lived. John was a woolcomber and practised his trade in several places, among them Saffron Walden and Stansted. He and Mary were ministers among the Friends and travelled separately or together on religious missions to different parts of the country. In Stansted, we are told, John 'was in good repute amongst his Friends there, for his labour of love in the ministry of the gospel, and for his orderly and upright walking in his daily intercourse in the world. Having laid before his Friends, in 1711 or 1712, a concern to pay a religious visit to America, he was set at liberty, and had testimonies of unity from a meeting at Colchester, and several other meetings.'[17]

He arrived in Philadelphia in 1712, and stayed for about two years. At this stage he enjoyed amicable and supportive relations with the Friends of Philadelphia, and when he went on to Barbados he took with him 'certificates of commendation' from those parts of America he had visited. He returned to England in 1714.

About the beginning of 1715, with a fresh certificate from his Monthly Meeting at Stansted, and another from the Second-day Morning Meeting at London, he again sailed for America. All went well at first, but in 1716 he became embroiled in a dispute with the Friends of Rhode Island. He not only spoke out against the ill-treatment of blacks, but when his criticisms were rejected he lost patience and published them as pamphlets, with several 'biting' remarks, and would not withdraw them. The Yearly Meeting of Philadelphia in 1718 refused to see him, and he then lost heart and gave up his ministry. It seems that he never returned to England and that he died at some time before 1725. Mary went to live in Saffron Walden and continued her work as a minister until she died in 1740.[18]

1. ERO Q/SBA 2/91. See also Sharpe (1983: 79).
2. Stephenson (1976: 284).
3. Morant (1760-68: 579).
4. Morris (2007). For the poll book, see ERO, D/DKw 04.
5. Cruickshanks, Handley and Hayton (2002: 819).
6. Duke Henning (1983: 62).
7. ERO, LlB/POL 1/2.
8. Cox (1720: I.667).
9. ERO, T/A 420/1.
10. ERO, Q/SR 396/78.
11. Davids (1853: 607-8); Bromley (1873: 5); *HEO*, 3 December 1898.
12. ERO, D/NC 2/19; Davids (1863: 474).
13. I have found no contemporary figures, but in 1829 out of 57,984 Essex Dissenters 30,919 were Independents.
14. ERO, Q/SR 408/93.
15. ERO. T/A 418/175/25.
16. ERO, D/P 109/3/1.
17. *Journal of the Friends Historical Society,* Vol. 28 (1855: 316).
18. *The Friend* [Philadelphia] vol. 28, 1926, pp. 316 et seq.; *Journal of the Friends Historical Society,* vol. 23, pp. 60-2. For Farmer's journal of his first visit to America, see *Journal of the Friends Historical Society,* vol. 22, 1925, and Henry J. Cadbury (1943).

10: THE HEATHS

The Montfichets, the Myddeltons and the Fuller-Maitlands have all left a powerful impression on the village and on our sense of its history. The village name and the castle remind us of the Montfichets, the superb monuments in the church of the Myddeltons, and, as we shall see, Stansted Hall of the Fuller-Maitlands. There is little to bring the Heaths to mind, apart from a few plain inscriptions in the church. Not even a local road is named after them, yet they were lords of the manor for almost a hundred years and at times a family of importance in the county.

Like the Myddeltons, the Heaths derived their wealth from trade. The first lord of the manor was Thomas Heath, but it was his father, William, who had established the family's fortunes. William's story is touched with romance. He went to sea in 1667 at the age of 15 as a cabin boy in a ship commanded by his uncle Thomas, and in 1677 was given command of Thomas's new ship, the *Welfare.* He was so successful that he was then chosen by the East India Company to be the captain of a well armed merchant frigate, the *Defence,* but at this point his record becomes chequered and controversial. He failed badly in his operations around Calcutta in 1688 and Canton in 1689: a contemporary criticised him for 'tripping from port to port without effecting anything', he 'rendered our nation ridiculous',[1] and one of the Company's historians has described him as 'the hot-headed, wrong-headed, capricious, and futile, feather-brained skipper' of the *Defence.*[2] On the other hand he played a commendable part in bringing the famous buccaneer and traveller, William Dampier, back to England on the last stages of his voyage round the world.[3] In any event, he did well enough to be appointed in 1713 as one of the directors of the East India Company, and he amassed a considerable fortune, retiring to Mile End in London, which, being close to the docks, was a popular place with merchants and seafarers.

Thomas Heath, the eldest of William's nine children, became a wealthy East India merchant in his own right, later becoming a director of the company, and in 1714 he added to his wealth by marrying Catherine Bayley, the daughter of a rich merchant adventurer with the Virginia Company, also a resident of Mile End. In 1715, at the age of 31, he purchased the Stansted estate, in this way emulating many others at the time who invested their fortunes from trade in land. He was already a Member of Parliament for the town of Harwich, which Thomas Myddelton had represented, and like Myddelton took his stand with the Whigs. In the 1722 county election 30 men from Stansted voted, of whom 24, Thomas Heath among them, supported the Whig candidate. His own Parliamentary career, however, was cut short: he lost his seat in 1722 and his attempts to regain it failed. He was not highly thought of: in 1733 one faction in the town was so determined to oppose Lord Perceval that it was prepared to accept anybody, even Heath, it said, 'a lousy fellow',[4] though in the event it chose another candidate. While maintaining his house in Mile End Old Town[5] he must have spent much of his time in Stansted, since he regularly chaired meetings of the vestry. He died in 1741 at the age of 57, stipulating in his will that at his funeral no more than four ministers were to precede his corpse, there were to be no supporters of his pall, and only his family should attend.[6]

Thomas was succeeded by his son, Bayley Heath, who had been named after his mother. He went to Felsted School in Essex, and then went on to Cambridge University. Like his father and grandfather, he served in the East India Company, in his case as a Captain of Marines, and he also commanded a Brigade of Engineers. Unlike his father he soon stopped attending vestry meetings in Stansted, but he played a full part in the affairs of the county. During the Jacobite uprising of 1745 he donated £100, one of the highest contributions in the county, to a fund to support King George and the Constitution against 'the wicked and traitorous Designs of a Popish Pretender and all his Adherents'. In 1747 he became High Sheriff of Essex, and in 1752 MP for Pevensey in Sussex.

He seems to have formed a close friendship with William Dawkins, the lord of the manor of Elsenham Hall in the adjoining parish of Elsenham. In 1747 Dawkins, who had no children, bequeathed both the hall and the manor to him.[7] Bayley and his wife Bridget continued to live at Stansted Hall, with Elsenham Hall being leased or used by close family relatives.

Bayley died in 1760 and was succeeded by his eldest son, William, who was only ten at the time, and so his mother Bridget had to manage the estate. The transition from trade to land continued. William went to Eton and then to Cambridge, and eventually became a landowner with an extensive acreage, with the lordships not just of Stansted Hall and Bentfield Bury but of Elsenham and Ugley as well.

In 1763, in a by-election contested by John Luther and John Conyers, who were Whig and Tory respectively, 14 of Stansted's 15 voters[8] voted for Conyers, which suggests some direction, if not from the teenage William himself, perhaps from his family. In 1768, however, Stansted's voters were more divided: the 27 men who went to the county town of Chelmsford, each with two votes to cast, gave 18 votes to one candidate, 13 to another, 12 to another, and 5 to another.

William, it seems, did not involve himself much in the doings of the parish – the last occasion on which he attended the vestry was in 1774 – and towards the end of his life he suffered from a long and painful illness. It was probably because of this that his brother, another Bayley, represented Stansted at a meeting in 1793 to counteract the threat of revolutionary influences from France, a meeting that will be described in more detail in the chapter on the French wars below.

The other representative from Stansted at the meeting, or at least the only one to be mentioned, was Henry Croasdaile. In the 1770s his family had built Hargrave House, which was described in 1848 as 'a large handsome mansion in the castellated style, with tasteful pleasure grounds'. The Croasdailes, it seems, had made much of their money through their ownership of estates and slaves in Jamaica and were now one of the leading families in the parish.[9]

William Heath died in 1797, and Bayley succeeded him. Graduating at Cambridge, he became a barrister and appears to have spent most of his time in London. He did not marry, and when he died intestate in 1809 after falling from a horse his large fortune was divided between his three married sisters. There is a striking parallel with the Myddeltons: after a century as lords of the manor there was no male heir and the Stansted estate went out of the family.

By this time Stansted Hall was in a bad way. Writing in 1770, Peter Muilman had described it as 'a fine large old building, situate not far from the church, upon the summit of a lofty hill ....' It was 'decorated with good gardens, plantations, nurseries, &c. &c. and from the many improvements made in it by the late and present worthy owners' it had been 'rendered a pleasant and convenient country residence'.[10] It must have deteriorated rapidly. In 1790 Humphry Repton, the great landscape designer, who had been called in by the Heaths to suggest improvements, described it in one of his celebrated Red Books as 'a vast shell ... without any rooms'. He believed that 'it would be very easy for an able Architect to make it internally comfortable, convenient, elegant and magnificent', and that its outward appearance would be transformed if its red brick was covered with stucco. Some of his suggestions for the park were carried out, since considerable improvements to the planting were made in or around 1795, but for the most part his Red Book was left to gather dust.[11]

So too was the Hall. In 1810, the year after Bayley's death and after the Fuller-Maitlands had acquired the property, the churchwardens reported that the chancel of St. Mary's needed some repair, but the Fuller-Maitlands had not yet moved into the Hall.[12] At the time of the census in 1811 it was still unoccupied.

27. St. Mary's Church in 1756.

1. Keay (1993: 164). More generally, see Keay (1993: 161-4, 205-7).
2. Sir Henry Yule, quoted in John Keay (1993: 161). Keay too had a poor opinion of Heath.
3. Dampier (1937: 347-367).
4. Romney R. Sedgwick, online member biography of Thomas Heath in *The History of Parliament*.
5. Morris (2002: 46). See also Morris (2002: 16). Brown (1996: 90) notes that Thomas Heath 'died in "his lodgings in Piccadilly"', which suggests that Stansted Mountfitchet was his home.
6. Morris (2002: 61).
7. Barker and Sayers (1999: 80-81).
8. These were men who were entitled to vote, not because they were resident in Stansted, but because they held land there: in fact eight of them lived elsewhere. There were at least five residents of Stansted who held land elsewhere, and four of these voted for Conyers.
9. I am grateful for this information to Ralph Phillips, who has been working on the history of the Croasdailes of Stansted.
10. Muilman, Vol. III (1770: 18). For a similar description see Britton and Brayley (1803: 412).
11. ERO, T/A 229/1. Repton's Red Books, with text and illustrations, were produced to help his clients to visualise his designs.
12. Reader, 'Stansted in the Last Century', *SMPM*, March 1941, p. 10.

11: POPULATION, GROWTH AND PROSPERITY

In 1086, at the time of the Domesday Book, the population of what would now be the parish of Stansted was about 260. By 1250 this figure would have risen to about 450. In the catastrophic years of 1300-1375 the population of the country as a whole fell by about 40%, a collapse that has left its mark in the archaeological record at Stansted and that would have brought the population of the parish down to about 270, roughly the Domesday level. Throughout the 1400s, if Stansted followed the pattern in the country as a whole, this level of population would have remained much the same. Over the next two centuries, 1500-1700, the national population roughly doubled. By the 1660s and early 1670s, as we know from the records of the Hearth Tax (i.e. the records of the tax that was payable on each hearth), there were about 120 households in Stansted, and if we allow between four and five people to each household we get an overall population of between 480 and 600, i.e. about double the 1500 level. We can check this figure against Bishop Compton's census of 1676. In response to the Bishop's questions it was reported that Stansted had 348 conformists, no papists and 20 non-conformists, a total of

28. Stansted's population.

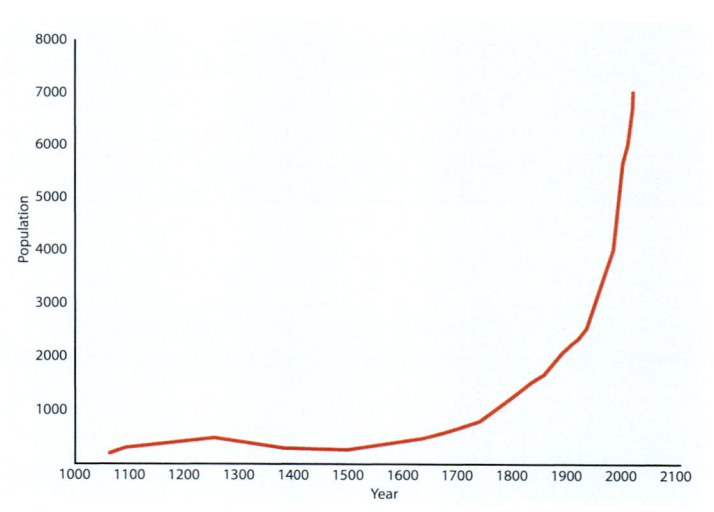

368. It is reckoned that these people, adults of 16 years or over, made up 60% of the population, which gives us an overall population of 613 or thereabouts.

In terms of overall size it is interesting to compare Stansted's estimated Compton return of 368 with the figures submitted by some of the nearby parishes. This shows that Stansted was one of the larger parishes, about the same size as Clavering (370) and Debden (368), bigger than Elsenham (180), Ugley (169), Arkesden (149), Quendon (74) and Birchanger (65), but not in the same league as the market towns of Thaxted (782), Saffron Walden (1000) and Great Dunmow (700).[1] Bishop's Stortford had an overall population of about 1,500.[2]

In the 18th century the population continued to increase, slowly at first but then very rapidly, as we can see from the numbers of baptisms in the parish. In 1650-99 the average number was 17 a year. In 1700-1749 it rose to 20 a year, and in 1750-1799 to 30 a year. In 1801, the time of the first national census, the population was 1,285, and by the census of 1831 it had risen to 1,560.

There were of course variations from year to year, with sudden increases in burials which were probably due to fever or plague. The worst years were 1726, 1727 and 1728, when the numbers were 23, 35 and 29, roughly double the numbers for other years around that time. In the great plague year of 1665, however, while there was a surge in the number of burials in Bishop's Stortford, there was only a small increase in Stansted. The registers also provide evidence about departures from the parish. Of the first 100 persons to be baptized in the 18th century 33 do not appear in the burial registers and 23 died young. So only 44 out of the 100 survived childhood and spent all their lives in Stansted. There was more mobility than we used to believe.

These were the overall figures. For the social and economic differences within them the Hearth Tax returns are revealing. Of the 120 householders in Stansted in the 1660s and 1670s more than a half had only one hearth and about a quarter had two. Of the rest, taking the 1662 returns, seven had three, 13 had between four and seven, two had nine, and one, Sir Thomas Myddelton, had no fewer than 31. About 40, or a third, were too poor to pay rates and were therefore exempted from the Hearth Tax, and nearly all of these had only one hearth. Using these returns as a guide to principal occupation, and following the suggestions of Spufford and Malcolmson,[3] we can say that about 70 of Stansted's 120 households were headed by labourers or cottagers, about 30 by craftsmen, shopkeepers or small farmers, about 20 by well-to-do yeomen, and at least three by members of the gentry who by definition did not have to work for a living. There must have been servants, mainly young, unmarried people, in about a quarter of these households, ranging from the occasional domestic servant to the troop of retainers employed by the Myddeltons.

29. The barn at Bentfield Bury farm.

11: POPULATION, GROWTH AND PROSPERITY

It was during this period, the 16th and 17th centuries, that what has become known as the Great Rebuilding took place. The Myddeltons were in a class of their own. With their prodigious wealth they were able to afford a new hall much larger than any other domestic buildings in the parish. According to the Royal Commission on Historical Monuments more than 30 surviving houses and cottages date from this period, buildings such as Hole Farm, Savages, Tudor House and the King's Arms, nearly all two storeys high, timber-framed and plastered, sometimes pargetted as well (though many have been altered and refronted), the roofs thickly thatched or red-tiled, and many still with the original chimney-stacks and hearths for which their owners were taxed under Charles II. Close to the farmhouses are several black weather-boarded barns, some of which date back to an even earlier period. The timbers of the superb barn at Bentfield Bury, for example, have been dated by dendrochronology to 1453.

30. The windmill, erected in 1787, and donated by Lord Blyth to the parish in 1935.

Agriculture of course was the mainstay of the economy. The old feudal system had long since broken down, with services for land being replaced by rent. Many of the strips in the old open fields had been sold off into private ownership, sometimes being joined with other strips, though some survived and were only finally tidied up in the nineteenth century. Enclosure had taken place gradually and piecemeal, and Stansted, like most of Essex, was spared the comprehensive and disruptive enclosure that stamped its straight and rectangular patterns on so many parts of the country. Fields have been enlarged since WW2, but many of the surviving lanes and hedgerows testify to boundaries that go back to the Saxon period and perhaps even beyond.

There were radical changes in farming. Partly in response to the rapidly growing demand from London's expanding populace and the rise in the price of corn, there was a great increase in productivity and production, especially in the period after 1750. Improved methods of farming were introduced and extended, especially in the cultivation of wheat and barley. Turnips and clover became part of a four-course rotation, drill sowing and hollow draining were increasingly adopted, and between 1700 and 1800 yields of wheat per acre more than doubled.[4] A windmill, a post mill, was built near the present site of Walpole Farm in 1720 or thereabouts, and another, a tower mill, in 1787.[5] In the view of one observer in 1795 'the general spirit and costly improvements of the Essex farmer stand unrivalled in any part of the Kingdom'.[6]

The drive for efficiency was matched by the drive for the consolidation of land holdings. In the 16th and 17th centuries the wills of Stansted's gentlemen, yeomen and husbandmen

11: POPULATION, GROWTH AND PROSPERITY

tell an interesting tale. We are accustomed today to think of farms centred on farmhouses surrounded by their fields in relatively compact blocks of land. The wills make it clear that for the most part this was not yet the pattern in Stansted. Only rarely was the word 'farm' used. The men who owned or leased the land had several fields dispersed over a wide area, generally described as crofts, closes, meadows and pightles, and also parcels of land in what still remained of the common fields, such as Stoney Common Field, Bargate Common Field, Callender Common Field, Northfield and the Common Meadow. Several owned land, not just in Stansted, but in one or more of the parishes around. Some of them lived in farmhouses in the countryside, but others still had their homes in one of the four hamlets. There were also men in other parishes who owned or rented land in Stansted. There was a lively market in land.

A good example of a yeoman with a scattered landholding is John Savell, who made his will in 1579. To his son John he left his messuage with the buildings and three acres of land in Alsa Street, three closes of land purchased of Richard Wylley, the seven-acre field that was one Littell's in Stansted, his parcel of meadow in the Common Meadow in Stansted, in the tenure of Thomas Stock, and ten acres of land bought of Mr. Parker of Berden lying in Ugley. To his son George he left his four-acre close of land called the Crouche, and three pieces of land amounting to three acres in all in Stoney Common Field and Bargate Common Field. To his daughter's son, James Walker, he left his messuage in Bradford Street (the name then given to Lower Street) in Stansted, and all his other lands and tenements.[7]

A more modest example is Richard Stockbridge, who described himself as a yeoman and who made his will just over a hundred years later, in 1684. He divided among his two sons the house where he lived, a five-acre croft called Marefield in Stansted, a two-acre croft called Barly Croft in Birchanger, a three-acre parcel of land in the common field called Stoneyfield in Birchanger, Dellcroft, about five acres lying in Stansted and Birchanger, and a close of meadow land in Stansted.[8]

Map 6. Part of Bentfield Green Farm in 1804, showing the strips in the common fields and the Stort split up into small streams.

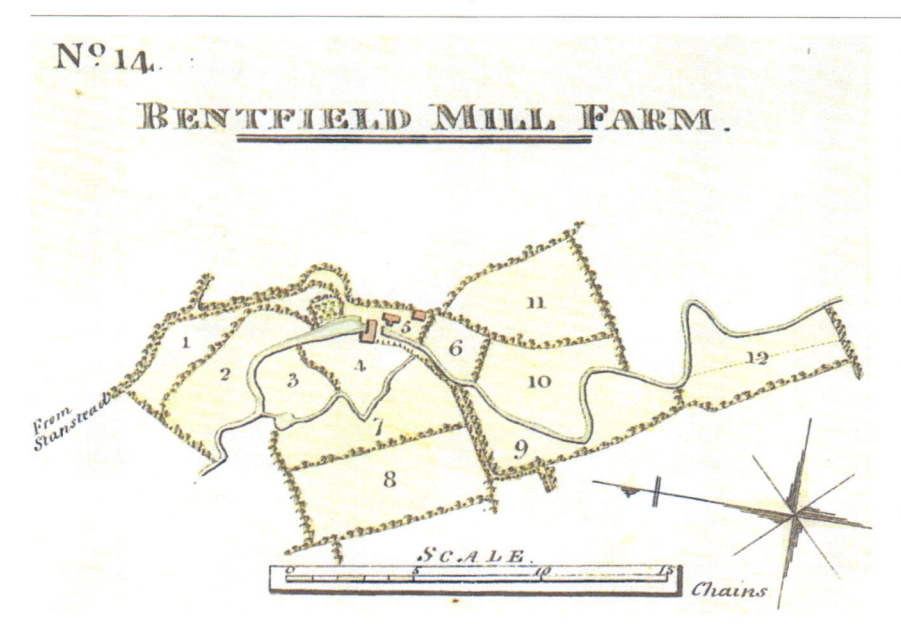

Map 7. This map of Bentfield Mill Farm in 1815, though not covering exactly the same area as Map 6, nevertheless shows how the fields were consolidated in the 1811 enclosure and how the Stort was more tightly controlled.

It was also common for well-to-do craftsmen and tradesmen to own some land. James Giffyn, a weaver, who made his will in 1631, had land not only in Stansted, but also in Little Hallingbury, Ugley and Bishop's Stortford, and John Nothage, a shoemaker, who made his will in 1645, had one and a half acres in Northfield in Stansted and a 'piece' of pasture land in 'Mellenden' (Manuden?).[9]

Gradually the process of consolidation continued, and landholdings were increasingly identified as farms. We can see the later stages of this process in the maps that were made for William Gosling, who lived mainly in London, but whose local base was in the neighbouring parish of Farnham, who began purchasing land in Stansted in 1804, and who was able to secure an enclosure settlement in 1811. The first map, covering part of Bentfield Green Farm (Swann's Farm) in 1804, shows the strips in the open fields and the way in which the Stort divided into several small streams. The second, covering Bentfield Mill Farm in 1815 and overlapping with the first, shows a much more compact landholding and also how the streams of the Stort were combined.[10] In 1847 the Fuller-Maitlands, whose estate covered most of the east of the parish, were able to push through a similar enclosure in order to consolidate their land.[11]

Over a long period the smaller farmers were bought out. To take one crude indicator of change, in 1710 47 men exercised their right to vote in an election, a right that was based on the tenure of freehold property, in 1768 27, and in 1830, in a fiercely contested election, only 19. As early as 1759 about half of the parish was in the hands of one man, Bayley Heath, the lord of the manor.[12] By the time of the census in 1831 there were only 16 occupiers of agricultural land in the parish: two of them worked their own farms without help, and the rest employed 183 labourers between them.[13]. The familiar pattern of a few large landowners, a middling number of prosperous tenants, and a crowd of landless and impoverished labourers had become increasingly established.

Inevitably the rise in the price of corn encouraged landowners to turn increasingly to arable farming, but other uses of land remained important, as we can see from the tithe records. These are such a rich and detailed source of information, and not just for farming practices, that I shall examine them at some length.

Tithes, which consisted of one tenth of the produce of the land, were of two kinds. The great tithes, or corn tithes, on cereal crops were paid to the rector, in Stansted's case the lord of the manor. Normally they were payable on hay as well, but in 1715 the last Thomas Myddelton bequeathed these tithes to the vicars of Stansted, excepting the tithe grass on his own lands and farms.[14] The papers relating to the great tithes probably went up in flames when Stansted Hall's manorial records were destroyed in WW2. The small tithes, or vicarage tithes, on livestock, vegetables, fruit and wood were paid to the vicar.

It was these payments, the small tithes, that John Leigh began meticulously recording when he became vicar in 1682. John Reynolds, who succeeded his 'Good Friend and Worthy Predecessor' in 1691, copied out Leigh's records in what he called 'The Book of the Small Tythes received by the Vicars of Stansted' and continued them until he died in 1728. His successors, John Allen (1728-1769) and Jonathan Judson (1769-81), also kept careful records, but under Richard Grant (1782-1827) the entries in the book degenerated into little more than random jottings. Reynolds in particular added many other transactions as well, such as Easter offerings and burial fees, and he even recorded payments for window tax and purchases such as the gardening tools that he bought from John Berry in 1728. Most tithes were paid in cash, but in many cases a note was made of the produce to which they related. Over the years payments were made for wood, grass (hay), hops, turnips, peas and beans, a horse, pigs, cows, bullocks and calves, sheep, lambs and wool, honey and wax, clover and osier grounds, orchards and fruit (mainly apples, but also pears, damsons, cherries and an apricot tree), ducks, chickens and eggs, and pigeons. A few payments were still made in kind and were recorded with a note of what they were worth. For the year ending in August (Lammas Day) 1697 the Quaker John Burnet brought a tithe pig which was valued at 1s. For the year ending August 1698 Richard Markewell paid 'Tyth Apples' to the value of 4s. and in the year ending August 1702 'a fat fowl in lieu of his chickens'. In the following year Reynolds noted that John Gurson was 'to pay Wax and Honey when he burns his Bees' - a reference to the old practice of burning skeps in order to get the wax and honey.

At the back of the first tithe book Reynolds noted down the tithable possessions of some of the wealthier parishioners, and these give us revealing insights into their domestic economies. In 1700, for example, Richard Woodley paid tithes on 40 lambs (£1), 5 cows (5s.), 3 calves (3s.), wool which he sold for 30s. (3s.), and nuts which he sold for above 20s. (2s.). He had no poultry that year, and so overall his tithes, together with his Easter offering (4d.), came to £1 13s. 4d., though Reynolds 'took of him but 20 [shillings]'. In 1704 Valentine Grave paid tithes on '4 Cows, No Calves' (16s.), 4 Bullocks (6s.), '10 Sheep ye Wool' (4d.), 4 Lambs (1s. 2d.), his Orchard (6d.) and Eggs (6d.). With his Easter offering (4d.) this came to £1 4s. 10d.

In the early years there were many entries relating to payments for hops, no doubt because many families brewed their own beer, but there were three other types of produce

11: POPULATION, GROWTH AND PROSPERITY

which Reynolds took care to note down in special lists drawn up at the back of the book. The first was 'Turneps in the Year 1726', which was a list of eight men who paid tithes on turnips, and we are reminded that this was the period when Viscount Townshend introduced the large-scale cultivation of this crop and was given the nickname of Turnip Townshend. The second was orchards, and twice, in 1713 and 1714, Reynolds recorded the names of the 30 or so parishioners whose orchards were subject to tithes, the main crop being apples. The third was wood, and in 1696 he noted down 'The Names of all The Woods in the Parish ... which pay Tyth Wood to ye Vicar ....' Thirty-one were listed, making up 275 acres in all. Alsa Wood, with 79 acres, was the largest, as it still is today, followed by Taylor's Wood, 37 acres, and Stocking Wood, 25 acres.

Although from time to time, perhaps all the time, the vicar employed an agent for collecting the tithes and so avoided at least some unpleasant personal confrontations, there are clear signs that in Stansted, as throughout the country, the collection of tithes gave rise to constant bickering and resentment. It was common for people to fall behind with their payments, sometimes by as much as 14 years – hence the bequests to the church in early wills for tithes 'negligently forgotten'. In the year ending August 1698 Goodman Keen paid 15s. to cover his tithes for two years, and Reynolds reckoned 'this should have been 20d. more, but he made me abate it upon his having (as he saies) broken up 2 or 3 acres', i.e. converted land from pasture to arable, for which no vicarage tithes would have been paid. In 1723 William Smith, a tenant farmer, paid 18s. He used to pay 20s., but his new landlord, 'one George Canning, an old purse-proud oppressour', would allow him to pay only 14s. 'and threatened to spend £100 in a Law Suit' – though in fact Smith ignored his landlord's instructions.

The Quakers were the only people against whom the vicar had to bring legal proceedings to enforce the payment of tithes, though neither side seems to have pushed the issue to extremes. I have already mentioned how in 1694 Reynolds and John Day, the Quaker shopkeeper, tacitly came to an arrangement, without recourse to legal proceedings on either side, whereby Day refused to pay his tithes and Reynolds refused to pay for the goods which he had bought from Day's shop. Day persisted in his refusal to pay, so that by 1708, by Reynolds's reckoning, he owed £1 8s. 6d. During this period, however, Reynolds had run up a bill of £1 9s. 'for Candles and other things sent for from [Day's] shop'. There was only 6d. between them, but in spite of Reynolds's entreaties Day refused to settle and draw a line under the account. In 1731, however, John Allen, Reynolds's successor, recorded that Day had agreed to pay tithes of 12s. a year for a house and land he had recently acquired, and for the year ending August 1739 that he had 'agreed for the future at £1 4s. a year and he has leave to sow Turneps ....' Allen 'forgave him the rest upon account of his circumstances' – a reference perhaps to his health, for he was now an old man and died two years later. His son, also John Day, paid £1 5s., 'as agreed', until his death in 1749, after which his widow continued the payments.

Quaker resistance persisted, however. On 25 June 1759 the first John Day's two grandsons, Tayspill John (commonly known as John) and Samuel, paid £1 6s. and £1 11s. respectively which were 'levied by distress', which no doubt means that they were seized under a warrant of distress. This was made more explicit in April 1765 when Samuel paid £2 8s. 'as seiz'd by Warrant of Distress which he approv'd on', which suggests that the vicar, then John Allen, took legal action to obtain a warrant of distress and that Samuel acquiesced in this. He might have been prepared to pay tithes if legally compelled to do so, but not voluntarily. The same pattern went on into the 1770s when tithes were twice 'seized' from Samuel Day.

The Days' resistance to tithes did not damage their standing in the village. In 1732 John Day, probably the son of the first John Day, attended a vestry meeting, and both Samuel and Tayspill John Day attended vestry meetings and held office as overseers of the poor. Samuel Day was respectfully referred to as Mr. Samuel Day.

Over the period covered in detail by the tithe book, from 1682 to about 1780, the amounts collected increased more than fourfold, from an average of about £29 a year in the 1680s through £101 in the 1730s to £133 for those years which were recorded in the 1770s. When an assessment was made in 1810 the vicarage tithes were reckoned at £303 6s. 6d., compared with the corn tithes of £928 0s. 6d.[15] Although there had been a substantial increase in small tithes during the French wars these were assessments only, and no doubt the actual collection fell short of these sums.[16]

In the late eighteenth century, with the price of corn rising and reaching new heights during the wars against France, many fields were turned over from pasture to arable, and in 1844, when a detailed and comprehensive survey was carried out, there were more than three and a half acres of arable land for every acre of meadow and pasture.[17] This is comparable with the figures quoted above for the payment of tithes in 1810 – three times as much for the corn tithes as for the vicarage tithes. It is interesting too that on the arable land almost as much food was grown for horses as for people – 1,500 bushels of oats compared with 600 bushels of wheat and just over 1,000 bushels of barley.

According to the 1801 census four out of every five adults worked mainly on the land, and those who did not made most of their money by serving those who did. The 1811 census listed 169 families, of which 81 were engaged in agriculture, 44 in trade, manufacture or handicrafts, and 44 in other occupations.[18]

The most prominent business in the village was that originally founded by John Day the Quaker in 1687. John had been a grocer, draper and chandler, and ran the business until his death in 1741, a period of more than 50 years. The shop was then taken over by his son, also John, who, according to Joseph Green, added "Sope boyling" to the business and was so successful that he carried on a considerable export trade in fancy soap with France.[19] After the second John Day died in 1749 the business was continued by his widow, Elizabeth, and their two sons, Tayspill John and Samuel. Samuel Day took over the sole running of the business in 1757, and, relying on tales handed down in the family, Green gives us a picture of him 'journeying to London in his coach with a pair of long tailed black horses to make trade purchases'.[20] The horses, it seems, had long tails because he would not follow the prevalent fashion of docking them.[21]

In 1780 Samuel entered into partnership with William Grover, another leading Quaker, a 'truly good man', and so admired that edifying selections from his letters and other writings were published after his death.[22] Under these two the firm continued to flourish, building up its premises on the Newmarket Road and steadily expanding its range of goods and services. Samuel died in 1796, and his place in the firm was then taken by his son, Samuel Tayspill Day. At some point the soap boiling came to an end, but one indication of the firm's continuing success is that in 1815 it was turning out about twenty tons of tallow candles each year. It would go on playing a major role in the village for the rest of the century and beyond.[23]

Women made a substantial contribution to the economy of the parish, and not just in their unpaid work in the home. On the farms, in addition to the men's employment, there was casual labour for women and children, such as weeding, stone-picking and bird-scaring. Right up to the latter part of the 18th century, with the wool trade in worsted and fustians still flourishing, the spinning wheel was a fixture in almost every common home. In the Poor Law records we find women being paid as midwives and for nursing and looking after their poorer neighbours, in some cases orphaned or abandoned children.

In the eighteenth century the whole parish benefited from two major developments in transport - the turnpiking of the main road and the opening of the Stort Navigation. The road from Bishop's Stortford to Newmarket had been improved considerably in the reign of Charles II, and then, in 1744, it was removed from the control of the parish and made the responsibility of the Hockerill Highway Turnpike Trust, which established a toll gate just south of Stansted.[24] The improvement was dramatic: 30 years later the diarist Parson Woodforde described it as the best of roads he had ever travelled.[25]

In 1772 Peter Muilman referred to 'the vast traffic of this much-frequented road'. There were travellers on foot or on horseback, visiting friends or relatives or engaged in business. Increasingly there were the coaches and post-chaises, some of them bound for the races in Newmarket, perhaps stopping at Stansted for a change of horses and refreshment for their passengers. And there were the farmers, tradesmen and carriers, carting their goods to Bishop's Stortford, either to the weekly market or, after 1769, to the head of the Stort Navigation.

For the people of Stansted and the nearby villages Stortford had always been the hub of the local economy, but it became even more important after the navigation to London had

31. The Bell, a sketch by P. Palfrey in Charles Harper (1904).

11: POPULATION, GROWTH AND PROSPERITY

32. The Three Colts, c.1850.

33. The White Bear, a sketch by P. Palfrey in Charles Harper (1904).

been opened. The engineer responsible could claim, with literal justification, that Stortford was now open to all the ports in the world.[26] Stansted's farmers sold grain in its markets and grew barley for its flourishing maltsters. By 1800 Stortford was sending more malt to the London brewers than any other town in England. There were plans to extend the canal to Cambridge, going through Stansted on the way, but they came to nothing.

34. The Rose and Crown, now private residences.

In Stansted the traffic of the Newmarket Road was catered for by at least four inns and alehouses - the White Bear, the Three Colts, the Bell and the Rose and Crown[27] – and large fields were provided where the drovers could leave their stock overnight. There were also several houses and 'a few neat shops, but not', wrote Muilman 'of any considerable trade'. Sixty years later, in 1836, Thomas Wright found Stansted to be a large and populous village, and referred to the 'numerous capital houses' on 'the great road from London to Cambridge and Newmarket'.[28] The de Veres' old wayside chapel, now used as a blacksmith's shop, still stood at the crossroads in this part of the village.

Economic change led to a widening of social divisions. The increasing price of corn, which brought so much wealth to the farmers, led directly to the increasing price of bread, which plunged many labourers and their families into abject poverty. With their new-found riches the larger farmers could afford to imitate the gentry, at least in their more attainable comforts and refinements. Previously they had hired their labourers by the year and provided those who were still young and unmarried with board and lodging. Now they hired them by the week or the day and they were unwilling to share their homes with men whom they regarded as their social inferiors. The old bonds of familiarity and friendship were snapped. Class divisions became sharper and more embittered. The word 'respectable' entered the fashionable vocabulary, and the unrespectable and at times disrespectful poor were feared as a threat to the existing order.

In the next chapter we shall consider what this 'order' was, what threats, real or perceived, it faced, and how these threats were averted or controlled.

1. ERO, T/A 420/1. No figures are given for Manuden and Farnham.
2. Cooper (2005: 31).
3. Spufford (1974: 37-45), Malcolmson (1981: 18-9). It is interesting to compare the Hearth Tax returns with the Ship Money assessments of 1636 (ERO, T/A 42). 107 persons were listed for Ship Money, of whom 31 were 'Out town dwellers', leaving 76 inhabitants. Of these inhabitants 10 (13%) paid £1 or more, 8 (11%) between 10s. and £1, 9 (12%) between 5s. and 10s., and 49 (64%) less than 5s. Unlike the records for the Hearth Tax the Ship Money assessments did not include householders who were too poor to make any payment. Timothy Myddelton was assessed at £6 11s.
4. Brown (1996: 24-5).
5. A third mill, towards Elsenham, was operative by 1820, but it seems that it was irreparably damaged in a storm in 1887. Only the tower mill survives today. For Stansted's mills, see Kenneth Farries (1988: 33-36).
6. Brown (1996: 25), quoting Arthur Young.
7. ERO, D/ABW 34/270.
8. ERO, D/ABW 72/22.
9. ERO, D/ABW 50/153 and D/ABW 60/104.
10. Maps in the possession of Frances and Toby Lyons of Hole Farm. Brown (1996: 173) says that there were many enclosures in the early 1800s because of the increasing price of land.
11. ERO, Q/RDc 36A.
12. ERO, Q/RJ 1/2 and D/P 109/3/4. See also Young, Vol. I (1807: chapter 4).
13. Census returns, 1831.
14. Local practice varied greatly. Muilman, Vol. III (1770: 26), says that 'From the papers of the late Mr. John Reynolds, vicar, it appears that a modus [i.e. a cash payment in lieu of a payment in kind] is payable to the vicar out of the parsonage and great tythes of Stansted of £12 yearly, which in 1664 was £12 12s.'
15. ERO, D/P 109/3/4. It is difficult, however, to reconcile this with the statement under Stansted in *White's Directory of Essex*, 1848, that tithes were commuted in 1840, the rectorial for £315 15s. and the vicarial for £306.
16. Brown (1996: 170).
17. ERO, C/CT 328. 2,900 acres of arable land, 800 of meadow and pasture, and 300 of woodland.
18. For this analysis of the 1811 census, see Reader,'Stansted in the Last Century', *SMPM*, June 1941.
19. When Green was writing in 1887 four of the iron soap boilers were still in existence, two of them on the original premises. He also says (1887: 6): 'The part of Stansted in Water Lane, called the Potash, is named from the place where the Days made potash for their soap manufacture.' There are still cottages there called Potash Cottages.
20. Green (1887: 5).
21. Paper by Barclay Lewis Day, 1908, 'Descent of the Days of Essex', now in Michael Day's possession.
22. Josiah Forster (1829).
23. Green (1887).
24. Maud (1957).
25. Bishop's Stortford and District Local History Society (1973: 56).
26. Bishop's Stortford and District Local History Society (1973: 61).
27. The White Bear surprisingly went out of business at some time between 1783 and 1820 - see ERO, Q/RLv series. The Three Colts was established in the 18th century. The Rose and Crown should not be confused with the public house of that name at Bentfield Green. The Bell should not be confused with what is now the Old Bell which was then in the parish of Birchanger.
28. Wright, Vol. II (1836: 155).

12: THE QUARTER SESSIONS AND CRIME

The activities of the Myddeltons and the Heaths on the national stage have been described. More important for the people of Stansted were their activities as Justices of the Peace, working locally with other JPs in the parish, who were usually members of the gentry or the clergy, and at the county level with JPs from every part of Essex. Sitting in the Quarter Sessions in the county town of Chelmsford these country gentlemen exercised a daunting array of judicial powers, which dated from the fourteenth century, and administrative powers, which had been massively enlarged in the Tudor period. When needed they could sit singly, or with one or two others, conducting their business locally, often in their own homes, a system which became formalised in the Petty Sessions.

In today's terms the JPs were both magistrates and local authorities. As well as trying criminal cases they could check on weights and measures, license alehouses, order the repair of bridges and highways, and maintain the county gaol and the houses of correction. They acted as a check on parish government, approving the parish rates and appointing the parish constables on the recommendation of the manorial courts. There were however many variations in practice: in Stansted, for example, it was the vestry that appointed the constables. For the monarchy JPs had the great merit of not being paid.

In their criminal jurisdiction the magistrates were supported, when necessary, by jurors who had to be owners of freehold or copyhold land worth at least ten pounds a year, a requirement more demanding than that for the parliamentary franchise, and in Stansted there were rarely more than ten men who could meet it. With these allies they dispensed justice, defended the interests and rights of all property owners and stamped down on any popular discontent. They enforced the Game Laws in their own class interest, and if their authority was threatened they could call on the militia.

To cover their expenses they raised a rate which was known at first as quarterage or bridge money and later as the county rate. Sometimes the parish resented having to pay money to the county. In 1653, for example, Stansted was one of several parishes which refused to contribute to the maintenance of the House of Correction in Saffron Walden. The magistrates sitting in Chelmsford ordered that £100 should be paid by these parishes, and the inhabitants, including Timothy Myddelton himself, were summoned to appear at the next Quarter Sessions to show reason if they argued that they should not pay.[1] As late as 1807 Stansted refused to pay the county rate, and a warrant was issued to seize the goods of the churchwardens and overseers to the value of £4 10s.[2]

Larceny (theft) was the most serious criminal offence to be tried at the Quarter Sessions, and more serious felonies, such as murder, rape, arson, grand larceny and burglary, were reserved for the judges in the Assize Court. As well as the county gaol at Springfield, near Chelmsford, there were Houses of Correction throughout the county, including one nearby at Newport, which was founded in 1691. Penal administration was not strongly developed, and sentences were rarely for more than one year. From 1787 onwards transportation to

Australia was another option, though the first case in which a Stansted parishioner was transported appears to have been in 1824.[3]

The only certain instance I have found of capital punishment was in 1786, when Thomas Brett was found guilty of burglary and hanged.[4] Lesser offences were generally punished by fines, and whipping was commonly meted out, either in one of the Houses of Correction or in public. In 1653, for example, Joan Browne, a widow, confessed to stealing three faggots of brushwood and was whipped.[5] The stocks in Stansted, according to Joseph Green, stood until about 1830 'near the bridge leading to the castle hill',[6] and perhaps the whipping post was in the same area.

The cases involving Stansted's parishioners were much the same as those in neighbouring parishes. Larceny and assault were the most common overall, and when required the inhabitants were ordered to mend a highway, repair a bridge or clean a ditch. There are several features of these cases, however, that stand out.

First, a negative observation. There were no convictions for witchcraft in Stansted. In the only case of alleged witchcraft brought to court, in 1593, Edwin Haddesley from Willingale Doe was accused of betwitching John Green so that he languished for a month and then died. Haddesley, however, was found not guilty.[7] There were a few witchcraft cases in the parishes nearby, such as Takeley and Elsenham, but the Puritan attack on witches, led by Matthew Hopkins in the 1640s, was concentrated in the eastern part of the county.

The second feature I have noted already – the large number of Quakers and Independents prosecuted after the restoration of Charles II for holding religious meetings or not attending the parish church. It was only with the Act of Toleration in 1689 that the holding of unauthorised religious meetings ceased to be an offence.

Third, there were many disputes with other parishes over responsibility for the poor. The underlying principle of the law was that each parish had a duty to care for those who had a right of settlement there. The maintenance of the poor was a heavy expense and each parish was determined not to take on anyone for whom it was not legally responsible. The measures that were adopted will be described in Chapter 14, but some cases where the right of settlement was disputed had to be referred to the courts, and in the first half of the eighteenth century, to take just that period as an example, we find Stansted at loggerheads with Great Hormead (1716), Rickling (1725), Birchanger (1728), Woodford (1728), Wakes Colne (1738) and Littlebury (1742).

Cases were also brought against men who were trying to evade responsibility for the illegitimate children they had fathered with women who lived in the parish, and if a case was proved to the court's satisfaction the most common outcome was an order for the payment of maintenance.

These Poor Law cases bring us to the fourth striking feature, the number of people convicted of being rogues and vagabonds. The economic changes of the Tudor period had led to a massive redistribution of wealth and a resultant intensification of poverty with all the attendant dangers of crime and disorder. As the poor and unemployed took to the roads there was a widespread fear of vagrants. Not only were they potential criminals, but they were also suspected of spreading smallpox, and if they slept out in barns and other buildings there was the danger that they might set fire to them. If they established a right of settlement they could become a liability on the parish rates, which was why it was an offence to harbour a newcomer without informing the authorities.

One of the measures introduced to strengthen control was to make it unlawful for any person to wander around as a vagabond and to beg without a licence. The constables were expected to enforce the law, and in 1700 Edward Nash, one of Stansted's constables, together with constables from other parishes, was punished because he had repeatedly, 'then and before and since', failed to arrest 'divers vagabonds, wanderers and sturdy beggars'.[8] In 1755 Bayley Heath, sitting locally as a JP, committed Elizabeth Want to be safely kept at the Newport House of Correction and to be whipped, if necessary, for being a vagrant and begging for relief in Stansted.[9] In most cases orders were given that the offender should be returned to his or her last place of settlement under the Poor Law.

The fifth feature, in no way surprising, is that the men prosecuted for larceny and assault were almost invariably labourers, and that among the women taken to court a high proportion were single.

1 Allen (1974: 34).
2 ERO, Q/SO 20.
3 CC, 2 April 1824. Joseph Smith was transported for 14 years for robbery and fraud.
4 ERO, D/DTu 235. In 1610 Parnel Payne, a spinster of Stansted, was found guilty of infanticide. She was sentenced to hang, but it is possible that the sentence was not carried out: Cockburn (1982: case 554).
5 ERO, Q/SR 355/16.
6 ERO, T/P, 68/31/2.
7 Cockburn (1982: case 156).
8 ERO, A.F. 35/141/3.
9 ERO, Q/SBb 204.

13: THE CHURCH COURTS AND MORALITY

Parallel with the secular courts were the church courts, which continued in operation until 1857. Stansted fell within the diocese of London and the archdeaconry of Colchester, and the church court for the archdeaconry, presided over by the bishop's appointee, was convened every few months in one of the local villages, sometimes in Stansted itself. Such courts, acting on information from the churchwardens and others, disciplined both clergy, on issues of faith, practice and conduct, and, much more commonly, ordinary parishioners, for misdemeanours such as not attending church, failing to receive the sacrament, 'scolding', which disturbed good neighbourly relations, brawling in the church or in the churchyard during divine service – and there were a surprising number of such cases – and, above all, immorality, so much so that they came to be popularly known as the 'bawdy courts'. They regulated the employment of what we might call certain professionals, making it unlawful for curates, schoolmasters, midwives and surgeons to practise without a licence; they supervised the administration of wills; and they made sure that the fabric of the church was properly maintained. As well as fines, two of the remedies available to them were excommunication and public penance.

In the sixteenth and seventeenth centuries these courts were active and vigorous in carrying out their duties. They frequently took action against persons who failed to attend church, especially when they compounded their offence by whiling away their time in an alehouse. In 1575, for example, Thomas Castelow and John Reynolds (not to be confused with the vicar of a century later), who had been playing cards and dice in service time, were ordered to work for two extra days on the highways.[1] In 1632 Richard Aylett was presented for mowing grass on the Sabbath day, but when he explained that he was using a scythe and that he only mowed six lengths of grass the case was dismissed.[2] In 1588 poor Elizabeth Mudge explained that she did not attend to receive communion because she could not say the Lord's prayer or the Ten Commandments.[3] In 1620 the churchwardens themselves were taken to court for failing to present 'certain maids' who had been playing stoolball when they should have been at church. (Stoolball, sometimes regarded as a precursor of cricket, was generally played by girls, traditionally milkmaids, who used their bucket as a wicket.) They explained that they had admonished the girls' parents and masters who had promised to reform their ways.[4] Couples who lived 'incontinently' before marriage were presented to the court, and so too were those who gave offence by living together without wedlock – though one couple, denounced by prurient neighbours, were able to demonstrate that they had been married in the neighbouring parish of Elsenham. In 1604 there was the sad case of Mary Cakebread, who had 'latelie had a child by one Paine who is dead: she is a very idiot, one that knows not her right hand from the left'.[5] Action was taken to check rowdy behaviour in church, as against Henry Eve in 1628, 'that he did kicke a dogg in the parish church' and then made a great din, for which he was fined 12d.,[6] and also against people who were troublemakers, as against Catharina

Golding 'for a person of an evill life and bad conversation and a user of bad language to her neighbours', and against William and Mary Linward for breeding 'great discord and disturbances amongst their neighbours'.[7]

Gradually this strenuous discipline was relaxed. Although it was the duty of the churchwardens to present to the courts any cases that arose of non-attendance, fornication and so on, in practice they were reluctant to lay information against their fellow parishioners. In 1719 the vicar John Reynolds was called upon to marry a couple who, according to him, 'to their Eternal Shame', had been 'guilty of Fornication before Marriage'. There was not any argument about this, since they were bringing their illegitimate child to be baptized on the same day as their wedding. In spite of Reynolds's demands, however, 'The Church Wardens would not present them'. All he could do was to add a thick black cross against their names in the marriage register as 'a Marke' of what they had done.[8] He was more successful in 1724. After the churchwardens had reported that 'We have none in our Parish who lie under a fame or suspicion of Adultery, Fornication or Incest', he was evidently able to persuade them to insert between the lines 'except Hannah Griggs and Elizabeth Layman Guilty of Fornication'. (No men were named.) On lesser crimes the churchwardens were more resolute: 'We cannot present any Persons as Common Swearers or Drunkards', they wrote, 'tho' doubtless there are some, but we know not who they are'. Reynolds was fighting a losing battle. There were no Papists, Jews or Heretics in the parish, but as early as 1707 the vicar and his churchwardens had to report that, in addition to the many 'Schismaticks' in the parish, there were 'Severall' persons 'who, we believe, frequent not any Place' but 'keep at home'. They were so little condemned by public opinion that it would serve no purpose to present them.[9]

Even before this time it was common practice throughout the diocese to report 'omnia bene', 'all well', and when a later vicar, Richard Grant (1782-1827), was asked a series of questions about his parishioners – 'Are there any in your Parish who are under a common fame or suspicion of adultery, fornication or incest ... any Common Swearers or Drunkards ... any who commonly absent themselves from the Public Worship of God on the Lord's Day ... any who keep open shop or suffer persons to tipple in their house on the Lord's Day?' - he responded briefly with a world-weary wisdom 'This pretty much the same as in other Parishes'.[10] The proportion of children born out of wedlock went up from less than 1% in 1650-99 to more than 5% in 1800-49.

The formalities of church practice were conscientiously observed, and by the standards of the early eighteenth century Stansted, as judged by the *Victoria County History*, was an 'exceptionally good church'.[11] In their presentments the churchwardens invariably expressed themselves satisfied with the way in which church affairs were conducted, and what they had to say was generally consistent with the vicars' answers to the set queries of the diocesan authorities. The church was kept in good repair. In 1692 the tower had been rebuilt 'at the sole charge' of Sir Stephen Langham, Thomas Myddelton's father-in-law, and the vicarage, which Reynolds had erected largely at his own expense, was 'perhaps one of the best in the diocese'. Two services were held every Sunday and the vicar preached at both. Reynolds evidently accounted it a great virtue that he preached in the winter as well as the summer, and he was said to preach 'distinctly and devoutly'. The sacrament of holy communion was held three or four times a year, though there were only about 30 communicants, and children were taught their catechism during Lent. Reynolds was dutiful in visiting the sick and was said to be a man of sober conversation and exemplary life. As a reward for building the new vicarage he was given the living at Thorley, in Hertfordshire, where he maintained a curate at his own expense. His church clerk sang the psalms well, kept the church 'neat and clean', and gave general satisfaction. It had to be acknowledged that there were many Dissenters in the parish, the Quakers having a small meeting house and the Independents a large chapel, though towards the end of the century it was noted that their numbers were not increasing.

Our evidence for schools is fragmentary, but it is clear that the church courts had little to do by way of licensing schoolmasters in Stansted. We know from the admissions registers of St. John's and Gonville and Caius Colleges, Cambridge, that there was a private school at Stansted under the mastership of Mr. Hales in 1584.[12] In 1589 Edward Hubbard, the lord of the manor, as noted already, had £100 which he was supposed to use to set up a free school, and he was penalised for not using it. Perhaps he did take action after that, because in 1594, according to the records of the church courts, there was a new schoolmaster in the parish who was required to produce his licence 'ad etudiend. liberos', for educating children.[13] He was not named, but later in the same year Justinian Watson was taken to the church court for laying violent hands on the new schoolmaster, whose name was given as Arthur Howsden. Unsurprisingly, Howsden did not stay long in his post, and three years later, in 1597, the church courts recorded Mr. Rydley as being a schoolmaster in the parish. He too did not stay long: in 1598 it was reported 'non est ludimagister', there is no schoolmaster.[14]

After this the record is silent. Perhaps some parishioners sent their children to the grammar school at Bishop's Stortford, founded in 1579, or the grammar school at Newport, founded in 1588. In every presentation by the churchwardens, however, it was acknowledged that there was no 'public' or 'free' school in Stansted. 'We have no Schoolmaster in Our Parish', wrote the churchwardens in 1727, 'only some Women teach Little Children'.[15]

By 1776, however, the Independents had established a school,[16] and this was the beginning of a sustained educational effort on their part. In 1810 the Anglican churchwardens had to report that there was 'a Boarding School for Boys and Girls kept by a Mr. and Mrs. White – They are Dissenters. Their Scholars go some to Church, some to Meeting. We know of no licence.' The Whites' school was a substantial enterprise: according to the 1811 census it had 35 boys and 44 girls. Mordaunt White, the Head Master, was evidently a man of some standing and ability: in the election of 1810 he was one of only two men in Stansted who voted for the radical candidate, and when he died in 1843 he left among other things two piano-fortes, some oil paintings and 400 books, including 20 volumes of the Encyclopaedia Britannica. For the Church of England the churchwardens could only report: 'We have a little School of our own, supported partly by voluntary Contributions. The Schoolmaster a decent young man – who does his duty well.'[17] Most children were untouched by formal education. Of the bridegrooms who married in St. Mary's Church between 1776 and 1812 only 42% could sign their names, and of the brides a mere 33% - figures that are about 20% below the average for the country as a whole.[18]

All this, however, was about to change in the Victorian period after the establishment of a National School by the Anglicans and a British School by the Nonconformists.

1 ERO, D/AZ 1/8, p. 126.
2 ERO, D/ACA 49, p. 58.
3 ERO, D/AZ 1/2, p. 105.
4 ERO, D/AZ 1/3, p. 15.
5 ERO, D/ACA 28, p. 24.
6 ERO, D/ACA 46, p. 80.
7 ERO, D/ACA 55, pp. 6, 363.
8 ERO, D/P 109/1/2. A black cross was added against the names of another couple who had been married a month earlier: the bride was four months pregnant.
9 LMA, Ms 9,583/11 and Ms 9,583/14.
10 ERO, T/P 68/17/2.
11 *VCH*, Vol. ii (1907: 74).
12 *VCH* Vol. ii (1907: 501).
13 ERO D/AZ 2/19 (21), p. 39.
14 ERO, D/ACA 23, pp. 172 and 174.
15 LMA, Gibson Papers, Ms 9583/15.
16 ERO, D/NC 2/13.
17 Reader, 'Stansted in the Last Century', *SMPM*, May 1941, p. 10.
18 Laslett (1983: 232-3).

14: THE PARISH VESTRY AND POVERTY

As a unit of administration the parish was at its height in the 17th and 18th centuries. By the end of Queen Elizabeth's reign the old manorial courts retained only vestiges of the powers they had exercised in the Middle Ages. They dealt with territorial infringements, such as unauthorised encroachments on waste land, and they appointed minor officials such as aletasters, but for the most part they were concerned with transfers of copyhold land, whether through sale or inheritance, and their rolls were little more than registers of ownership. They were usually chaired not by the lord of the manor but by his steward, and several years often passed between one meeting and the next.

For day to day parochial administration it was the vestry and its officers that mattered. They exercised many functions which today would be described as social services, and a rudimentary health service was provided for the poor. The vestry's meetings, held once a month, were open to all adult ratepayers, but in practice they were controlled by those who paid the highest rates, the wealthier farmers and to a lesser extent tradesmen. The minutes of these meetings survive from 1642 onwards, and throughout this period they were signed or marked by a small group of men, usually about seven or eight, who included, in addition to the churchwardens and the overseers of the poor, a nucleus of four or five who went on from year to year. Until 1742, when Bayley Heath evidently decided that he had other things to do, the squire usually attended and took the chair, and the vicar stood in for him if he was not there. Richard Grant, however, who was vicar from 1782 to 1827, rarely attended.

At Easter the vestry elected one of the two churchwardens, the other being appointed by the vicar. In any list of parish officers these men always came first. They were residents of substance and standing, and since their duties were not very heavy some of them were willing to be re-elected for several years. The overseers, who were also chosen by the vestry, were drawn from the same class as the churchwardens – they had to be 'substantial householders' by law – but their work was so demanding that, until their number was increased to four, very few served for more than two years. The constables were usually more humble men: they were appointed by the vestry but rarely attended its meetings, except to present their accounts. The office of surveyor was unpopular and shunned, though because of the special importance of the Newmarket Road several men of standing took on this post, even Sir Thomas Myddelton in the late 1670s.[1] Each householder was under an obligation to work on the roads for four days each year. None of these officers was paid, and the poor never held office of any sort.

At the Easter vestry the officers who had served in the previous year had to present their accounts, and the officers who were to serve in the coming year were granted a rate of so much in the pound in order to raise the income they needed. The churchwardens were responsible for maintaining the fabric and property of the church and for providing bread and wine for communion. In most years the little they spent was covered by rents from church lands, and if they had to levy a rate it was rarely a heavy imposition. In some years they had to incur a heavy item of expenditure, such as a major repair to the church or the purchase of new church bells, and their rate was then much higher. They also made reports to the Bishop of London on the spiritual state of the parish. Everyone, they said in 1724, paid the church rates, except the Quakers, but no action was taken against them.[2] The Independents were evidently more prepared to compromise.

The main duty of the overseers of the poor, as defined by the Elizabethan Act of 1601, was to relieve those who were unable to support themselves because of age, illness or infirmity. They also had to provide the children of the poor with training to work, and they were supposed to find work for the able-bodied unemployed, which they were rarely able to do. Under the Act of 1662 their responsibilities extended to all those who had a right of settlement in the parish, whether through birth, marriage or authorised residence, and they and their fellow officers made every effort to stop outsiders coming in and becoming a burden on the parish. It was their duty, as they saw it, 'to save the parish harmless'. If an outsider was likely to make demands on the rates they would apply to two magistrates for a removal order.[3] Alternatively, not insisting on removal, they would obtain from the newcomer a certificate of his or her last place of settlement so that they could be sent back if they could not support themselves. It is significant that all the surviving certificates related to skilled or propertied men, such as a woolcomber (1697), three cordwainers (1714, 1746 and 1769), a husbandman (1721), a silk comber (1724), a carpenter (1759) and a bricklayer (1760). None were for labourers. The neighbouring parishes were equally vigilant.

A less stringent alternative to removal was to allow the newcomer to stay, even if they needed relief, so long as they obtained this relief from their parish of origin. I have found no examples of Stansted's officers allowing this to happen, but we can see it in reverse in 1813 in the case of Elizabeth Shepphard, who had left Stansted some time previously and was living in Leyton in Essex. On 19 September she wrote to the authorities in Stansted:

> *Sir I take this oportunety of writing to you and send to let you Know that I ham vary poorly hand if you plese to send me my months money I should be vary glad by Return of post No Mor at Prsent from your humble Servent Elesebeth Shepphard.*[4]

Illegitimate children were a constant source of anxiety, since they could easily become a burden on the parish. Even when the father was ready to assume liability he could be required to enter into a bond undertaking to reimburse the parish for any expenditure it might incur in relation to the child. In 1770, for example, Ward Shepherd, a young bricklayer from Ugley, acknowledged that he was the father of 'a male bastard child' by Sarah Robinson and entered into a bond for £40 to pay for any expenses incurred in bringing up that child, but 'if Ward Shepherd shall keep the parish harmless in respect of the maintenance, education and bringing up of the said Bastard Child then this Obligation to be void'.[5] There were many other certificates of this kind.[6] In 1743, however, Robert Halls, a servant of a miller in Poplar, who had begotten a 'male bastard child' by Frances Gray, was not so ready to acknowledge his responsibilities and a warrant was issued for his arrest.[7]

The overseers' expenditure was nearly always much heavier than the churchwardens', and their rate was correspondingly higher. At the vestry meeting at Easter 1728, for example, the churchwardens were granted a rate of a penny in the pound, while the overseers were granted eight pence in the pound,[8] and on Easter Monday, 1743, it was recorded that the overseers had disbursed £175 19s. 3d. compared with the churchwardens' £3 5s. 5d.[9]

The pattern of expenditure was at first very simple. For those who needed regular help, sometimes called pensioners, there were weekly payments, 'the weekly collection', and they might also be given help over and above these payments. For the 'casual' poor there were occasional payments as the need arose. It was the vestry that decided who should be included in the weekly collection, and sometimes what extra or casual relief should be granted. Sometimes the claimants appeared before the vestry to make their case, and their claims were 'granted' or 'denied'. At a meeting on 6 January 1789, for example, among the many claims considered, Samuel Warwick's wife was denied 'shoes and firing', while Peter Judd's wife was given 'Druggets [a coarse woollen fabric] for a coat'.[10] After the vestry had determined the rate to be granted the overseers had the authority to collect the money and to make the required payments. The whole scheme was carried out under the watchful eyes of the magistrates, two of whom had to confirm the appointment of the overseers, authorise the poor rate and approve the accounts. They could also hear appeals from the vestry's decisions. In 1742, for example, Samuel Schooling and his wife appealed to a local magistrate, who then wrote to the overseers:

Whereas Samuel Schooling Labourer ... is by age and infirmitys rendered incapable of earning a Subsistance by his Labour for himself and his Wife who is now so lame with Rheumatick pains that she can do no work, not even so much as to dress herself, and her eyesight so bad she can scarce guide herself about the house, And the said Samuel Schooling [says] that he applied himself to the Parishioners at your last Easter Vestry for relief which you refuse to give him, sufficient to support him and his wife, I do hereby Order you to pay to this Samuel Schooling for the support of himself and his Wife Four shillings a week.[11]

The relief of poverty was by far the most demanding and important of all the vestry's activities, and the overseers' accounts, dating from 1744, record literally thousands of transactions. For the early years, up to about 1770, this part of the Poor Law was administered without undue strain on the parish. So long as there was employment for the men the main beneficiaries were women, especially those who had been widowed or left alone with children by husbands who had died or absconded, and the elderly who could no longer work. In 1730, a typical year in the first half of the eighteenth century, the weekly collection was given to 24 people – 16 widows, two single women, four men and two children, and the total disbursed each week in this way amounted to £1 13s. 6d., giving an annual total of £87 2s.[12] Taking into account also the payments to the casual poor, expenditure amounted to £120 18s. 3d.

It is difficult to assess how humanely the law was administered. No doubt there were proud and oppressive vestrymen who made the poor painfully aware of their position. The poet George Crabbe, in *The Village*, wrote of 'churchwarden stern, or kingly overseer', and in *The Parish: a Satire*, John Clare was fiercely critical. Historians on the whole have a poor opinion of the system. Dorothy Marshall, for example, emphasises the heartless limitations of a law that was administered by men who were unwilling and untrained to hold office and whose main concern was to keep expenses down.[13] Arthur Brown, however, who made a detailed study of prosperity and poverty in rural Essex during this period, gives a more favourable account. Officers in the country parishes, he writes, were on the whole hard-working and efficient, purposeful, honest and free from corruption, and in a community as small as a parish the impact of the system was 'softened' by 'neighbourly feelings'.[14] Stansted's records were meticulously kept, and the impression given is that the officers were sensitive and sympathetic to the many needs of the poor and made varied and appropriate provision insofar as they had funds to do so. In some cases those who handed out relief and those who received it were not only neighbours but relations.[15]

The overseers' accounts recorded the full range of provision in careful detail.[16] Cash payments, whether through the weekly 'collection' or on a casual basis, were often supplemented by gifts of clothing, which in many cases were approved by the vestry – for the women shifts, stockings, petticoats, coats and gowns, and occasionally hats and pairs of gloves, and for the men shirts and breeches. Shoes were given to both men and women, though for 'Widdow Sarl [Searle?]' in 1750 'Second Hand shoes' were specified. Often, instead of a finished garment, ells of brown cloth were handed out, with thread, strings and lining, either to the recipient herself or to another woman in the parish who would make up the garment for her. Bedding was occasionally given out – in 1749, for example, a pair of sheets for old Schooling. In the winter many faggots of firewood were purchased and distributed.

For the homeless there was accommodation in property that was owned or rented by the parish, or they were looked after by neighbours and the parish paid the rent. At some point a poorhouse was acquired on the site of what is now Linden House in Silver Street. Orphaned or abandoned children were looked after for a small sum each week. One of these was 'the child of Osborne Ware', a 'negro', no doubt a servant, who had evidently fathered an illegitimate child with one of the village girls and then disappeared. For eight months in 1771 this child was looked after by a carpenter, John Sanders, and his wife Jane at the rate of a shilling a week.

In some cases laundry services were provided. In 1745, for example, the overseers paid a shilling to Goody Says for 'washing for Widd. Brewer' and 1s. 4d. to Sarah Williams for 'Lodging and Washing for Abraham Palmer'.

For those who were ill there was nursing on the parish. Sometimes this was provided by a member of the family, by someone we would today call a carer. In 1776, for example, John Peacock's wife was paid 2s. for looking after her mother. More often it was provided by someone outside the family. One of the earliest entries, for 20 November 1744, records a payment of 2s. 6d. to 'Widdow White' for 'a week's nursing for Goody Collins'. Several entries relate to nursing for smallpox, which was better paid: on 3 December 1765, for example, Widow Savill was paid £2 19s. 'in full for nurseing the Small Pox'. There was an isolated pest house for smallpox sufferers who had to be kept out of the way, such as Widow Stone in 1789, who was 'carted' to the pest house at a cost of 5s.

Medical treatment was also provided. As early as October 1746 Mr. King the Surgeon presented a bill for £1 3s. 6d. and in 1759 Mr. Rowley was paid 9s. 'for bleeding Henry Keen and Edward Nash'. In 1748 a young woman was given 4s. to go to and from London 'to have advice about her eyes'; and in 1765 the parish paid 6d. for a pair of spectacles for

Widow Reid. In 1768 one of the vestrymen, John Headland, took John Robertson's boy, presumably to London, to be 'cured of the [King's] Evil' [i.e. scrofula] and was given a guinea to cover his expenses.

The local doctor from the 1770s onwards, George Welch, charged heavily for his services - £23 2s. 6d. in March 1776, for example, and £25 17s. in April 1780. Among the treatments that he gave were two purging powders for Richard Phillips, antirheumatic drops for Richard Wright's wife, bleeding at home for Henry Wybrow, drawing a tooth for Mary Saville, a narcotic draught for Warwick's wife, and a blister for the back of John Bullinger's wife. Another bill included a payment for one guinea for 'amputating Old Turnival's finger, dressing and care'. In 1788 Welch's son, also George, entered into an agreement with the vestry whereby he was to attend the poor of the parish as surgeon and apothecary for three years for the annual sum of eighteen guineas, midwifery cases excepted,[17] but in 1791 this sum was reduced to twelve guineas.[18] Eight years later, in 1799, the parish reached an agreement with him whereby for the same sum he was to attend to the poor in all cases except fractures and smallpox, and to receive 10s. 6d. for every pauper child he delivered.[19] Vaccination for smallpox was introduced only in March 1825, when George Welch, grandson of the first George, agreed to vaccinate the children of the poor for two guineas a year, by which time the annual fee had gone up to 30 guineas.[20] Although the vicar reported to the church courts that no midwives had been licensed in the parish, there were several instances of village midwives being paid for delivering the children of the poor.

When a sick person seemed close to death it was common for a neighbour to sit up with them and, if they were poor, to be paid by the parish. In the 1760s 6d. a night was the going rate, and it was sometimes included in the funeral expenses as a whole. In 1758, for example, 2s. 6d. was paid 'for Setting up with old Harris and Laying him out', and there were regular payments for coffins, shrouds and carrying the body to the church - usually a long journey and thirsty work, since St. Mary's was a long way from most homes in the parish and the bearers had to be refreshed with beer. (Years later I was told of a Victorian funeral when the coffin was seen propped up outside the door of the King's Arms while the bearers were fortifying themselves inside.) Sometimes a modest contribution was made to the funeral refreshments: in 1760, for example, 6d. was given 'For eating and drancking when Bearyed Blacks wife'. The full run of services provided is reflected in the following entries for the last days of Widow Vinson in June 1763:

10 June	Paid to Widow Vinson	1s.
12 June	Paid to Elizabeth Martin for nursing Widow Vinson	2s.
13 June	Paid to Widow Laine for Siting up with Widow Vinson	6d.
14 June	Paid to Elizabeth Martin for Laying out Widow Vinson and beer	3s.
30 June	Paid to John Sanders the charge of Widow Vinson's Funeral	£1.

In a few cases help was given with the expenses of baptisms and weddings. In 1789 a guinea was paid to the parish clerk for the baptism of the child of Hannah Sanders and in 1811 17s. was paid to cover 'Expense of ring and marrying John Whybrew'.

There were many incidental expenses, such as travelling expenses to and from Saffron Walden to get the accounts approved or in connection with legal proceedings. Carters were paid for moving the poor and their goods, and in 1762 Mr. Stock was paid 14s. for looking after Widow Savil's cow for seven weeks. Drink was sometimes provided, and not just for the bearers of coffins. In November 1808, for example, a shilling was spent on 'Beer for men carrying Poor Rule to Workhouse'. From 1789 onwards, as a service to the farmers, boys were paid for killing sparrows at a rate of a farthing a bird.

Very little was done to provide work for poor children or for the unemployed. Normally boys were put out to work as labourers and girls to domestic service, but they did not all go willingly. In May 1747 the vestry resolved that 25 youngsters, 8 boys and 17 girls, 'should be ordered to service forthwith', but to what extent this instruction was obeyed is not recorded. Apprenticeships were costly, and it would seem that between 1686 and 1836 only a dozen or so boys were indentured.[21]

Spinning wheels were commonly provided. Two wheels at 2s. each, for example, were purchased for Widow Gilbey and Elizabeth Wiberer (Wybrow). The vestry also instructed the overseers to provide a mattock for the use of the poor, to be marked SM.[22] When the overseers were asked in 1787 how much they had spent on 'setting the Poor on Work' they replied that in the years 1783-1785 the average annual amount spent was 8s. 8d., compared with the average of £475 12s. that was 'paid for the poor'.[23]

In the latter part of the eighteenth century, driven by rampant inflation, the costs of administering the Poor Law rocketed throughout the country. With the increase in population, particularly in the towns, the price of wheat per quarter went up from an average of 38s. 6d. each year in 1761/5 to 73s. in 1796/1800, reaching almost 114s. at the end of that period.[24] Labourers' wages failed to keep pace. According to a near-contemporary set of calculations they would buy 15 loaves of bread a week in 1792, 12 in 1803, and 9 in 1812.[25] At the same time work for women dried up as the woollen industry in Essex was stifled by competition in the north of the country.

From the 1770s onwards a new category of claimant emerged – the able-bodied labourer. Whereas in 1730 the weekly collection had consisted of 24 people, more than half of them widows, now payments were made to literally scores of able-bodied men who were either unemployed or could not earn enough to maintain their families.

To deal with this torrent of claims and expenses the parish had to improve and enlarge its administration. In 1764 the number of overseers was increased from two to four, and soon a committee of overseers was set up which met once a week. Later, during the French Wars, a permanent and salaried official was appointed, John Seamer, who was given the title of assistant overseer. It was also in 1764 that the parish decided to erect a workhouse, presided over by a master, though it was 1772 before the building was bought.[26] It had room for 40 inmates.[27] In these ways the shift began from unpaid parish officers working for a year to salaried officials employed on a permanent basis.

The intention was to deter claims for outdoor relief and so to keep down the rates, and also to raise some income for the parish. A workhouse was meant, quite literally, to be a house of work, and at first some of the inmates helped to pay for their keep by spinning. Forty spindles were purchased in 1783,[28] and there are many entries for income from this work, not just in the daily accounts, but also at the back of the account book which covers 1779-1787.[29] Yarn was sold to Braintree and Dunmow clothiers, and at one point the income from this source equalled about a quarter of the parish's Poor Law expenditure. With the decline of the wool trade in Essex, the parish turned to silk-spinning, but that

35. The old workhouse. Sketch by Joseph Green, 1890.

lasted only a few years.[30] In one year the workhouse grew potatoes which produced an income of £75,[31] but other activities brought in very little. In 1788 and 1789, for example, small payments, all except one less than £1, were received 'for the Workhouse Orchard', 'for Boy's Work' (this from the vicar), 'on account of Girl', 'for wood sold', 'Of Mr. Packer for Workhouse Children's work', and 'Of Mr. Phillips for pulling docks'. But by the turn of the century the workhouse was more of a poorhouse than a workhouse, containing mainly children or the old.

There were also many expenses connected with the workhouse, not just the master's salary, but payments for repairs and improvements to the building and provisions for its inmates. The records list firewood, coal, cheese, beer and pigs, half a bushel of white pears and clothes for the workhouse boys. One of the earliest expenses, recorded in 1776, was 'carrying ye Brew House to ye Workhouse 2s.', and so presumably the workhouse brewed its own beer.[32] In many cases the tradesman or the farmer supplying the house was a member of the vestry or a close relation, and no doubt they profited from the deal. Although there is no evidence of any impropriety it is significant that under the new Poor Law, which came into force in 1834, the process of tendering was carefully applied. In 1787 the overseers reported that in 1783-5 the average annual 'Expenses of Entertainments at Meetings relative to the Poor' were a mere 2s.[33] In April 1801, however, two guineas were laid out on a 'vestry dinner'.

Other measures were taken to try to cut back on expenditure. In 1791 two local JPs, William Heath and Robert Raynsford, examined 29 people to determine 'the places of their last legal settlement'. Most of them were from Bishop's Stortford or villages nearby, and they were presumably expelled.[34] In another economy in 1810 the vestry agreed that nothing but cheap drugget should be given for gowns and petticoats.[35]

It was all to no avail. In 1730 £120 18s. 3d. was disbursed by the overseers; by 1761 this had risen to £253 14s., by 1793 to £661 2s., by 1801 to £2452 17s. 6d., and by the peak year of 1802 to £3194 11s. 4d. After that it levelled out at between £1000 and £2000 a year.[36]

With such an increase in the number of claimants and payments, the whole tenor of the parish administration changed, becoming less 'neighbourly' and more impersonal. In the register of burials a large letter P was insensitively stamped on the entries for pauper burials. In 1774 six out of 23 burials were stigmatised in this way, in 1788 10 out of 28, and in 1793 13 out of 43.[37] As the labourers became more impoverished so the farmers became more prosperous, and the social divide widened to a chasm. All this will be the background to the events that will be described in the next chapter, to the wars with the French from 1793 to 1815, and to the events that will be described in the next part of this book – the Swing Riots of 1832, the comparable 'riot' in Stansted in 1834, and then, in the same year, the harsh severity of the Poor Law Amendment Act.

The church was closely involved in the administration of Stansted's charities. In 1723 the vicar, John Reynolds, acknowledged that these were only 'small benefactions', but he assured his bishop that they were administered 'without the least Fraud or Abuse'. At that time there were eight charities in the parish – Hubbard's (1582 and 1593), Cooke's (1604 and 1609), Browne's (1609), Palmer's (1616), Buck's gift (1620) and Peck's (1705). In the Charity Commissioners' Report in the 1830s two more were added, Rush's (1811) and Brent's (1827).[38] Even so, by 1874 the total amount being distributed was valued at only £50 a year.[39]

The ways in which these charities were organised varied a great deal. The gift set up by the draper, Robert Buck, was given in Stansted every third year, Ugley and Manuden benefiting in the other years, and the recipients, three poor men and three poor women 'of honest name and fame', were each given enough cloth to make up a suit of clothes, together with a hat, shoes and stockings, which they were obliged to wear to church on each of the following three Sundays to satisfy the churchwardens that they had used the cloth for the purpose intended. More commonly a legacy would be used to purchase a few acres of land, the rent on which would be given to the parish authorities to buy loaves of bread for the poor to be handed out after the morning service at church. These arrangements changed over time. By the 1830s, when the Charity Commissioners submitted their report, the incomes of five of the charities were being paid into the churchwardens' general account. The Commissioners regarded this as improper, but noted that each year the parish was spending £6 18s. 8d. on bread, which was made up into penny rolls, and about 33 of these were given, every Sunday, after morning service, to as many poor parishioners. The Commissioners recommended that the income of all the property appropriated to the poor by charity should be distributed by the minister and churchwardens to poor parishioners of good character and, if possible, not receiving parish relief. The churchwardens and assistant overseers undertook that this would be done.

Every charity was connected with the church in one way or the other. Buck's stipulation that the recipients of his charity should wear their new clothes to church on each of the three following Sundays is just one example. Browne made arrangements for 20s. to be distributed among the poor yearly on Christmas Day at the discretion of the vicar and the churchwardens. The sums involved might have been small, but the recipients no doubt valued them, and the connection with the church added to its influence and authority in the village.

1. ERO, D/P 109/8/4.
2. LMA, Gibson Papers, Ms 9,583/14.
3. For orders for the removal of persons who had 'intruded' themselves into Stansted, see ERO, D/P 109/13/2. For orders for the removal of persons to Stansted, see ERO, D/P 109/13/3.
4. Thomas Sokoll (2001: 601).
5. ERO, D/P 109/15/1.
6. ERO, D/P 109/15/1-3.
7. ERO, D/P 109/15/2,3.
8. ERO, D/P 109/8/4.
9. ERO, D/P 109/8/4.
10. ERO, D/P 109/8/1.
11. ERO, D/P 109/18/4, John Maryon to the overseers of the poor, 1 May 1742.
12. ERO, D/P 109/8/4.
13. Marshall (1926: Introduction: Summary of Contents).
14. Brown (1996: 151, 162).
15. E.g. Sanders (1989: 8).
16. Except where otherwise indicated, the details of these transactions are taken from the overseers' accounts in the D/P 109/12 series.
17. ERO, D/P 109/8/5, 24 March 1788.
18. ERO, D/P 109/8/5, 25 April 1791.
19. ERO, D/P 109/8/5, 25 March 1799.
20. ERO, D/P 109/8/5, 25 March 1825.
21. A file on indentures in the ERO, D/P 109/14/1, contains only 10 indentures. The register of apprentices, D/P 109/14/2, contains only two names, and I have found only five relevant entries in the overseers' accounts and the vestry minutes.
22. ERO, D/P 109/8/4, 20 January 1749.
23. ERO, Q/CR 1/1, 'Abstract of the Returns made by the Overseers of the Poor ... to certain Questions ... relative to the state of the Poor', 1787.
24. Cole and Postgate (1961: 77-8).
25. Hampson (1934: 216), quoting J. Denson, *A Peasant's Voice to Landowners* (Cambridge, 1830).
26. ERO, D/P 109/12/1C, 2 July 1764. See also NA, MH 12/4536/217, Folios 500-505, Dobede to Poor Law Commission, 14 November 1836: the workhouse was bought in 1772. In the overseers' accounts the first references to the workhouse are in 1773. On 10 April 1773 it was agreed that £50 'shall be applied towards the Workhouse now enlarged by an additional building and lately purchased by the parish': ERO, D/P 109/8/5.
27. Drury (2006: 14). ISC: the original village poorhouse, which stood on the site of Linden House in Silver Street, was discontinued c.1773 when the property was sold, the proceeds being devoted to the extension of the new workhouse.
28. ERO, D/P 109/12/5, 9 February 1783.
29. ERO, D/P 109/12/5.
30. Brown (1969: 149).
31. *Ibid.*
32. ERO, D/P 109/12/4, 24 April 1776.
33. ERO, Q/CR 1/1.
34. ERO, D/P 109/8/5, 19 October 1791.
35. ERO, D/P 109/12/10, 10 November 1810.
36. These figures come from the vestry minutes, D/P 109/8/4,5. For figures for Essex see Brown (1996: 153).
37. This practice was stopped in 1794.
38. See Morant (1760-68: 579), Muilman Vol. III (1770: 24-5), and the Charity Commissioners' Report (n.d., 1830s). There are several discrepancies between these accounts on points of detail.
39. *Post Office Guide 1874.*

15: THE WARS WITH FRANCE

It was against this background of increasing poverty and strain, exacerbated by bad harvests, that Britain absorbed the impact of the French revolution and of the wars with France that followed. The propertied classes feared that the overthrow of the Bourbons and the establishment of a republic would incite the populace to take up arms, all the more so when it seemed that the French were bent on spreading revolution by conquest. In January 1793 a meeting was held of 'the Gentlemen, Clergy, Yeomanry and other Inhabitants of the Hundreds of Uttlesford, Clavering and Freshwell', with Lord Howard of Audley End in the chair. Worried about the evils which were likely to result from the 'seditious libels and inflammatory publications' which had been spread throughout the kingdom by 'unprincipled levellers, designing republicans, and desperate men, acting in conjunction with our foreign enemies', those present resolved to appoint a committee to support the constitution and to do all in their power to suppress sedition. These resolutions were left at an office in Saffron Walden and at the White Bear in Stansted 'for the signature of such persons as approve thereof'.[1] Two men from Stansted helped to make up the committee - Bayley Heath, representing his brother, William, who was ill, and Henry Croasdaile.

These fears were exaggerated. There was little revolutionary fervour, and when riots broke out in Saffron Walden, Thaxted and Dunmow in 1795 the aim was not to overthrow the constitution but to bring down the price of bread to its pre-war level. In the same year there was a riot in Bishop's Stortford 'in consequence of the scarcity of bread and flour'.[2] More serious was the threat of invasion. In February 1793, a month after the meeting presided over by Lord Howard, France declared war on Great Britain. Although the British navy was supreme it could not guarantee the complete blockade of the French navy in the Channel ports, and if the French had been able to break out their massed armies, based on conscription, would have overwhelmed the forces on the British side.

In 1793 the number of men in the regular army on home soil was a mere 17,344, a number which was increased to 48,609 by 1798. This force was supported by the local militia that in Essex, as elsewhere, fell under the control of the Lord Lieutenant of the county, was officered by local gentlemen, and was recruited by ballot, though if a man was wealthy enough he might pay for a substitute, or if he was not the parish might pay on his behalf. Such was the poverty and hardship of the labourers at that time that many were prepared to volunteer for service. Soldiers' families were supported as a matter of course. The numbers to be enrolled in the militia rose from 30,740 men in England and Wales in 1792 to 64,000 men in 1796. In Essex 960 men were required, one in ten of those who were eligible, and a year later this quota was raised to 1,756, almost one man in five. The county was split into 12 sub-divisions, and Stansted fell within the Walden and Freshwell sub-division. There were two battalions of the Essex Militia, the Western and the Eastern, and, oddly, the Walden and Freshwell sub-division was in the recruitment area for the Eastern.

After the militia the most important and popular support for the regular army came from the volunteers, of whom there were 51,380 in the country as a whole by 1798. In 1811 there were 23 corps in Essex with more than 2,000 volunteers in all, one of them being the Saffron Walden Infantry.[3] There were also three companies in Bishop's Stortford with a total of over 200 men.[4] One of the great attractions of volunteering was that men were exempt from service in the militia.[5]

Sailors were required for the Royal Navy too. In 1796 the villages and towns of Essex were called on to supply 316 men in all, and Stansted would have been included.[6]

The threat of invasion rose and fell. The alarm aroused by the French landings in Ireland in 1796 was intensified when the first Army of England, l'Armée de l'Angleterre, gathered on the Channel coast in 1798. All plans for invasion, however, were put aside when Napoleon attacked Egypt instead, and the threat seemed to have fallen away completely with the Treaty of Amiens in 1802. It was renewed, however, in the following year when war broke out again. As well as conquering his enemies in a series of devastating victories on the continent, Napoleon assembled another Army of England, based at Boulogne, and built up a fleet of 1,500 flat-bottomed barges. He was thwarted once again by the blockade imposed by the British navy. If he were given control of the Channel for six hours, he declared, he would conquer the world, but when he tried to create a diversion and in this way to open up the Channel his fleet went down to defeat, a humiliation that was then completed by the battle of Trafalgar in 1805. The camp at Boulogne was broken up and the fleet of barges dispersed. After that there was no longer any serious possibility of invasion, and the focus of British attention was turned on the Peninsular War, the campaigns in Portugal and Spain.

The parishioners of Stansted were affected in several ways. First, there was service in the regular army. The first man from Stansted to have enrolled appears to have been James Poole, who served from 1794 to 1814, being discharged when he reached the age of 45.[7] He served in the First Life Guards, and would have fought under Wellington in the Peninsular War. There were also several men – we know of five - who, having been enrolled in the militia, then volunteered for the Line.

Second, there was service in the militia. The most detailed return that survives for Stansted dates from 1813, when 30 men were on the lists, 20 who had been balloted and 10 volunteers, their ages varying from 18 to 24.[8] Other Lieutenancy papers record the names of individuals who were balloted and of those who served as substitutes for them. In 1803 alone Stansted paid £31 for substitutes.[9]

There are also Quarter Sessions papers recording the financial transactions that took place when a man from Essex was serving as a substitute for a man in another county and when payments had to be made to the substitute's family by the overseers of the poor. For example, William Tyler of Stansted Mountfitchet, a married man, served in the militia as a substitute for William Sapseed of Hertford from April to December 1793, and 1s. 2d. a week was transferred from Hertfordshire to Essex and paid to his wife. When a child was born this payment was increased to 2s. 4d. a week.[10]

Conversely there were men from other counties who served as substitutes for men of Stansted. For example, Daniel Mumford of Hunsdon, Herts, a married man with no children, served as a substitute for Thomas Carter of Stansted from April 1805 to March 1807 and 1s. 6d. a week was paid to his wife.[11]

As for volunteers, no doubt there were some from Stansted who served in the Saffron Walden Infantry, but there is no record of them in the surviving papers. One of the attractions of volunteering, as noted already, was exemption from the militia, and we know that in 1815 39 men in Stansted were listed as exempt.[12] None of the Stansted gentry are recorded in the lists of those who took part in the more elite corps.[13]

But perhaps the most profound impact of the war was economic. Enormous profits were made from farming, especially from the cultivation of wheat. Rents rose rapidly and the price of land rocketed. It was only the labourers and their families who missed out, and the advent of peace did nothing to help them.[14]

At the close of hostilities there were no doubt celebrations, as in other villages throughout the country, and in 1815 the parish gave £15 12s. to the subscription for the families of the men who had been killed or wounded at Waterloo or in other battles in the recent fighting. Of this £11 was 'Received at the Doors of the Parish Church' after a sermon preached by the vicar, Richard Grant.[15]

---

1   ERO, D/P 109/28/6.
2   Cooper (2005: 63), quoting *The Times*.
3   ERO, L/L 1/2.
4   Cooper (2005: 97).
5   Brown (1996: 165).
6   Brown (1996: 164).
7   NA, WO 97/8/79.
8   ERO, L/R 5/1.
9   Brown (1969: 147).
10 ERO, Q/FAc 3/22.
11 These cases are taken from ERO, Q/FAc 3/8. See also ERO, D/P 109/17, instructions to the churchwardens and overseers of the poor to pay militia men or their substitutes.
12 ERO, L/R 6/2.
13 Andrews (1954: 73-4).
14 Brown (1996: 168, 170, 186).
15 Reader, 'Stansted in the Last Century', *SMPM*, May 1941, p. 13.

PART IV

FROM THE NAPOLEONIC WARS TO WORLD WAR I

16: THE FARM LABOURERS' 'RIOT' OF 1834

After the French Wars Great Britain was the greatest power in the world, a position it was to hold and consolidate for most of the coming century. Its citizens were buoyed up by a sense of national pride, which was deliberately fostered and encouraged by those in authority. But beneath this proud and patriotic surface was the disturbing reality of a society divided against itself, the people poor and embittered, the rulers fearful and repressive. This reality was clearly reflected in Stansted.

The Heaths' period as lords of the manor had come to an end with the death of Bayley Heath in 1809. The manor of Bentfield Bury then passed into the hands of William Gosling, whose family had made its fortune in banking. Gosling lived mainly in London but his local base was just a few miles away, at Farnham. The manor of Stansted Hall was acquired by Ebenezer Fuller-Maitland, then aged 29, whose family had made its fortune in commerce and banking and had extensive estates in Berkshire and Breconshire. The Fuller-Maitlands would later play a major role in the administration of the parish, but in these early years Ebenezer and his family spent little time in the village, preferring to live at their Berkshire home and in London. The building of Stansted Hall, which had been left derelict by the Heaths, was pulled down in 1812. Gosling, not being resident in Stansted, played no part in its affairs apart from the management of his estate. So power was exercised mainly by the leading farmers, and perhaps by the vicar, backed up when needed by the full array of the county gentry.

    Landowners and farmers had done well during the war, but towards the end of the conflict the price of bread fell and they began to feel dangerously at risk. The Corn Laws, which imposed steep import duties on foreign grain, shored up their position to some extent, but the wartime prosperity did not return. It was the labourers and their families, however, who suffered most and who became increasingly impoverished and discontented. The increase in population over the past century and the shift from pasture to arable worsened their plight. The fields of oats, wheat and barley provided only seasonal employment, such as spring sowing and harvesting. In between, and especially in winter after the cereals had been threshed, there was little demand for labour.

    Many able-bodied men had to turn to the parish for relief. Poor Law expenditure, which had peaked at over £3,000 a year during the French Wars, came down in the peace that followed, but it was still high – £1,500, for example, in 1818-19, and in 1832/33 and 1833/34 it was still running at about £1,600. Many turned to poaching. This was a time when the gentry were building up their reserves of pheasants, and mantraps and spring guns were used to protect them, though I have found no evidence of these practices in Stansted. More generally, the administration of the law became increasingly harsh and savage, and transportation to Australia became a common punishment.

    In 1830 and 1831 the southern counties of England were convulsed by the Swing Riots, the last great rural uprising in this country, when farm labourers protested against low

16: THE FARM LABOURERS' 'RIOT' OF 1834

wages and unemployment by going on strike, burning hayricks, breaking up threshing machines (which put men out of work in the winter) and maiming animals (anything to strike a blow at the farmers). No one was killed, but much damage was done. Like the food riots in the French Wars, the Swing Riots were not revolutionary. The men who went on strike were not seeking to overthrow the existing order. What they wanted was justice, a living wage for a full week's work. Nineteen men were executed in all, and 481 transported to Australia, wrested away from their families and shipped 12,000 miles away.

There were riots in several villages near Stansted, such as Henham, Clavering, Arkesden, High Easter, Finchingfield and Steeple Bumpstead, but not in Stansted itself. The only related disorder in Stansted was that two men, Griggs and Warwick, maimed a lamb. Typically they were young - Griggs was 23 and Warwick 19 - presumably because it was the men without family responsibilities who had less to lose and were therefore bold to take action. Griggs, who seems to have taken the lead, was found guilty. The chairman of the magistrates said that the offence was of such 'malignity' that he could have transported him for life, but he would be merciful, not severe, and he gave him only seven years. Griggs laughed as he left the bar, saying 'Thank ye, my Lord, if that's all you can do for me'.

At the beginning of 1834 about 100 people in Stansted were receiving poor relief each month. Some men were being paid to work on the roads, and farmers were being paid to employ others. Because of the increased expenditure in the country as a whole the Poor Law was about to be reformed, and in preparation for this the Poor Law Commissioners sent a questionnaire to all the parishes in the country. In response the authorities in Stansted reported that there were 14 men who were regularly out of employment; that the average labourer earned 12s. a week with beer in summer and 10s. a week with beer in winter; that if he was married with four children his family would bring in a further 5s. a week; and that they could not 'without the strictest economy, subsist on these Earnings, unless they debarred themselves from wheaten bread, and potatoes were generally their sustenance'. It was 'certainly impossible' for a labourer to lay anything by. As for the Swing Riots (though they were not named as such), 'Nothing of the kind took place in this parish; but there is reason for believing that want of employment and inadequate relief in some instances and increasing depravity in others, have a strong tendency towards exciting vindictiveness and desperation'.[1]

In fact conditions were much worse than the authorities had reported, for in September 1834, after the harvest had been gathered in, the farmers in Stansted, or at least some of them, reduced the wages of their common labourers from 9s. a week with beer to 8s. a week with beer. They were responding to the agricultural depression at the time, and there were reductions in wages elsewhere, but it was only in Stansted that the labourers went on strike, and it was this that led to the disturbances which took place on 22 September. A month later two of the leaders, George Sapseed, aged 20, and George Willis, aged 22, both of them labourers living in Bentfield End Causeway, were charged with conspiracy, riot and assault.

What we know of the strike comes from the court proceedings in Chelmsford, but it is only the evidence of the prosecution that we have, since the defendants did not go into the witness box. When wages were reduced, the labourers gathered together and resolved that they were going to go on strike until the farmers put the shilling back on. They must have been desperate, for they would have been well aware of the punishments meted out in the

Swing Riots. They were also determined that no one was going to break the strike, and at two farms at least there were men who went on working – at Hole Farm, where the 43-year-old Edridge Phillips was the farmer, and at Bentfield Bury Farm, where the farmer was the 21-year-old Charles Spencer. Both Philips and Spencer were tenant farmers of the Goslings.

On the morning of 22 September 100 or more labourers gathered together, perhaps at Bentfield Green, and went down the road to Hole Farm. It was 5 a.m. Edridge Phillips – he was the first witness – went out to ask them what they wanted. They told him that they were going on strike until the shilling was put back on. Phillips advised them to return to work, but they ignored him. Phillips's ploughman was already out with his horses in the fields, but two of his men at the farm joined the strikers who then moved on to Bentfield Bury Farm.

There Charles Spencer, the second witness, came out to meet them. He had 15 labourers in all, he told the court, but that morning nine were not there. His ploughmen, however, had turned up, and he had already sent them out to start work. As Spencer came out the strikers surrounded him and said that they would make him put back the shilling. He told them that he was not going to be frightened by them, even though they were so many, and that he could do without them for a fortnight. They said that they would be damned if his men or his horses were working for him the next morning, and they moved away. Spencer then left home, and while he was out he saw the men go up to Phillips's ploughman and unhook the horses, and when he returned at ten o'clock he found that all his own horses were back at the farm, which meant that the ploughing on his own land had been stopped.

The next witness was John Savill, one of Phillips's workmen, a man of 61 who lived in the cottage in the Causeway now known as Corner Thatch. He had not been at Hole Farm when the crowd came, since apparently he had been out collecting reeds and flags, but around ten o'clock he returned with his wagon piled high. While he was there, he said, he turned his head and saw six of his master's horses coming home from the plough, and just after them came 'a throng of men'. They told him to come down from the wagon, but he would not. So Willis and Sapseed climbed up and Sapseed, putting up his hands, 'desired' him to come down. He said 'Don't hurt me, and I'll come down', which he did, but he was so terrified that he ran into the house, where the farmer's wife, Elizabeth Phillips, let him in. At the same time the ploughman, Griggs, rushed in.

Elizabeth Phillips, the fourth witness, claimed that the mob, as she called them, had tried to stop Savill and Griggs getting into the house, but once they were in she bolted the door and Griggs was so terrified that she locked him in the cellar. They were glad to escape.

What followed then was a legal argument. Dowling, the lawyer for Willis and Sapseed, tried to show that no violence was intended. What happened that morning, he said, was merely a meeting, and it was perfectly lawful for men to hold a meeting and to ask for an increase in wages. They were not armed, they did not even shout out. There had been no violence, and no threat of violence. There were over 100 of them. Surely, if they had wanted to inflict violence on Spencer, Griggs or Savill they could have done so.

The prosecutor argued that it was more than a meeting and that violence had been threatened. That was why the strikers had marched on the farms, why Spencer had said that he refused to be frightened, why Griggs and Savill had taken refuge in the farmhouse, and why the farmer's wife had locked the door.

36. Notice of District Ploughing Match to be held on 24 September 1834, now on display in Saffron Walden Museum.

The chairman of the magistrates, J.J. Strutt, summed up. The prisoners had the right to meet and decide what action they should take, but he reminded the jury of the definition of a riot - an assembling together of three or more persons in a riotous and routous manner calculated to excite terror. Was this, he asked, a meeting of a quiet and peaceable nature, or was it an assemblage using expressions towards others which were calculated to excite alarm? The men had threatened the masters: they had said they would *make* them put up their wages. They had told Spencer that neither his men nor his horses would be at work the next morning and they had terrified Savill and Griggs.

The jury took a long time to agree – one juror, it was said, wanted to acquit – but in the end they found both Willis and Sapseed guilty. It was then for the magistrates to impose the sentence. The chairman referred back to the Swing Riots: he had hoped, he said, that the punishments meted out then would have been a sufficient deterrent, and he was sorry that this type of case had occurred again. 'There were no extenuating circumstances. There was an agricultural depression. The farmers had to reduce wages, and the wages that were paid in the parish were not as low as in many others.' In fact they were 'sufficient to enable the men to maintain themselves creditably' - this was in stark contradiction to the evidence given to the Poor Law Commissioners – 'and even if they were not that was no excuse for their behaviour'. So he sentenced both prisoners to one year's hard labour.

Such was the story of Stansted's 'riot'. It appeared to have been a complete failure, both in its immediate objectives and its effect in the longer term. The farmers did not put the shilling back on and the labourers had to return to work. Nor was there any improvement in their condition. On the contrary, the harshness of the new Poor Law of 1834 made their plight even worse. In reaction to the Swing Riots in general, however, there was widespread astonishment that the labourers could achieve such a degree of organisation, and perhaps they made the farmers hesitate before lowering wages in future. It is surely significant that there were no threshing machines in Essex in 1835.

Shortly before the strike took place notices appeared throughout Stansted and the neighbouring parishes advertising the fourth District Ploughing Match to be held in Stansted by the District Agricultural Society. Organised by the local gentry and farmers, it offered prizes, not just to the best ploughman and the best ploughboy (for each a Glazed Hat and a Jacket with Sleeves), but also to those labourers and servants who had done the most to win the approval of their masters, such as 'the Labourer in Husbandry who shall have brought up the largest Family without any, or with the least parochial relief', 'the Labourer or Servant who shall have worked the greatest number of years without intermission (except from illness) upon the same occupation, or with the same Master', and 'the Labourer who shall have subscribed the greatest number of years to a Benefit or Benefit Societies'.[2] This Ploughing Match, with its display of heavy paternalism on the one hand and submissive deference on the other, was to be held on 24 September, just two days after the 'riot' took place. It is possible that it was cancelled, but if it was held it is unlikely that any of the strikers were among the prize-winners.

We know from the census records that George Sapseed and George Willis, the two ringleaders, were back in the village by 1841, while the two farmers, Phillips and Spencer, became overseers of the poor. Spencer, in fact, became one of the leading figures in the parish, retiring as churchwarden on his 76th birthday in 1888.

1   The Poor Law Inquiry Commissioners (1834).   2   Notice displayed in Saffron Walden Museum.

17: THE NEW POOR LAW

For the well-to-do farmers of Stansted the suppression of the labourers' strike was not the only cause for satisfaction in 1834. They also benefited from the passing of the Poor Law Amendment Act, under which the responsibility for the relief of the poor was transferred from parishes to Poor Law Unions, each consisting of several parishes. In each Union the law was administered by a Board of Guardians elected by the ratepayers and responsible centrally to the Poor Law Commission. Stansted was one of 20 parishes, ten from Essex and ten from Hertfordshire, which made up the Bishop's Stortford Poor Law Union.[1]

The number of Guardians varied over the years, but it was normally between 25 and 30. In 1847, for example, there were 27, four for Bishop's Stortford, two each for Sawbridgeworth, Stansted, Braughing and Much Hadham, and one each for the rest. Most of the Guardians were farmers, in many cases the same men who had administered the old Poor Law. In 1846, for example, 22 were described as farmers (among them William Parris and Charles Hicks of Stansted), one as a yeoman, one as a farmer and maltster, two as maltsters and one as a brewer. The brewer and one of the maltsters were from Bishop's Stortford.[2]

The provision of relief continued to be financed by rates collected by local officials, and in Stansted John Seamer, the assistant overseer under the old Act, was appointed first as a rate collector and then, again, as an assistant overseer.[3] The brothers George and Samuel Welch became Medical Officers, Samuel serving Stansted and Henham and George serving Birchanger, Manuden, Elsenham and Ugley.

The Welches were a constant thorn in the side of the authorities. John Walsham, an Assistant Commissioner, asserted that the Medical Officers in the Stortford Union were better paid than any others in the district, and yet they gave endless trouble, more particularly the Welches, by their disrespectful behaviour to the Guardians and (as the Guardians alleged) by their careless treatment of the poor.[4] In 1847 George Welch was reprimanded for giving gin and beer, without exercising proper control, to four paupers who were suffering 'the infirmities of age', and he finally resigned in 1848. Samuel was alleged to have been negligent in his treatment of one poor woman, for which his contract was terminated in 1847, only for it to be renewed again in the following year because it was difficult to find anyone to replace him.

The aim of the new law was not to improve the condition of the poor but to reduce the burden of expenditure on the rich. To this end outdoor relief was to be discontinued, and indoor relief would be given, not in the parish workhouses, which were to be sold off, together with other parish property such as pest houses and poor houses,[5] but in the new, purpose-built Union workhouse, in Stansted's case in the workhouse in Bishop's Stortford, where conditions were to be so grim that no one would want to go there unless they were in dire need. The workhouse in Stortford 'was deliberately designed, for surveillance and austerity, to look like a prison'[6], and it was built to contain 360 people since the Guardians intended to fulfil the expectation that all relief would be provided there.[7] It was soon realised that this policy would have to be modified, since for many people indoor relief was inappropriate and outdoor relief was often less expensive. Even so the workhouse had to be enlarged to hold 425, and in the 1890s, when standards were higher and there were fewer than 200 inmates, it was considered to be inadequate even for them, and it was noted that the higher numbers of earlier years had been accommodated only by the use of bunk beds.[8] Two important parts of the workhouse complex were the infirmary for looking after sick paupers and the school for educating the workhouse children.

An early measure to reduce pressure on the rates, and in part to reduce pressure on the workhouse, was a scheme for the emigration of paupers to Canada, and we know of three who went from Stansted – Charles Ward, a shepherd, an orphan aged 19; George Patmore, a maltmaker and a general labourer, aged 19 (no father and his mother had married again to a 'bad character'); and Mary Jordan, 19, an inmate of the workhouse.[9] There were also schemes from time to time to send children to the cotton mills near Stockport, or more generally to the 'manufacturing districts' in the north. No doubt some of them came from Stansted.[10]

The new law was a great success at first in bringing down the rates. Alfred Power, the Assistant Poor Law Commissioner responsible for making preparations for the Union, had drawn up a table setting out for each parish several important indices. This showed that in 1831, under the old Poor Law, Stansted, with a population of 1560, had 20 male persons out of work, 127 persons receiving relief each week, 264 poor persons being relieved at one time, and 20 inmates in its workhouse. Its average annual expenditure on the poor in the three years from 1832 to 1834 had been £1,391, which worked out at a little under £1 per head of the population. This was significantly less than the other nine Essex parishes, with the exception of Little Hallingbury, but more than that of Bishop's Stortford, where the population was 3,958 and the expenditure £2,643. Power referred to the whole district, with the exception of Stortford, as being an 'extremely pauperized agricultural district', and to the extent that Stansted might have had a more diversified economy than the smaller villages this may account for its lower expenditure per head of population. Power also commented on the high numbers of men out of work in the parishes - 'The practice of throwing men out of employment for a time is also very general among the farmers of this district'.[11] In 1842 new averages of expenditure were submitted for the three years ending 25 March 1841. Stansted had an annual average of £799, just 53% of the earlier figure. There were comparable reductions in the other parishes, while Bishop's Stortford went down to £1381, 52% of the earlier figure.[12]

The farmers had good cause to be pleased, but the Union workhouse, and the system of which it was an expression, immediately acquired an evil reputation among the poor. Even before it had been built there were arson attacks on the old parish buildings in Stortford and Saffron Walden,[13] and the Guardians were so fearful of disorder that they asked for two policemen from London to be attached to the workhouse. They were granted one, and allowed him to go only when they were satisfied that most of the inmates would not be able-bodied men but children and the old.[14]

It is easy to see why 'the house' was so loathed. Men and women were separated, even husbands and wives, and so were brothers and sisters over the age of seven. The inmates had to wear Union clothing, and were put to work on wearisome tasks such as oakum-picking and stone-breaking. If they refused to work they could be taken to court. The Poor Law Commissioners expected every economy to be observed, but in one case at least the Stortford Guardians went even further than the Commissioners required, providing inadequate medical arrangements, and explaining when called to account that it was their deliberate policy 'to administer relief in a sparing and obnoxious manner to some who, from misconduct, wilful improvidence or determined sloth have become a burden upon the poor rates'.[15] The diet which they chose consisted of four ounces of bread daily and half a pound of potatoes. Meat days might be added at the Guardians' discretion,[16] and it was reported in 1838 that the meat supplied to the workhouse consisted of 'clods and stickings free from bone', i.e. the cheapest cuts of beef.[17] When potatoes were unavailable rice and bread were provided.[18] There were improvements over the years. In 1847, for example, tea and butter were allowed for breakfast and supper, but only for the infirm,[19] and in 1880 the Guardians called for tenders for the supply of

grocery, butter, cheese, new milk, tea, peas, rice, wine, spirits, ale, porter, soap, oil, candles, coals, firewood, hosiery, drapery, woollen drapery, haberdashery, brushes, brooms and other articles for the workhouse and beef and mutton for the outdoor sick poor for 26 weeks, also with the best seconds bread and flour for the workhouse and outdoor poor for 13 weeks, ... Also for the supply during the like period of 13 weeks of brandy and gin and good port and tarragona wine for the outdoor poor....[20]

The spirits were for the infirm and the sick.

A festive dinner was provided on Christmas Day, when members of the royal family were toasted, and in later years outings and entertainments were organised. There was increasing sympathy for the sick in the infirmary, and in 1894 the *British Medical Journal* carried out an inspection and published its findings:

The sick are treated with humanity and consideration; the wards are bright with sunshine, pictures, and plants, and it was a pleasant sight to see the old people seated round the fire in comfortable armchairs, the women with soft bright-coloured shawls on their shoulders, some working, knitting or mending, and men spelling their slow way through a magazine or newspaper. In bed were some sad cases of helplessness – complete paralysis, spinal disease, cancer, bronchitis – such illnesses as overtake the aged poor when their day's work is over; but we felt sorry to see that the nursing staff was so inadequate to cope with these old and sick people; kindness and thoughtful care they had, but it is quite beyond the power of one nurse, however capable, to do all that could be done for over seventy patients more or less ailing, more or less helpless .... At night there is no one to wait on them, or to help them in their necessities, but an inmate sleeping in the same ward. We have no reason to think they are not kind and helpful, but it is a makeshift for skilled attention, and the night must be dreary and painful to many a bedridden inmate in the dark silence of the ward.

Although at first the new law was successful in bringing down expenditure and so reducing the rates, in later years its application was relaxed, and in spite of the original policy of confining relief to those who went into the workhouse there was a substantial increase in the number of outdoor paupers. In the Bishop's Stortford Union, in the half year ending in Michaelmas 1855, 545 people were accommodated in the workhouse for varying lengths of time (201 men, 144 women and 200 children), while the number of outdoor poor was 2,306, more than four times as great (616 men, 812 women and 878 children). The comparable figures for Stansted's workhouse poor were 20 men, 15 women and 25 children, making a total of 60, and for the outdoor poor 47 men, 63 women and 54 children, making a total of 164. Of the 60 indoor poor 11 were there on more or less a permanent basis.[21] By 1872, in the country as a whole, there were five outdoor paupers to every one in the workhouse.[22]

In spite of the improvements made, people had a horror of the workhouse and put up with terrible hardship rather than go there. In December 1862 John Chapman, 'an oldish-looking man', was found sleeping in an unoccupied stable in Stansted 'in a wretchedly weak and dirty state'. Parishioners were afraid that he would freeze to death, but he refused to go into the workhouse, being prevailed upon to enter only when he was charged with vagrancy in the Petty Sessions at Saffron Walden.[23]

Emma Jocelyne, a blind woman, 69 years old, was equally determined to maintain her independence. She acted as housekeeper to an 'infirm old man', and one morning in February 1876, after the old man had lit his fire and gone out, she was found in flames, being burnt alive. At the inquest the local doctor gave evidence that there had been many attempts to get her to go into the Union Infirmary, but 'she had a great horror of it'. She had been on outdoor relief of 18d. and two loaves each week, and one of the jurymen commented 'that she ought to have been compelled to go into the workhouse', but the Coroner, 'although admitting that the sum was quite inadequate to maintain life', stated that there was no law to compel a person to go into the workhouse: 'all the Guardians could do was to withhold the allowance and then if the person starved they were equally held culpable'. It is a telling indictment of the system that no one suggested that her relief should have been increased.[24]

A year later, in 1877, Jane Mumford, a difficult old woman who refused to pay her rent, was evicted, inhumanely it was alleged, from her one-roomed thatched hut with her effects, and took refuge in a gravel pit, where she was taunted and tormented by local children, obstinately 'refusing an asylum which would readily have been obtained for her at the Union Workhouse'.[25]

In 1891, in another case which provoked accusations of inhumanity, William Cook, about 44 years of age, who had 'been leading a sort of vagabond existence for some time' and was well known in all the villages around, was found one night lying by the side of the main road leading to Stortford. He was lame, and it was thought he was drunk, but in fact he was ill and dying. He had been in the workhouse at Braintree and when he came out 'he said he would sooner die by the side of the road than attempt to go into the Union again'. Though the police and the relieving officer were called, that was where he was left, by the side of the road, and where he was found dead in the morning.[26]

In the early years of the twentieth century the administration of poor relief was moved even further from the parish and began to be organised on a national scale. An old age pension of 5s. a week for men and women over 70 was introduced in 1908, and in 1919 it was raised to 10s. and in 1946 to 16s. The National Insurance Act became fully operational in 1913. Sickness benefits and widows' pensions were provided, and for those out of work there was the dole, which was payable for a period of up to six months. After that the claimant had to rely on 'transitional payments', though from 1931 onwards, as an economy measure, these were subject to a means test, which aroused more bitterness than any other aspect of welfare provision. In 1930 the Boards of Guardians were abolished. The parish as such no longer had a role.

1. The ten Essex parishes were Berden, Birchanger, Elsenham, Farnham, Great Hallingbury, Little Hallingbury, Henham, Manuden, Stansted Mountfitchet and Ugley. The Hertfordshire parishes were Albury, Bishop's Stortford, Braughing, Little Hadham, Much Hadham, the Pelhams (Brent, Furneux and Stocking), Sawbridgeworth and Thorley.
2. NA, MH 12/4538/328, folios 467-8, Taylor to Chadwick, 11 April 1846.
3. NA, MH 12/4536/248, folios 569-70, John Dobede Taylor to Poor Law Commission, 11 February 1837, and NA, MH 12/4536/355, folio 759, Taylor to Poor Law Commission, 14 December 1837.
4. NA, MH 12/4539/33, folios 57-9, annotated remarks by John Walsham, 30 March 1847, on Samuel Welch to the Poor Law Commission, 23 March 1847.
5. For the sale of parish property in Stansted, see NA, MH 12/4536/252, folios 575-82. Taylor to Chadwick, 28 February 1837.
6. Cooper (2005: 88).
7. NA, MH 12/4536/176, folios 404-6, Taylor to Poor Law Commissioners, 8 July 1836.
8. *HEO*, 12 February 1898. In January 1901 there were 146 paupers in the workhouse: *HEO*, 12 January 1901.
9. NA, MH 12/4536/59, folios 158-60, Woodley and Cornell to Poor Law Commission, 16 February 1835, and MH 12/4536/69, folio 177, Woodley and Cornell to Poor Law Commission, 1 June 1835.
10. See, e.g. NA, MH 12/4536/44, folios 358-61, Taylor to Poor Law Commission, 8 June 1836, MH 12/4538/335, folios 475-6, Taylor to Poor Law Commission, 9 May 1846, MH 12/4538/336, folios 477-8, draft letter from Poor Law Commissioners to Taylor, 12 May 1846.
11. NA, MH 12/4536/36. Folios 112-120, Power to Poor Law Commissioners, 16 February 1835.
12. NA, MH 12/4537/347, folios 559-60, Sir John James Walsham, Assistant Poor Law Commissioner, to the Poor Law Commission, 16 Nov. 1842. These reductions are confirmed by the parochial records: see ERO, D/P 109/8/5. In the last two years under the old Poor Law John Seamer, the assistant overseer in Stansted, spent £1623 in 1833/4 and £1449 in 1834/5, and in the first two years under the amended law £1065 in 1835/6 and £945 in 1836/7.
13. For Saffron Walden see Drury (2006: 276), and for Stortford see NA, MH 12/4536/120, folios 262-3, Chaplin to Poor Law Commission, 25 December 1835, and Cooper (2005: 87).
14. NA, MH 12/4536/225, folios 517-8, Taylor to Poor Law Commission, 8 December 1836, MH 12/4536/226, folios 519-20, Poor Law Commission to Taylor, 9 December 1836, and MH 12/4536/227, folio 521, Poor Law Commission to Taylor 12 December 1836.
15. Cooper, J. (2005: 88).
16. NA, MH 12/4536/121, Folios 264-7. Taylor to Poor Law Commission, 20 December 1835.
17. NA, MH 12/4537/33, folios 42-3, Wade to Poor Law Commission, 5 March 1838.
18. NA, MH 12/4539/37, Folio 64, Taylor to Poor Law Commission, 3 April 1847.
19. NA, MH 12/4539/82, folio 142, Phipps to Poor Law Commission, 21 June 1847.
20. *HEO*, 18 September 1880.
21. ERO, D/P 109/19/2.
22. *HEO*, 11 December 1875.
23. *HEO*, 2 January 1863.
24. *HEO*, 19 February 1876. In 1898 one of the Guardians proposed that the allowance of the aged outdoor poor should be increased by 1s. 6d. a week, but his motion was lost because there was opposition to having an 'expensive' outdoor system as well as a good indoor system: *HEO*, 12 November 1898, 'Notes of the Week'.
25. *HEO*, 15 and 22 September 1877.
26. *HEO*, 18 September 1891.

18: ARSON, THE 'REVOLT OF THE FIELD' AND EMIGRATION

As well as keeping the rates down, the amended Poor Law might well have had the effect of suppressing wages, because the farmers would have known that their men would work for a pittance rather than enter the dreaded workhouse. In the words of Arthur Brown, 'The New Poor Law crushed the labourer'. And he quoted Rider Haggard's judgement after speaking with an old labourer in Witham in the 1850s: 'with labour in overflowing supply, to lift up his voice against an employer, however tyrannous, means instant dismissal and the hell of a poorhouse ... or a roadside ditch to die in'.[1]

Heartened by the failure of the Swing Riots and of the strike in Stansted, and buttressed by the stricter provisions of the amended Poor Law, the farmers were firmly back in control, and the supposed tranquillity of rural Essex was complacently compared with the discontent and poverty of the urban areas where Chartism was riding high. The only threat to their well-being, it seemed, was the movement against the Corn Laws which kept the price of bread artificially high, though on this issue the parish was divided, and when the Corn Laws were finally repealed in 1846 there were no doubt mixed reactions.[2] Another development which benefited the more prosperous farmers was the final enclosure of what remained of 'two large commons', involving several exchanges of land, which, together with the land given up for the proposed railway, necessitated a major revision in the rates.[3]

It was therefore all the more of a shock when this supposedly peaceful idyll was shattered by a wave of incendiary attacks that revealed an underlying discontent, indeed a hatred of the farmers and their landlords. At 8 o'clock on the night of Thursday, 4 January 1844, a haulm wall, that is a wall consisting of stalks of potatoes, beans, etc., was set on fire. The property of Edward Hicks, it stood next to a barn by the side of what was now called the Cambridge Road. The fire was detected almost at once and quickly extinguished.

Three hours later, at 11 o'clock, a more serious fire was detected at Bentfield End on the property of William Clarke. A barn had been set alight in which there were almost ten quarters of wheat, and the flames quickly spread to a large cow-house and piggeries. All the buildings were burnt down, and it was only because of help given by Clarke's neighbours and the village fire-engine that the fire did not spread to Clarke's house and stables.[4]

These were not the first cases of incendiarism in the area. In the previous week there had been a fire in the neighbouring parish of Manuden, and two months before that another fire in the same parish. The local landowners and farmers were alarmed. On Friday, 5 January, on the very next morning after the Stansted fires, a meeting was held at the Bell Inn, chaired by one of the leading farmers, Matthew Woodley, following which a reward of £200 was offered for information about any of the fires. It was also decided, because of the difficulties of obtaining evidence in such cases, since the fires were started secretly and at night, that a letter should be sent to the Home Secretary asking that the Queen should issue a pardon to any accomplice who came forward with information, and shortly afterwards an officer was sent from the Metropolitan Police to help with the inquiries.

(The Essex Police had been formed only in 1840 and there were no officers stationed yet in Stansted. The nearest police station in Essex was in the village of Newport.)

A second meeting was held on the Tuesday of the following week, 9 January, which led to the identification of a suspect, Charles Patmore, a young man residing with his parents at Bentfield End, who lived next door to Clarke's yard where the second of the Stansted fires had been started. He was arrested and committed for trial, but the case against him broke down. Though listed for the Assizes it was not in fact heard, but was thrown out by the grand jury.[5]

In September 1844 a fire broke out at the farm of John and George Raven. It began in a thatched shed at some time between 11 and 12 at night. Fortunately the members of a friendly society, the Odd Fellows, were holding a celebration nearby at the King's Arms at the time, and they were able to pull down the shed before the fire had done any material damage. The *Essex Chronicle* had little doubt that it was the work of an incendiary, but although a reward was offered for the discovery of the arsonist he or she escaped detection.[6]

Three years later, in July 1847, Stephen Griggs, a labourer aged 30, was accused of setting fire on the night of 1/2 June to a barn, stable, shed and outhouses at Down Farm, which was occupied by one of Fuller-Maitland's tenant farmers, William Parris, who was one of Stansted's Guardians of the Poor. Forty quarters of wheat were destroyed, some wagons and carts, and three valuable horses. The damage was estimated at £450-£500. This time there was evidence about the possible motive. Griggs had been out of work for several months and the farmers in the parish would not employ him: just a fortnight before the fire he had openly declared that 'he should like to see them burnt alive' and that he would 'serve them out'. Moreover Parris testified that he had quarrelled with Griggs because Griggs had stolen goods from his father. Although the evidence was only circumstantial Griggs was found guilty, and he was transported for the term of his natural life.[7]

These arson attacks in and around Stansted were part of a widespread spate of attacks at that time. It is impossible to be precise or certain about their number, but in *Horrid Lights,* their study of 19th century incendiarism in Essex, Stephen

37. 'The Home of the Rick-Burner' by John Leech, Punch 1844.

Hussey and Laura Swash calculated that out of 452 reported attacks in the 19th century almost half, 211, occurred in the 1840s, and that the heaviest year of all was 1844, with 58. They ascribed this to the deteriorating fortunes of the poor. They also demonstrated that the fires were concentrated in a band across the north of the county, where, because of the emphasis on arable farming, the problems of seasonally variable employment were particularly severe.

The Home Secretary tried to place the blame on irresponsible vagrants. Others blamed the Anti-Corn Law League, whose propaganda, they alleged, inflamed the labourers against their masters. In fact, as the correspondence in the press clearly demonstrated, the connection between poverty and incendiarism was well understood. A cartoon in *Punch* showed a labourer brooding over his wrongs in a run-down cottage, his cupboard bare and his children begging for food, and the devil in the background tempting him with a flaming firebrand.

Unlike the strike, which was a collective and open form of protest, incendiary attacks were carried out by individuals and in secret, often by men with a grievance. They aroused fear and endangered life, and were commonly described as 'diabolical'. In the *Punch* cartoon it was the devil who incited the unhappy labourer. Until 1837 they were punishable by death, and after that transportation. But in fact they were an acknowledgement of weakness, a recognition that open protest was ineffective and risky, and they did not pose a serious and systematic threat to the established order. They were not part of a co-ordinated campaign for more employment or better wages, and the responses of other parishioners varied. At Manuden in December 1843 a 'mob' of disorderly persons turned up at the fire and the police had a hard time in preserving property and good order,[8] but at Stansted in 1844 neighbours helped to put the fires out.

After the spate of attacks in the 1840s there was a marked decline of incendiarism in Essex. The figures given by Hussey and Swash are probably too low,[9] but they clearly indicate the trend – 211 in the 1840s, 78 in the 1850s, 34 in the 1860s, 10 in the 1870s, 13 in the 1880s and 1 in the 1890s. They attribute this to a period of relative prosperity in the 1860s in which labourers' wages slowly increased.

In Stansted incendiarism continued, but only sporadically. In 1863 the property of William Parris was attacked again, a haulm stack at his farm in Burton End, and the man who was accused of setting it alight was William Griggs, no doubt a relative of the Stephen Griggs who had been convicted in the earlier case. This time there were witnesses ready to give evidence for the prosecution – a labourer in Parris's employ, and an ostler at the King's Arms whom Griggs asked for 'five or six lucifers'. At the trial, however, he was found not guilty.

There was yet another fire at Parris's farm in 1868, when five stacks were destroyed, but the cause was not known, and in 1877 there was a supposed case of incendiarism when some maltings were burnt down. In 1878 a barley stack was destroyed at Bentfield Bury, at Edward Spencer's farm, and since it stood in a field some distance away from any buildings suspicion pointed to 'some diabolically disposed person'.[10] Another suspected case occurred in 1879, when a stack of trefoil seed, the property of Charles Hicks, was destroyed. In 1897 there was a supposedly incendiary fire at Burton End, when a barn owned by the squire, William Fuller-Maitland, was burnt to the ground.[11] Finally, in 1901, there were two fires at farms owned by the Goslings, one at Bentfield Place Farm, where the cause was unknown, and one at Hole Farm, where incendiarism was alleged.[12]

These fires at Stansted, however, were few compared with those set alight across the parish boundary in Manuden. Here, according to Hussey and Swash, there were 11 arson attacks for the century as a whole, the second highest parish total in the county, West Bergholt being the first, but again this figure may well be understated. Incendiarism in Manuden received much popular support. We have already noted the behaviour of the 'mob' at the fire in December 1843. At another fire in 1870 the hose of the fire engine was cut and poultry were taken from the henhouse, and at another in 1883 an 'unruly element' ran off with the pigs and poultry that had been burnt, and some half-cooked pork was thrown at the police. In 1888 Manuden Hall itself went up in flames and the *Herts and Essex Observer* reported that over the last 15 years there had been 16 fires on the Goslings' Hassobury Estate. None of the perpetrators had been convicted.[13]

No matter how many fires there were, or how much popular support they attracted, or how much alarm they gave rise to, in the long term they had little or no effect, even in Manuden. If the labourers wanted to improve their lot there were two other courses open to them, trade unionism and emigration. They were connected. By reducing the size of the workforce emigration gave the labourers a stronger bargaining position, and it was partly for this reason, and partly to better the labourer's lot, that the National Agricultural Labourers' Union (NALU) encouraged and organised emigration.

NALU was formed in May 1872 under the leadership of Joseph Arch, a Methodist lay preacher, and within two years its membership numbered 86,000, one tenth of the farm work force in Britain. In Essex NALU had 7,000 members, one fifth of the labouring work force, and of these 1,800 were in north west Essex.[14]

What gave rise to this dramatic development, this 'revolt of the field' as it came to be known? The third quarter of the century was the so-called golden age of Essex agriculture. In the words of the Essex historian, Arthur Brown, 'From the 1850s the unemployment which since 1815 had so weakened the labourers' bargaining power began slowly to diminish ... while continuing migration from the villages prevented any growth in the amount of available labour'.[15] In the 1851 census 275 men in Stansted identified themselves as agricultural or farm labourers out of a population of 1719, i.e. 16%. In 1881, 30 years later, the number of labourers had gone down to 176 out of a population of 1924, i.e. 9%. Labourers' wages, though less than those of most industrial workers, were slowly improving. In 1874 one of the speakers at the Essex Chamber of Agriculture ascribed the betterment in the condition of the poor mainly to emigration.[16]

When this improvement came to a halt in the early 1870s, when wages reached a ceiling and began to come down again, the resulting resentment gave rise to the birth of NALU. There was a campaign to get wages raised from 10s. a week to 15s. a week, but in Suffolk the farmers responded by locking out the work force and eventually the men were compelled to go back. A prolonged strike in 1874 depleted the Union's funds, and when this was followed by the agricultural depression, caused mainly by the import of cheap corn from America and Canada, the Union collapsed. By 1889 its membership had slumped to 4,254.

Stansted was largely unaffected. On the evenings of 12 and 13 April 1874 the Union held open-air recruiting meetings at Bishop's Stortford and Stansted respectively. The

Herts and Essex Observer commented dismissively that the remarks of the speakers made little impact.[17] On 13 May, however, another open-air meeting was held in Stortford. About 200-300 men were present, including no doubt some from Stansted, and a Bishop's Stortford branch of the Union was formed with about 80 members. The *Observer* reported condescendingly at this stage:

> The delegates are no doubt fair examples of others of their class at present stumping the country on behalf of the downtrodden and oppressed British peasantry, as they style their fellow agricultural labourers. Their manner and mode of speaking incline one to the belief that they have first come to the front in public as local preachers. They talk freely though occasionally somewhat wildly and there is a degree of shrewdness and eloquence in some portions of their addresses that could hardly have been expected from men in their position in life.[18]

No branch was formed in Stansted. Arthur Brown, in his study of the union, found this puzzling since branches were formed in comparable villages such as Kelvedon and Earls Colne. The squire, William Fuller-Maitland, was a Liberal, as at Kelvedon, and the labour market was not unfavourable. The main cause, Brown believed, 'may have been the power of the thirteen farmers occupying almost all of the parish's 4,193 acres, mostly men of substance and with deep roots in the place, in whose hands parochial power probably, and economic power certainly, were firmly held'.[19] Another possible reason was the presence of a branch in Bishop's Stortford only three miles away. Whatever the cause, by the turn of the century the labourers in and around Stansted were the worst paid in the county, earning wages of 11-12s. a week compared with the county average of 13s. 9d.[20]

The failure of the union gave a new impetus for emigration both to the north of England, mainly to Yorkshire, where farm labour had been drawn off to the factories, and abroad, especially to Canada, Australia and America. In April 1873, even before the decline of the union, an agent from Yorkshire held meetings in Harlow and Saffron Walden to engage men for farm work.[21] The *Observer*'s correspondent at Saffron Walden wrote that

> During the day some 150 men had an interview with him, but as he had previously intimated that no one would be engaged without a character from his late employer or a clergyman many were disappointed and had to return back home without making an engagement. Some 40 or 50 strong, able, single young men, from 18 to 25 years of age, were engaged at 18s. per week, with their fare paid to the scene of their future labours but no 'Union men' were taken on.

A typical advertisement was that which appeared on 28 March 1874:

> Agricultural labourers wanted for Yorkshire – 49 respectable young lads from 14 years and upwards, also a few married men. Board and lodging will be given to single men and a house and garden to married men. The full railway fare will be paid and wages will be liberal. None however need apply who are not thoroughly trustworthy and not in possession of two good suits of clothes and a substantial box. The agent will be at Audley End at 9 a.m. on Tuesday, 31st March, and at 2.30 p.m. at Rayne, when all must be in perfect readiness to return with him. No union or militia men will be engaged.

There were many similar advertisements. Whether any men left Stansted for Yorkshire we do not know, but given the high numbers involved it seems very likely.

At the same time there were repeated advertisements for assisted passages to Canada paid for by the Canadian government. Farm labourers were wanted, navvies, female servants and country mechanics. In Manitoba (the province most eager to attract settlers from this part of the country, followed by the North West Territories) free grants of prairie land of 160 acres were offered[22], and in March 1898 the same province announced that it wanted 'capitalists, persons with moderate income, farmers, farm labourers, young men wanting to learn farming': special arrangements would be made for domestic servants.[23] In 1897 Western Australia advertised for farmers, farm labourers and others, and the newly discovered gold fields were an added attraction. Ships leaving Liverpool every fortnight for America and Canada were advertised.

There was encouragement nearer home as well. In February 1889 an Anglican vicar from Stepney gave a lecture in the Central Hall on 'The Advantages of Emigration'. It was arranged by Joseph Caygill, Fuller-Maitland's steward, and it was primarily directed at the unemployed lads and young men of Stansted and its neighbourhood. About 70 attended.[24]

Those who emigrated tended in fact to be younger men and, if they were married, their families. There must have been many who went from Stansted, but there is no complete record of them and we have to pick up information fortuitously. Henry and Nancy Clark emigrated to Canada, Nancy being a daughter of Thomas Levey, and we know about them because when Nancy died of smallpox in 1874 in Montreal Henry had her death announced in the *Herts and Essex Observer*.[25] In March 1907 the *Observer* reported that four daughters of David Saggers, a farmer at Burton End, had left for British Columbia on the SS Canada, and had been seen off from the station by many friends and school companions.[26] It seems that Saggers went to join them, because in October that year he was summoned for not paying his rates and it was reported that he had left the country.[27] John Wilkins, gamekeeper for the Fuller-Maitlands, happened to remark in his autobiography that his brother-in-law, Edward Humphries, had gone to Australia many years before.[28] Harry Yeomans emigrated to Canada shortly before WW1,[29] and we learn of about a dozen men who went to the colonies, mainly Australia, because they returned with their colonial regiments in the war and were killed. There were also emigrants from the wealthier families. In or around 1886 C.J. Stammers went to South Africa and died when visiting Stansted in 1904.[30] Other emigrants to South Africa were two sons of Henry Douglas, the Head Master of the National School,[31] while in 1906 Edward Spencer resigned from the Parish Council because he was leaving the country.[32] Robert Fuller-Maitland, the squire's youngest son, had settled as a farmer in British East Africa when he was killed there in 1912 by an elephant.[33]

1. Brown (1990: 12).
2. In the *CC* of 18 March 1842 it was reported that 'Lord Ki[n]naird presented a petition [to the Queen] from the inhabitants of Stansted in favour of the total repeal of the corn laws'. On the other hand J.O. Nockolds, a land agent in Stansted, was a committee member of the local Agricultural Protection Society, which campaigned for retaining the Corn Laws: *CC*, 22 December 1843.
3. NA, MH 12/4538/213., folios 283-4, Taylor to Chadwick, 31 March 1845.
4. *Essex Standard,* 12 January 1844.
5. *Essex Standard,* 12, 19 and 26 January 1844; *Ipswich Journal,* 9 March 1844.
6. *CC,* 4 October 1844.
7. *CC,* 4 June, 9 July and 1 October 1847.
8. *Essex Standard,* 15 December 1843.
9. For example, only two cases are identified in Stansted, but there were several more.
10. *HEO,* 16 February 1878.
11. ERO, T/P 181/10/19, unascribed newspaper cutting: 10 September 1897.
12. *HEO,* 30 November 1901. There were other fires believed to be due to causes other than arson. There were also fires outside Stansted in which Stansted men were involved either as the farmers or the alleged arsonists, e.g. the fires at Matthew Woodley's farm in Clavering (*CC* 11 February 1848), at William Parris's farm in Elsenham, for which George Parker was arrested (*CC* 18 November 1853); and at Dunmow, for which Arthur Brace was arrested (*CC* 31 October 1856).
13. For these Manuden cases, see *Essex Standard,* 15 December 1843, *HEO,* 26 March 1870, 23 and 30 March 1878, 6 April 1878, 10 November 1883, 1 December 1883, 26 October 1888.
14. Brown (1990: 50).
15. Brown (1990: 21).
16. *HEO,* 11 December 1875.
17. *HEO,* 18 April 1874.
18. *HEO,* 16 May 1874.
19. Brown (1990: 150-1).
20. *VCH* vol. ii (1907: 328).
21. *HEO,* 12 April 1873.
22. *HEO,* 14 April 1873 and 5 February 1898.
23. *HEO,* 5 March 1898.
24. ERO, T/P 68/10/2, Caygill to Harford Green, 22 January 1889; *HEO,* 9 February 1889.
25. *HEO,* 5 December 1874.
26. *HEO,* 23 March 1907.
27. *HEO,* 26 October 1907.
28. Wilkins (1976: 306, 439).
29. *HEO,* 16 January 1915.
30. *HEO,* 16 July 1904.
31. *HEO,* 21 April 1917.
32. *HEO,* 17 March 1906.
33. *HEO,* 6 July and 10 August 1912.

19: FRIENDLY SOCIETIES, CLUBS AND ALMSHOUSES

A more direct form of self-help was membership of a friendly society, which provided a disciplined framework for insurance against sickness. In return for regular contributions a member of a society who fell sick could draw on the society's funds rather than turn to the parish, and payments were also made for funerals. Each society was based on a public house, which provided the hospitality that was at the heart of its ethos. Unlike NALU, friendly societies were actively sponsored and supported by the gentry, many of whom became honorary members, seeing them as a way both of encouraging independence and of reducing the burden on the rates. Prizes were offered at agricultural shows to men who had subscribed longest to a friendly society. They did not challenge the ordering of the village, but helped it to work more harmoniously.

Friendly societies began in the late 1700s, and one of the earliest in Essex was a society in Dunmow, which had a flourishing branch in Stansted. By 1839 the custom had been established of holding the Dunmow society's annual meeting on Whit Monday. As well as 130 honorary members, it had 536 ordinary members of whom 39 were women, 174 servants and artisans, and 343 agricultural labourers (figures that do not add up to 536, but no explanation is given for this). In that year the rules were changed, so that payment of 1s. a quarter ensured the provision of sickness allowance, and 1s. 6d. a quarter ensured free medical attention as well.[1] These payments remained much the same for the rest of the century.[2]

The Stansted branch held its annual meeting on the same day. Its members gathered at the Rose and Crown, proceeded to the church for a service there, and then returned to the Rose and Crown for a celebratory dinner. Fifty-eight members attended, and 24 honorary members, among them the vicar, two of the leading farmers and one of the local doctors. The curate, Collin, was the secretary.[3] No occupational breakdown of Stansted's members was given, but at the annual meeting in 1845 it was reported that there were 107 members in all, honorary as well as ordinary, and Collin declared that the increase in the number of ordinary members over the past year 'proved that the humbler classes of society, for whose benefit it was formed, have increasing confidence in it as an instrument of good'.[4]

But the Stansted branch of the Dunmow society failed to make progress. In 1875/6 it had 90 members, in 1884/5 73, and by 1905 it had sunk so low that no chairman could be found, no meetings were being held and there seemed little prospect of revival.[5] This was probably because of the rise of other societies, notably the Ancient Order of Foresters (AOF) and the Order of Ancient Shepherds (OAS), both of which were based at the Barley Mow on Chapel Hill.

The AOF Court Prince Arthur, named after Queen Victoria's son, was founded in 1869. At the opening ceremony at the Barley Mow Brother Gomme, the Chief Ranger of the district, explained the principles of forestry and recounted the history of the society from its beginning in 1813 to an organisation with a membership of 380,000.[6]

The Court Prince Arthur was carried along on the wave of this success. By the end of 1898 it had 183 members, with its complete complement of Rangers, Woodwards and Beadles, and among its honorary members were William Fuller-Maitland, Sir Walter Gilbey, the farmers Edward and Frank Spencer, and Joseph Caygill, Fuller-Maitland's agent. Its funds amounted to £1,549, of which £1,472 consisted of the Sick and Funeral Fund. £880 was invested in eight freehold cottages, and £654 was deposited in the bank.[7] By 1904 it had 240 members and 14 honorary members, its capital was £1,900, and it had a quarterly income of £70. 1903 had been a year of heavy expenditure, £276 in all, but even so it had been covered by income.

38. The Order of Ancient Shepherds gathered outside the Barley Mow public house on Chapel Hill, c.1900.

The AOF's main rival, Lodge Excelsior of the Loyal Order of Ancient Shepherds, which had been opened in or shortly before 1882, had more members but less capital. In 1904 it had 333 members and its funds amounted to £1,183. In the previous year £67 had been paid in sick pay to its members, and the net gain had been £192.[8] In November 1907 it held a supper for 20 members to celebrate the building of a block of cottages at Bentfield End: it had a 5% return on money invested in this way, compared with 2½% before. Like the AOF it was based at the Barley Mow and had a junior as well as a senior lodge.

By 1911 Dr Haynes was working for six clubs in Stansted, for which he was paid £197 5s. each year, an average of 4s. 4d. per member. He claimed that in a single year there were 3,448 attendances at his surgery from club members and that he travelled 3,500 miles to see them in their homes.[9]

19: FRIENDLY SOCIETIES, CLUBS AND ALMSHOUSES

Forester funerals were impressive occasions. Members gathered at the Barley Mow, sometimes as many as 50, wearing green scarves with strips of mourning attached, each carrying a wreath of laurel. They followed the coffin in procession to the church and the bearers carried it to the grave. The Foresters' address was delivered at the graveside, and on one occasion the vicar, Canon Luard, being an honorary member, delivered the address himself.[10]

Up to 1889 it was the custom to have an annual Friendly Societies' Church Parade and Dinner. This lapsed, but was revived in 1903 on Easter Monday. The Foresters took the lead, inviting the Shepherds and others to join them. They all met at the Barley Mow and, with full regalia and banners, went in procession to the church headed by the Bishop's Stortford band. The vicar, George Oakshott, who had been initiated into both Orders, gave a sermon to a packed congregation, no doubt extolling the virtues of thrift and foresight, and the members of the societies then proceeded to the homes of those members of the gentry who had given them help and encouragement over the past year. At the dinner in the evening Oakshott proposed success to the Stansted Benefit Societies, and Reginald Vercoe on behalf of the societies said that 'He wished to thank the gentry of Stansted and neighbourhood for … contributing towards such a successful and eventful day'. Special thanks were given to Oakshott for his 'kindly interest'.[11]

This celebration, being moved to Whit Monday, became once again an annual occasion.

39. Procession in Lower Street led by the vicar, Ethelbert Goodchild, 19 July 1919. The banner is that of the Court Prince Arthur of the Ancient Order of Foresters. The Working Men's Club is the timber-framed building on the right.

In 1905, for example, over 200 Foresters and Shepherds met at the Barley Mow and went in procession to the church, where they paraded and a service was held. In the afternoon a cricket match between the two societies was played, for which a cup had been donated by Ormond Blyth, and sports were added to the programme, with the gentry acting as starters and judges. Oakshott took the chair at the dinner in the evening, toasts to the royal family were drunk, songs were sung and prizes handed out. The Edwardian period was probably the peak of the friendly societies' importance. The passing of the Old Age Pension Act of 1908 and the National Insurance Act of 1911 not only cut across the Poor Law, which was finally abolished in 1926, but also reduced the need for the benefits provided by the friendly societies and over time diminished their role in the village. It was another manifestation of the way in which the state was becoming responsible for functions that were once the preserve of the local community.

Another major initiative in the village was the Girls' Friendly Society, which in spite of its name was not a friendly society in the same way as those already described, for it was only marginally concerned with the payment of benefits. The national organisation had been founded in 1875, and the Stansted branch, covering 11 parishes in all, was founded in 1881. At the national level the driving force came from a group of women who were concerned about girls who had left home to take up employment and, being cut off from friends and family, were often in need, as they saw it, of guidance and support. In Stansted it was the women of the gentry who took the lead, the wife of the squire and the wife of the vicar, and the secretary was Mildred Chester, the wife of a local lawyer. Although the organisation was non-denominational it was in fact dominated by the Church of England and the Anglican clergy were heavily involved.

The Society had two classes. There were the members, girls from the age of 12 upwards, and there were the associates, the ladies who would befriend and guide them. Within two years of its foundation the Society had over 200 members and 20 associates. In 1889 there were 290 members, of whom 170 were in service, 11 in business or in teaching, and the rest living at home.[12]

The aim was to provide every girl with a friend who came from a class above her own. There were regular quarterly meetings of the Society, but the groundwork was done in smaller meetings or classes. In 1884/5, for example, Mildred Chester was holding fortnightly meetings for religious instruction and needlework, and two other Stansted associates were doing the same. In this way the associates got to know the girls and to take an interest in their welfare. Help was given in finding jobs and in looking after girls who fell sick.

The highlight of the Society's activities was its Annual Festival which was held each summer or autumn. The centrepiece was a short church service, usually but not always at Stansted, and the centrepiece of the service was a sermon which was directed to the members rather than the associates. In 1882, for example, Thomas Luard 'laid special stress on the value and dignity of the humblest work when done from a high and Christian motive'.[13]

After the service there would either be a visit to some nearby attraction, such as Hatfield Forest or Audley End House, or the party would enjoy refreshments in the grounds of one of the associates, such as the park at Stansted Hall or the vicarage gardens. Prizes were handed out for the best answers to Scripture questions, and premiums for good service and bonuses on savings. In 1884 the Honourable Victoria Grosvenor, the diocesan GFS President, gave a short address on the benefits accruing to both member and associates 'from the relations of mutual interdependence which it is one of the great objects of the GFS to foster between women and girls belonging to the different classes in which society is necessarily divided'.[14] In other years there were prizes for needlework and knitting.

In 1912 a pageant, 'G.F.S. in the Empire', was held to mark the annual festival of the Stansted and Bishop's Stortford branches. It is worth describing it in detail, since it expressed so vividly some of the ideals that inspired the women who ran the GFS. It was organised, and the script written, by Miss Chisenhale-Marsh of Bishop's Stortford, who among many other roles was a leading Conservative, a member of the Education Committee of the Essex County Council and one of the Guardians in the Bishop's Stortford Union. It opened with the entrance of the "Spirit of the Past" (Miss Chisenhale-Marsh) 'attired as an old woman in grey robes' and dramatically reciting in rhyme that she was now revisiting the land she knew of yore, and that whereas in her time there had been 'hunger, strife and warfare', now there was peace and freedom. 'Why was this?' she asked. Then entered the Spirit of the Present (Mrs. Ival Williams), 'attired as a young girl in pink robes, who explained that the change was due to 'our country's noble work', bringing 'the Gospel message', 'light, peace and love', to the growing Empire. 'And who has dared to do this?', asked the Spirit of the Past, whereupon the Spirit of the Present called forth England, Scotland, Wales and Ireland, each represented by 20 girls carrying banners, singing 'national songs' and dressed in appropriate colours. The Spirit of the Present then summoned

Britannia, symbol of the might
That rules our empire and upholds the right.

Britannia (Mrs. Arthur Browne) then entered, attended by two Boy Scouts. They mounted the dais and sang Rule Britannia, and then 'Britannia, in a clear and beautiful voice', hailed the Colonies:

Though wide seas roll between us, long years pass,
Nor time nor space may break the sacred ties
Which hold us still akin. From East and West!
From North and South! Come forth my Colonies!

Then came forth Newfoundland, South Africa, Australia, Canada and the West Indies, all in appropriate costumes, and formed up on either side of Britannia and sang 'God is working his purpose out, as year succeeds to year'. The Spirit of the Present then proclaimed her message:

.... Everywhere
That Britain's name is known the tidings go.
Darkness is changed to light, and strife to peace
Where love divine in human hearts doth glow.

The Spirit of the Past naively asked if this had been done with armed force. To which the Spirit of the Present replied that in these glad days she would show

How girls and women,
Knit in friendship's bands
Moved by this friendship send Christian love,
The Gospel's teaching to far distant lands.

19: FRIENDLY SOCIETIES, CLUBS AND ALMSHOUSES

This was followed by tableaux of missionary work, and representatives of each parish came with their parochial banner and a purse of money collected in the parish which they laid at Britannia's feet. Britannia addressed them:

Daughters of Empire! Workers in the field
Where souls are harvested and lives are won
Back from the shadow of the heathen night
Into the radiance of the Eternal Sun.

After two more verses in this vein all those who took part marched round with their banners singing 'Now Thank We All Our God' followed by the National Anthem.

'It was', said the *Herts and Essex Observer*, 'from beginning to end an extremely ennobling and picturesque performance'.[15]

Those who ran the Society, the associates, regarded it as a great success. As early as its report for 1883 it claimed that one of the main objects of the GFS had been realised, 'that of creating a bond of sympathy and of confidence between the girls and the Associates'.[16] What the girls thought of it is more difficult to ascertain. The press reports and the Society's annual reports say how much they enjoyed the Annual Festival and the Society's various activities, and the fact that the Society was so well supported suggests that the girls did appreciate what it had to offer. In their old age Ellen and Ena Sylvester, who were members soon after WW1, remembered it with pleasure: it provided new outlets, enjoyable and interesting social occasions. Years later Mildred Chester took a close interest in Ellen's daughter, Margaret, encouraging her, for example, to do her homework. Margaret remembers her as an old woman, very upper class and very kind, and slightly eccentric.[17]

Other initiatives, such as coal clubs and clothing clubs, were on a smaller scale. They were largely run by the gentry – Mrs. Luard's Boot Club for example - and were often based on the church or the schools. The usual arrangement was that the club members made small weekly contributions, and at the end of a set period what they had saved was supplemented by gifts from the patrons of the club and they were given tickets to spend on the appropriate goods. In 1874/5 the vicar bought 32 blankets to be loaned out for the winter.[18]

In 1883 a new two-storey block of almshouses was built on Church Road, close to the centre of the village, on a site given by William Fuller-Maitland. These were the Fuller Almshouses, and they were being moved from Hoxton in London because the trustees of the charity responsible for them wanted their inmates to enjoy a more healthy environment. They had originally been built and endowed in 1795 by William Fuller, the wealthy grandfather of Bethia Fuller-Maitland (about whom more in Chapter 21 below), for 28 'aged women of good walk and conversation', who had to be at least 60 years of age or incapacitated. Each almswoman was provided with coal and a weekly allowance of money.[19] It was entirely appropriate that William Fuller-Maitland should make himself responsible for the almshouses in this way, but he also found it convenient for accommodating some of his retired retainers.

40. The Fuller Almshouses, c.1913. Now private housing.

The agricultural depression persisted, and although the real value of farm labourers' wages increased in the last quarter of the century they remained among the most poorly paid workers in the country. Yet the population of Stansted continued to rise, and it was often referred to at this time as a flourishing and prosperous village. In the next chapter I consider why this was so.

1. *CC*, 24 May 1839.
2. ISC, *A Report of the Church and School Accounts ... 1884-85.*
3. *CC*, 24 May 1839.
4. *CC*, 31 May 1844.
5. ISC, *A Report of the Church and School Accounts and other current expenses for the parish of Stansted Mountfitchet 1875-6,* and *A Report of the Church and School Accounts and a Statement of the Various Charities, &c. of the parish of Stansted Mountfitchet, Essex, 1884-85*; *HEO*, 4 February 1905.
6. *HEO*, 23 January 1869.
7. *HEO*, 11 March 1899.
8. *HEO*, 27 February 1904.
9. *HEO*, 10 June 1911.
10. *HEO*, 12 November 1870. For other accounts of Foresters' funerals see, e.g., *HEO*, 5 November 1887 and 14 November 1896.
11. *HEO*, 18 April 1903.
12. ISC, *Report of the Stansted Mountfitchet Branch of the Girls' Friendly Society for 1889.*
13. *HEO*, 10 February 1883.
14. *HEO*, 9 August 1884.
15. *HEO*, 15 June 1912.
16. *HEO*, 10 February 1883.
17. For posters and early reports of the Stansted branch of the GFS, see ERO, T/P 68/12/2.
18. ISC, *A Report of the Church and School Accounts and other current expenses for the parish of Stansted Mountfitchet 1875-76.*
19. *HEO*, 15 and 19 September 1883.

20: 'SUCH A PROSPEROUS VILLAGE'

41. The Central Hall, c.1908.

In 1854 a Central Hall was erected on Chapel Hill to provide a place for public meetings and for the Reading Room and Library of the Stansted Literary Institution which had been founded five years before. In 1882 extensive additions and alterations were made, and when they had been completed there was a grand reopening at which, according to the *Herts and Essex Observer*, there was a numerous audience 'representative of all grades of society'. In the *Observer*'s opinion the Central Hall now represented 'the spirit of enterprise which has characterised Stansted for the last quarter of a century or more'. The chairman, Henry Gilbey, older brother of Walter and Alfred Gilbey, 'ventured to say that there was scarcely another village of the same size in the country that possessed such a Hall as the one they were assembled in that evening'. Joshua Green declared that in 1854 the Hall had been 'almost unprecedented', and going back 50 years 'he compared the Stansted of 1832 with the Stansted of today and asked [his listeners] to picture what the place would be like without the schools, railway, Post Office, telegraph, etc. He noticed the improvements in private residences.' The Fuller almshouses were about to be erected in the village and he was confident that a second church would soon be built. 'Let their motto be ever "Onwards and upwards, higher and higher".'[1]

Stansted's prosperity was celebrated on other public occasions – at a Liberal Party rally in 1885, since the Liberals put themselves forward as the driving force of progress,[2] and at a Parish Dinner in 1890 soon after the building of the new church, St. John's.[3] These encomiums reached a new height at a Tradesmen's Dinner in the Central Hall in 1898. According to the *Observer* about 50 sat down to the meal under the 'genial chairmanship' of Harford Green, the son of Joshua and the brother of Joseph Green, who had been left in full charge of Green's Stores since Joseph had retired from business. The main purpose of the gathering was 'to recognise the impetus given to local trade by the two important industries recently introduced' into Stansted, namely Rochford's Nurseries, part of a much greater enterprise with its headquarters near Cheshunt in Hertfordshire, and the Mica Manufacturing Company, an American firm which had taken over the buildings near the railway which had been used by Fuller-Maitland for a dairy.

After Green had proposed the loyal toasts, W.F. Haynes, the local doctor, proposed 'the trade and commerce of Stansted': 'he instanced evidences of the advance which had been made in the place in recent years - the great increase in the number of houses, the improvement of the poorer dwellings, and the erection of handsome residences which had made Stansted more nearly a place approaching a town than a village'. He mentioned the local gas supply and the public waterworks. 'All about their little town they saw evidences of advance and prosperity in trade. A fresh sign of enterprise met them in the recently completed factory for the manufacture of mica insulators as applied to electrical apparatus... the only one of its kind in England at the present time. It employed something like 60 hands and he was told it was likely to go on until the number reached 300.' He also referred to 'Mr. Rochford's extensive nurseries, now employing about 150 hands'.

Harford Green reinforced this message, stating 'that it was his lot to drive through 30 or 40 villages and towns every month and in many of them he found empty cottages, and village shops which in his recollection used to be doing £30 or £40 a week were now doing only £5-£10 a week. He need hardly remind them that those places were in purely agricultural districts [and therefore in districts in the grip of the depression], but in Stansted they might look in vain for empty cottages or houses. It was all the other way.'

Green adduced two reasons for Stansted's prosperity. 'First of all they had ... a number of rich gentlemen living there who were liberal in spending their money in the place and who employed a good many servants and so forth.' Secondly he mentioned Rochford's nurseries, which admittedly were as much in Birchanger as in Stansted - but 'Birchanger really belonged to Stansted' - and the Mica Manufacturing Company. For all these reasons 'he believed there was a very big future for the place' and he thought that soon people would be referring, not to Stansted near Bishop's Stortford, but to Bishop's Stortford near Stansted.[4]

Harford Green's explanation for Stansted's increasing prosperity was fine as far as it went, but the village had been thriving well before Rochford's Nurseries and the Mica Manufacturing Company had appeared on the scene, and we have to ask why it was so attractive to trade when many of the villages around were in decline.

The answer was given just a few months later in the unexpected forum of the bicentennial celebrations of the Independent Church in Stansted. Among those attending was the Rev. Ebenezer Ault from Clavering, who reminded his audience that in the seventeenth century the church at Clavering had been much better supported than the church at Stansted, but now the railway had come to Stansted and Clavering had been 'left

42. Stansted railway station in 1916.

in her seclusion, where the railway had never come, and where the engine's whistle was never heard ... with her small population going through a slow but certain exodus'.[5]

Ault was right. If there was one factor more than any other that accounted for Stansted's increasing prosperity it was the railway, run at first by the Eastern Counties Railway Company, then by the Great Eastern Railway. The population figures speak for themselves. Between 1851 and 1901 Stansted's population increased from 1719 to 2208. Compare this with villages which did not have stations on the line: Clavering went down from 1220 to 835, Berden from 418 to 286, Farnham from 558 to 434, Manuden from 752 to 660, and Ugley from 450 to 305. Of the other villages that were on the line Elsenham, the next station to the north, went down from 517 to 453, a similar reduction to Manuden's but otherwise much less than the other villages listed, while Newport went up from 898 to 914.[6] The only village to buck the trend was Birchanger, where the residential pattern was such that, as Harford Green had commented, it 'really belonged to Stansted', so much so that the adjacent part of the parish was transferred to Stansted in 1987: there the population went up from 371 to 469 in 1891, and then to 753 in 1901, the spurt at the end being due to the coming of Rochford's Nurseries. Neither Rochford's Nurseries nor the Mica Insulation Company would have come to Stansted but for the railway, and the wealthy families who provided so much employment were no doubt drawn by the easy access to London. Any doubts which the Fuller-Maitlands might have had about letting the railway cut through their property – and there were mutterings from 'gentlemen' all along the proposed line about the intrusion into their pleasant parklands - were swept away by the generous payment of over £10,000 by way of compensation and purchase and the appointment of Ebenezer Fuller-Maitland as one of the company's directors. The first train ran through the village on 29 July 1845. Until then the line from London had stopped at Bishop's Stortford. Now it went on to Norwich, and the inaugural train, decked with streamers and flags, replete with dignitaries and company directors, accompanied by a band of the Coldstream Guards and cheered on by enthusiastic crowds, ran triumphantly from London to Ely, where it met another train coming from Norwich.

The coaching trade collapsed. Over the next two weeks no fewer than 500 horses were sent for sale at Cambridge, and the revenue of the Hockerill Highway Turnpike Trust from road tolls plummeted from £105 a week in 1844 to £22 a week in 1846. (In 1870 the Trust was dissolved.) At first the train service was limited - just two trains each weekday to Shoreditch station in London, leaving at 11.03 a.m and 11.59 a.m., and two trains from London, leaving at 9.30 a.m. and 2.15 p.m. The journey through Stratford took nearly an hour and a half, and fares were expensive, the first class fare being 6s. 6d. (32.5p.), the second class 4s. 6d. (22.5p.), and the third class 3s. (15p.)

By 1848, however, there were several trains each day, and between 1850 and 1885 some of the fastest trains in the country operated on the line, reaching speeds of 70 mph. Wealthy travellers from Stansted could now go with ease to and from London, and every evening there were horse-drawn carriages at the station waiting to take them home. By 1900 there were complaints that at times there were so many horse-drawn vehicles at the station that pedestrians found it difficult 'to scramble out among horses' heads'.[7]

In addition to the normal service there were excursion trains to Newmarket for the races, to seaside resorts such as Yarmouth, Frinton, Brighton and Hastings, and to London for the Christmas pantomime, the Lord Mayor's Show, the Oxford and Cambridge boat race or a performance of a Handel oratorio at the Crystal Palace, all of which must have broadened the horizons and added to the pleasures of many of the villagers and their children, for these outings were well patronised. In August 1882 98 passengers left Stansted for Hunstanton, and a month later 84 went to Yarmouth while 21 took the longer and more expensive trip to Brighton. For those of a more serious and sober disposition there were special excursions to the builders' exhibition at the Agricultural Hall and the National Temperance Fete at the Crystal Palace.

To meet the growing demands of the population many new houses were built, mainly to the south of Chapel Hill, and within a few years of the railway line being opened one of the attractions most advertised for properties in Stansted, whether residential or commercial, was the proximity of the station. Local businesses and farmers profited as well as landlords and home owners. Before the coming of the railway, as Ralph Phillips has noted in his history of the local station, heavy goods, such as coal from Yorkshire and slate from Wales, had been brought to London by sea and then by barge to Bishop's Stortford, and from there had to be carted to Stansted by road. Now they could be delivered by the truck load into the heart of the village, and in return livestock and farm produce could be sent to the London markets within a very short time of their delivery to the station. When Fuller-Maitland's steward advertised timber for sale from the Stansted Hall estate he could say that it lay a mile and a half from the station. When Edward Hicks and Sons advertised their lime they could offer delivery to 'any station on the railway'. As in other villages and towns along the line, maltings, granaries and warehouses were set up close to the station, and a coal depot too, complete with sidings. The most extensive development was the tramway which connected Rochford's Nurseries with the railway sidings in Stoney Common, 'one of the most ambitious tram-way schemes in Essex'.[8]

The result of all this development was a diversification of the economy, so that the parish was less dependent than before on agriculture. We have already noted that in the 1851 census 275 men in Stansted identified themselves as agricultural or farm labourers out of a population of 1719, a percentage of 15%, and that by 1881, just 30 years later, this figure had gone down to 176 out of 1924, a mere 9%. By comparison the population of Clavering in 1881 was 1039, of whom 208, 20%, were identified as agricultural labourers, more than twice the Stansted percentage.

In 1902 *Kelly's Directory* listed six county magistrates, two schools, 85 'residents' (the upper echelons of the parish), and no fewer than 115 entries under the heading of Commercial, of whom only nine were farmers. Some of these enterprises were tiny. David Player, for example, was listed as a shopkeeper of Burton End, but we know that in fact he worked as a farm labourer and that the shop was kept by his wife in the front room of their house with the cash being kept in a cupboard under the stairs. Others combined several trades. In 1902 Richard Archer was both a pork butcher and a tinplate worker, while George Potts, 'a decidedly ingenious man', had been listed in 1890 as a photographer, but was also a 'tailor, ... market gardener, bird stuffer, frame maker, hair cutter, horse clipper, and general dealer'.[9] Many craftsmen and tradesmen worked on their own or with just two or three assistants, but others were major employers, drawing their labour force not just from Stansted but from Bishop's Stortford and the villages around. In 1868, when Charles Spencer and Sons erected a new and substantial malting close to the railway station, they celebrated with a dinner attended by 150 employees.[10] In 1881, when the builder Arthur Sanders completed some extensive work for Henry Gilbey and James Blyth, his two patrons provided a substantial supper at the Bell Inn for no fewer than 60-70 men.[11] Green and Marsh - after Marsh's death in 1884 to become Joshua Green and Company - employed scores of men and women. In 1890 they were listed as 'general drapers, milliners, outfitters, tea dealers, grocers & provision merchants, ironmongers, dealers in earthenware & glass, wholesale & retail'. Thomas Newman, a manufacturer of agricultural implements, also had a considerable workforce, sufficient to put out a cricket team,[12] and above all there were the newcomers, Rochfords Nurseries, located in Birchanger but with many workers from Stansted, and the Mica Manufacturing Company, which produced mica for electrical insulation and employed over 100 workers.[13] In 1903 the Mica Company sold out to its managing director, A.H.S. Dyer, who with his partner Young operated a factory on the same site, manufacturing commutators, and continuing to employ a large number of people, though not as many as the Mica Company before him.[14] There were always two or three brickmakers in the parish: when James Smith gave up the Alley Field Brick Ground in 1881 he advertised '150,000 capital red facing bricks' for sale, and assured prospective buyers that they were 'well situated for carriage, being close to the Stansted station on the Cambridge line of the Great Eastern Railway'.[15] In 1897 E.M. Wood and Company acquired the Stansted Hall gravel pits, tar paving and limeworks, and announced that they were 'prepared to supply same by rail or cart at very low prices'. They also supplied 'breeze, house refuse, street sweepings and manure', and almost immediately entered into a contract with the Enfield District Council to supply 1,000 tons of gravel.[16] There was a growing band of professional workers, such as doctors, solicitors, land agents, insurance agents, music teachers and a bank manager.

The spirit of enterprise and invention was apparent on every side. By 1881 Charles Spencer and Sons had patented and were manufacturing malt cake which they had analysed as being more nutritious than malt, and in 1883 they exhibited it at the Royal Agricultural Society's show at York where it 'excited a considerable amount of interest': the agent for the Prince of Wales gave orders for an immediate supply. In 1891 Thomas Newman, the manufacturer of agricultural implements, sent two 16-horse steam plough engines to Germany, where they were to be used for ploughing beet fields, and in 1898 he was advertising acetylene gas, which he claimed had 15 times the illuminating power of ordinary coal gas. By that time he had also invented and patented an automatic scoop for clearing out silt and mud deposits from the bottoms of lakes and ponds and shallow streams.[17] Another mechanic, Mr. G.O. Gooday, invented a 'sewing machine for making thatch'.[18]

There were several tradesmen with more unusual services and wares to offer. In the 1870s George Spalding advertised himself as a 'Family Chymist and Dentist', paraded his qualifications, experience and connections, and offered 'Fashionable Perfumery, Stationery, Choice Cigars, Tobaccos, Cattle Medicines, etc., Prescriptions Dispensed, Teeth extracted and Medical Galvanism performed'. He was also an 'Agent for Spratt's Famous Dog and Poultry Cakes, Thorley's food, Horniman's Pure Teas, Schweppe's Mineral Waters and Baker's Lavendar Water'.[19] Another versatile trader was R.B. Little, 'Shawl, Furniture and Dress Cleaner', who practised 'French Dyeing and Cleaning in all its branches'. Silk dresses were cleaned without being taken to pieces, and feathers were cleaned and curled.

All this activity was supported by a growing infrastructure of public utilities. In some of them the parish led the way. In others it dragged its feet, mainly because it did not want to raise more in rates. Towards the end of the century an increasing role was played by the new and more democratic bodies set up by the Local Government Acts of 1888 and 1894. Under the 1888 Act the newly created Essex County Council took over the administrative functions of the Quarter Sessions, including the repair and maintenance of main roads, which in Stansted's case meant the Cambridge Road, and in 1902 it became responsible for education. Every county was divided into electoral divisions, each returning a single councillor, and in Essex William Fuller-Maitland, elected unopposed, represented the district of which Stansted formed a part.[20]

Under the 1894 Act two new bodies were set up. The first was the Stansted Rural District Council (RDC), consisting of representatives from Stansted and nine of the neighbouring parishes, which assumed responsibility for a wide range of subjects, most importantly those relating to public health. (Harford Green later became chairman of the RDC.)

The second was the Parish Council, which took over the administrative functions of the old vestry, whose responsibilities were now confined to the church and church charities. An inaugural meeting in the Central Hall, chaired by William Fuller-Maitland, was attended by 'a large and representative number' of parishioners, and it was carefully arranged that 11 councillors were nominated, seconded and elected to the 11 seats on the Council, thus avoiding the trouble and expense of an election. It is worth saying who the 11 were, since they were no longer confined, as the old vestry had been confined for so long, to the leading farmers and landowners, and the clergy, whether Anglican or Nonconformist, were strikingly absent. They were John Brett, blacksmith;

C.B. Brown, brewer; Joseph Caygill, Fuller-Maitland's steward; George Gray, agricultural labourer; Harford Green, 'merchant'; W.F. Haynes, surgeon; Charles Hicks, farmer; John Keddie, James Blyth's steward; C.A.Norman, mineral water manufacturer (he is now remembered mainly as a ginger beer manufacturer); William Ramsey, coachbuilder; and William Spencer, maltster. William Fuller-Maitland was co-opted as chairman.

One of the earliest initiatives came in 1864, before the local government reforms, when a prominent gas company would not take the risk of investing in the village and the leading parishioners set up the Stansted Gas Company under William Fuller-Maitland's chairmanship with James Marsh as the first secretary. At a well attended meeting in the Central Hall it was agreed that £1,500 should be raised in 300 shares of £5 each, and £800 was raised on the spot. The remaining shares were soon sold, and the gasworks were set up in Water Lane close to the railway. At the opening ceremony a band from Bishop's Stortford played 'lively airs' as each lamp was lit and the Central Hall was brilliantly illuminated by a splendid gas star. While private users paid for commercial and domestic consumption it was an essential part of the scheme that street lighting should also be provided out of the rates, though not in the summer months. In 1903 the company was taken over by the Bishop's Stortford Gas Company.

In 1896, after several private and partial schemes, the Stansted Water Company was formed with an initial capital of £2,000 which had to be increased within a year to £3,500. Harry Chester was the Company Chairman, and Harford Green his Deputy.[21]

Other initiatives were less popular. In 1889 or 1890 unsightly telegraph poles were erected along the Cambridge Road. There were objections from Joshua and Joseph Green and others – Henry Gilbey referred to them as a 'disfigurement of our village' – but laying the wires underground would have been too expensive and apart from the Greens none of the private landowners concerned would agree to the alternative of poles being erected across their land.[22]

A much longer battle was fought about drainage and sewage. From the 1860s onwards there were complaints about the sanitary condition of the village. With the population growing rapidly more cess pits were being dug, and there were increasing complaints about their offensiveness, especially in the summer. In the Street, the lowest part of the village, some of them overflowed into the brook, and in 1898 the village was described in the RDC as 'a blot on the sanitary condition of the district'. Fuller-Maitland, leading a delegation on behalf of the parish, said that they were content with the cess pit system and saw no need for change since for many years the village had enjoyed a clean bill of health.[23] The main reason for resistance, of course, was expense. In the Chapel and Bentfield End Henry Gilbey installed a private sewer along Silver Street (a stretch of the Cambridge Road), and this served several of the leading families in that area, but it did nothing for the lower part of the village, the Street, where the stench and the filth were most offensive.[24]

In 1901 the Parish Council completely reversed its policy when, for the lower part of the village, it agreed to the RDC's entering into a contract with a French company, the Liernur Syndicate, for the installation of a vacuum system, adopting at the same time a separate scheme for the Lower Woodfield area. In 1902 it bought out the Silver Street sewer which had been laid by Henry Gilbey.[25] The reason for this about turn was simply money. The company had installed its system in several important centres on the continent – at Trouville in France, for example, Amsterdam in the Netherlands, Hanau in Germany and Prague in what is now the Czech Republic – but it had been unable to get a footing in the United Kingdom because the Local Government Board was refusing to sanction loans until it could be shown a comparable scheme that had been operating successfully for at least two years. Somehow the company came to hear of Stansted's position, and Liernur himself came to Stansted for discussions with Harford Green. Here was a thriving village not far from London (so members of the Local Government Board could come and inspect it without too much trouble), in need of a scheme (or so the RDC argued), relatively small (so avoiding prohibitive expense), but large enough to demonstrate the benefits of the system. As an inducement to the parish to adopt the scheme the company was prepared to pay all the costs of installation itself and to operate it for two years at only a small charge, and if at the end of the two years the parish was satisfied it could then purchase the scheme

43. 'The visitors at the pumping station', several of them identified, namely Watts, the surveyor (A), Harford Green (B), Rev. Oswald, chairman, Stansted RDC (C), Luther Norman (D), Sir James Blyth (F), M. Liernur? (G), Sir Charles Gold (H), Walter Gold (J) and Tresham Gilbey (K). 1907.

at cost price. For the parish this was the ideal solution, disarming its critics but at minimum cost to the ratepayers.

At the opening ceremony, a champagne lunch for 100 guests given by the company in the Central Hall, Harford Green expressed his confidence that the parish would take over the operation in two years' time.[26] But the system kept breaking down. The pipes leading to the central vacuum were much narrower than those of an ordinary gravitational system, and villagers repeatedly blocked them up by throwing in their rubbish, such as rabbit skins, tin cans, sacks, old boots and broom heads, and it was 1907 before these problems seemed to have been overcome. Harford Green, now chairman of the RDC, laid on another celebratory dinner in the Central Hall, proudly declaring that the system was working well, that it was the first such installation in England, and that it marked a new chapter in local history.[27] He was clearly excited by the prospect that Stansted might become a trail-blazer for other parts of the country.

There was further conflict between the parish and the RDC, represented, as it had been in the sewage dispute, by its sanitary inspector, E.T. Watts, this time on the issue of 'scavenging', that is refuse collection. In 1909 30 householders petitioned the Parish Council for dustbins to be regularly emptied, since it was 'most injurious to health, especially to children, to inhale the poisonous germs that arose from the decaying substances placed therein'. The response of Councillor Luther Norman tersely expressed the majority view: 'There's nothing we can do. The rates are enough already.' But William Tissiman, a well-to-do tailor who was acting as chairman, said the problem could not be ignored. Watts said the job could be done for £25 a year, and on that basis tenders were called for. None of those received was as low as £25 and so the matter was shelved.

As the rubbish piled up so too did the pressure on the Council. Watts pointed out that in the Alley Field you could pick up a wagon-load of tin cans (which unlike most rubbish did not rot down), and in 1912 the Clerk to the Essex County Council called on the parish to reconsider the matter. Eventually an agreement was reached with Albert Smith of Ugley who undertook to collect the rubbish and take it to a gravel pit in his home village for 7s. 6d. (37½p) a day, the total cost not to exceed £25 a year. Then there was further delay because many parishioners, Luther Norman among them, refused to provide dustbins. Under further pressure, including the threat of legal proceedings, there was some measure of compliance, and by October 1912 80 of the 116 householders concerned had fallen into line, even, it seems, Luther Norman. By July 1913, a year after his tender had been accepted, Albert Smith had been paid just £15, £10 lower than the £25 limit – which the Council deemed very satisfactory.

The other main dispute between Stansted and the higher authorities concerned the imposition of a speed limit in the village, but this time it was the Parish Council that was applying the pressure and the higher authorities that were dragging their feet. There were motorists who drove through the village at 30-40 mph, giving all the others a bad name it was said, and the councillors were all agreed that an application should be made to the County Council asking it to apply to the Local Government Board for a speed limit of 10 mph on the Cambridge Road and on Chapel Hill. That was in September 1910, and five months later the County Council replied asking the Parish Council to send a map of the roads where the speed limit was wanted. This was done, but then there was a further long delay, until in February 1912 the County Council wrote to tell the parish that it was not prepared to proceed until the parish councillors undertook that, if the Local Government Board decided to hold an inquiry, they would be prepared to appear before it and to hire a properly qualified legal representative to present their case. Even the mild-mannered Tissiman was exasperated. He had been ill at home recently during Newmarket week, and had counted 50 cars passing through the village in a single hour. Another councillor, Mr. Buck, claimed that some of these Newmarket cars were going at a rate of 50 mph. The councillors said they would appear at the inquiry, and they secured the help of a local lawyer, Harry Chester.

In May 1912 a notice was published that an application had been made to reduce the speed limit to 10 mph in the two roads concerned, and that the AA and the RAC were objecting to this. It was also worrying for Tissiman that the maverick Luther Norman had now discovered the joys of speeding: he liked to go up Chapel Hill at 20 mph when there were no people about, he said, and he had also taken up motor cycling.

The inquiry was held in November 1912, and in March 1913 a notice appeared in the local press to the effect that a speed limit of 10 mph had been granted on Chapel Hill and in the Cambridge Road – two and half years after the Parish Council had first raised the matter.[28]

There were two other sources of disagreement between the Parish Council and the County Council. First, Essex had taken over responsibility for maintaining the Cambridge Road as a main road: Stansted wanted it to take responsibility for the road between Stansted and Elsenham as well. The county refused on the ground that it could only take through traffic into account, not local traffic, and there were only 32 through cars every day.[29] Second, in the days when most roads were not tarred there was the constant nuisance of dust from the roads, and the parish was repeatedly asking for the water cart to be deployed more often.

There was one other issue that twice agitated the village: it involved every tier of local government and was eventually settled by a House of Commons Committee. This was whether or not Stansted and the other Essex villages which formed part of the Bishop's Stortford Union under the Poor Law should be transferred to Hertfordshire.

The issue first came up in 1888 as one of several changes put forward by the Boundary Commissioners under the Local Government (Boundaries) Act of 1887, and in response the Local Government Board set up an Inquiry to be conducted by a Commissioner. The proposal relating to Stansted and its neighbouring parishes made sense administratively since it was inconvenient for the Stortford Board of Guardians to have to deal with two sets of local authorities. Some of the parishes affected had no strong views one way or the other, but there was fierce opposition from others, especially Stansted. There were some minor practical objections to the proposal, and there were arguments about whether or not it would bring any financial advantage, but the overwhelming reason for opposing the transfer was 'sentiment'. It was Joseph Green who expressed it best in an impassioned letter to the local press in April 1888. Stansted and the adjoining villages, he wrote, had been 'part and parcel of the County of Essex proper since the days of Alfred the Great'. He invoked the memory of Richard de Montfichet and his part in securing Magna Carta, 'the great Charter of our liberties', and urged his readers 'to make the most strenuous efforts to be allowed to remain peaceful inhabitants of a thriving Essex village, and loyal to a county of whose history we should be justly proud'. Referring to Essex as 'our dear old county', he urged the parishioners affected to hold meetings, pass resolutions and raise petitions 'to obviate the operation of one of the most meddling policies that has ever been mooted'.[30]

A petition was indeed raised in Stansted and was submitted to the Essex County Council by the parish's representative, William Fuller-Maitland. He too was opposed to the transfer, but in a lukewarm way, merely reporting to the Council that 'he had received a petition signed by most of the principal ratepayers of the Stansted district',[31] and later he told parishioners that 'He found there was a strong feeling that they preferred to remain in Essex, and he was in favour of that himself, but perhaps it was more a matter of sentiment than anything else'.[32] The Essex County Council, with many other reasons for holding on to the parishes, then threw its weight against the proposal.

By the end of May 1888, when the Commissioner appointed by the Local Government Board held an Inquiry in Stortford, the opposition campaign was in full spate. Even the Board of Guardians had come out against the proposal, and Stansted's representative at the Inquiry, Henry Trigg, said the people of Stansted wanted the boundary to remain as it was.[33] The Commissioner reported all this to the Local Government Board, and such was the strength of the opposition that eventually the proposal was rejected.

The issue was raised again in 1904,[34] apparently on the initiative of the Stansted RDC, and this time the proposal for transfer commanded wider support. Again the conflict was between the administrative convenience of having all the parishes of the Bishop's Stortford Union in one county and the local people's 'sentiment' of attachment which bound them to Essex. The man leading the charge locally was Harford Green. He had opposed transfer on the first occasion, but since then he had been elected as chairman of the Stortford Board of Guardians and as a result of his experience in that post he had changed his mind, as indeed had the Board. Not only that, he was also chairman of the Stansted RDC, where he argued powerfully for transfer and was able to secure a majority of six to two in favour. Finally he was the vice-chairman of the Stansted Parish Council, and on 1 November 1904 a general meeting of the parish voted in favour too. Of the ten parishes affected six were for transfer, two were against, and two offered no opinion.

In the Local Government Board Inquiry that followed a lively meeting was held in Stansted, where once again Harford Green spoke in favour, and the Board came down in favour of transfer.[35] But the Board's decision had to be ratified by Parliament, and it was at this stage that the opposition swung into action. The Essex County Council raised a petition against transfer, and in Stansted a request to the Parish Council to hold another parish meeting was signed by several leading parishioners, among them the vicar, George Oakshott, and the Congregational minister, Eustace Long. At the subsequent meeting it was the vicar who took the lead, and at the end of the debate only 13 parishioners voted for transfer and 105 voted against. Harford Green was mortified, claiming that the facts had been misrepresented, but there was nothing he could do. A year later, when the issue reached a House of Commons Committee, it was decided after a five-day hearing not to confirm the Local Government Board's Provisional Order, and 'the weightiest point' in the Committee's deliberations was 'the sentiment of many of the people in the affected area', a sentiment which was referred to as 'the groundwork of patriotism'.[36]

1. *HEO*, 9 December 1882.
2. *HEO*, 30 May 1885.
3. *HEO*, 19 March 1890.
4. *HEO*, 6 August 1898.
5. *HEO*, 3 December 1898.
6. For the effect of the railway on Newport, see Archer (1995: 2). The population of Bishop's Stortford rose by 75% in the 30 years after the railway's arrival: Cooper (2005: 71).
7. *HEO*, 5 May 1900.
8. Phillips (n.d: 14).
9. *HEO*, 23 August 1890.
10. *HEO*, 22 August 1868.
11. *HEO*, 15 October 1881.
12. *HEO*, 8 July 1899.
13. *HEO*, 20 May 1899.
14. *HEO*, 5 September 1903. The Mica factory was sited at Elms Farm. A siding to the railway was needed, but this was refused because it would have cut across a public footpath. The company therefore went back to London, to Walthamstow, and Dyer and Young took over the premises.
15. *HEO*, 5 March 1881.
16. *HEO*, 15 May 1897.
17. *HEO*, 28 February 1891, 5 March 1898 and 29 July 1899.
18. *HEO*, 16 December 1871 and 28 February 1874.
19. *HEO*, 26 March 1870.
20. *HEO* 29 March 1890.
21. *HEO*, 18 September 1897.
22. ERO, T/P 68/10/1.
23. *HEO*, 5 March 1898.
24. *HEO*, 19 February 1898.
25. *HEO*, 8 December 1900, 28 September 1901, 8 March 1902.
26. *HEO*, 27 September 1902.
27. *HEO*, 12 January 1907 and ISC, unscribed press cutting, 11 January 1907.
28. ISC, press cuttings from *HEO* on Parish Council meetings.
29. *HEO*, 6 October 1906, 16 February 1907.
30. ERO, T/P 68/11/1-5, unscribed press cutting, 23 April 1888.
31. *HEO*, 3 May 1888.
32. *HEO*, 29 March 1890.
33. *HEO*, 2 June 1888.
34. *HEO*, 12 November 1904.
35. *HEO*, 6 May 1905.
36. *HEO*, 15 July 1905. See also ERO T/P 181/10/19, unscribed press cuttings, 26 May and 2 June 1904.

21: 'A NUMBER OF RICH GENTLEMEN': THE FULLER-MAITLANDS

At the tradesmen's dinner in 1898 Harford Green, asking why Stansted was such a prosperous village, put forward as part of the explanation that 'First of all they had ... a number of rich gentlemen living there who were liberal in spending their money in the place and who employed a good many servants and so forth'. J.A. Rush, writing in 1897, described that part of Essex bordering on Hertfordshire as 'a most charming neighbourhood' and commented on 'the number of gentlemen's houses': 'in fact, Stansted has of late years become quite rich in its aristocratic residents'.[1] The gentlemen – and ladies – of Stansted not only provided employment but set a decidedly 'aristocratic' tone.

At the top of the tree were the Fuller-Maitlands. After Bailey Heath's death in 1809, while the manor of Bentfield Bury had been bought by the Goslings, a banking family with their local base in Farnham, who played little part in the public affairs of Stansted, the manor of Stansted Hall had been purchased by Ebenezer Fuller-Maitland – or, to be more accurate, by the trustees of his wife Bethia.

The Maitlands were descended from an old Scottish family, and as Presbyterians they were committed to the Dissenting cause. It was Ebenezer's father, also Ebenezer, a merchant in the City and for many years a director of the Bank of England, who enlarged the family fortune. He was a noted philanthropist, and when he died in 1834, aged 82, the sermon given by the minister officiating at his funeral was published under the title 'The life of Christ in Glory: the death of Ebenezer Maitland'. His wife Mary, the daughter of a Dissenting minister, died in 1835, aged 83.

Their only son, the younger Ebenezer, inherited their fortune, but the great bulk of his money came from his wife, Bethia Ellis, who was commonly described, for very good reason, as the grand-daughter of William Fuller rather than the daughter of Joshua and Esther Ellis. Fuller had worked as a writing master (teaching the art of penmanship or calligraphy) for the first part of his life, but had then become a banker for the last 40 years and built up a prodigious fortune. He died in 1800 at the age of 95. According to one damning obituary, 'The pleasure of amassing wealth reigned unrivalled within his soul'.[2] Others were more generous. One conceded that he had followed 'a system of rigid economy, bordering on penuriousness' and that his 'extreme frugality' had 'exposed him to ridicule'. Another admitted that 'his habits, formed in early life, were rigidly parsimonious': he never, for example, kept a carriage but rode everywhere on horseback. But it was also noted that his morals were 'derived from the schools of Calvin', that he had established a reputation for hard work and unbending probity, and above all that he had given generously, often privately, to several charities, including a school for orphans in London, almshouses in Hoxton and an academy in Rotherham in which he was associated with the older Ebenezer Maitland. In fact he was in much the same tradition as the Maitlands – a banker, a Calvinist and a philanthropist - and no doubt it was because of this that the two families came together.[3]

By 1807 or 1808 most of Fuller's wealth had found its way into the hands of his only grandchild, Bethia Ellis, who had married the younger Ebenezer Maitland in 1800, and it was in acknowledgement of this and in honour of William that the couple changed their name to Fuller-Maitland. They then embarked on a spree of acquiring properties in different parts of the country, and in 1809 Bethia's trustees purchased their Stansted estate.

Ebenezer and Bethia did not go to live in the Hall. Bethia had taken a dislike to the old place, and, already neglected and vacant for some years, it was allowed to fall into ruin, being demolished, except for one tower, in 1812. They had country seats at Park Place, Henley, in Berkshire, and Garth House, Builth Wells, and they came to Stansted, it seems, only on occasion. While Ebenezer held high public office in Berkshire and Breconshire, and while he became a Tory MP for Lostwithiel, Wallingford and Chippenham, he never sat as a magistrate in Essex. In 1848, adding to his Brecon, Berkshire and Stansted estates, he purchased High Barcaple, Kirkcudbright, in Scotland, from another branch of the Maitland family. When he died in 1858, however, he was buried in the family vault in Stansted, being described as E. Fuller Maitland of Park Place in the County of Berkshire and of this parish. Bethia, who died in 1865, was also buried in Stansted.

Ebenezer and Bethia had twelve children, and it seems that some time before Ebenezer's death his eldest surviving son, William, had taken over responsibility for the family's estate in Stansted. In 1842 William had married Lydia Prescott at Florence in Italy, and it was probably then that he and Lydia had come to live in Stansted House, which had been built in or around 1819 on Upgrove Hill overlooking the valley of Stansted Brook with the ruins of Stansted Hall on the opposite skyline. Ebenezer had formally continued to be Lord of the Manor, but in William the village at last had a resident and active squire again, and by 1846 he was sitting as a local magistrate.[4] He soon took up the usual country pursuits, one of his first acts being to engage John Wilkins as his gamekeeper,[5] and he also became one of the driving forces for the progress described in the previous chapter. His wife Lydia died in 1851 at the age of 39, and in the following year he married Charlotte Dick Macnabb, a widow, described by Joseph Green as 'an excellent christian woman'.[6] In spite of his Dissenting background William attended St. Mary's, and when his father died he took on the squire's role as the patron of the vicarage. It may in part have been due to the Fuller-Maitlands' influence that relations between the Anglicans and Nonconformists in Stansted were so good for the rest of the Victorian period.

William was a keen sportsman, fond of his gun and his dogs, but he had broader cultural interests as well. He had a deep knowledge of natural history, built up a valuable

44. Ebenezer Fuller-Maitland.

45. Stansted House, c.1920. Destroyed in 1958.

collection of coins and Delft china, but above all was a perceptive art collector. During several journeys to Italy he came to know the works of the early Italian masters at a time when they were largely unappreciated, and by 1872 he had built up a magnificent collection of over 160 paintings, including 43 by Italian artists (among them Botticelli, Fra Angelico, da Vinci and Bronzino), 19 by early Flemish artists and 24 by Dutch artists (including Rembrandt, Rubens and Ruysdael), 73 English landscapes (including works by Cotman, Crome, Constable and Morland), and a painting by Poussin. He also had one of Holbein's

46. The Recreation Ground, 1916, with the mill in the background.

47. Stansted Hall, from the back. Now the Arthur Findlay College.

works and some drawings by Blake. He was a friend of Millais, who visited him in Stansted, and owned his famous painting of Ophelia. Millais also painted Mary, his only daughter by Charlotte. He was closely associated with the Royal Academy, often lending pictures for its annual Old Masters' Exhibitions, and after his death nine of his most important paintings were sold to the National Gallery, including two Botticellis, the Adoration of the Kings and the Mystic Nativity. He sometimes opened up his pictures for display in Stansted, so that the villagers had the extraordinary privilege and opportunity of seeing the works of the great masters in their own parish.

To the art world Fuller-Maitland was a man of refined taste, a distinguished connoisseur. Joseph Green remembered him as 'a decidedly aristocratic and not particularly accessible squire', though he was careful to add that he was 'upon most friendly terms with my father, with whom he maintained kindly relations to the end of his life and used to send him game and grouse from the Scottish moors. He not infrequently presided at lectures, soirées and penny readings etc. at the Central Hall', and he 'gave' a recreation ground at Woodfields to the parish, where there is still an obelisk recording the gift - it does not record that he received land elsewhere in return. He also gave land for the new British School that was built in 1862. Finally he was an active Liberal, a commitment which was to be strengthened in the next generation.

William and Charlotte continued to live at Stansted House, but in 1871 they pulled down the last remains of the old Stansted Hall and began work on a new building on the same site, a great red-brick pile designed by Robert Armstrong, a more fitting setting for William's paintings. By the February of 1876 the building was complete and the family was due to take up residence within the next few weeks. On Saturday, 12 February, William sat on the bench of magistrates at Saffron Walden, and walked the whole way home, and on Sunday he paid a visit on foot to Elsenham Hall. On Monday he was 'as active and lithe as ever'. On the morning of Tuesday 15 February he rose at 8 a.m. and 'went to his dressing-room to bathe'. The gong sounded at nine for the household to attend prayers, which he invariably read himself, but he failed to appear and was found dead on the bathroom floor, having suffered a stroke. He was 63.[7]

His memorial in St. Mary's Church described him, rather coolly, as 'A just man, and one that feareth God'. According to his obituary, he was beloved and known most in the 'home circle', and his dependants ever found in him 'a kind and indulgent master'.

William's son and heir, also William, was by this time living partly in London and partly at Garth House, near Builth Wells, where he had been elected as the Liberal MP for Breconshire in 1875. So once again the Lord of the Manor was an absentee, and he leased out the newly completed Stansted Hall to Lord Alan Gardner, Baron of Uttoxeter, who seems to have taken over the role of the squire. According to Joseph Green the Gardners became very popular in the village

> by their goodness to the poor, and unostentatious kindness generally. Lady Gardner drove in an aristocratic looking carriage with cane fittings, and her charming daughter [Evelyn] used to drive a pretty pair of ponies and would visit the poor and with her own hands decorate their houses with pictures etc. Indeed, this good lady took Stansted by storm,[8]

48. The younger William Fuller-Maitland.

all the more so in 1881 when she married William Fuller-Maitland.

Though the wedding took place in London it was also the occasion of great festivities in the parish. More than 1,000 adults were treated and entertained in three large marquees, 'each being set apart for various grades of visitors', with 'the principal marquee' given over to the tenantry and tradesmen with their wives and families and the other two supplying 'the creature comforts of the teachers, band, cottagers and labourers, ... everyone receiving a cordial welcome'. The park and grounds were studded with flags and banners, the Union Jack flew from the nearby tower of St. Mary's, the band played and the church bells rang. Sports were arranged for the children, and at the end of the day the festivities were brought to a close by fireworks and the release of 'fire balloons'. With a subscription organised by Joshua Green the parishioners were able to present William and Evelyn with a gift of an ebony and gold chiming hall clock.

At that time William was listed as one of the great landowners in Great Britain, with 3,128 acres in Essex (value £4,103), 3,841 acres in Brecon (value £1,547), 211 acres in Berkshire (value £440), and 1 acre in Middlesex (£348).[9] Lord Alan Gardner died in 1883, and in the following year Lady Gardner, his widow, left Stansted Hall and went to live nearby in Great Dunmow. In spite of his duties as an MP in Wales William now returned with Evelyn to Stansted and took up the full range of his responsibilities as squire.[10] He was more approachable than his father, and it is clear from the many accounts of public meetings, when he was almost invariably asked to take the chair, that he was held in great respect and even affection. Years later, at the celebrations to mark the coming of age of his eldest son, Harford Green declared that his name was associated with 'the cause of progress and reform which had made the village of Stansted Mountfitchet one of the happiest and pleasantest places in the country'.[11] His memorial in St. Mary's says that he was 'greatly loved', and many years later Hilda Seymour, who worked as a lady's maid for a family which often entertained him, told me with great warmth that she remembered 'Mr. Fuller-Maitland, a dear little gentleman.... I loved him, and he wore a very pale grey suit, and of course a bowler hat.'

His main claim to distinction was that he had won blues for cricket and athletics at Oxford. He was a 'devastating' slow bowler, his best performance being 8 for 58 against the MCC in 1864. As the Liberal MP for Breconshire he served on a Parliamentary committee on forestry and was said to be hard-working and conscientious, but he was not outstanding in any way. His brother-in-law, Herbert Gardner,[12] made a much greater impact. While the Fuller-Maitlands moved into Stansted Hall, Gardner moved to Debden Hall, another of their properties, about six miles to the north. He was young and good-looking, a poet and the writer of several light comedies for the stage as well as being an amateur actor himself, and he was so successful a shot that a cartoonist showed the pheasants quaking when they heard of his approach. The Conservatives belittled him as 'a drawing-room exquisite',[13] but in fact he worked very hard. In 1885 he was elected as a Liberal MP for the constituency of Saffron Walden, of which Stansted formed a part, and from 1892 to 1895 he served under Gladstone and then Rosebery as President of the Board of Agriculture. In 1895 he was elevated to the peerage as Lord Burghclere. In later years he became the chairman of the Royal Commission on Historical Monuments in England, and his youngest daughter married Evelyn Waugh.

The Fuller-Maitlands and the Gardners formed a close-knit and well-connected alliance. In Stansted they enjoyed enthusiastic support, and Fuller-Maitland had a good relationship with Lord Rosebery, who described him as an old friend. When the Liberal Unionists broke away from Gladstone's Liberals on the issue of Irish Home Rule Fuller-Maitland and Gardner remained loyal to Gladstone, and Stansted, or 'radical Stansted' as it came to be known, was swept by political excitement to an extent not experienced since the Civil War. But the squire and his brother-in-law were not the only active Liberals in the parish, and before we return to Stansted's involvement in national politics we need to consider the role that was played by the other 'rich gentlemen', some of them Conservatives but most of them Liberals, who had come to make their homes in the village.

1. Rush (1897: 157).
2. Edmund Burke (1801), *The Annual Register*, the 'Chronicle' section.
3. The two more favourable obituaries are from the *Monthly Magazine and British Register*, Vol. 9, pages 289-90 and *The Gentleman's Magazine* 1800, Vol. 70, Part I. Obituary.
4. *CC,* 14 August 1846.
5. Wilkins (1976: 195).
6. Charlotte's letters to her parents are preserved in the British Library (MSS EUR F 206/35 and 127). They reflect her deep Christian faith, but are also concerned, at great length, with financial matters. See also MSS EUR F 206/36 for William Fuller-Maitland's correspondence with his father-in-law.
7. *HEO,* 19 February 1876.
8. ISC, Joseph Green's 'autobiography'.
9. Bateman (1883: 272). His Scottish land was not included.
10. *HEO,* 16 August 1884.
11. *HEO,* 21 May 1904.
12. Herbert's father, Lord Gardner, had three illegitimate sons by an actress, Julia Fortescue. He then married her and they had two daughters. The eldest son, Colonel Alan Gardner, fought at Isandlhwana against the Zulu and later became an MP for Herefordshire (Ross Division). Clarence, the second son, died young, and Herbert was the third son. One daughter became the Countess of Onslow, and the other, Evelyn, married William Fuller-Maitland. Because they were illegitimate none of the three sons could take their father's title.
13. *HEO,* 14 December 1889.

22: MORE 'RICH GENTLEMEN'

In the 1860s and 1870s a cluster of 'gentlemen' came to live in the parish who were not only rich, but extremely rich. They were related to each other, and they were all directors of the firm of W & A Gilbey, the wine and spirit merchants, one of the most successful family businesses in the country. They did not belong to the old landowning class, though they acquired or built grand houses and farms, but rather to a new plutocracy. They were also Liberals.

49. Sir Walter Gilbey.    *50. Henry Parry Gilbey.*

51. Hargrave House.

52. Blythwood House, c.1908.

In 1864 Walter Gilbey, the chairman of the firm, took out a lease on Hargrave House in the Cambridge Road, where he was to live with his family until 1874, when the lease came to an end. After a short interval he went to settle at Elsenham Hall. Two or three years earlier his brother-in-law, Charles Gold, had taken up residence at The Limes, also on the Cambridge Road, a house which he had had built himself and which was in that part of Birchanger that was later incorporated into Stansted. Also around this time Henry Parry Gilbey, Walter's elder brother, had the house that was misleadingly called The Cottage built on the site of what is now Bentfield Gardens. Finally, in 1875 Walter's nephew, James Blyth, bought Wood House, next door to The Limes, and later had the imposing Blythwood House built on the site. Designed by William Caroe, who had recently designed St. John's, the new village church, it was a grandiloquent statement of Blyth's social pretensions. All four men had London houses as well and continued to work for the company.

Other members of the family lived in Bishop's Stortford, and between them all they had literally dozens of children and grandchildren. Walter Gilbey, for example, had 9 children, Charles Gold 13, and James Blyth 7. With so much money at their disposal these families, as Harford Green had observed, provided employment to many people in the parish, not just directly as employers but indirectly through the purchase of goods and services, and the younger members, lively and energetic, invigorated its social life. They left a strong visual legacy in the village. Henry largely funded the building of the Liberal Club in Lower Street, he and Walter erected the fountain on the site of the de Veres' old chapel (which was demolished) and both the club, now the Social Club, and the fountain are still there today.

The Gilbey family had long connections with Stansted and the area around. Walter's grandfather, Daniel, had run the White Bear, and his father, Henry, had run the Bell. But then Henry had decided to take advantage of the flourishing coaching trade, moving to

Bishop's Stortford, starting as a coachman himself and eventually setting up his own company and running coaches between Saffron Walden, Stortford and London. He was ruined by the coming of the railway, reverted to his old trade as an innkeeper, and died in 1842 at the age of 53.

Walter and Alfred, the founding members of the firm, were the tenth and eleventh of Henry's 13 children and were only 11 and 9 when he died. For some years they went their separate ways, supported by a network of older brothers and sisters, but in the early 1850s they were living together in London with their elder brother, Henry Parry Gilbey, who was already a successful wine merchant. In 1853 they set off for the Crimea, not as soldiers but as pay clerks in the Army Pay Department. There they started to display the commercial initiative that was to characterise the rest of their lives, selling goods sent out by their brother Henry, such as saddles, bridles and above all wine.

In 1857, on their return from the Crimea, they set up the firm of W & A Gilbey. On Henry's advice they traded in wines from the colonies, on which the duties were only half of those on French wines. These appealed to the growing middle classes, who could not afford the French wines enjoyed by the upper classes but saw wine consumption as one of the hallmarks of high-class living. Their success was phenomenal. They were joined by their two brothers-in-law, Henry and Charles Gold, and by their cousins Henry and James Blyth, and they opened branches in Edinburgh and Dublin.

In 1860 it seemed that their enterprise might collapse when Gladstone's budget harmonized the duty payable on French wines with that on colonial wines, but they turned this to their advantage by sourcing and selling French wines, passing on the full benefit of the tax reduction to the consumer, and in this way attracting trade from their longer-established competitors who kept the profit for themselves. A second measure in the budget allowed wine to be sold by the bottle by agents whereas before it had only been possible to buy it by the case for consumption at home. Seizing on this opportunity the Gilbeys quickly established a network of more than 2,000 agents, mainly grocers, throughout the country. In this way the off-licence trade came into being. Their cousin Henry Grinling became a partner in 1865, and Henry Parry Gilbey, their older brother, joined them in 1866. In 1867 they moved their London headquarters to the splendid setting of the Pantheon building in Oxford Street. James Blyth was the company's main buyer of wine, and Charles Gold developed its whisky interests in Scotland.

Alfred died in 1879, but other members of the family joined the firm and throughout the rest of the Victorian period it maintained its pre-eminence in the trade. When Henry Parry Gilbey died in 1892, however, the death duties to be paid were so heavy that it was decided to turn the firm into a private limited company. The shares were allocated to the partners on the basis of the capital they had invested, and James Blyth was so dissatisfied with his allocation that he ceased to have a major role in running the company.

While he was in Stansted at Hargrave House Walter Gilbey had bought land and built up one of the finest herds of Jersey cattle in the country. When he left the village he had to sell this herd, but soon afterwards he set up and became president of the Shire Horse Society, and at Elsenham Hall he built up a highly successful stud which received a stream of interested visitors, among them the Prince of Wales. He also became the President of the Royal Agricultural Society. This was not a case of a businessman taking on the

53. The Prince of Wales at Blythwood Dairy, 17 October 1892. From left to right, back row: Charles Gold, James Blyth, Walter Gilbey, the Countess of Warwick, ?, ? Front row: the Earl of Warwick, the Prince of Wales, a daughter of James and Eliza Blyth, Eliza Blyth.

trappings of rural gentrification: since his days as the son of a coachman Gilbey had been devoted to horses and he wrote several books on the subject. In 1903 he was made a baronet for his services to agriculture, and he had high hopes of being made a peer, but in this he was disappointed. He had even more cause for disappointment when his nephew, James Blyth, with whom he had fallen out over the allocation of shares, was ennobled as Lord Blyth of Blythwood and Stansted Mountfitchet in 1907.

For some years Blyth had followed a similar path to the Gilbeys'. He acquired land and built up a herd of Jersey cattle and a flock of Southdown sheep, and he became President of the British Dairy Farmers Association, on one occasion entertaining over 700 of its members to a lavish reception at Blythwood. He was a great showman as well as a generous host, and erected not only a glass shelter from which visitors could admire his animals, but also a Model Dairy lined with Carrara marble and equipped with electricity, which was opened with great ceremony in 1892 by the Lord Mayor and Lady Mayoress of London. At his London home in Portland Square he entertained aristocrats and politicians, singers and actors, foreign princes and potentates, and above all the Prince of Wales, who is said on one occasion to have been taken aback by the size of the glasses in which the port was to be drunk - 'Port in buckets?' he asked.[1] He also entertained many distinguished visitors at Blythwood, among them again the Prince of Wales, who came on to Stansted with the Countess of Warwick, 'Darling Daisy', after visiting her at her nearby home of

Easton Lodge. Blyth's daughter Nora married Alan Gardner, Herbert's brother, and Agnes, another daughter, married Plum Warner, the England cricketer. All these occasions were recorded in great detail in the local press and added to his standing and prestige. The honours heaped on him were exotic and extensive – the Order of Leopold, the Order of the Medjudie from the Khedive, the Order of Merito Agricola of Portugal, Vice-President of the Royal Society of Arts, Vice-President of the Royal Statistical Society, to name but a few.[2]

In 1902 Blyth gave up his farms in Stansted and one of his houses in Silver Street for the use of the Royal Commission on Tuberculosis, which carried out important research based largely on experiments on cattle and monkeys. It was for this, and his support of the Liberal Party, that he was awarded his peerage. Pushy and self-promoting, he was not well liked, but he was clearly a man of considerable ability.

Charles Gold, the first of the Gilbey directors who had come to live in Stansted, remained committed to the business, but was prevailed upon to stand as the Liberal candidate for Saffron Walden in 1895 when Herbert Gardner went to the House of Lords. He was elected with a reduced majority and became an expert on the licensing laws, but he found the work tedious and exhausting and gave up his seat in 1900. For his services as an MP he was awarded a knighthood.

Henry Parry Gilbey was the elder statesman in the company, much valued for the advice and support he gave to his younger brothers. Genial and generous, he was more closely involved in the affairs of the village than the other directors. In a Liberal meeting in 1887 Harford Green said that there was 'no more popular man in Stansted'.[3]

54. Charles Gold as a Parliamentary candidate in 1895.

There were several other 'rich gentlemen' who came to live in Stansted, and the family that left the greatest mark on the village was the Pulteneys, whose forebears had been connected with the Countess of Bath, and whose name is still preserved in Pulteney Bridge in Bath. Richard Pulteney, the rector of Ashley in Northamptonshire, owned Hargrave Park, which he let to Walter Gilbey, but after he died in 1874 his widow Emma and several of their younger children came to live there and Gilbey had to leave. Emma died in 1884, but the unmarried daughters stayed on, and at least three of their brothers lived there at various times, among them William, who became a General in WW1. They gave generously to village causes and took part in entertainments to raise money for them, but their most striking contribution was the land and the money they gave in memory of their mother towards the building of the new church in the centre of the village, St. John's, which was designed by William Caroe and consecrated in 1889. The initial cost of St. John's was £5,000, of which the Pulteneys gave £4,000, and they went

55. St John's Church and the war memorial.

on to meet most of the costs of the tower, between £1,500 and £2,000, and to provide an endowment of £1,500 towards the maintenance of an assistant clergyman.[4] The Pulteneys left the village in 1898.

Gilbert Alder, who came to live in Hargrave House in 1900, was another 'rich gentleman' who became heavily involved in village activities. So too was Sir Thomas Jackson, who had formerly been the manager of the Hong Kong and Shanghai Bank and who went with his wife and family to Stansted House. When Jackson chaired the annual dinner for the staff of the railway in 1907 Harford Green toasted him as

> a genial and kindhearted neighbour. At Stansted they were particularly fortunate in the gentlemen who lived among them. Sometimes squires made their country home a sleeping place only and took little interest in their neighbours, but that, he was pleased to say, was not the case here. Sir Thomas stood for the best type of the English country gentleman and since he had been in this neighbourhood had greatly endeared himself to the people of the place.[5]

Though not the richest, perhaps the most prominent family in the life of the village was the Greens. They were not new to Stansted: in 1887 Green and Company celebrated their bicentenary, and Joseph Green marked the occasion by producing a brief history of the company from the time when John Day had set up his shop in Stansted in 1687. Typically he called it *Ye Hystorie of a Countrie Business at Stanstede in ye countie of Essexe. 1687-1887.*[6] About the same time the shop's premises were transformed by the addition of an

56. 'View of the premises at Stansted now Green's Stores Stansted Ltd. From a photograph of a model executed in 1840.'

57. Green's Stores after the renovation in 1877/78.

imposing red-brick Gothic frontage, complete with a shield bearing the initials JG (for Joseph's father, Joshua Green) and the two dates, 1687 and 1887.

The early history of the business has already been described – how the Quaker, John Day, a grocer, chandler and general dealer, set up his shop in 1687, how its activities were extended in the eighteenth century by 'sope boyling', and how in 1780 the much respected William Grover had been taken into partnership with Samuel Day. When Grover retired from the firm in 1820 Samuel's son, Samuel Tayspill Day, became the sole proprietor. (Going against family tradition he married an Anglican wife and became an Anglican himself, and in the 1830 election he voted Conservative.) According to Joseph Green, the firm's activities were extended again, this time to take in wines and spirits, drapery and undertaking, which, as Green noted, 'became an extensive department in the days of elaborate mourning and paraphernalia'.[7] Although the business more than paid its way Day seems to have taken little interest in it. None of his children wanted to take it over, and so in 1840 he made it over to Joshua Green, his cousin, and to Joshua's close friend, James Marsh. By this time, no doubt because of Samuel's neglect, the premises 'were in a forlorn condition, and the business to some extent corresponded. It therefore required many years of hard plodding work by both partners before it was placed on a better and more thriving footing.'[8] New departments were added, such as outfitting and bespoke tailoring and millinery, and new offices and warehouses were added, the biggest alterations, already described, marking the bicentenary of the business. The trade in wines and spirits, however, was discontinued, no doubt because of the family's prominence in the temperance movement, and so Green and Marsh, as the business was then called, never became agents for W & A Gilbey. At the same time the trade in drugs and gunpowder was discontinued, and Green adds, with a humour worthy of Mr. Pooter, that 'what was once a large trade, that of snuff, has, thanks to good sense, been virtually snuffed out'.[9]

Both James Marsh and Joshua Green became heavily involved in objects they believed likely to benefit the village, such as the founding of the Literary Institution, the building of the Central Hall, and the formation of the Gas Company in 1863. They employed a substantial workforce, and the memorandum drawn up for their assistants imposed a strict regime of working discipline and religious observance. The shop was to be open by 7 a.m. and closed at 8 p.m. (10 p.m. on Saturdays); the young men were not allowed to be absent from the Scripture reading at 9.30 p.m. on Sundays; they were not to be out after 10 o'clock at night; they were not to frequent public houses; they were expected to attend their respective places of worship twice on Sundays; and it was 'earnestly requested that no book having an immoral or anti-christian tendency, may be introduced into the establishment ....' Smoking was not allowed indoors, and – an enlightened provision for the period – a fortnight's holiday was given each year.[10]

Marsh retired from the business in 1871. Joshua Green went on until 1885 when he retired in favour of his two sons, Joseph and Harford. The three Greens, with support from their wives, were at the heart of almost every progressive movement in the village, and it is interesting to compare them with the other 'gentlemen' who contributed so much. With their fabulous wealth the Gilbeys, the Golds and the Blyths came to stand on an equal footing with the landed gentry, and James Blyth, patronised by the Prince of Wales, no doubt regarded himself as a cut above them all. The Greens, however, were always 'trade' and were very conscious of this. In a letter to the *Observer* in 1883 Joshua Green firmly identified himself as middle class, as distinct from lower class or the aristocracy. The middle classes, he wrote, were 'the very backbone of the nation' and he quoted Earl Russell with approval: 'If you want to find morality, you must go not to the top or to the bottom, but to the middle classes.'[11] Joseph Green's 'autobiography', which was more in fact a social portrait of the village, was steeped in deference to the gentry. The Greens, of course, were not as wealthy as the Gilbeys, the Golds, the Blyths and the Pulteneys, nor were they landowners, except to the extent that they had a meadow off Chapel Hill which was useful for occasions such as sales of work and Queen Victoria's diamond jubilee celebrations.

They remained faithful to and indeed proud of their Quaker traditions, and they were active and consistent Liberals.

The three men were very different from each other. Joshua, the father, was highly respected and admired, not just in Quaker and Liberal circles, but throughout the village. In 1882, at the reopening of the Central Hall, Henry Gilbey described him as 'a friend of mine and yours, and as good a friend as Stansted ever had', and when he rose to speak he was 'warmly applauded'.[12] In 1883, when because of illness he was absent from a big meeting of the Stansted and District Liberal Association, Davies, the Congregational Minister, said he 'had been the very backbone of the association', a statement that was greeted with loud applause.[13] Though a Quaker, he was on excellent terms with the vicar, Canon Luard,[14] gave money for the restoration of St. Mary's, and supported both the Congregationalists and the Primitive Methodists, presenting prizes to their Sunday school children and making his meadow available for their treats. While he was not afraid to engage in controversy – he campaigned vigorously for an end to church tithes[15] – he did so in such a measured and straightforward way that he still commanded the respect of his opponents. He was a natural chairman when lectures were given, and took a prominent part in the meetings and entertainments of the Temperance Society. His daughter, Henrietta, became a medical missionary in Hankow.[16]

Joseph Green we have already met – bookish and a collector of autographs, ready to write letters to the local press on matters that concerned him, but not a leading public figure like his father, mainly no doubt for reasons of temperament, but partly perhaps because he did not enjoy good health. While conscientious in carrying out his commercial duties he was much more at home in the world of Quaker history, and when, for health reasons, he retired from the business in 1891 and left the district it was to Quaker history that he devoted his energies for the remaining years of his life.

By contrast Harford was lively, witty, energetic and outgoing. There were three main aspects of his public life.

First, there was the business, which he expanded rapidly. Under his direction Green's was by far the biggest advertiser in the local press, for long periods taking up half a page in each issue and trying out one bold promotion after another. In 1894 he took the company into the furniture business, a few years later he started Greens Motor and Transport Company, and in or around 1908 he plunged into the mail order business in a large way.

Second, he was a noted 'entertainer', and over a period of more than 30 years he must have given scores of performances in aid of village societies and organisations. He delighted in amusing and mystifying his audiences, especially the children, and his main act was his conjuring tricks, otherwise called sleight-of-hand or prestidigitation. He occasionally gave 'spirited' comic readings, provoking 'roars of laughter',[17] and in 1898 he took a major part in the variety entertainment given before a full house by the assistants at his company's establishment. Though head of the firm and sole proprietor, he did not stand on his dignity, but delighted the audience with his conjuring tricks, his impersonations and lastly

> *'the Resuscitation of the Head of Princess Thebia' who, the audience was informed, was beheaded 4,000 years ago, but her head comes to life every 100 years for a short period, and by special arrangement appeared this evening.*

> *This little exhibition was very capitally done, both by Mr. Green himself and by Miss Douglas, the young lady who assisted him in the character of the princess.*[18]

Presumably his performance with his daughter at a Temperance Society entertainment was more serious – 'Drunken sailor visited by a sister of mercy'.[19]

Third, there was his public service, which reached a dizzying peak in the 1900s, when he was a JP, Chairman of the Bishop's Stortford Board of Guardians, Chairman of the Stansted RDC, Vice-Chairman of the Parish Council, and Deputy Chairman of the Stansted Water Company. He later became the Essex County councillor for Stansted. He was nearly always on the platform at Liberal meetings, and he was constantly in demand on other occasions: if a chairman was needed for a jury conducting an inquest into a suicide, Harford Green was the man, and in 1904 he chaired a meeting on women's suffrage in Bishop's Stortford. He seemed to be everywhere, if not taking the chair, then proposing toasts and votes of thanks, moving or opposing resolutions, taking part in delegations. He clearly enjoyed the confidence of those around him. He was a 'genial' chairman and never had any difficulty in being re-elected. In the Parish Council elections in 1904 he and Irvine Rowell received more votes than anyone else,[20] and when for the first time there were elections to the RDC he received 285 votes, 90 more than Walter Gold, his nearest rival.[21] In 1906, when he was re-elected as Chairman of the RDC, the voting was unanimous and his fellow councillors acknowledged that they could not get a better man.[22] In answer to an admiring questioner he said he spent five hours a day on public activities.[23]

But Harford Green was flying too close to the sun. In 1909 he began to feel unwell, or so he said, and went on holiday to Okehampton in Devon, and from there, on 23 February, he went for a walk on Dartmoor and did not return. All efforts to trace him failed, and it then transpired that he had plunged too heavily into the mail order business and was in debt to the tune of £20,000. He was declared bankrupt, his estate was realised, and 'an amount' was paid to his creditors.[24] The firm was saved by help from other members of the family and their friends and associates. A private limited company was formed, Green's Stores, and continuity was maintained as much as possible. The new Managing Director, Charles Hatch, had previously worked for the company for six years and the new Company Secretary, E.E. Tunbridge, for 17 years, and every effort was made to retain the existing staff.[25]

That seemed to be the end of the story. Five years later, however, in May 1914, Harford Green suddenly reappeared, as if in one of his magical entertainments. According to the *Observer* he had 'just been found to be living at Winchmore Hill [where his wife and daughter had been living since his disappearance]; ... he had been in Canada and the Argentine, ... he had visited the offices of the Bankruptcy Court officials, and was now preparing a statement of affairs with a view to obtaining his discharge from bankruptcy'. He was claiming 'that he had lost his memory, until he read a paragraph in a newspaper whilst sitting in a club in Buenos Ayres'. He then 'remembered his identity' and immediately took ship back to England.[26]

It was a dramatic fall from grace, and there could be no return. Harford Green lived on until 1931, and the firm continued in business, in one form or another, until 1982.

As well as these wealthy families, some of them outstandingly wealthy, there were the solid, dependable, respectable families, some of them engaged in farming over several generations, such as the Triggs and the different branches of the Spencers and the Hicks, whose men served as churchwardens, overseers and guardians, party officials and parish councillors, and whose wives were often pillars of support. They did not capture the headlines as much as the gentry, but they made a powerful contribution to the public life of the parish.

1. Patrick Streeter, 'The Blyth family', talk to Stansted Mountfitchet Local History Society, 6 April 2000.
2. *HEO*, 29 June 1907.
3. *HEO*, 12 November 1887.
4. Freeman (1989).
5. *HEO*, 16 February 1907.
6. Another edition – or perhaps it was just the title page of this edition - was more straightforwardly called *Two Hundred Years' History of a Country Business, 1687-1887*.
7. Green (1887: 6).
8. *HEO*, 24 February 1894.
9. Green (1887: 10-11).
10. The Friends House, London, V 252 a. See also a longer version in ERO, T/P 68/39.
11. *HEO*, 20 January 1883.
12. *HEO*, 9 December 1882.
13. *HEO*, 29 December 1883.
14. *HEO*, 21 November 1885.
15. See, e.g., *HEO*, 1 July 1882.
16. *HEO*, 27 September 1913.
17. *HEO*, 24 November 1877.
18. *HEO*, 15 January 1898.
19. *HEO*, 31 December 1881.
20. *HEO*, 12 March 1904.
21. *HEO*, 30 March 1907.
22. *HEO*, 5 May 1906.
23. *HEO*, 14 December 1907.
24. *HEO*, 22 May 1914.
25. The Friends House, London, L 14/47.
26. *HEO*, 22 May 1914.

23: THE ELECTIONS OF 1830 AND 1831[1]

The farm labourers' 'riot' of 1834, described in Chapter 16 above, was the most dramatic expression of the deepest division in the parish, the division between those with property and those without, in that case between those who owned the land and those who worked on it. Among those with property, however, there were also political divisions, and in the elections of 1830 and 1831 these were concentrated on the issue of electoral reform. A secondary issue was the abolition of slavery.

Standing for election was expensive, more so in the county than in the boroughs. In Essex the voters had to be conveyed to Chelmsford and provided with accommodation, and although bribery was illegal they were 'treated' to generous dinners. Because of these heavy expenses many elections were uncontested. The gentlemen of the county met beforehand and decided who should represent them, and it was only if they could not reach agreement, or if some outsider tried to break in, that, to use the phrase current at the time, 'the peace of the county' was disturbed and an election had to be held. In 1774 the leading men went even further, for they reached an agreement whereby the county was to be represented by a comfortable coalition of one Whig and one Tory MP.

After that, over a period of more than 50 years, there were only two elections in the county, in 1810 and 1812, and in both Montague Burgoyne tried to break in, describing himself as a radical and unofficial Whig. He was heavily defeated on both occasions, but in Stansted, in 1810, he got two votes, one from a doctor, George Welch, and one from a schoolmaster, Mordaunt White, who as professional men could afford to take an independent line. In 1812, however, White gave his vote to one of Burgoyne's opponents and Welch did not vote, though it would be unwise to read too much into this because Burgoyne, seeing how hopeless his cause was, pulled out of the contest after the poll had lasted five days when it could have gone on for another ten. Burgoyne was a man before his time. The great causes which he championed, the reform of Parliament and the abolition of slavery, were the issues that were to be at the heart of the elections in 1830 and 1831.

After Burgoyne's intervention the peace of the county was not disturbed for almost 20 years. Then, in 1830, George IV died, and at that time the death of a monarch had to be followed by a general election. The pressure for Parliamentary reform was now intense, and there were two main issues.

First was the redistribution of constituencies. In Essex there were four constituencies returning eight MPs. The three ancient boroughs of Colchester, Maldon and Harwich each returned two MPs, and the rest of Essex, the county, was also represented by two MPs. This was blatantly unfair, especially as Malden had only 32 voters. This pattern was repeated throughout the country.

Second was the extension of the franchise. In the counties only the 40s. freeholders could vote, i.e. men who had freehold property which was valued for the land tax at 40s. a year. In the Reform Bill £10 copyholders and long leaseholders were to be added, and £50 short leaseholders and tenants at will. There were to be comparable changes in the towns, and the overall effect would be to increase the national electorate from 435,000 to 652,000.

Essentially the struggle for reform was a struggle between those who wanted the country to go on being ruled by squires, parsons and wealthy landowners, and those who wanted to recognise the rights of the new classes produced by industrial expansion and commercial enterprise. It was a crucial debate, and the history of the United Kingdom was to turn on its outcome.

There were two main parties - the Tories under the Duke of Wellington, the party of the Church and King, who wanted either no reform or very slow reform, and the Whigs under Earl Grey, who wanted reform along the lines of the Reform Bill. The first candidate to declare himself in Essex was William Wellesley, a nephew of the Duke of Wellington, who wore both the orange of the Whigs and the blue of the Tories and stood as an Independent. Like Burgoyne, he had not been chosen by the men of the county. He had simply burst in on the scene. The Whig candidate was the veteran Charles Callis Western. At first it seemed that the Tories would not be able to put up anyone at all, since their sitting MP declared that he could not afford to stand, but in the end Colonel John Tyrell, a young squire, was persuaded to put his name forward with the support of a public subscription to lighten the expense.

Wellesley stood firm for Parliamentary reform and the abolition of slavery. So did Western, and Wellesley hoped for his support. But it soon became clear that Western and Tyrell were fighting as a Whig/Tory coalition in the traditional way. In spite of all the turbulence and excitement in the country the gentlemen of Essex were determined to arrange the election on the same old basis. Wellesley complained loudly of this unprincipled alliance, particularly on the part of Western, 'the greatest of all political apostates' as he called him, but Tyrell and Western denied that there was any formal agreement, claiming instead that there was a unanimity of sentiment against Wellesley. In the words of one of Tyrell's supporters, 'the voice of the gentlemen of the county' was against him. And he provided a good target for abuse. His opponents attacked him for his political unreliability, because he had previously been a Tory and had now changed sides. And they attacked his personal morals. Having married one of the wealthiest heiresses in the country he had gambled away his fortune and at times had to go to the continent to escape his creditors. He claimed he was not hostile to the Church of England, but the Church was certainly hostile to him, and he later complained of 'the blue Clerical Gentry on their sporting nags, scampering from hamlet to village, and even from the Church door on the Sabbath to the farm house, to solicit votes for Tyrell and Western'. In spite of his extravagant and colourful lifestyle, however, he had not alienated the Dissenters, who stood firmly behind his two main causes, Parliamentary reform and the abolition of slavery.

This was certainly the case with the Independents in Stansted. As Dissenters they were often ill at ease with the Church of England, which was strongly hostile to reform, and they were passionately committed to the abolition of slavery. For reasons which will be explained in Chapter 27 below, there were now two Independent Churches in Stansted, the Old Meeting and the New Meeting. A missionary society had been set up in 1812, and when slavery was abolished in 1834 the Old Meeting set aside the whole of one Sunday 'in thanksgiving to God for the emancipation of the negro slaves in our British colonies'.[2]

The hustings were set up in front of the Shire Hall in Chelmsford, strong enough to

23: THE ELECTIONS OF 1830 AND 1831

withstand any riot or disorder, and bands of special constables were sworn in. The poll was due to open at ten on the morning of 5 August, and from seven onwards there were peals of bells from the parish church and three bands marched through the town. Flags flew from every public house, crowds thronged the streets, and the windows, according to the local press, were 'filled with all the beauty and fashion of the town and neighbourhood'. At half past nine the candidates and their trains of supporters rode in, colourful with bows, cockades and streamers and holding up their banners – 'Western, his country's friend', 'Colonel Tyrell and the Essex True Blues', and, for Wellesley, 'Equal Laws and Equality of Rights'.

After the formal speeches of nomination the poll was thrown open, and at the end of the first two days Wellesley was slightly in the lead. Gradually, however, Western and Tyrell pulled ahead. The crowd around the hustings were mainly Wellesley's supporters, and in the speeches at the end of each day Western was regularly shouted down. There was continual scuffling and uproar: banners were pulled down, stones were thrown, and effigies of the different candidates were torn apart. As Wellesley fell further behind he became more and more desperate, railing against both the squirearchy and the clergy. By the end of the poll, on the 15th day, Tyrell had received 2,638 votes, Western 2,556 and Wellesley 2,301.

Nineteen electors from Stansted voted, and there was no question this time of their following a lead set down by the landowners. Eight of them voted for Wellesley alone or for Western and Wellesley. Six of these can be identified as Independents, including the minister of the Old Meeting, Robert May, and none can be identified as Anglicans. Eleven voted for Tyrell alone or for Tyrell and Western. Six of these can be identified as Anglicans, including the vicar, Josias Torriano, one as a Quaker, Edward Hicks, and one as an Independent, John Atkin. Although the pattern of voting was not entirely clear cut, on the whole the Anglicans resisted reform while the Independents supported it. Wellesley had been justified in his attacks on the Anglican clergy: in the county as a whole 259 of them voted against him, while only nine gave him their support.

Less than a year later, in May 1831, another general election was held. The Reform Bill of Earl Grey's Whig government had passed the first reading of the House of Commons, but only by a single vote, and William IV had dissolved Parliament. Tyrell, Western and Wellesley again stood for the county of Essex, but this time the gentlemen's compact could not hold under the intense pressure for change. Tyrell's support for reform was lukewarm and limited, Western had to join forces with Wellesley, and by the end of the poll Western had received 2,367 votes, Wellesley 2,250 and Tyrell 1,701.

The issues were clear, and so was the voting of Stansted's 14 electors, five fewer than before. Eight of them voted for Western and Wellesley, and of these seven were Independents. Robert May, the minister, was again one of their number, and so now was John Atkin, who had shifted his support since the previous election. Only six voted for Tyrell, and this time the vicar did not vote.

In the country as a whole the cause of reform was triumphant, and in 1832 the Bill became law. Two years later slavery was abolished. Stansted's electors, in however small a way, had played their part.

1. This chapter is based on the poll books and on an anonymous publication, *Essex County Election. Report of the Speeches delivered at the Hustings, and of the interesting proceedings during the contest of fifteen days, for the representation of the County of Essex, Commencing on Friday, the 6th of August, 1830, and terminating on Monday, the 23rd, ...* (Chelmsford: 1831).
2. ERO, D/NC 2/1/1, p. 218.

24: RADICAL STANSTED

After the Reform Act of 1832 Essex returned ten MPs – two for North Essex, two for South Essex and two each for the boroughs of Colchester, Harwich and Maldon. In all the general elections held under this Act the constituency of North Essex, in which Stansted was situated, returned two Conservatives, except in 1865, when the Liberal candidate squeezed in as the second MP. In five elections there were no Liberal candidates – in 1835, 1837, 1841, 1857 and 1859 – and there was no need for a poll.

Under the 1867 Reform Act, which almost doubled the electorate to 2.5 million, taking in many more men in the towns, Essex still returned ten MPs, but the distribution was different – East, West and South Essex returning two each, Colchester also returning two, and Maldon and Harwich each reduced from two to one. Three general elections were held under this Act. Nationally the Liberals won two of them and the Conservatives one. Stansted's constituency of West Essex, however, was represented by two Conservatives throughout. The Conservatives were also dominant in Essex as a whole: in 1874 they achieved a clean sweep of all ten seats.

Stansted was as Conservative as the rest of West Essex. Joseph Green declared that his father and James Marsh 'were at one time the only voters in the Liberal interest resident at Stansted, and drove with flying colours to the poll at Saffron Walden into the midst of Lord Braybrooke's tenantry'.[1] He was exaggerating, but the Conservatives were firmly in control. In the 1847 election, for example, there were three candidates, two Conservative and one Liberal, and the poll book listed 48 voters from Stansted: 34 of them voted for the Conservative candidates, 12 for the Liberal candidate (including Joshua Green and James Marsh), and two for one Conservative and one Liberal.[2]

As William Fuller-Maitland acknowledged later, up to this time the Liberal Party had hardly been active in the area,[3] but then his brother-in-law, Herbert Gardner, who was soon to be chosen as the prospective candidate, threw himself into the fray and a party agent was appointed. In March 1881 the Stansted and District Liberal Association was inaugurated at a meeting in the Central Hall. Fuller-Maitland was the President: though he was MP for Breconshire and spent much of his time there, he was still affectionately known as 'the squire of the parish'.[4] The vice-presidents were Herbert Gardner, no fewer than five of the directors of W & A Gilbey - Henry Parry Gilbey, Walter Gilbey, Charles Gold, James Blyth and Henry Blyth - and the Congregational Minister, Daniel Davies. Among others at the inaugural meeting were Joshua Green, Joseph Green (secretary), James Marsh and Thomas Hicks. At this meeting and others that followed three main themes emerged. The first was loyalty to Gladstone. The second was the great advances that had been made in the country as a whole, and more particularly in Stansted, under Liberal Governments over the past 40 years, mainly because of their policy of free trade. The third was the campaign to extend the franchise to working men in the rural areas. Why, it was asked, should men in Stansted not have the vote when men of the same class in Cambridge did?

24: RADICAL STANSTED

The Conservatives fought back, but they did not have the same guns at their command as the Liberals. One of their local leaders was Robert Gosling, the lord of Bentfield Bury manor, but, living in Farnham, he had less influence in Stansted than the popular William Fuller-Maitland. Others who gave their support were the Pulteneys, the Spencers, the lawyer Harry Chester, the farmer Henry Trigg and, surprisingly, Robert Fuller-Maitland, William's younger brother. The Conservatives' anathema was free trade, and they banged the drum for protection, or *fair* trade as they called it. Whereas the Liberals had pointed to the increasing prosperity of Stansted as proof of the success of their policies, the Conservatives pointed to the decline of the villages around and the agricultural depression as proof of the opposite. It was free trade, they argued, that was ruining the farmers, since it allowed in wheat from the New World so cheaply. Finally, a stance that did them no good with the agricultural labourers, they had no enthusiasm for extending the franchise. In fact the man they selected to oppose Gardner, Charles Strutt, argued against it on the grounds that it would not be conducive to the happiness and contentment of the people and that the artisan class had quite enough power already.[5]

58. Herbert Gardner. Sketch by Spy in Vanity Fair, 1886.

In 1884 Gladstone's Reform Act was triumphantly passed: the enfranchisement that had been granted in the towns under the 1867 Act was extended to the countryside, and more than two million voters were added to the registers. Essex was to return 11 members, each by a single constituency, and Stansted was to form part of the Saffron Walden Division.

In the election campaign that followed in 1885 the Liberals were carried along by a great wave of excitement and expectation. Herbert Gardner was adopted as their candidate at an 'enthusiastic' meeting in Saffron Walden, and over 400 people came to hear him in the Central Hall in Stansted. The room

> *was crowded to excess. All the doors were kept open, and the front entrance and the ante-room were thronged with people, while others flocked around the windows outside. .... Such an enthusiastic political demonstration had probably never been witnessed in the Hall before, and Mr. Gardner evidently created a most favourable impression upon the great majority of his hearers for the cheering at times was simply deafening.*[6]

Fuller-Maitland was in the chair, hammering home the message that the country owed its prosperity to the Liberals and their policy of free trade, and Joshua Green urged the new electors to vote for the Liberals, who had given them the franchise, and not the Conservatives, who had fought against it.

The climax was reached in November when once again the Central Hall was filled to its utmost capacity. The *Observer* reported that no Liberal candidate in the whole of Essex had received a more hearty reception than Gardner. His coach was met by an excited band of admirers who unharnessed the horses and drew him through the village themselves. When he arrived the audience rose to its feet, and the speeches that followed were constantly interrupted by cheers and applause. Much play was made of the franchise issue, and Gardner quoted Gladstone to good effect: 'the policy of the Liberal Party was trust in the people, qualified by prudence. The policy of the Conservative Party was mistrust in the people, qualified by fear.' When Gardner left at the end of the meeting the crowd outside escorted his carriage for some distance out of the village, singing and cheering.

The Conservatives responded in July with an open-air demonstration of support for their candidate, Charles Strutt, and then in September with a meeting in the Central Hall, chaired by Robert Gosling. Although these occasions were described as successful, there was nothing like the enthusiasm that greeted Herbert Gardner. As the Conservatives themselves ruefully acknowledged, Stansted was 'one of Gardner's strongholds'.[7]

So too was the Saffron Walden division as a whole. In the election, held in December 1885, there was a transformation in Essex, where the Liberals won six of the 11 seats, and by far their largest majority was in the Saffron Walden Division, where Gardner defeated Strutt by 4,755 votes to 3,006. In the country as a whole the result was less clear cut. The Liberals won 332 seats, the Conservatives 252, and the Home Rule Party, the Irish MPs led by Parnell, 86. So the Liberals depended on Parnell's support to stay in power.

Almost immediately Gladstone dropped his bombshell – Irish Home Rule. This was not an issue on which the election had been fought, but Gladstone was convinced that it was necessary for a peaceful solution to the Irish question. The Conservatives opposed it to a man. It would lead, they said, to the dismemberment of the empire. Worse still for Gladstone, there was opposition from within his own party, and in 1886 his Irish Government Bill was defeated by 30 votes. The Government fell and another election had to be held. Henceforward, on all issues affecting Home Rule, the Conservatives would fight in alliance with those Liberals, the Liberal Unionists, who had broken away from Gladstone.

Gardner, who was again the Liberal candidate for the Saffron Walden Division, remained loyal to Gladstone, and so did Fuller-Maitland, who had been re-elected as MP for Breconshire, and most Liberal supporters in Stansted. The Conservatives chose George Brewis as their candidate. The sole issue was Irish Home Rule, and the passions generated were even fiercer than in the 1885 election. The Liberals saw it as a moral question, the Conservatives as a matter of life and death for the British Empire. There were always disturbances at election times. In 1885 Liberal posters had been smeared with blue paint, a Conservative speaker in the Central Hall had been interrupted so frequently that he had been unable to complete his speech, and Robert Fuller-Maitland and Strutt, the Conservative candidate, had had mud and stones thrown at them on the streets of Stansted and would have suffered worse but for police protection. It was just as bad in 1886. When Gardner addressed a meeting in the Town Hall at Saffron Walden a great crowd outside kept up a constant din – Joseph Green referred to 'the dismal howlings, yellings and groanings of human hyenas' – and threatened Gardner with 'horrid gesticulations' as he left the meeting.[8]

The poll itself passed off quietly, but as the counting got under way in the evening the tension mounted. Seventy policemen were on duty outside the Town Hall in Saffron Walden, and 'as time wore on the streets became more alive and knots of men with yellow and blue were to be seen standing about the corners ....' Around 11 pm Gardner and then Brewis drove up to the Town Hall, and both were greeted by hissing and boos from their opponents and cheers and wild applause from their supporters. Finally the results were announced – Gardner had received 4,059 votes and Brewis 3,319. Gardner was declared to be the duly elected MP, but when he tried to speak he could not make himself heard above the uproar. Brewis appealed in vain for calm and fighting broke out when some of his supporters attacked the home of a Liberal activist.[9]

Gardner's majority had been reduced by 1,009 since the election a year before, but it was remarkable that he had won at all. In 1885 Essex had returned six Liberals and five Conservatives to Parliament. In 1886 it returned one Liberal, Gardner, and ten Conservatives. Gardner was not only the sole Liberal MP in Essex: he was the only MP to support Gladstone in the Home Counties.[10] Such was the extent of the Liberal collapse, and such was Gardner's achievement, backed up as he was by his strong support in Stansted. In the country as a whole the Conservatives swept back to power with 316 MPs, with support against Home Rule from 78 Liberal Unionists, while the Liberals had only 190 MPs, and Parnell's Home Rule Party 86.

There was no slackening of political activity. The Conservatives, determined to stamp out the only radical constituency in Essex, held several well supported meetings of the recently formed Primrose League in the village, while the Liberals embarked on the bold initiative of establishing a Stansted Working Men's Liberal Association with a grand new club house, complete with assembly room, library, billiards room and bar. The main benefactor was Henry Parry Gilbey, who became the Association's first president, and the building was formally opened in 1887 by Fuller-Maitland's 'old friend', the future Prime Minister Lord Rosebery. It was a grand occasion: the village was 'en fête', flags flying on every side, 'while above the railway bridge at the entrance from Stansted Hall was a triumphal arch of evergreens bearing across the top the word "welcome" in bold Liberal colours on a red ground'. Even the public houses flew Liberal flags. A conference was held in the afternoon in the Central Hall, a banquet in the evening in the new assembly room of the Club, and then a mass meeting in a marquee on Castle Hill which 1,200-1,400 attended. In such a setting Gilbey could not resist the temptation of placing the Liberals in the tradition of Richard de Montfichet and Magna Carta.[11] But this Liberal triumphalism was misplaced. Gilbey himself had wanted to establish a social club for all working men in the village, not a political club for Liberal supporters. Political clubs, he felt, were acceptable in large towns, but were unpleasantly divisive in villages. But party feeling was running so high that the men he consulted were insistent that a political club should be established.[12] The Conservatives were offended and dismayed: Harry Chester described the new building as a 'huge and hideous excrescence' and accused the Liberals of trying to attract support by selling cheap beer.[13] Over the years, however, party animosity became less intense, and in 1892, at a ceremony attended by the leading men from both Liberals and Conservatives, the club was refounded as the Stansted Working Men's Club, open to men of every political persuasion and supported and patronised by the gentry from every party.[14]

Gardner held his seat in 1892 with an increased majority of 1881 (4,564 against 2,683), a victory which reflected the upturn of Liberal fortunes in the country as a whole, and he then took office for three years as President of the Board of Agriculture. He rarely visited the constituency because of the demands of office and declining health, and for this he was subject to increasing criticism. In 1895, after he had been elevated to the House of Lords as Lord Burghclere, and after a reluctant Charles Gold had been persuaded to take his place, the Liberals held the seat again. The Liberal majority, however, was reduced from 1,881 to 425, and nationally there was a Conservative landslide.

The next election was held during the Boer War.

1   Green (1887: 8). The tenants of Lord Braybrooke at Audley End would have followed his wishes and voted Conservative.
2   ERO, LIB/POL 1/23.
3   *HEO*, 10 November 1906. See also ERO, T/P 68/25/4, Minutes of the Stansted and District Liberal Association.
4   *HEO*, 29 December 1893.
5   *HEO*, 11 July 1885.
6   *HEO*, 6 June 1885.
7   *HEO*, 11 July 1885.
8   *HEO*, 17 July 1886.
9   *Ibid.*
10 *The Daily News*, 26 July 1888, in ERO, T/P 68.
11 *HEO*, 22 October 1887.
12 For the rules of the club see ERO, T/P 68/25/1-4.
13 *HEO*, 29 October 1887.
14 *HEO*, 7 May 1892.

25: THE BOER WAR

In 1899, while Charles Gold was MP, the second South African war broke out, commonly referred to as the Boer War. Stansted was profoundly affected. There were several Stansted men in the regular battalions who served in the war, and there were others who stepped forward as volunteers. On the home front funds were raised for the support of the troops and for their widows and orphans.

To understand the politics of the second South African War we have to understand what happened in the first. In 1878 the British annexed the Transvaal, which was bankrupt at the time – this was before gold was discovered – but then the Boers rose in rebellion, the British troops were defeated, astonishingly it seemed at the time, at Majuba and Laing's Nek, and in 1881 the Liberal Government, under Gladstone, made terms and withdrew. Many still regarded this as a national humiliation and held the Liberals responsible for it. Since then the world's richest gold deposits had been discovered on the Rand and thousands of immigrants had flocked in. The Boers, under President Kruger, determined not to lose control in their own land, refused to give the vote to these newcomers. The British Government made heavy demands which Kruger refused to meet in full, and war broke out. On the one side were the two Boer Republics - the South African Republic, i.e. the old Transvaal, and the Orange Free State. On the other was the whole might of the British Empire.

In spite of the experience of the first South African war the Government was confident that the fighting would last only a few weeks. But the Boers were now wealthier and better armed than before, and within months British troops were cut off in Ladysmith, Mafeking and Kimberley. When Redvers Buller, the Commander-in-Chief, tried to relieve Ladysmith he suffered a series of terrible defeats in what became known as 'black week' for the British army. The worst disaster was that at Spion Kop on 24-25 January 1900.

One of the regiments under Buller's command was the 2nd Royal Lancaster Regiment, and one of the soldiers in that regiment was William Hutley of Stansted. Now in his late 30s, he had previously been a general labourer living with his parents on Grove Hill. On 14 February, just three weeks after 'black week', he wrote to his mother from Chieveley Camp, Buller's headquarters in Natal. He had been heavily involved in the fighting but had come through unscathed. He told of the physical hardships - 'not a mouthful of bread have I had since the 9th January ... the heat here is something awful'. At times he postured with a devil-may-care bravado – 'it's awful fun, this killing one another'. At times he let his real feelings show through – 'but when you see your chums getting knocked over all round you it makes you think of those at home'. The lessons of patriotism drummed into him in Stansted were not forgotten: 'Still, we keep on going just to let them know we're Englishmen and not to be beaten'. One theme was common at this time, that the Boers were crafty and deceitful foes: how else to account for their success over the British army? 'They are a bad lot to trust,' wrote Hutley, 'so we give them no quarter if they want it'.[1]

Reinforcements poured in, Lord Roberts took over as Commander-in-Chief with Kitchener as his Chief of Staff, and Ladysmith was relieved on 28 February. Hutley's next letter was written a week or two later. He had taken part in the relief and had seen terrible things. The Boers' trenches were choked with dead and wounded, but 'they deserved all they got'. One survivor threw down his rifle and asked Hutley not to bayonet him: 'So I didn't, but I turned my rifle round and bashed his brains out on the rocks'.[2]

At home the Essex Soldiers Relief Fund was set up to help the wives and families of Essex soldiers, and in Stansted funds were raised at 'patriotic services' in the churches and at patriotic dances and entertainments organised by members of the leading families. In January a 'Patriotic Concert' arranged by 'Mrs. Breeks, a daughter of Mr. H.A. Blyth', was held in the assembly room of the Working Men's Club. The account given in the *Herts and Essex Observer* captured and reflected the spirit of the occasion:

> *Mr. Sidney Lamb opened with a piano solo, 'God Bless Victoria' .... The lady vocalists were Mrs. Tresham Gilbey and Miss Marie Bailey ... Mrs. Gilbey giving 'There's a land' and 'When I'm Big I'll Be a Soldier' .... The audience were also treated to two recitations by Mr. Robert Lorraine, who was announced as being about to join the yeomanry. The first was Kipling's 'Flag of England' ... Mr. Charles Loder's songs, 'The Soldier's Goodbye' and 'Sons of the Empire', were greatly enjoyed, particularly the latter which was ... loudly redemanded and repeated. Mr. Oscar Wigan too had a capital new patriotic song, 'Valete' ... and his other song, 'Soldiers of the Queen', gave the audience a good chance to take their part in a chorus .... Mr. Tresham Gilbey danced a hornpipe and was encored, and Mr. Gerald Gold sang 'Tommy Atkins' and 'The Absent-Minded Beggar'.*
>
> *The musical programme ... was interspersed with some really excellent tableaux. [Among them were] 'Abuses of the White Flag' [a reference again to the alleged deceitfulness of the Boers] ... 'Scarlet Fever' (showing the attractions of Tommy to the fair sex), 'Red, White and Blue', and 'The British Empire'. The concert raised £36 18s.*[3]

As news of the disasters came in more calls were made for volunteers, and the gentry were particularly receptive to the appeal of the Duke of Cambridge, who formed his own corps, the Duke of Cambridge's Own, the DCOs, as part of the Imperial Yeomanry. These men were the cream of country society – the sons and grandsons of the aristocracy and gentry, masters of foxhounds, and also their gamekeepers and estate managers. They were to provide their own uniforms and equipment, to pay for their own passage, and to devote their pay to the fund for soldiers' dependants.

Among those who enrolled were Audley and Rupert Blyth, sons of Sir James Blyth, and Philip and Guy Gold, sons of Charles Gold. Another volunteer was John Keddie, Sir James Blyth's agent. Alfred Gosling, one of the sons of Robert Gosling at Farnham, also joined the DCOs – in the middle of the hunting season, it was noted with surprise. Before they set off Sir James Blyth, with his customary flair for showmanship and publicity, entertained about 30 DCOs at his home at Blythwood, giving them lunch and toasting the Queen and 'a glorious victory for our forces in South Africa'.[4] A week later the DCOs set off for Cape Town.

By this time the war was going better, or so it seemed. Lord Roberts was steadily advancing, defeating the Boers in set battles. In March, the month in which the DCOs arrived at Cape Town, he captured Bloemfontein, the capital of the Orange Free State, and in May the relief of Mafeking was greeted with scenes of wild rejoicing in London. Stansted contented itself with a display of flags.[5] In May Johannesburg was captured, in June Pretoria, and in October the Transvaal was annexed by the Crown.

In the midst of this triumphal progress the DCOs ran into disaster. In June they entered the Free State town of Lindley. They thought it had been deserted, but in fact de Wet's Boers were in hiding, lying in wait, and no sooner had the DCOs entered the town than they were surrounded and placed under siege. Within a few days, after losing nearly 100 men, they had to surrender, and they were marched off to Nooitgedacht in the Transvaal, where they were confined in an area of about 200 square yards surrounded by barbed wire. Five Stansted men were there – the two Blyths, the two Golds and Keddie. Another DCO captive was Alfred Gosling.

The DCOs were not badly treated. They were allowed to send letters home and to receive food parcels and letters in return. Sir James Blyth made sure that Audley's lively account of his prison experiences was reprinted in the local press, and there was publicity too for Blyth's generous food parcels, sent to all the prisoners, not just his sons, and his gift of £1,000.

As the British advanced most of the prisoners were released and others escaped, among them the two Blyths and Keddie. For the men of Stansted that was the end of the fighting. They returned to the village where they were welcomed as heroes by admirers and estate workers who 'cheered them heartily', unyoked their carrages and drew them home.

With the capture of Pretoria it seemed that the war was almost over, and it was at this point that the Conservative Prime Minister, Lord Salisbury, surprised his opponents by calling an election. He was clearly hoping to take advantage of the enthusiasm engendered by the war: it was to become known as the khaki election.

Charles Gold, who had been elected in 1895 with a majority of 425, stood down, for reasons of health as he said, and a new candidate was drafted in at short notice, Armine Wodehouse from Norfolk. The Conservative candidate was Charles Gray, who had contested the seat before. The campaign centred on the war in South Africa. The Conservatives claimed that they were the patriotic party, that the Boers were hoping for a Liberal victory, remembering how Gladstone had abandoned the Transvaal after the first Anglo-Boer War, and that a vote for the Liberals was a vote for the Boers. The Liberals argued that they were just as patriotic as the Conservatives - no doubt they pointed to the military service of the Blyths and the Golds - but they were not jingoists. What was needed now was not just firmness in winning the war, but fairness and moderation in the peace terms.

In the country as a whole the Conservatives were returned with a large majority, but in the Saffron Walden division the result was a Liberal victory, though only by 3,247 votes to 3,137. In spite of the Government's sanguine expectations after the fall of Pretoria, the war dragged on. The Boers changed their tactics: they no longer engaged in pitched battles, but their commandos, under inspired leaders such as Jan Smuts and Louis Botha, embarked on a guerrilla war. To counter this Kitchener, the new Commander-in-Chief who succeeded Lord Roberts, set up a system of wire fences and blockhouses and rounded up the local population in concentration camps. At home many people were tired of the war, and were far from sure that it was being fought for the right reasons or in the right way. At Stansted enthusiasm dwindled: fund-raising events were no longer held for the soldiers and their families but, once again, for the repair of the church organ or the local nursing fund.

Armine Wodehouse, the new MP, was a relatively young man, but he died unexpectedly and in June 1901 a bye-election had to be held. Charles Gray was again the Conservative candidate, while the Liberal candidate was Joseph Pease, a mine-owner from Yorkshire. The Conservatives persisted with their argument that every vote for the Liberals was a vote for the disgrace of England, for the smashing up of the Empire and the upholding of the tyrant Kruger. The Liberals made much play with the argument that at the last election the Conservatives had claimed that with a Conservative victory the Boers would surrender, but in fact there was no sign of an end to the war. This time the result was 3,994 votes for the Liberals and 3,202 for the Conservatives, a majority of 792.

At last, in May 1902, the Boers came to terms in the Peace of Vereeniging, and there were celebrations throughout the country. In Stansted the streets were gaily decorated with flags, the church bells were rung, the schoolchildren paraded the streets singing patriotic songs and at dusk there was a bonfire on the Recreation Ground. But in general, as the local press reported, there was no triumphalism, just a sober and quiet spirit of gratitude.[6]

As well as the Blyths and the Golds and James Keddie, several others from Stansted, or with Stansted connections, served in South Africa. Jack Watney, a grandson of Charles Gold, was killed in the assault by de Wet's troops at Tweefontein on Christmas morning, 1901. He was 19. The memorial service for him was held at Birchanger, but there is a monument to his memory in St. Mary's. William Alan Fuller-Maitland, the squire's eldest son, went out with the Coldstream Guards in January 1902. And Sergeant-Major Chappell, who was to be awarded a Distinguished Conduct Medal for gallantry in WW1, also held a medal for service in South Africa. When we interviewed John Speller in 1988 he told us that he knew of five men who had fought in the Boer War, and all had come back, though one, Alf Griggs, had a bullet that had gone through his cheek.

1 *HEO*, 10 March 1900.
2 *HEO*, 14 April 1900.
3 *HEO*, 27 January 1900.
4 *HEO*, 17 February 1900.
5 *HEO*, 26 May 1900.
6 *HEO*, 7 and 14 June 1902.

26: NOT SO RADICAL STANSTED

After the elevation of Herbert Gardner to the House of Lords and the political retirement of Charles Gold the leadership of the Liberal Party in the constituency became centred again on Saffron Walden and Stansted no longer played a distinctive role. The Liberals held on to the constituency, with a brief Tory interlude in 1910, but later, from 1922 onwards, Saffron Walden became a Conservative stronghold. In one of the elections in 1910 William Fuller-Maitland was so inactive that it was rumoured, falsely, that he had withdrawn from politics altogether, and by 1911 Charles Gold had defected to the Conservatives, describing himself as a sheep that had strayed from the fold but had now found its way back.[1] The tag 'radical Stansted' was no longer to be heard.

This was reflected in local government. In 1894, at the first parish meeting under the Local Government Act of that year, there had been general satisfaction that, 11 candidates being nominated for the 11 seats on the Council, there was no need to call for a vote. There was also a widely held view that party politics had no part to play in local government. Councillors held office for three years and then had to stand for re-election. If there were more candidates than seats there was a vote by a show of hands at a general meeting, but if five electors asked for a poll it had to be held, even though it cost £25 of the ratepayers' money. As the Council attracted more interest there were several contested elections, and every now and then party politics raised its head.

The election that gave rise to the most excitement was in 1913. At the parish meeting in March there were 20 nominations for 11 seats, and it was noted that a leaflet had been sent round in advance on behalf of 11 of the candidates. The existing Council consisted of eight Conservatives and three Liberals, and the persons behind the leaflet – who were not named at the meeting but were condemned on all sides – wanted nothing less than a full slate of 11 Conservatives. When this was pointed out by one of the councillors the cry went up 'No politics'. William Fuller-Maitland, who was in the chair, agreed: 'We must have no politics …. It is only an election of the Parish Council tonight'. There was further disturbance when one of the candidates, Miss Ralphs, asked if she could address the meeting for five minutes on the cause of women's suffrage. In this respect local authorities were more advanced than Parliament. Before the 1894 Act single women were allowed to vote and to stand as candidates as long as they had sufficient property: under the Act this right was extended to married women. The people of Stansted were unsympathetic: Fuller-Maitland's refusal of Miss Ralphs's request met with applause.

There was then a show of hands and a list was drawn up of the 11 who had received the most votes. But each elector had been allowed to vote 11 times, which gave rise to some confusion, and five of the electors demanded a poll, a proposal which was met with 'booing and hissing' but which Fuller-Maitland had no alternative to granting.

The election was held on Monday, 7 April.

> *Lively proceedings attended the polling [reported the Observer] … the excitement being quite equal to that displayed at a Parliamentary election. For*

the first time ... party politics were introduced into the contest, with the result that whereas the constitution of the retiring Council consisted of eight Conservatives and three Liberal members, the new body is composed entirely of Conservatives. The poll was taken at the Central Hall ... and during the day Mrs. J.E. Walker, of the Friends' School, Saffron Walden, sold and distributed Women's suffrage literature in the parish. During the evening a good deal of amusement was caused by Miss Ralphs, the lady candidate, mounting a temporary platform outside the Central Hall and attempting to address the crowd which had assembled there. ... Miss Ralphs was unable to get a hearing and she had eventually to abandon the attempt.

Of the 575 voters on the parochial list 288 went to the poll. The most popular candidate, Gilbert Alder, who lived at Hargrave House, received 267 votes. Miss Ralphs came bottom of the poll with 40. Apart from women's suffrage there was no reporting in the press of the issues between the parties, if indeed there were any issues, but the result, said the *Observer*, 'occasioned an outbreak of enthusiasm among the supporters of the victorious candidates'.[2] It was indicative of the general attitude to the women Suffragists in Stansted that Miss Ralphs's attempts to address the crowd gave rise to 'a good deal of amusement' and that she had to abandon her attempts to get a hearing.

In 1884 squire Fuller-Maitland, who had ruled Miss Ralphs out of order at the parish meeting, had voted as an MP for Breconshire against women's suffrage.[3] In June 1904 a society had been formed in Saffron Walden to promote the cause of votes for women,[4] and a week later it had held a meeting in Stansted with a view to establishing an association in the village. Harford Green was in the chair and expressed his support, though he declared that he was not yet ready for women in Parliament. A visiting speaker, Miss Manning, spoke mainly about the experience of New Zealand and Australia, where the cause had made more progress, but confessed that she had not found 'a great deal of keenness' for women's suffrage in Stansted. A committee was formed, but we hear no more about it.[5]

After what seems to have been a period of inactivity, certainly so far as Stansted was concerned, a meeting was held in 1909 in the Central Hall under the auspices of the Saffron Walden society. The hall was crowded, the case was well argued, but still no local organisation was formed.[6] A year later, in the first general election of 1910, Suffragists throughout the Saffron Walden constituency stood outside the polling stations getting signatures to support their campaign.[7]

In the country as a whole the women's movement was divided between the Suffragists and the Suffragettes. The Suffragists wanted to promote their cause through legal and constitutional methods. The Suffragettes were prepared to break the law. At Saffron Walden it was the Suffragists who were in control, and in March 1910 they held another meeting in the Central Hall. They stressed their moderation. In spite of a constant buzz of conversation from the back of the hall the main speaker, Miss Bathurst, was 'particularly anxious to bring home to the men in that audience that women who were asking for the vote were not unfeminine and anxious to avoid the duties which their sex imposed on them. They were anxious to do those duties better. At this point there was considerable interruption at the lower end of the room and the President had to call for order.' In the end she asked the men at the back to leave: there was no point in their coming, she said, if they would not listen.[8]

Again there was no great flurry of activity, and two years passed before another meeting was held, again under the auspices of the Saffron Walden society, and again in the Central Hall. This was more successful. Two 'charming little plays' were produced by the Actresses' Franchise League, and the main speaker, Lady Meyer from Newport, stressed that her organisation was not militant and had nothing to do with party politics. She was well received, and the laughter this time was in response to her humour and not against her. But the press reports made no mention of anyone from Stansted taking part, and there was still no question of a Stansted branch being formed.

In the country the campaign was hotting up. The Suffragettes were smashing windows, and at the beginning of March 1912 Christabel Pankhurst, who had taken a leading part in organising this, fled the country to France to avoid arrest. It was against this background that the Saffron Walden society held a further meeting in Stansted. The speaker was the local President, Mrs. Baillie Weaver. She took great pains to dissociate the society from the window smashers and to stress its moderation, but she was constantly interrupted. 'Where's Christabel?' she was asked. 'What about the woman who tried to burn down the General Post Office?' The next speaker, Mrs. Bailey, declared that it used to be said that it was the duty of men to go out to work and the duty of women to stay at home: 'Quite right', said a heckler. 'That is their place.' And when Dr Coates, another speaker, asked if it was fair that men should make laws for women, 'Certainly', one man in the audience replied, 'women are told to love, honour and obey'. When Coates asked the interrupter if he was a married man she was asked in turn: 'How many Suffragettes are there who would like to get married?' Coates gave up in despair: it was difficult to speak, she said, with so many interruptions. Lady Meyer said, forlornly, that she hoped they had been able to stimulate some thought on the subject in the village, and she hoped – again a vain hope – that supporters in Stansted would form a branch of the Saffron Walden society.[9]

Although Harford Green had been sympathetic to the Suffragist cause, the local Liberals were now unhelpful, some even hostile. Both Suffragists and Suffragettes were seen as fair game. At a Liberal Social Evening in January 1913, among the 'capital entertainment' provided, a sketch entitled 'The Suffragette' 'caused great amusement'.[10] In a speech in Parliament Cecil Beck, the Liberal MP for Saffron Walden, was dismissive of women's suffrage.[11] When the football club put on a comic football match, Stansted Rovers vs Funnyoldies, a demonstration was made on the field by a supposed Suffragette armed with a hammer and parasol.[12]

Perhaps most revealing of local attitudes was a curious incident in June 1914. The press report leaves many questions unasked, but even as it stands it shows a striking degree of prejudice:

> *Supposed Visit of Suffragettes. A good deal of uneasiness has been felt at Stansted this week in connection with a supposed visit of Suffragettes to the Parish Church. Soon after dark on Monday evening Mr. Jolly, the sexton, saw a motor cycle and a lady's cycle standing in the road against the Church fence and heard a rustling noise among the shrubs near the Church. Suspecting that Suffragettes were about, he at once sent his son down to the village to inform*

the police and about fifty of the inhabitants immediately ran up to the Church and searched the immediate neighbourhood, but by that time the two bicycles had disappeared and no trace of them could be found. Had any Suffragettes been found they would undoubtedly have had a rough time. The Police and several of the parishioners remained in the vicinity of the Church that night, and they have been on duty there each evening this week.[13]

It seems extraordinary that, seeing a motor cycle and a lady's cycle against the fence and hearing a rustling noise in the bushes, Mr. Jolly did not form a more obvious suspicion. Perhaps he and his fellow parishioners were obsessed by the fear that the church windows might be broken.

With the outbreak of war just six weeks later both Suffragists and Suffragettes called off their campaigns. In 1918 women who were over 30 and met certain minimum property qualifications were given the vote, and in 1928 all women over 21 were placed on the same footing as men. Stansted's part in the struggle had been negligible.

1 *HEO*, 29 April 1911.
2 ISC, press cuttings from *HEO* on Parish Council meetings.
3 *The Times*, 13 June 1884.
4 *HEO*, 18 June 1904.
5 *HEO*, 25 June 1904.
6 *HEO*, 20 March 1909.
7 *HEO*, 29 January 1910.
8 *HEO*, 3 March 1910.
9 *HEO*, 16 March 1912.
10 *HEO*, 1 February 1913.
11 *HEO*, 10 May 1913.
12 *HEO*, 2 May 1914.
13 *HEO*, 20 June 1914.

27: THE CHURCHES: THE INDEPENDENT SCANDAL OF 1822

In May 1822, in a letter to a ministerial colleague, the Reverend William Chaplin, the pastor of Bishop's Stortford's Independent Church, described Stansted as 'that unfortunate village'. 'My heart bleeds over that place', he wrote, 'The souls of the faithful are cast down. The cause of the Redeemer suffers. The wicked laugh and triumph.'[1] The reason for Chaplin's distress was that the Independent Church of Stansted had been split apart by the so-called immorality of its newly appointed young minister, Josiah Redford. Some in the church condemned it. Others condoned it. For more than 100 years, since 1698, the church had met near the bottom of Chapel Hill where the Stansted Free Church still meets today. Now Redford was leading a breakaway church, and, financed by a public subscription, a new Meeting House was being built in the Great Newmarket Road, in what is now called Silver Street. Within two months it was completed, and Redford was overjoyed. 'This was the Lord's doing', he wrote later, 'and it was marvellous in all our eyes. Hallelujah! Praise the Lord!' But it was not marvellous in everyone's eyes, and William Chaplin described it, not as the Lord's doing, but as 'a public monument of disgrace brought upon the Dissenting cause'.[2]

One of the reasons for Chaplin's distress was that the split among the Independents, between what came to be known as the Old Meeting and the New Meeting, exposed them to the mockery and derision of the Anglicans. There had long been a simmering antagonism between the two churches, and it had boiled over in 1766 when a certain Mr. Robert Poole, encouraged, as the minister believed, by the vicar, dug a pit in the grounds of the meeting house on Chapel Hill as a forceful demonstration of his claim that the land belonged to him. The Independents took legal action, and Poole was 'compelled to relinquish his pretensions' and to make good the damage he had done.[3] Later this religious rivalry became an educational rivalry as well, with the Independents founding the British School in 1835 and the Anglicans the National School in 1838. In 1830 and 1831, as already related, there were also political divisions.

It seems, though, that in 1822 the Anglican vicar was not a powerful and vigorous presence. Richard Grant had been the incumbent since 1782. His monumental inscription in St. Mary's Church refers not only to his easiness of access and the great kindness of his manner, but also to the great energies of his mind, which he retained to the last. But the evidence points the other way. He rarely attended meetings of the vestry, the parish registers were so badly kept that parts had to be copied out again later, the tithe records were reduced to a few random jottings, and the church buildings fell into such a state of disrepair that within three years of his death in 1826 at the age of 82 they had to be substantially renovated.

The Independents in Stansted had always been strong, and 300-400 attended church. They were drawn from neighbouring villages as well as Stansted, and they included 30 members. They placed a high value on respectability, and their sermons, their letters and the church books of both Meetings reveal them as men and women of intense religious sensibility. One deacon at the Old Meeting, for example, signed off one of his letters 'beseeching the divine presence to direct and rest upon you and yours, Your humble servant ....' And the same man began his will: 'I desire to commit my immortal soul into the hands of a covenant God in Christ Jesus to be washed in the precious blood of Christ the eternal son of God to be made meet to be a partaker of the Saints in light'. The Anglicans, if they mentioned religion at all, were more restrained.

The Independents, or Congregationalists, were so called because each congregation was independent and not subject to any overall control, and this was to be an important issue in the events of 1822. They appointed their own ministers and they elected their own deacons, who normally represented them in matters of discipline and administration. For 17 years, however, from 1807 to 1824, the Old Meeting was without deacons. There were two services every Sunday, one in the morning and one in the evening, and the pattern of service was much the same as today. Then, as now, the high point was the sermon, and from 1827 onwards a selection of sermons was published annually in a little pocket book, *The Essex Congregational Remembrancer*. The titles alone convey the full weight and import of their listeners' concerns. In Stansted there were sermons on 'Mourners Comforted', 'Divine Forgiveness', and 'The Burdened Sinner Directed to Christ', and other titles included 'Satan's Malice defeated by Christ's Intercession', 'Continuance on Earth not desired by the Believer' and 'Memory the Source of the Sinner's Torment in Hell'.

In addition to their services they had prayer meetings, which were normally held on Sunday afternoons or on weekday evenings, and in the church books these were described as interesting, serious, delightful, encouraging (if many people attended) or refreshing (as in a time of refreshing in the Lord). They prayed for the divine blessing on their services, that 'backsliders' might be reclaimed, and that the Spirit of the Lord might be poured upon them from on high. They deplored the general desecration of the Lord's day, the spread of infidelity and, in 1831, the incendiarism of the Swing Riots. They also had a missionary society, founded in 1812, and they were caught up in the anti-slavery movement.

A Church Meeting was held once a month which only the members attended. As well as choosing their own ministers and deacons, they admitted candidates for membership. Entering the church was no formality. Normally the deacons would 'wait upon' the candidates and question them closely on their religious experience. In most cases they were satisfied and recommended acceptance, but in 1824, at a time when the Old Meeting was without deacons, one candidate was examined by the whole church, which rejected him, 'finding him ignorant of the great principles of salvation'.

The Church Meeting also dealt with cases of discipline, a responsibility that was taken very seriously. In 1813, for example, Robert Tyler was 'suspended from the Lord's Table', i.e. barred from Holy Communion, for cruelly beating his father. In 1823 Mrs. Gaffee was dismissed from membership after admitting that she had been guilty of the sin of fornication. (This was a particularly painful 'wound' because Mrs. Gaffee was the widow of a former minister.) And in 1834 John Munchall was solemnly excommunicated for profanely violating the Lord's day by selling goods secretly and by artifice.

After the death in 1818 of Benjamin Gaffee, their minister, the members had to find a replacement. As on similar occasions in the past, they approached the Evangelical Academy at Hoxton in London, whose Treasurer, Thomas Wilson, sent up a series of students who were just coming to the end of their training and who were looking for a ministerial appointment. They would preach for a few months, and the church would then decide if it wanted them. On this occasion the church was badly divided, and was wracked by what a later minister called ill will and angry feeling, but in the end everyone was agreed that the man they wanted was young Josiah Redford. So in October 1821, three years after Gaffee had died, Redford was appointed as the minister at a service at which five of the neighbouring ministers presided, including William Chaplin from Bishop's Stortford. At last the church's difficulties seemed resolved, and when, in January 1822, Redford went away for a few weeks to carry out a previous engagement in Bristol, he believed he was leaving the church 'in Unity and prosperity' - or so he said.

What happened after this is disputed, and there are two main accounts. The first was written by Redford later in the same year. The second was written by Robert May, Redford's successor at the Old Meeting.

Redford says that 'On his departure, it transpired that he had privately entered into a matrimonial engagement and connection with the younger daughter of Mr. John Tyler of Bentfield End'. This caused 'much dissatisfaction' among the members. On 24 January, while Redford was still in Bristol, he received 'a very condemnatory letter' from William Chaplin, the minister at Bishop's Stortford, and on 30 January the church met and passed a vote of suspension.

Robert May says that he would gladly draw a veil over Redford's 'most gross and scandalous behaviour', but 'This much ... is due to the cause of Truth and good morals ... that he was found to have been living in fornication at the very time of his Ordination'. This must obviously have been the charge, and in fact when Redford married Ann Tyler of Bentfield End, as we know from the baptism of their son in May, she was already several months pregnant.

Redford hurried back from Bristol, and on 3 February, a Sunday, assuming that the majority were against him, he publicly tendered his resignation. According to his own account, however, this turned out to be 'both premature, and quite contrary to the feelings of a large majority'. A petition was got up, signed by 27 of the 31 Members, and by 194 'attendants', condemning the severe measures taken against their 'beloved, & highly esteem'd Minister', and asking him to continue among them, if necessary, 'in some more humble spot'.

May's account is again different. He says that after Redford had admitted his 'criminality', 'It was deemed prudent, by neighbouring Ministers, and pious people in general, that he should be advised to leave the village'. But, says May, Redford would not listen: 'he ...was destitute of any personal property, and finding himself wrecked as to all prospect of rising in the esteem of the Religious public, he appears to have determined upon making one grand and powerful struggle for the possession of the Meeting House where he should continue to exercise his ministry'. He accused Redford of drumming up support by enlisting new subscribers who would vote for him at a decisive meeting which was about to be convened.

This meeting was to be held on the evening of Tuesday, 12 February, and two ministers from London were invited - Thomas Wilson, the treasurer of the Evangelical Academy, and John Clayton, who had been Redford's pastor in London. So Redford's opponents were wheeling in the heavy guns of the Independent establishment. Redford, on the other hand, was taking his stand on the strict principles of Independency, and argued that only church members could exercise discipline over the ministers. His supporters did not want any outsiders, and one of them publicly protested that the members had not invited Wilson and Clayton to the meeting and that the church was being deprived of its rights.

On the Tuesday evening the meeting house was packed. According to May, Redford had been 'mustering his newly enlisted forces in a neighbouring barn' beforehand, and when Clayton and Wilson arrived

Nothing could exceed the vexation and dismay which the hostile party displayed ... a mob in the galleries shouted out "Redford for ever!" and heaped upon [their opponents], especially the Visitors, the most opprobrious epithets. In vain did Mr. Clayton remind them of the awful impropriety of their behaviour; his voice was drowned by the ... rabble. At length, however, ... Mr. Redford came forward and finding that his plans were frustrated, he made a long harangue to the audience, occasionally cheered by the shouts of his party, and surrendered his pastoral office, together with the keys of the meeting house .... At the breaking up of the assembly nothing could exceed the riot and disorder that prevailed. Not content with abuse, the lives of many were threatened; stones, and other missiles were hurled against Mr. Redford's opponents, and one of the members of the Church ... was severely wounded in the face, others owing their escape to the protection of peace officers or to flight!!! Such alas! was the unhappy termination of Mr. Redford's ministry at the Old Meeting.

But May's account, though detailed and colourful, does not explain how it was that Redford's plans were frustrated and why he had to resign and hand over the keys of the meeting house. Redford's own account places a different construction on what happened. At the beginning of the meeting, he claims, his opponents produced their trump card - the original trust deed of the church. This showed, in Redford's words, that the power of decision was not vested, as it ought to have been in Independent churches, in the church members, but in the Trustees. And the Trustees were the Independent establishment, including several people from outside Stansted. According to Redford, the multitude begged him to stay, but his hand was forced, and he signed the paper.[4]

This may be correct, but in a private letter written two months later, on 25 April, Chaplin gave yet a different account. Redford, it seems, had made some confession, and his resignation, according to Chaplin, was 'universally understood' to be occasioned by the presence of Wilson and Clayton, and their determination 'to make some public communication if he did not give way'. And Clayton, in one of his letters to Chaplin, said he was 'possessed of more ample materials than Redford's own confession', which he had been prepared to produce had it been necessary.[5] If this is right, it was the fear of yet further public disgrace which forced Redford to give way.

Whatever the true explanation, this was only the beginning of the affair. Redford's supporters had already indicated that they wanted him to continue among them, if necessary, in some more humble spot. An old carpenter in the village, Guiver Sanders, offered a site in the great Newmarket Road, and that was where the New Meeting was established. 'The mischief', wrote Chaplin, 'is now in full force.'

Seventeen of the 31 members went with Redford, and many of the congregation. The

Old Meeting was left crippled, with no minister and its attendance sometimes reduced to a handful. Robert May was appointed a year later, and the Old Meeting gradually recovered. By 1828 it claimed to have about 300 'hearers', but the New Meeting claimed about 100 more. The local ministers continued to ostracize Redford, but May in turn had reason to complain of Redford's 'malevolence and repeated annoyances'. Occasionally there were moves towards reconciliation, but as long as Redford remained pastor of the New Meeting there was no real possibility of a reunion. The Independents of Stansted remained divided.

Disagreements were common in Dissenting Churches. The Anglicans jibed: 'Where look we for dissent but among Dissenters?' John Binfield, in his study of Nonconformity in East Anglia at this time, ascribes this to the fact that each congregation felt it was autonomous, that it could speak directly to the Lord and get guidance. There was an independence of spirit as well as organisation.

In this case the cause of the split was essentially the division of feeling over Redford's 'immorality'. But there appears to have been more to it than that. There was evidently strong local feeling, a resentment of interference from outside, especially from Stansted's big neighbour, Bishop's Stortford, and Redford, with his insistence on the strict principles of Independency, was able to exploit this. There was a fusion of morality and religious principle with more worldly sentiments.

Whatever the causes, as May wrote in 1833,

The sin and mischief which have resulted from this unhappy affair have been such as would scarcely be credited. Envy, bitterness, wrath, uncharitableness, and every evil work have grown out of it and now, at this distance of time, when it is beginning to appear in the light of an historical fact, and God has in great mercy begun to repair the breach, the Writer can with difficulty call to mind any schism in the Church of Christ which has been (ceteris paribus) a more fruitful source of evil.

The consequences were no more edifying. The New Meeting continued to be plagued by constant bickering, members were excommunicated and then reinstated. There were more allegations against Redford, the church book refers to litigation, and at one point a pistol was brought out and flourished. Redford's account of these happenings in the church book was later crossed out as being 'a tissue of falsehoods'. Eventually, after Redford left in 1844, a new minister was appointed, John White, but he did not give satisfaction either. In 1848 the members were asked why they wanted to get rid of him, and

The general feeling expressed, was, that no Spiritual edification was derived from Mr. White's sermons, his sermons being composed principally of texts of Scripture, in no wise bearing on the text announced. There was also something in his manner and mode of address and in his Pastoral visits, which was not in accordance with their feelings and wishes.

He refused to budge, a dispute broke out over control of the building, and there was more litigation. But this, the church book recorded with relief, was resolved by divine intervention: 'The Allwise disposer of all events delivered them from all fears, by his taking away by death the said Mr. J. White on May 26th 1851'.

27: THE CHURCHES: THE INDEPENDENT SCANDAL OF 1822

Not surprisingly, the number of adherents had fallen away sharply, and in March 1851, two months before White's death, it was reported that no services were being held in the morning or the afternoon and only 30 were attending the evening service.[6] In 1875, when the church was reformed as a Union Church of Baptists and Independents, there were only four members. This too met with little success, and in 1884 the building was handed over to the Old Meeting, which was now the Congregational Church, for the purposes of a Sunday School.

The New Meeting was no more, but the building still stands. It is a large, red-brick edifice standing back a few yards from the pavement. When I began this research some of the older people in the village still remembered going there to Sunday School. In 1934 it was sold to Joscelyne's, a large store in Bishop's Stortford, who used it for more than 50 years as a warehouse, 'Joscelyne's Depository'. Now it is occupied by several enterprises, such as the Mountfitchet Gallery and Leisure Plan. The style and grim ornament of the front, however – the arching pattern of the brickwork over the wooden doors with their Gothic hinges, and the small stained-glass squares in the lower windows - declare unmistakeably that it was once a Dissenting chapel.

59. The Independents' New Meeting House in Silver Street, which became the Sunday Schoolroom for the Congregational Church. This photo was taken in 1917 when it was being used for the armed forces by the YMCA.

1 DWL, L.52/4/44, Chaplin to Blackburn, 14 May 1822.
2 *Ibid.* Except where otherwise indicated, this chapter is based on the church books of the Old and New Meetings in the ERO, D/NC 2/1/1 and D/NC 2/2/1.
3 ERO, D/NC 2/1/1, p. 11.
4 I have not been able to trace the trust deed.
5 DWL, MS 201.41(h).118, Chaplin to Wilson, 25 April 1822.
6 NA, HO 129/139.

28: THE CHURCHES: ANGLICANS AND NONCONFORMISTS, HIGH AND LOW

Even a cursory glance at local newspapers in the Victorian period will indicate how important a part the churches played in the public life of rural communities throughout the country. For Stansted the *Herts and Essex Observer* carried detailed reports of activities and occasions such as Easter and Christmas services and Harvest Festivals, vestry meetings and clerical conferences, missionary gatherings, temperance rallies and Bible Society meetings, Sunday School anniversaries and treats and outings, feats of prolonged bell ringing, the comings and goings of the clergy, disputes over church rates and tithes, controversies between high church and low church, and the raising of funds for repairs, improvements and new buildings, sometimes by public subscriptions but also through concerts and entertainments which brought people together in a good cause and shared enjoyment. The churches also controlled most of the formal education in the parish, the Anglicans running the National School and the Independents and Quakers the British School.

In 1851 a national religious census was conducted, the central question being how many people had attended religious worship on Sunday, 30 March. At St. Mary's the vicar, Josias Torriano, reported that 332 attended the morning service with 73 Sunday

60. Primitive Methodist Church in the Cambridge Road, c.1890.

schoolchildren, and 330 the afternoon service with 76 Sunday schoolchildren. At the Old Meeting, which had now fully recovered, Daniel Davies, the Independent (or Congregational) minister, reported that 245 attended the morning service with 64 Sunday schoolchildren, 365 the afternoon service, again with 64 children, and 150 the evening service. We have already noted that at the New Meeting of the Independent Church there were no morning or afternoon services, and 30 attended in the evening. At the Society of Friends (the Quakers) Joshua Green reported that there were 28 attendants in the morning and 18 in the afternoon.[1]

In 1876 a Primitive Methodist Church was opened in the Cambridge Road. Although it had only 13 members at first, about 80 people attended services. By 1899 the membership had increased to 52, but after that there was a sharp decline. 'Camp Meetings', all-day, open-air mission meetings, were held both in Stansted and in the villages nearby, and the tenor of their appeal can be gauged from the texts on the side of the camping van – 'Be sure your sins will find you out. Flee from the wrath to come. He that believeth on me hath everlasting life. He that believeth not shall be damned. Christ died for the ungodly. Reader, are you saved or lost?'[2]

The fierce antagonism between church and chapel which embittered many other communities seems to have played little part in Victorian and Edwardian Stansted. We do not hear, for example, of Quaker and Independent tradesmen being boycotted by Anglican customers. On the contrary, the Greens, though Quakers, supplied many of the leading families in the parish, and Arthur Sanders, the Independent grocer in Lower Street, often provided food and drink for Anglican gatherings. The Anglicans had the assurance and confidence that derived from being part of the established church, and it was against this stance and tradition that the Nonconformists nurtured their own distinctive identity. The very name Dissenters implied a body of doctrine and practice from which they dissented. No doubt these divisions gave rise to animosity at times, but it is striking how often Anglicans and Dissenters worked together and shared the same platform, particularly on issues such as teetotalism and missionary work. The Greens and others contributed to the restoration of the parish church, and in 1891 Elizabeth, Joseph's wife, even contributed to the salary of the Anglican curate.[3] The leading residents of all denominations worked together to promote organisations that they believed were for the public good, such as the Literary Institution, the Bible Society and the Gas Company. There were bonds of personal affection too. When Canon Luard, the vicar, was ill, Joshua Green made a special point of declaring his admiration and friendship for him and his hopes for his recovery, while Luard contributed to a leaving present for Daniel Davies, the Congregational minister. No doubt the Fuller-Maitlands, with their Dissenting background, were in part responsible for this. As patrons of the living they appointed vicars who were, for the most part, low churchmen and for that reason would have been more in sympathy with Dissenters.

It might have been expected that there would have been outspoken hostility between the temperance movement and the directors of W & A Gilbey, but there is little evidence of this. In 1876 Henry Parry Gilbey, responding to a question about teetotalism, condemned the abuse of alcohol but was against total abstinence. Banning alcohol, he wrote on another occasion, only made drink more attractive.[4]

61. Daniel Davies, Congregational minister 1845-1883.

62. Eustace Long, Congregational minister 1884-1899.

63. Arthur Cook, Congregational minister 1900-1920.

Throughout the nineteenth century, and indeed to the present day, the Quakers maintained their Meeting House on Chapel Hill. If individuals left the community, such as Samuel Day and Alfred Hicks, it was usually because they had married an Anglican. The Quakers were never numerous, but they were influential, especially the Greens, and they enjoyed a network of local support based on the flourishing Quaker community in Saffron Walden. Descriptions of their meetings in the local press were always couched in terms of respectful interest, and even during the Boer War there appears to have been no overt criticism of their pacifism.

Meanwhile the Independent Church, which was renamed as the Congregational Church in or around 1869, was flourishing, and enjoyed mutually supportive relations with other Independent communities in the neighbourhood, such as those at Bishop's Stortford, Clavering and Newport. By the late 1870s the conflicts that had divided the church in the 1820s had at last been resolved, and the New Meeting House in Silver Street became the Sunday Schoolroom for the Old Meeting on Chapel Hill.

From 1844 to 1883 the minister was Daniel Davies. He enjoyed a happy relationship with his congregation. He was a strong supporter of the temperance movement and missionary work – his niece and adopted daughter married a minister from Newport, J.J.K. Hutchens, who went out as a missionary to Rarotonga – and he was heavily involved in Liberal Party activities. On his retirement a purse of £225 was presented to him, with contributions coming from all denominations.

In 1835, a decade before he began his ministry, an elementary school, known as the British School because it was set up under the auspices of the British and Foreign School Society, had been founded in a small schoolroom on Chapel Hill. It was mainly supported by the Nonconformist community, and in 1862, during Davies's ministry, a much larger building was erected next to the Independent Church. But the most striking visual monument to Davies's ministry was the new chapel, built in the 'Lombardo-Venetian' style and opened in 1864, to replace the old building that had served for so long. It cost £1,200, and it was a testimony to the vigour of the Independent cause that the debt was paid off within a few years.[5]

64. The Stansted Free Church, originally the Independent Church, next to what used to be the British School.

In 1884 Davies was succeeded by Eustace Long, who also enjoyed a long ministry, retiring in 1899. He followed very much in Davies's tradition, being a strong supporter of the temperance movement and an active Liberal. Long was followed by Arthur Cook, who was minister for 20 years, from 1900 to 1920. His services, we have been told, lasted an hour and a half, and his sermons a full half-hour, and one member of his congregation confessed to being bored.[6]

I have suggested that at the beginning of the nineteenth century the Church of England in Stansted, under the elderly William Grant, was sunk deep in lethargy. There was however a significant change in 1825 when a new organ was purchased for £125, no doubt replacing the old church band – the accounts record the sale of violincelli for £3.[7] When Grant died in 1827, aged 82, he was succeeded by Alan Gardner Cornwall, 'an earnest evangelical minister of the Clapham sect, brought up on intimate terms with William Wilberforce and Lord Macaulay, and well connected socially' – just the sort of vicar we might have expected Ebenezer Fuller-Maitland to choose. But, for whatever reason, Cornwall stayed only a year.[8]

He was succeeded by Josias Torriano (1828-51), who had been born in India in 1788 and had served as a captain in the Indian Army, but had then gone to Cambridge and entered the priesthood. He was described as an evangelical.[9] Almost at once he set about restoring the dilapidated church building, an essential undertaking, though he clearly went too far when he removed the pillars defining the north aisle and integrated that part of the church with the nave – a change which was reversed in the later restoration in 1888. We

28: THE CHURCHES: ANGLICANS AND NONCONFORMISTS, HIGH AND LOW

may also regret the removal of the carved stalls which until then had remained entire along the north side of the chancel and of a large pew with sliding lattice-work on the south for the use, it was said, of penitents.[10] It was perhaps at this time that the doorway shown in the centre of the 1756 picture of the church (illustration 27) was moved westwards to its present position.

In 1838 Torriano personally paid for the erection of a school in Lower Street, a development that will be described in more detail in the following chapter. Like most Anglican priests, he voted for the Tory candidate in the election of 1830, but he abstained from voting in 1831. In 1850, when the appointment of Nicholas Wiseman as cardinal and archbishop of Westminster was regarded as an act of 'papal aggression' and aroused fierce opposition, Torriano, together with William Fuller-Maitland, was among 1050 'Noblemen, Gentry and Clergy' who called on the High Sheriff of the County to convene a county meeting of protest.[11]

65. Thomas Luard, vicar 1851-86.

Torriano's successor, Thomas Luard (1851-86), also came from a wealthy background, and his generosity to the poor and to the parish was widely acknowledged and admired. He was conscientious and hard-working, and though 'very reserved' he enjoyed respect on every side and even affection. He was low church but not aggressively so. Together with his predecessor, Torriano, and while still a curate at Henham, he had signed the appeal to the High Sheriff of Essex to protest against 'papal aggression', and in the *Christian World* of 19 November 1885 he was classified as evangelical, as distinct from ritualist.[12] He was

66. St. Mary's Church, 2016.

particularly friendly in his relations with Nonconformists.[13] He took a strong line on drink, and was in the chair when the local Temperance Association was formed.[14]

In 1845, a few years before Luard became vicar, Stansted, together with several other Essex parishes, was transferred from the diocese of London to the diocese of Rochester, and in 1877 it was transferred from Rochester to St. Albans. In 1861 Luard was made a Rural Dean of Newport and in 1882 a Canon of St. Albans. His wife, Jane, who died in 1871, left £300 for a new organ in the church, which presumably replaced that which had been installed in the time of William Grant. After a ministry of 34 years Luard died in 1886. According to the *Christian Weekly News* he was 'greatly esteemed by the parishioners of all denominations',[15] and one of his successors, looking back on the history of the church in Stansted, referred to him as 'good Canon Luard'.[16]

One of the most contentious issues that Luard had to face was whether to renovate the old parish church, St. Mary's, which had fallen into disrepair since Torriano's restoration, or to build a new church in the centre of the village. This gave rise to strong feelings on both sides, and at the time of Luard's death no agreement had been reached. McKinney, the next vicar (1886-91), tackled the problem with the aid of a high-powered committee, and it was decided that both should be done. At St. Mary's the whole of the nave was taken down to the foundations and the north aisle was restored, the pillars between the nave and the north aisle being raised from the same foundations as the pillars that had been taken down in Torriano's restoration. This work was completed in 1888 and was paid for mainly with funds donated by wealthier parishioners, above all by William Fuller-Maitland and Henry Gilbey, who each donated £1,000.[17]

St. Mary's continued to be used as the parish church, but meanwhile, with the help of money provided by the Pulteneys, the new church of St. John's was built on Chapel Hill as a chapel of ease and was consecrated in 1889. The cost of maintaining two buildings, the difficulties of finding two sets of churchwardens and sidesmen, and the effort required to maintain two choirs, became a heavy burden on the parish for many years to come.

McKinney was popular and comparatively young, but left after a few years and went to Liverpool, mainly because he felt he had a calling to preach in a more deprived area. He also lacked Luard's financial resources and felt unable to meet all the expectations that were placed on him.

67. Alexander McKinney, vicar 1886-91.

It was after McKinney's departure, however, and the arrival of George Valentine that the church's troubles really began. So far Stansted had steered clear of the divisive low church/high church controversy. There had been the odd spat. Anonymous complainants to the press alleged that musical services were banned because they smacked of Roman Catholicism.[18] But feelings were running high. In 1899, at a meeting of the British and Foreign Bible Society, the Chairman, Harford Green, said that for more than 700 years religious controversy had 'not waxed so fiercely as it did now. They could not take up a secular newspaper, let alone a religious one, without being made aware of the fact that there was a tremendous conflict going on between different shades of religious opinion.'[19] It was against this background that George

Valentine became vicar of Stansted. He was about 55 years old, and he had been vicar at Holme-Eden, near Carlisle, for 22 years. He immediately established his evangelical credentials, and Joseph Green wrote later that when Valentine first came to the village his sympathies were 'very much with him as representing the evangelical and Protestant party in the Church'. He worked closely with Eustace Long, the Independent minister, and at one time they were holding special meetings for men on Sunday afternoons that were described as brief, bright and brotherly, when Moody and Sankey's hymns were sung.[20] In January 1899 a proposal to put a cross in the church at Bishop's Stortford aroused a storm of opposition. A meeting of the Protestant Reformation Society was held, and when Valentine spoke he declared that he was against not only the proposed cross but also the retention of the screen. What they required was 'the Reformation over again', and although it had been said that they should retain the screen, yet nevertheless it might be said that it was 'a relic of Romanism'. For that reason he would get rid of it.

> *Although it might be very beautiful that was the very danger of it - because it was so beautifully carved. He read in his Bible that Hezekiah, when he found the brazen serpent a lure to idolatry, had it ground to powder (Hear, hear). And so in regard to the screen he would say if it lured people away from the Reformation let it be burnt. He knew his views upon that subject were very different to those prevalent today, and the reason was that he had been brought up as a thorough Protestant.*[21]

With views such as these George Valentine inevitably clashed with those who were less evangelical, but he made matters worse by what were regarded as personal attacks from the pulpit on some of his more eminent parishioners. He was like the Puritans of an earlier generation, an 'uncomfortable preacher', ready to condemn looseness of morals wherever he saw it or even, it seems, heard rumours of it – but with this difference, that his attacks were often veiled rather than open, and this, coupled with the reluctance of the press to spell matters out, perhaps for fear of an action for libel, often makes it difficult for us to grasp what charges he was making and against whom he was making them. When he was challenged, he fell back on obfuscation and denial. Joseph Green, though supportive of the vicar's evangelical stance, was critical of him for introducing 'personal matters ... into the pulpit, a course which experience has long shown to be disastrous'. And he added darkly, 'Other controversial matters I will not allude to, but all tend to rupture'.[22]

The first recorded confrontation occurred at the Easter Vestry of 1892, within a year of Valentine's arrival at Stansted. Old Henry Trigg was retiring after 33 years' service as the vicar's churchwarden, and there was the question of who was to take his place. The vicar suggested Alfred Welch, but he refused on the ground that he was not in harmony with the vicar's religious views. Two others were proposed, but they refused as well. There were complaints about the way the Sunday School was being managed, there were concerns about a decline in the offertories, and there was anger about what Valentine was supposed to have said in the pulpit about the royal family. The Duke of Clarence had died recently, and Valentine had allegedly suggested that this might be regarded in many quarters as a divine judgement on the nation for the sins of the upper classes. He denied this, but the bad feeling aroused rankled for several years.

He had also made an attack on the English Church Union, a high church organisation which Welch supported, and Welch was indignant about what he saw as an assault on his religious convictions: 'I don't care a snap what you call me', he said, 'or if you call me a Roman Catholic'. Valentine retorted that if Welch was a Catholic – and he did not say that he was – then he ought to leave the church. 'If a person is in the Church of England and has at heart Roman Catholic principles, the sooner he goes to the Church of Rome the better.'

But this was a polite and mild-mannered disagreement compared with what happened in 1898. The church was falling increasingly into debt, and at the Easter Vestry it was decided to hold a public meeting to explore how this debt could be cleared. But before the meeting could be held Valentine preached two sermons on Sunday, 17 April, which infuriated his congregation. Some very unpleasant and scurrilous rumours were being spread abroad about three leading parishioners. What these rumours were and who the parishioners were is not clear, but we are told that the gossip was so vicious that no reasonable person could believe it to be true. It seems, however, that Valentine believed that there was something in it and in his sermons he alleged, without naming any names (though everyone knew who was being referred to), that attempts were being made to sweep things under the carpet. This caused great offence, and when the public meeting was held to discuss the deficit the vicar's sermons came under attack as well. The *Observer*'s headlines speak for themselves:

STANSTED, ESSEX. THE VICAR'S SERMONS AND LOCAL SCANDAL. INDIGNANT PARISHIONERS DEMAND APOLOGY. EXTRAORDINARY PROCEEDINGS. THE VICAR HISSED.

The meeting, which took place in the Central Hall, was packed. Fuller-Maitland took the chair, and all the leading parishioners were there. The proceedings were reported almost verbatim in the press. When Fuller-Maitland invited proposals for meeting the deficit, William Pimblett, a farmer at Bury Lodge Farm, proposed that the meeting should refuse to consider the question until Valentine had withdrawn and apologised for the observations made in his sermons on 17 April. This was seconded to great applause, and Henry Wood, a 'contractor', called upon the vicar to name the persons he was accusing. Fuller-Maitland asked the vicar to respond – 'I suppose, Mr. Valentine, you would wish to say something on the matter' – but the vicar said he had not heard what Wood said - 'he happens to be on the side I don't hear'. Wood repeated his challenge, and when Valentine denied making any charges Dr. Haynes contradicted him, saying that he had distinctly heard Valentine say that the alleged offences were being hushed up and that this was a scandal. Others corroborated what Haynes had said, and Thomas Newman, the head of an engineering firm, moved a resolution to loud applause declaring that Valentine was not a fit person to be vicar.

Valentine fell back on two lines of response. First, he stressed that he had not 'particularised' in any way. In other words, he had not named names. Second, he turned to his religion: 'I have discharged my duty to God and ... I am not to be judged by man's judgement. I have done that for which I shall have to give an account before the Lord at the last, and ... I am not afraid to appear before the Lord having made [these statements] in all sincerity for the welfare of the community .... And I considered it to be my duty as Vicar of the parish not to pass over such things as were being bandied about in the place.'

Haynes and others insisted that he should name the people he was accusing – that he should in fact 'particularise' – since otherwise they would all be under suspicion, and when Valentine refused the doctor stormed out. Valentine was then called upon to withdraw and apologise for his observations, but again he refused, and was hissed as he left the meeting.

Following this a petition was sent to Valentine asking him to resign, signed by well over 100 parishioners, including the Fuller-Maitlands, the Blyths, the Golds and the Greens. A copy was sent to the Bishop of St. Albans, but he said he had no power in the matter. Still Valentine refused to budge. Feelings became even more inflamed when someone, presumably one of Valentine's sympathisers, added comments to the petition that were insulting to the petitioners and hung it up by the church door and outside the house of the church clerk on Chapel Hill.[23]

The struggle was renewed in the following year, again at the Easter Vestry. The central issue was a deficit of £80 in the churchwardens' accounts. Pimblett put the question clearly: 'Why is it that the churchwardens can get no money in Stansted, which is a very rich place?' Newman asked who was responsible, which provoked another moment of farcical disrespect. Valentine 'didn't quite catch' what Newman had said. 'Come closer, Mr. Newman', Charles Spencer said, 'the poor chap's deaf'.

Having protested about this rudeness, Valentine once again tried to take the moral high ground. Could they not let bygones be bygones? 'I stand with a clear conscience before God and God is my judge.' There were cries of 'No sermons!', but Valentine ploughed on: 'And if I haven't a clear conscience I couldn't go before God in prayer. But I do and the Lord hears me and answers me.' To which Newman snappily retorted, 'But that don't settle this account!'

68. George Valentine, vicar 1891-1901.

There was another cause for complaint. The vicar now had an ally, Harold Smith, a low churchman who had agreed to be his churchwarden and who seems to have become as unpopular as the vicar himself. Valentine's well liked assistant, A.E. Tollemache – he was not formally a curate, but had offered to help the vicar at St. John's - had left the parish, apparently because Smith had criticised his conduct of services, and the choir at St. John's was refusing to continue. Smith was heavily criticised for the part he had played, but Valentine denied that he was in any way to blame – Smith had acted 'nobly' he said. He also denied driving anyone away himself - 'unless they go away because they don't like God's truth. I preach the word of God and keep to it.' He even compared his position in Stansted to that of Christ. He kept asking those around him to shake hands, but Charles Spencer said he would shake hands only on the day that Valentine left the parish.[24]

But Valentine took his time. It was October 1900 when he finally resigned, and December that year when he preached his last sermon. He retired to Somerset, and two years later he was dead. He was 69. William Fuller-Maitland and other 'friends' from Stansted sent wreaths, for which Mrs. Valentine expressed herself grateful.[25]

George Oakshott, the next vicar, was 32 and had been the curate at Great Hallingbury for two years. The transformation was immediate. Fuller-Maitland became his churchwarden, good relations were re-established with the leading parishioners, the Blyths and the Golds willingly served as sidesmen at St. Mary's, the money started flowing in, two new choirs were formed, the church's deficits were paid off, and Oakshott found there was so much work to do that he was soon asking for a second curate. The Easter Vestries were the occasions at which this happy progress was most celebrated and recorded. In 1903 the Easter offering for the vicar was a generous £71, and Maitland gave his 'warmest thanks' for all that Oakshott had done. 'He thought anybody who knew Stansted a few years ago must admit that a marvellous change had taken place.'[26] In the same year, 1903, the number of communicants on Easter Day was 315; by the following year it had risen to 365, in 1905 it was 388 and in 1906 430. Sometimes congregations were so large that there were difficulties in seating everyone.[27] Oakshott warned against measuring success purely in terms of numbers, but they were indicative of a new and harmonious spirit.

Oakshott's vigour and energy were poured into new initiatives. As recounted already, on Easter Monday 1903, after a lapse of 14 years, the old custom of having a Friendly Societies' Church Parade was revived. He also started the parish magazine, with a leading article by himself each month.

Unlike his Congregationalist counterparts, Oakshott did not play a prominent political role, though we have seen how he threw his weight against the proposal to transfer Stansted and other parishes to Hertfordshire. He did not like the Education Act of 1902, which stipulated that all schools should be supported out of the rates and he was afraid that this would weaken the Church's control, but his opposition was muted, since he had to recognise that throughout the country as a whole 'Church people' had not supported the schools as they ought to have done. As a loyal Englishman, he said, he had to make the best of it.[28]

69. George Oakshott, vicar, 1901-8.

70. Augustus Manley Winter, vicar 1909-15.

In church politics, however, he was always mindful of the mistakes made by his predecessor. In terms of high and low church he seems to have been middle of the road. He was strongly critical of the Roman Catholic Church, and he condemned the 'misdirected zeal' of those who were high church Anglicans.[29] But he was critical of low churchmen too, and in 1903, when leaflets entitled 'Why Am I a Protestant?' were circulated around the parish – the sort of propaganda of which George Valentine would no doubt have approved - he dismissed them contemptuously as 'foolish literature' designed to stir up strife.[30] In 1902, at the funeral service of Evelyn Fuller-Maitland, William's wife, he made use of a processional cross, which was what she had asked for, and, partly in commemoration of her, he wanted to introduce it for other services. He knew that he would have to approach this cautiously. 'You all know', he wrote in the parish magazine, 'how very very careful we have been, since I came here, that nothing in Church should be "a cause of offence", and your confidence in me shall not be misplaced.' He got his way, apparently without any trouble or opposition.[31]

In 1905, however, complaining that for three years he had been 'exposed to a continuous persecution, while in the pulpit of the Parish Church', and that his private remonstrances had failed, he issued a warning in the Parish Magazine that he would initiate legal proceedings and asked his readers for support.[32] What this related to I have been unable to discover. No proceedings followed.

More seriously, his ministry was undermined by his poor health. As early as 1902 he had to take a long break in the Canary Islands, and in 1908 he resigned. His place was taken by Augustus Manley Winter, whose ministry was relatively uneventful. He was happy in his work and in his relations with his congregation, the squire served as his churchwarden, and the church finances gave no cause for concern. It was during his ministry, in 1914, that the parish was transferred to the newly created diocese of Chelmsford. When WW1 broke out Winter supported the war effort, encouraging volunteers to come forward, but was not especially prominent. In September 1915 he exchanged churches with Ethelbert Goodchild, the vicar of Stokesay in Shropshire.

1 NA, HO 129/139.
2 Ralph Phillips, 'The Primitive Methodist Connexion', n.d.
3 ERO, T/P 68/17/2.
4 *HEO*, 11 March 1876, 10 January 1880. See also Kidd (1997: 43).
5 *HEO*, 18 January 1868.
6 SMLHS, Interview with William Bunting, 11 March 1987, p. 14.
7 ERO, D/P 109/8/5, 5 October 1825.
8 As rector of Owlpen and Bagpath he wrote memoirs which have been described as 'a valuable social history' and can be read on the internet.
9 DWL, New College MSS, 297/5, May to Wilson, 10 December 1828.
10 *HEO*, 19 September 1863 and 16 June 1888; *SMPM*, June 1938.
11 *CC*, 22 and 29 November 1850.
12 ERO, T/P 68/36/2.
13 See, e.g., *HEO*, 10 August 1861 and 14 July 1866.
14 *CC*, 13 April 1855, and *HEO*, 28 November 1862.
15 *Christian Weekly News*, 15 January 1886.
16 *SMPM*, June 1902.
17 For full details, see ERO, T/P 28/36/2.
18 Letters in *HEO*, 4 and 18 August 1878.
19 *HEO*, 13 May 1899.
20 *HEO*, 25 February and 18 March 1899.
21 *HEO*, 14 January 1899.
22 *HEO*, 22 April 1899.
23 *HEO*, 20 April 1898, 7, 21 and 28 May 1898.
24 *HEO*, 8 April 1899.
25 *HEO*, 26 April 1902.
26 *HEO*, 18 April 1903.
27 *SMPM*, July 1905.
28 *SMPM*, June 1902 and March and December 1903.
29 *SMPM*, July 1904.
30 *SMPM*, January 1903.
31 *SMPM*, June 1902.
32 *SMPM*, July 1905.

29: THE SCHOOLS

Before the Victorian period educational provision in Stansted was patchy and its results poor. The children of the gentry and some wealthy parishioners went away to boarding schools or were taught by tutors at home. In 1811 there were several private schools, among them, as noted already, the establishment run by Mordaunt White and his wife, which catered for 35 boys and 44 girls. In 1832, just over 20 years later, three 'academies and schools', boarding and day, were listed in *Pigot's Directory* – Mary Murray's, Welsh's Charity School for girls, and Mordaunt White's school, which was now just for boys. Murray's and White's establishments no doubt catered for the children of the more well-to-do farmers, tradesmen and craftsmen, and Welsh's might have reached out to some of the poorer parishioners. There must also have been humble dame schools that *Pigot's* did not deem worthy of mention.

At that time there was no great enthusiasm for the education of the poor. It was widely held that teaching them to read and write would give them ideas above their station. As one visiting speaker in Stansted said later, looking back to this time, there were fears that it would give rise to political disturbances, 'habits of irreverence and want of submission'.[1] But gradually the idea took hold that children should be instructed in the Word of God and should be able to read it, and that an elementary education would benefit both those who received it and society at large. In 1811 the Anglicans founded the National Society for the Promotion of the Education of the Poor in the Principles of the Established Church, and in 1814 the British and Foreign School Society was established, formally undenominational but in fact drawing most of its support from Nonconformists. In due course both societies received grants from the state which they spent on founding and supporting schools throughout the country. By 1851 there were 17,000 National Schools and 1,500 British Schools. While the two societies were sometimes in conflict, they both agreed on one thing – that elementary education was essentially a religious enterprise, and that apart from giving them cash the state should have nothing to do with it.

In Stansted it was the Independents who moved first. In 1829 some 'benevolent persons … [feeling] the need of a school for the benefit of the poor, established on liberal and unsectarian principles', set up what they called The Free School of Industry,[2] though it is not mentioned as such in *Pigot's Directory*. This was held in the chapel vestry, and in 1835 it was developed as the British School, fully established upon the principles of the British and Foreign School Society. In 1862 it was moved to larger premises, still on Chapel Hill, on land donated by William Fuller-Maitland.

In 1838, the Anglicans founded a school in Lower Street with the aid of money given by the vicar, Josias Torriano, on land made available on a long lease by Ebenezer Fuller-Maitland. This school had its origins in a charity school, but a stronger organisation was now needed. If nothing else, the Church of England could not afford to be seen to be neglecting its children's education when the Dissenters had built their schoolroom just three years before. The new school was commonly known as the National School because it was conducted under the auspices of the National School Society, and it accommodated 250 children.

Both the British School and the National School were financed by school fees, usually a penny per pupil per week, by grants from their parent societies (which were in turn supported by grants from the state), and by generous support from their local patrons, and they were each run by a board of managers controlled in effect by the churches. There were still some small independent schools for children whose parents did not want to send them to the village schools.

The extension of the franchise gave an added impetus to the need for more education and so did the need to build up a literate and numerate workforce to maintain Britain's industrial supremacy. In 1870 Forster's celebrated Education Act made the provision of elementary education compulsory, and in parishes which did not make adequate provision the state could establish a Board School, i.e. a school run by a board of elected ratepayers, to fill the gap. A further Act in 1880 made school attendance compulsory to at least the age of 10, and this age was raised to 11 in 1893 and to 12 in 1899. At this stage Stansted had no need of a Board School, since the British and the National Schools provided all the education that was needed. In 1891 fees were abolished and schooling was then free.

By 1902 many of the voluntary schools were in financial difficulties and the Education Act of that year therefore made provision for rate funding for secular education in those schools. Many Anglicans, such as Stansted's vicar, George Oakshott, were worried about this because of the potential for more ratepayers' control, but they had to face up to the unwelcome fact that many church schools were being replaced by Board Schools because they could no longer pay for themselves. Nonconformists had even more cause for complaint, because so many more Anglican than British schools were now being supported from the rates. Under another provision of the Act school boards were replaced by local authorities acting as Local Education Authorities, and these LEAs were allowed to provide secondary education.

In Stansted the crunch came in 1909, when the British School could keep going no longer. Expensive repairs had been carried out, but more accommodation was needed and the money was not there. In 1912 the school was transferred to the Essex County Council acting as an LEA, which duly erected the new buildings that were needed, providing a separate department for girls and infants. After this most children in the village went either to the 'Church School' in Lower Street or to the enlarged 'Council School' on Chapel Hill.[3]

In spite of the resistance of the churches the state had assumed increasing control over the schools. In 1862, as part of this process, it issued a code of practice which made grants dependent on the students' performance in an annual examination of the three Rs, plus a satisfactory level of attendance. From 1867 additional grants, 'subject grants', could be given for English grammar, geography and history.

The code also made it compulsory for each Head Teacher to keep a log book. At Stansted the earliest log books of the British School can no longer be traced, but for the National School two sets of log books, one for the infants school and one for the mixed school, are now preserved in the Essex Record Office.[4] As well as an account of the school's activities as seen by the Head Teachers, they give many insights into the life of

29: THE SCHOOLS

the village outside the school. The rest of this chapter is devoted mainly to a study of the first log books of the mixed school, with occasional references to the first log book of the infants school. (Later log books in the ERO will not be open to the public until 100 years after their last entry.)

The first entry is dated 2 March 1863: 'This day marks the commencement of the New Code in this School'. The last is dated 22 January 1901: 'Death of Her Most Gracious Majesty Queen Victoria'. In the 1860s there were about 80 children in the mixed school, divided into six classes, and about the same number in the infants. By the time of the Queen's death there were about 180 in the mixed school and about 130 in the infants.

The number of teachers varied, but normally there was a Head Master of the mixed school, whose wife would be the Head Mistress in the infants school and would teach the girls needlework. The Head Master was helped by an Assistant Teacher and two Pupil Teachers, i.e. teachers whose own schooling had just ended, but who continued to be given lessons and who gave lessons as well. They were really apprentice teachers. If and when they passed their exams they could go on to be trained as Assistant Teachers, often in places very distant from Stansted. Teaching was a mobile profession, and there was a constant procession of Pupil Teachers and Assistant Teachers. The Assistant Teachers were often women, but men were thought to have 'more teaching power'.[5] There were also monitors, schoolchildren themselves, who helped with the teaching.

The first Head Teacher under the Code was John Bourne, who was described as weak in both teaching and discipline. The visits of the Inspectors, which generally took place in February or March, clearly put him into a state of agitation. In January 1864, for example, he noted that one class would need 'an easy book to read out of at the coming inspection'. But it made no difference: the Inspectors judged that he should acquire more power of discipline and management, and after further adverse reports in 1865 and 1866 he was given his notice.

Bourne's replacement, Joseph Smart, was dismayed by what he found. In October 1866 he regretted to state 'that the Discipline of the School seems to be of the lowest kind. The children seem to do everything with as much noise as possible, and instruction and general conduct of classes by the Teachers betray a thorough absence of all knowledge of teaching and keeping order.' Smart turned the school around, and in 1867 the Inspectors noted a big improvement: 'Order and instruction in this school are very satisfactory'.

Smart, however, retired in 1868, and he and his wife were replaced after a short interval by Henry Douglas and his wife, who ran the school for more than 30 years. During this period the Inspectors' reports were satisfactory on the whole, though towards the end Douglas's health began to fail and they became more critical. He retired in 1902, but his wife continued after his retirement.

Throughout this period the school was controlled by a Board of Managers, usually about four or five in number, most of them being local farmers and tradesmen who were pillars of the Anglican Church. The most important was the vicar, who was the 'corresponding manager', i.e. the manager who corresponded with the National Society and with the Inspectorate. For most of the period covered by the first log book the vicar was Thomas Luard, and he and his successors kept a close and watchful eye on the school. The log book records many visits by them and their curates, while their wives mainly visited the infants school. They often took scripture lessons, and Luard in particular would test the children's reading and his wife would look at the needlework. Sometimes the Luards brought their friends, or other leading members of the church, who would also inspect the children's work or hear them sing. Sometimes they gave prizes for needlework or attendance. Whenever there were problems over equipment, the buildings or discipline Luard was referred to (or his wife, if girls were involved). The impression given is of a supportive and involved community: the Church School was their school, and as churchmen and churchwomen they took responsibility for it. They also raised funds for it by organising entertainments, which were well supported by the parents, while the teachers organised entertainments by the children.

The subscriptions made by these local supporters were crucial for the school's finances. In the year ending March 1885, for instance, receipts amounted to £350. Of this sum £180 came from the Government grant, £81 from school pence and stationery sold (i.e. from school fees and purchases by parents), £74 from subscriptions by 24 donors and £15 from church offertories. On top of this the school treat cost £17, which was paid for by donations. Luard was personally generous. In 1883, for example, he paid £50 of the £93 that was needed for a new fence, and in most years the school treat was held in the vicarage gardens. Even so the National Society was not always satisfied with the level of subscriptions. In January 1898, for example, it expressed the hope that more would be forthcoming.

The children were expected to bring in their pence on Mondays, but some fell seriously behind with their payments. There were the usual delinquents, such as the little boy in 1866 who spent his money in a shop on the way to school. The children had to buy their own pencils and pens and if a slate was broken 2d. had to be paid for it to be replaced. Parents also had to pay for copybooks, which some of them were reluctant to do. In 1891, when school fees were abolished, Douglas noted that attendance improved.

The school buildings in Lower Street, which are still standing, were added to over the years. At first there was one room for the infants and one for the mixed school, and they were separated only by a partition, to which a thick baize curtain was later added. Another room was added for the mixed school in 1871, and the two lowest classes were put there, while the top four classes stayed in the main room. There were constant complaints over the years about overcrowding, and the Inspectors repeatedly demanded improvements.

The rooms were heated by stoves, which every now and then caused trouble, belching out filthy black smoke, and the local blacksmith had to be called in to mend them. Fires were started late in the year, usually at the end of October or early in November. The dates when they were stopped were not recorded, but on 6 March 1867 it was noted that they had to be resumed because of a return of cold weather.

There was no caretaker, and the children did some of the caretaking work themselves. The girls cleaned out the school and swept the yard, and one girl had the duty of lighting the stoves, for which she was paid. Occasionally complaints were made about the condition of the toilets. In July 1863 boys were sent to fetch two bushels of lime to throw into the closets.

If the weather was fine the children were taken outside to be taught in the playground or on the hill above the school. School dinners were not provided: the children either brought their own or went back home to eat.

School hours were from 9 to 12 in the morning and from 2 to 4.15 in the afternoon, or

29: THE SCHOOLS

from 1.45 to 4 in the winter. The times when children joined and left the school were not always fixed by the terms. Some left, to Douglas's regret if they were bright, as soon as they became old enough to go to work, even if it was in the middle of a term, and many joined in mid-term as well. Some children did not go to school full time: in May 1875 Douglas recorded that he 'Admitted two half-timers from Mr. Gosling's brickyard'. During the winter there was a Night School for about 20 boys, who in 1878 were paying 2d. a week each for two nights' instruction in writing, spelling and arithmetic.

The six classes in the mixed school were each under the direction of a teacher or monitor. The education was basic – reading, writing and arithmetic forming the core, with geography, history, drawing, singing and religious education, and also needlework for the girls. In 1873 the oldest children were reading Robinson Crusoe, and for the inspections they recited poems. Both teachers and inspectors criticised the reading for its want of life and intelligence. In April 1880 Douglas 'ordered that every endeavour should be used to get the children to read more intelligently. The peculiar way of talking in the neighbourhood seems to affect the Reading making it a complete drawl.' The writing was usually described as fair, and so was the arithmetic, though one of the biggest difficulties was to get the children to stop using their fingers. Geography was admirably global, but history was almost entirely British and no doubt nourished the patriotism that was so important to the leaders of the parish.

Religious education was central – in the eyes of many it was the main reason for having a school at all - and from 1873 an examination in religious knowledge was held each year by a neighbouring pastor. The children were tested in scripture, the catechism and the liturgy, and always won glowing reports. On Fridays there was singing in church in preparation for the Sunday service, which they were expected to attend.

Discipline was strict. At first the children had to sit with their arms folded, but in 1866 Bourne made them sit 'with hands behind' instead. They marched in and out of class rooms, saluting as they left the room, and they had to curtsy and bow to the teachers. There were the usual offences, such as throwing stones, copying from the work of other children, blocking up the drain in the ditch, the occasional theft (especially of dinners), breaking windows (for which they had to pay), swearing and saying 'evil words'. In 1863 a boy was made to apologise for being rude to Mrs. Luard in church. Punishments were also meted out for bad behaviour in the streets.

The vicar and his wife were sometimes called in to impress upon the children the seriousness of their misdemeanours. In January 1871, when the new classroom was being built, a serious accusation was made against Alice Levey, one of the monitors, and found to be true, that 'she had been in secret company with one of the men working at the new class-room'. She was sent with a note to Mrs. Luard and received 'a severe reprimand', while the vicar reprimanded the man. In February 1867 Eliza Banks was 'very rude' and it was found that she had been 'busy in teaching her rudeness to two other girls'. When she was called before Mrs. Luard she confessed what she had done, and she was punished and expelled for 'very disgraceful conduct'. In the same month Luard and the Head Teacher, Smart, punished five boys severely, since 'there was not the slightest doubt that the boys had behaved in the grossest possible manner' - which did not stop two of the girls, one a Pupil Teacher, from sending the boys Valentines a few days later.

The punishments given were rarely specified, and they must have varied according to the severity of the offence. Children were sent home for bad behaviour, and in the worst cases expelled. Caning must have been a common punishment for the boys, and we know that in March 1880 one boy was given 'a sound caning' for theft. Sometimes parents wanted their children punished, and in one case at least they brought two of their boys to school for this purpose. But others protested. Pupil Teachers and even Assistant Teachers were sometimes disciplined for hitting children in the playground. On one occasion Douglas

Dismissed the Kerry family from the school. Through the mother abusing Mrs. Douglas for correcting one of her children at the Sewing Lesson. She said "She was not going to have her children corrected by any one in the School. That she sent them with their pence to keep Mrs. D and self and that we were the servants of all the poor persons in the parish", etc. etc. etc.

There was also a hidden social curriculum. Joseph Arch, of the National Agricultural Labourers' Union, attacked rural schools and Sunday Schools 'where the children of the poor were taught to submit themselves lowly and reverently to their betters, and to bow and scrape to the moneyed lords of the soil'. The curtsies and the bows to the teachers at Stansted were no doubt due to the vicar and the squire and their wives as well. How much this was resented is difficult to tell.

Over and above the education given, however, there were advantages in going to the Church School. In the earlier period Mrs. Luard handed out bonnets and capes in May for the summer, and in October the girls were given cloaks for the winter. Brent's gifts, one of the parish charities, were given out at Christmas and it was Douglas who prepared 'Brent's Charity list'.

The main holidays were five weeks in summer for the harvest, from the first week in August to the second week in September, and a week at Easter and a week at Christmas. There were other religious holidays – Ash Wednesday and Whit Monday – and later bank holidays as well. Holidays were given after inspections, and sometimes Mrs. Fuller-Maitland would ask for a half-day holiday after handing out prizes. The school was closed when there were national celebrations, such as the marriage of the Prince of Wales in March 1863, and when the Prince and his wife passed through Stansted station a few days later the children were allowed to go and wave to the train. Sometimes they went on their own initiative. On 10 December 1889, when the Prince of Wales went to visit Walter Gilbey at Elsenham, several children stayed away from school to catch a glimpse of him. On 25 April 1881 no school was held on account of the marriage of William Fuller-Maitland to Evelyn Gardner.

Naturally there was no school when the school treat was held, but sometimes children stayed away for other treats. Some went to the British School treat, and in 1864 they even stayed away when there was a Temperance Tea Meeting. On 23 October 1895 there was a poor attendance because of a bazaar at the Independent Church.

The weather wreaked havoc with attendance. Snow kept many away, especially children who lived at a distance. On 19 January 1881, after one of the heaviest snowstorms for 50 years, only six children attended. Roads were impassable, and in some places the snow lay five to six feet deep. Many stayed away when the weather was cold. At the beginning of 1879 the school was almost empty for a whole week because of the freezing weather.

29: THE SCHOOLS

Heavy rain had the same effect. On 13 November 1866, for example: 'Very wet morning indeed, only 20 present'. And on the same day, coincidentally: 'Found that several stopped at home in the afternoon to be ready to attend the Magic Lantern entertainment at night'.

For many parents and children the five weeks allowed for the harvest holiday were not enough. If the harvest began early many children stayed away to look after younger brothers and sisters so that their parents could go harvesting, and almost every year many were away gleaning when the school reopened. In some years children stayed away for the hay-making in June, and for some picking acorns for pigs was more important than going to school in October and November. In 1864 and 1867 some children stayed away in the spring peeling osiers or picking stones. Sometimes they were engaged in fetching coals. In at least two years, 1867 and 1868, some girls stayed at home to help their mothers with the washing. Others stayed away in anticipation of holidays, or after them, since their parents did not think it worthwhile to send them to school and to pay their pennies for part of a week.

In October 1872 the Infants Log Book recorded that many children from Burton End would not be coming to school until the spring because the distance was too great, which was a 'severe drawback' to their education since they forgot nearly all they had learned during the summer. In January 1899 in the same Log Book it was noted that several children would now be absent for some months since their parents were leaving for London 'with the various families in whose employ they are'.

Often the reason for absence was pleasure rather than work. On Guy Fawkes Day children went round the village with their Guy collecting money and on Valentine's Day they went round singing songs. In one year, 1889, they sang songs on Royal Oak Day. They would also go off to Bishop's Stortford to see the circus making its colourful procession through the streets, and boys would go to watch cricket matches there. Some children slipped away to the fairs at Stortford and Ugley, but most of all of course they went to the fair at Stansted, which was held at the beginning of May and virtually emptied the school every year. On 29 April 1864 attendance was 'low in prospect of the fair next week' and on the days of the fair the school rooms were 'almost empty'. The average attendance for that week was 16, compared with over 70 normally. As railway excursions became more popular they also affected attendance.

Sometimes children stayed away for apparently no reason at all. In 1867 Smart regretted to state that 'It is evident that the Parents care little about Education. Children are kept away upon the slightest excuse or rather without any excuse at all.' In 1886, almost 20 years later, Douglas made the same complaint: 'Lately several children have absented themselves upon most paltry excuses'.

After 1880 attendance was compulsory, and School Attendance Officers were appointed to enforce it. But only the most hardened and persistent offenders were ever taken to court, and the log books show clearly that absenteeism remained a problem.

There was one reason for absence, however, that took precedence over every other consideration, and that was illness. Health and cleanliness were constant worries. Children were repeatedly told to come to school cleaner, and some were sent home if they were not clean enough, particularly if they had lice in their hair. In April 1870 a child was sent home because he or she had ringworm.

Colds and flu were of course common, and on two occasions, in January 1867 and January 1879, there are references to children being away because of chilblains. Presumably their toes were so swollen that they could not get their boots on.

Smallpox was no longer the great killer it had been in the 18th century. In October 1864 it was found on inspection that out of 170 children (in the infants as well as the mixed school) only 14 were not vaccinated. Mumps was still dangerous and so was whooping cough. Chickenpox was mentioned only once, in July 1870. Measles was common and was sometimes so severe that the school had to be closed, and in December 1872 only 30 children were present. In November 1896 the Managers decided to close the school for a week, and when it reopened there was a very small attendance.

In the summer of 1894 measles coincided with scarlet fever, which was much more serious. Half the children were away on 5 June, and then it became so bad that the medical authorities closed down the school for five weeks. People were scared of it: in November 1869, for example, 'Several children away because of the menace of Scarletina'. In January 1885 some children were sent home to stop the illness spreading.

But the worst menace was diphtheria, as shown by the following entries:

4 December 1876.   *Eliza Patmore died of the diphtheria which is very prevalent in the parish.*

11 December 1876.   *The diphtheria is still on the increase. Little Tom Levey and Ellen Patmore taken with it.*

13 December 1876.   *Death of Tom Levey from the disease prevalent in the village.*

14 December 1876.   *Ellen Patmore died of the disease so prevalent in the parish.*

21 December 1876.   *Broke up the school for Christmas holidays.*

1 January 1877.   *Reopened school. .... Diphtheria on the increase still. The whole family of Snows suffering from it.*

5 January 1877.   *The family of Ratcliffs in Woodfield, Ratcliff in the Street, Smiths of Bentfield End taken with the diphtheria.*

10 January 1877.   *Little Annie Ratcliff died this morning of the disease, this making the fourth child belonging to these Schools who have succumbed to the epidemic.*

16 January 1877.   *Little Harry Ratcliff died this morning of diphtheria ....*

19 January 1877.   *School much thinner today on account of the sickness. The family of Corbys taken with it. Another death in the Ratcliff family, and one in Sanders.*

26 January 1877.   *The attendance of the School improving. The Epidemic abating.*

16 February 1877.   *The attendance this week has been better. The sickness in the parish disappearing.*

Only nine months later, in November 1877, diphtheria broke out again. Three children died and school was closed for a week while the buildings were 'thoroughly disinfected, coloured and cleaned'. One of the last entries in December 1900 records a further outbreak of diphtheria in the village.

29: THE SCHOOLS

In the absence of the earliest log books much less is known about the British School on Chapel Hill. In the papers collected by Joseph Green, however, there is the minute book of the Managers' meeting, beginning in 1861.[6] It is striking how strongly the Quakers were represented, at least in the early days. At the first meeting, on 18 August 1861, eight men were present, five of whom can be identified as Quakers - Joshua Green, James Marsh and three members of the Hicks family.

The British School had the same arrangement as the National School, in that it usually employed a husband and wife team, with the wife looking after the infants – though at one time there was a brother and sister team. No doubt the Independent minister played much the same role in the British School as the vicar in the National School.

The school was subject to Government inspection in the same way as the National School, and occasionally the Inspectors' reports were quoted in the local press. They were almost invariably favourable, but the report which catches our interest most does so, not because of its content, which was fairly bland – the examination was 'very satisfactory' and the Head Teacher had 'brought this school to a high point of efficiency' - but because the Inspector was the great poet and critic, Matthew Arnold.[7]

Similarly favourable reports were given in 1890, when Mr. Bradford was the Head Master, and in 1891, by which time John Woolley had taken over.[8] Woolley was to remain in post until the 1920s, and his daughter Irene became a teacher in the same school. The increasing pressure on the school, which led to its transfer to the Essex County Council in 1912, is reflected in the number of pupils. In June 1867 81 children were on the books. In 1909, when the crisis struck, there were 212 children on the books but accommodation for only 185. By comparison the National School had 233 children on the books and accommodation for 267.[9]

71. This photo of the British School infants is said to have been taken c.1905. The teacher is said to be Miss Woolley. See Paul Embleton (1998: 128).

1. *CC*, 7 November 1862.
2. *HEO*, 8 November 1862: speech by Rev. D Davies at 'opening of the new British Schools'. See also *House of Commons papers, volume 41, Abstract of Education Returns 1833.*
3. Jane Freeman's article in *The Link*, June 1983.
4. The infants school log book is ERO, E/ML 307/1, and the mixed school log book is ERO, E/ML 308/1.
5. ERO, E/ML 308/1, 2-3 December 1870.
6. ERO, T/P 68/21/6.
7. *HEO*, 18 June 1870.
8. *HEO*, 15 May 1890 and 20 June 1891.
9. *HEO*, 31 July 1909.

30: FROM EDUCATION TO ENTERTAINMENT

For the leading families and the emerging middle classes Stansted's economic growth was matched by its rich and varied cultural life, ranging from high-minded lectures and ambitious concerts to popular entertainments in aid of good causes. For the labourers there were not only the songs and sociability of the public house, but also penny readings in the 1860s, and at every level of society there was a proliferation of sports and societies.

The great centrepiece of Stansted's high culture was the Stansted Literary Institution, founded in 1849.[1] This was not an isolated initiative. Organisations of this sort had become widespread throughout the country, and already there were similar societies in Saffron Walden, Bishop's Stortford, Dunmow and Harlow. It was unusual however for an institution to be established in a village, albeit a large village, as distinct from a market town. The main driving force was Joshua Green with the help of his old school friend and business partner, James Marsh, and the local doctor, George Welch. They were supported and encouraged by the squire, the first William Fuller-Maitland, who became the President of the Institution, and by the Independent minister, Daniel Davies, who became one of the two Vice-Presidents. The vicar, Josias Torriano, was not involved, but his successor, Thomas Luard, was later chosen as the other Vice-President.

The inaugural meeting of the Institution was held at the King's Arms on 2 February 1849. Its aim, as formulated later in the Rules, was 'the dissemination of useful knowledge by means of a Library, a Reading Room and Occasional Lectures'. After the election of the President and Vice-Presidents William Canning was chosen as the first Secretary and Joshua Green as the Treasurer. There was a ten-man Committee, and in the first year there were 88 members. The founders were determined that the Institution should not be unsettled by religious or political animosities. The choice of newspapers and magazines would be politically impartial, and no works would be allowed 'inculcating sentiments of sectarian principles or injurious to the moral welfare of society'. There would be three classes of member – honorary members, whose annual subscription would be not less than one guinea; members whose subscription would be not less than ten shillings; and members whose subscription would be not less than six shillings, 'but no Masters or Tradesmen shall be admitted into the third class'. At the Annual General Meeting the three classes of member had differing numbers of votes, and although five of the original 88 members were women it was stipulated that ladies 'shall not be able to take any part in the management of the Society, nor be admitted into the Lecture or Reading Room, except when Lectures are delivered and to obtain books and papers'. The Stansted Literary Institution had much of the ethos of a gentlemen's club.

The Committee's reports reflected the lofty idealism of those who had founded the Institution. In its first report, for 1849, it expressed its gratification that the Institution now embraced as its members and supporters 'those who for many years have been active in every good work, and who have ever been ready to promote the physical and moral improvement of mankind'. The committee was 'sanguine' about the future. The most difficult task had been performed: the 'Castle of Indolence' had been invaded, and it only remained to throw the stone and the giant would die.

In its fourth report, while congratulating the Institution on its success so far, the Committee urged

> *the necessity of an untiring energy on the part of each member, in order that you may not only maintain the position you have already achieved, but that you may still more efficiently assist in that work which is now engaging the attention and employing the energies of so many noble hearts, viz – the removal of that veil of ignorance which still unhappily envelops the minds of such large numbers of our countrymen. For it should ever be remembered that your Society forms a part of that mighty lever that has done so much during the last quarter of a century [a period which took the reader back to the Reform Act of 1832] towards elevating our common humanity from its ignorant and degraded condition.*

The Rules of the Institution laid on the Committee the duties formulated when the Institution was first founded, that they should do everything in their power 'to prevent the introduction *of party spirit*, either in *politics or religion*, through the means of the books and papers they may select, or the lectures they may permit to be delivered', and we have a list of the newspapers and journals they provided in 1878:

Dailies:	*The Times, The Telegraph, The Standard, The Daily News.*
Weeklies:	*the Chelmsford Chronicle, the Herts and Essex Observer, the Illustrated London News, Punch, Fun.*
Magazines:	*Cornhill, Leisure Hour, All the Year Round, Good Works, Chambers Journal.*

We also have a complete but undated list of all the 203 books in the library. They are categorised under Biography (38), Poetry (10), Fiction, Tales, Essays &c. (24), Geography, Voyages, Travels, &c. (38), History (22), Natural History, Electricity, Astronomy and Chemistry (17), and Miscellaneous (54). They make up a solemn and improving collection, heavy going for the average reader, with titles such as 'The Lives of Illustrious Greeks', 'The Memoirs of the Marquise de la Rochejaquelein' and 'Lives of Men who raised themselves from Poverty to Eminence or Fortune'. The small number of works under fiction, tales and essays reflects the founders' intentions as expressed in Rule XII: 'That no Novels shall be purchased by the funds of this Society'. Novels were too frivolous for the serious purposes of the Institution. Members might donate them, but the Institution was not to buy them.

The Institution's third method of disseminating useful knowledge, after the Library and the Reading Room, was the 'occasional lecture', of which there were about three or four annually. In the early years George Welch lectured on 'The Ancient Britons: their Religious Worship and Monumental Remains', and there were lectures on Optics, Galvanism and Mechanics, the Life and Character of Socrates, and the Poetical Works of Milton. Daniel Davies lectured 'On Wales and the Welch', and Joshua Green on 'Atmospheric Electricity'.

These lectures were held in a large room at the King's Arms, and it became increasingly clear that more spacious and more suitable premises were needed for public meetings generally and for the Institution's Reading Room and Library in particular. On 14 March 1854 a meeting was held in the Bell for forming a Society for the erection of such a building, and the outcome was the formation of the Central Hall Company.[2] £500 was raised in £5 shares, half of them being bought by Joshua Green and James Marsh. Green was Secretary and Treasurer until 1880, when his son Joseph took over, and when Joseph retired in 1892 his brother Harford took his place. The Literary Institution would be the Company's main tenant, but the premises could be used for a fee by other organisations as well, 'societies of an unobjectionable nature', such as the Bible Society and in later years the Girls' Friendly Society and the Horticultural and Cottage Garden Association.

The Central Hall was formally opened with a soirée for 300 persons on 1 February 1855. It contained a hall and reading room, together with accommodation for the village Post Office and the home of the Postmaster, who was also the Institution's Librarian and Caretaker. Improvements and additions were made over the years. In 1857 the public clock was added, though many would argue that this was not an improvement, because, having been made in 1697 for the Dunmow Town Hall, it was already 'lamentably aged'.[3] In 1882 four rooms were added to the back of the building.

For its opening soirée the hall was adorned with evergreens, engravings and floral embellishments. Edward Ball, MP for Cambridgeshire, took the chair and there were several representatives from other literary institutions. The speeches emphasised once again the seriousness and idealism of the men who had brought the Institution into being. Ball declared that, since there was so much talk of extending the franchise, it was essential that the electorate should be educated and well informed; George Welch read an essay on the education of the people; the Reverend Flower from Clavering, while not objecting to light literature, asserted that a man of industry and perseverance would find more in Bishop Butler's Analogy of Religion than in any novel; and Mr. Stevens, a Quaker from London, gave a stern warning against the introduction of amusements.[4]

Consistent with the high tone of the speakers one of the paintings on display was a Madonna by Antonio da Correggio, 'at present the property of several gentlemen in shares'. At a later soirée the same picture was displayed again, together with several others lent by William Fuller-Maitland from his priceless collection. Among them were paintings by Andrea del Sarto, Francisco Granacci and Hans Holbein.[5]

At first the Institution remained true to its mission of disseminating useful knowledge. Some lectures were dauntingly recondite, such as the lecture given in 1863 by the Rev. J. Wilkins, 'On the Babylonian Captivity elucidating the books of Ezekiel, Daniel and the prophecies relating to the captivity of Judah': not surprisingly the attendance was 'small'. Others were heavily weighted with moral precepts, such as 'Golden Deeds and How To Do Them'. But subjects which might be regarded as a little more popular were also introduced. In 1869, for example, talks were given on 'The Tower of London and its Celebrated Prisoners' and 'The House of Commons and its Oratory'. Mrs. Bessie Inglis of London was a favourite lecturer, being called upon on at least three occasions. She spoke on 'Female Influence', 'The Importance and Advantages of Self-Cultivation', and 'The Mothers of Great Men'.

In 1861 the Institution began to reach out to a wider audience. Even for some of its serious lectures, like that on the Civil War in 1856, cheap tickets had been made available for members of 'the Labouring Classes'. Now it started a series of Penny Readings, which lasted until 1868, at which the Committee members and others read extracts from poems and novels to an audience which could not read for itself. They were called Penny Readings because the charge for admission was 1d., though 2d. would secure a reserved seat.

At the same time, mainly because of the need to make money, and in spite of the grim warnings of Mr. Stevens at the opening soirée, the Institution moved beyond its task of conveying useful information and began to hold entertainments, which consisted mainly of songs and readings, 'amusement and instruction blended together', as Walter Gilbey described them,[6] or 'grave and gay, humorous and pathetic', as they were once described in the local press.[7] They were regarded as being a cut above the Penny Readings, and the price for entry, 1s., was beyond the reach of the ordinary labourer.

For the most part it was members of the most prominent families who took the lead. Sometimes they performed themselves, sometimes they called on friends from neighbouring villages and towns, sometimes they engaged entertainers from London and elsewhere. They were 'ladies and gentlemen doing their utmost to please' and enjoying themselves in doing so, and their repertoire ranged from Shakespearean recitals in full costume to comic songs. While the women might have been barred from playing any part in running the Institution, they were just as prominent as the men in its entertainments, perhaps concentrating more on the delightful and sentimental while the men revelled more in the comedy. Patriotism was prominent, many readings reflecting Britain's great history and many songs celebrating the British soldier and sailor. In this way the people of Stansted took to heart the Death of Nelson, the Battle of Waterloo and the Charge of the Light Brigade.

In 1863 a sumptuous 'soirée' was organised to celebrate the wedding of the Prince of Wales, when the Hall was decorated with flags, banners, flowers and festoons, and Luard expressed the hope that on the day of the wedding itself they 'would have such a holiday ... as would awaken reminiscences of our old merrie England'. The lofty aims of the Institution were not forgotten, for the mottoes displayed were all of an improving nature, such as 'The greatest foe to eminence is ignorance', 'Justice is the badge of virtue', and 'The light of learning is the day of the mind'.[8]

Concerts too were held, with a grand piano provided by the Pulteneys or another leading family. The main items were songs and piano solos, and it was not unusual to hear pieces by Beethoven, Handel and Rossini as well as many minor composers. There were also plays, typically humorous and farcical, and dramatic recitals, with amateur companies coming in from Bishop's Stortford, Saffron Walden and Harlow. At a less elevated level there were evenings of 'innocent fun and wonder'[9] provided by the occasional illusionist, humorist, ventriloquist or magician. Tableaux vivants, a phrenologist and a spelling bee (an American 'craze') added to the variety, and in 1876 there was an exotic display of Arab life by Seyyid Mustafa Ben-Yusuf, supported by fourteen persons dressed in Eastern costumes.[10] There were often floral displays drawn from the gardens and greenhouses of the wealthier families.

These entertainments were a great success, and the following press report from March 1868 is typical of many others:

> On Tuesday evening another of those now highly popular entertainments was given in the Central Hall. Long before the doors were opened people were quietly waiting outside determined if possible to avoid the necessity of standing all the evening, as many were obliged to do on the last occasion. But all were not fortunate in that respect, for before the time arrived for opening the

30: FROM EDUCATION TO ENTERTAINMENT

proceedings of the evening, every seat was occupied and almost every available standing place was taken up, and several were turned away from the doors.[11]

The local press noted with condescending approval the good behaviour of the audiences, which it described variously as 'respectable and orderly', 'highly respectable and thoroughly appreciative', 'intelligent and good-humoured', 'distinguished', and even 'aristocratic'. In 1864 the audience for a Penny Reading was described as 'crowded and highly respectable'.

The repeated use of the word 'respectable' implied the worrying possibility of the opposite, and indeed a 'rough element' was sometimes present, not rowdy enough to disturb the performance, but obtrusive enough for its absence on one occasion in 1877 to be noted with relief: it had been 'enticed away' by some travelling exhibition in another part of the village.

The shift from education to entertainment was not uncontroversial. In 1876 the Committee resolved that there should be 'a higher class' of entertainments, but its efforts in this direction came to nothing. In March that year, when a distinguished elocutionist gave a rendering of one of Lord Lytton's plays, very few villagers turned out to hear him, and the Committee concluded that 'the better the lecturer and the more expensive the talent, the less it is appreciated by a Stansted audience'.[12] A Black Diamond minstrel troupe from Bishop's Stortford was much more successful: twice the rush of people when the doors were opened was so great that several who had tickets could not get in. In later years the Stansted Amateur Minstrel Troupe always attracted large audiences, and so did the GGG Minstrels, named after the Golds, the Gilbeys and their cousins, the Grinlings.

Although other organisations used the Central Hall for meetings and fund-raising events, the Literary Institution was its tenant and mainstay. As long as the Institution flourished so did the Company, and its shareholders could look for a 3% return on their investment. But in the 1880s the Institution began to run into financial difficulties. Concerts and entertainments were held to raise funds, and Harford Green pulled out the full range of his conjuring tricks. In 1882, when the church choir gave a concert in the parochial schoolroom, the vicar was publicly criticised for not using the Hall instead.[13]

The schoolroom, however, was never a serious alternative to the Hall, for it was uncomfortable and the acoustics were bad. But when the Working Men's Club replaced the Liberal Association in 1892 and, as well as a large and convenient Assembly Room, held out the attractions of beer and billiards, the Institution could no longer hold its own and was forced to close down. This was a great blow to the Central Hall Company, and it suffered another blow when the Post Office moved into new premises specially built for it next door. In 1893 Harford Green, now the Company Secretary, wrote to inform the shareholders that 'in consequence of the removal of the Post Office, and the compulsory closing of the Literary Institution, owing to the rival attractions of the Working Men's Club', the income of the Company had been reduced by over £20, and since repairs and alterations were necessary there would be no balance available for dividends.

The Company badly needed a new tenant. From time to time local businessmen hired a room or rooms, but it was 1897 before the Hall was leased out on a long-term basis as a magistrates' court, complete with two detention rooms. Thereafter Petty Sessions were held there on a monthly basis – a very different purpose from that first envisaged by the Company's high-minded founders.

Entertainments of course continued, sometimes in the Central Hall and sometimes in the Assembly Room of the Working Men's Club, which in 1902 became the Parish Room and was then much used by organisations connected with the church. The wealthy families still took the lead, but the high seriousness of Joshua and Joseph Green had now given way to the high spirits of the dashing young sons and daughters of the Directors of W & A Gilbey, a lively and wealthy social set drawing in friends and relations from London and elsewhere – a local reflection, perhaps, of Victorian piety and seriousness giving way, or at least some way, to Edwardian jollity and frivolity. In the early years of the Literary Institution Joshua Green had lectured on Atmospheric Electricity: in 1903 Gerald Gold, as a member of the Stansted Amateur Minstrel Troupe, sang 'Sambo kept smiling', which was the 'hit of the evening'. In this kind of light entertainment, it was reported in 1906, Stansted had made quite a name for itself.[14]

The musical endeavours of the parish had followed a similar path. Much good music was heard at the occasional concert to raise funds for the Literary Institution or some other deserving cause, but anything more ambitious, such as the establishment of a musical society, an orchestra or a choir (outside the church) was short-lived. In 1877 a Musical Society linked with the Literary Institution was founded and performed works by Handel, Rossini, Brahms, Gounod and others, but it then lapsed into silence. In 1883 a Choral Union was formed, so called because it was said to unite all the musical talent in the village. It was supported by the 'elite of the town',[15] with Fuller-Maitland as President and eight Vice-Presidents, including Luard and Davies, two Blyths, a Gilbey and a Pulteney. All this was thought 'to augur well' for the future, but after a few performances the Union was disbanded. The most disastrous failure was the Orchestral Society, founded in 1888 at the instigation of Charles Hoby, the newly appointed organist and choirmaster at St. Mary's, and presided over by the vicar, Thomas Luard. It gave only one concert, which Hoby appears to have organised on his own, calling in violinists and singers from outside. He received little support from the big families. Reviews in the *Observer* were usually fulsome in their praise of the performers, but on this occasion only one artist was picked out for mention, and all that could be said of her that 'we would like to hear her under slightly less depressing circumstances'. Hoby's mistake, according to the reviewer, was to aim too high, the programme consisting of works by Rubenstein, Mendelssohn and Chopin, and several by Hoby himself – or, as the exasperated reviewer put it, 'Hoby ... Hoby and Hoby again'.[16] He was so dismayed by this failure that he threw up his post as organist and choirmaster and emigrated to New Zealand.

In 1890, at a less elevated level, a Drum and Fife band was formed, and in 1902 the Stansted String Band, which for several years performed at dances and played carols at Christmas. In 1899, however, new opportunities for enjoying music were opened up by a wonderful new instrument that was advertised for sale in Bishop's Stortford: 'No up-to date Christmas Party is fully catered for without a Gram-o-phone, which will talk, sing and play', and the price was 'within reach of everyone'. In the early years of the new century whist drives with dances became a popular way of raising money.

Stansted did not have its own cinema, but in 1912 the Empire Picture Palace and the Bishop's Stortford Cinema were opened in South Street, Bishop's Stortford. The Picture

Palace closed soon after the beginning of WW1, but the Cinema remained open for many years and was a great attraction for the people of Stansted.

The entertainments attracted good audiences, but the event that drew in the greatest crowds was the annual show organised by the Stansted Horticultural and Cottage Garden Association, founded in 1891 and extended in 1892 to include Birchanger. The Association's first President was William Fuller-Maitland, and he was supported by several Vice-Presidents and two secretaries, Markwell Freelove and the ubiquitous Harford Green. Like the Literary Institution it had different categories of membership – gentlemen's gardeners, who paid 5s. a year, amateurs who paid 2s. 6d. and cottagers who paid nothing (a cottager being defined as a person living in a house with an annual rental of under £8). It had two main objects – to encourage thrift and industry among the poor and to give pleasure as well.[17]

The attractions of the show changed over the years, but the centrepiece was always the competitive displays of flowers, fruit and vegetables for which prizes were awarded by the Association. There were also prizes for the best cottage gardens and special awards were added by a ladies' committee for dinner table decorations (in which the daughters of the wealthier families excelled) and for items designed to encourage self-help, such as home-made loaves, rugs, shirts, shawls, woollen stockings and 'the best Darned and Patched *Old* Garments'. Wood carving, drawing and fretwork were soon added. Already by 1892 there were more than 600 entries, by 1893 there were prizes for more than 130 categories, and the names of the proud winners and runners-up were printed over many column inches in the local press. Sometimes the show was held at Stansted Hall, at Blythwood or in Harford Green's meadow, but the most common venue was Hargrave Park, where the owners, the Pulteneys, were enthusiastic and hard-working supporters and after them so too was Gilbert Alder.

The show's organisation reflected the social order. The big families, such as the Fuller-Maitlands, the Blyths and the Golds, displayed exotic and hothouse plants which the ordinary villager could not hope to emulate, and there were extensive displays by horticultural companies from Cheshunt, Waltham Cross and elsewhere. These entries were 'not for competition': the gentry were above the fray, though their names were given due prominence in the press, with the names of their gardeners added after them in brackets. Then came the entries from four classes – gentlemen's gardeners, amateurs, artisans and cottagers. Over the years the event became as much a festival as a flower show. At different times there were cricket matches, athletics, with tugs of war between the men of the different hamlets, tennis tournaments (begun in 1895 with over 100 competitors), a cycle gymkhana (in 1897), roundabouts, swings, shooting galleries, coconut shies and aunt sallies, and bands which played during the day and for dancing in the evening. As long as the weather was fine the local press hailed every show as a triumph and congratulated the great and the good who had been responsible for its organisation.

Royal weddings, jubilees and coronations also gave rise to celebrations organised by committees of the community's leaders and generously funded by public subscriptions. The earliest festivities recorded were the coronation of King George IV in 1821, when

£46 4s. was raised and Colonel Welch gave 80 lbs of beef and 25 quartern loaves of bread valued at £2 18s. 9d.[18] The enthusiastic response of the Literary Institution to the marriage of the Prince of Wales in 1863 has already been described, and for the village as a whole £60 was raised. A pound of beef was given to every adult and half a pound to every child, and Green and Marsh gave a pound of plums for every family and an orange for every child. A large bonfire was lit in the evening and there was a fine display of fireworks. Those taking part already saw themselves in the historic tradition of loyal Englishmen: Luard's hope at the celebrations at the Literary Institution has already been quoted, that on the day of the wedding itself they 'would have such a holiday ... as would awaken reminiscences of our old merrie England'.

72. The committee responsible for organising the celebrations for Queen Victoria's Golden Jubilee in 1887. From left to right, back row: Joshua Green, William Spencer, Henry Trigg junior, M.F. Freelove, Charles Hicks. Front row: J. Caygill, Thomas Hicks, Harford Green, Charles Spencer, Henry Trigg senior, Edward Spencer, Alfred Hicks.

The next great occasion was Queen Victoria's Golden Jubilee in 1887, and for the first time we have a public celebration recorded on camera. The gentry of the village did not take part in the committee that did all the hard work and organised the event, though one of the committee members was Fuller-Maitland's steward, Joseph Caygill. They contributed generously to the jubilee fund, which raised £300, and on the day itself Fuller-Maitland opened up his extensive park where the celebrations took place and entertained the committee and their friends to tea in Stansted Hall, while the Blyths provided new sixpences for the children, which were graciously handed out by the daughters of the family. But the committee members themselves were farmers, such as Henry Trigg and Alfred Hicks, maltsters, such as the chairman, Charles Spencer, and William Spencer, or tradesmen such as Joshua and Harford Green. Markwell Freelove, the secretary, was a commercial traveller. About half of them were Quakers, and they nearly all held or had held office as churchwardens, overseers or surveyors of the highways.

The weather was brilliant, and everything was done, the *Observer* noted, 'in a thoroughly patriotic and popular manner ....' The villagers gathered at the fountain at midday, and then set off in procession to St. Mary's with the Royal Standard in front, followed by a brass band, then the ministers of religion, the parish officers, the villagers themselves, marshalled by members of the committee, and lastly the schoolchildren.

After a thanksgiving service at St. Mary's dinner, a substantial fare called 'Old English', was served to 900 adults, up to 250 at a time, in a large marquee. Two bullocks had been roasted and boiled, 150 plum puddings prepared, each 5-6 pounds, and there were two pints of beer for every man and one for every woman, with ginger-beer for abstainers and sandwiches for the children. In the afternoon there were races and sports and amusements, prizes were distributed (hats and ties for the young men, spades, forks, scythes and shovels for the older men, and a pound and a half of tea for the women), the Blyths' new sixpences were handed out to the children, and the committee members and their friends were entertained to tea, coffee and refreshments in Stansted Hall. In the evening there was 'dancing on the greensward'. Again villagers were encouraged to see themselves through a premature haze of patriotic nostalgia. 'Nothing occurred to mar the harmony of this "day of days" in Great and Greater Britain's calendar', wrote the *Observer*, 'and generation after generation will hand down the tradition

How well was kept Victoria's Jubilee
In the brave days of old.'

Three at least of the entertainments were unofficial in the sense of not being organised by the committee – a Punch and Judy show, a coconut shy and climbing the greasy pole. Their inferior status was all part of the move towards respectability that we shall discuss below in the context of the May fair and harvest celebrations.

73. The committee responsible for organising the celebrations for Queen Victoria's Diamond Jubilee in 1897. From left to right, back row: Watts (?), T. Hicks, E.E. Tunbridge, L. Norman, J. Caygill, E.S. Spencer, J. Francis, - Jordan, W. Clarke, G. Little, J. Amey, A. Ratcliffe, F. Bedlow. Front row: A. Bright, J. Woolley, J. Richardson, J. Caister (sec), Harford Green (chairman), E.S. Spencer, H.H. Gayford, H. Bass, - Atkins(?), I. Reynolds. Seated on ground: W. Prior, - Lovell, Wm. Prior.

Ten years later, in 1897, came the Diamond Jubilee. This time Harford Green chaired the organising committee, and the celebrations were held in his meadow. They were not as ambitious as those for the Golden Jubilee. The amount subscribed was £174, compared with £300, and there was no public dinner, though beef was distributed a day or two before. An open air service was held in the meadow conducted by Eustace Long, the Independent minister, since the vicar, the unpopular George Valentine, was away. After sports and entertainments in the afternoon, about 400 children and 1300 adults were given tea, and the children were given commemorative medals.

In 1902 £277 was raised for the coronation of Edward VII and Queen Alexandra, but because of the King's illness the coronation was postponed and the celebrations were cancelled. When the coronation was eventually held on 9 August the day was quietly spent, with several stores and the Working Men's Club being decorated with flags and fairy lights but little more.

For the coronation of King George V and Queen Mary in 1911 the organising committee was chaired by Charles Gold – by this time the bankrupt Harford Green had 'disappeared' – and the Independent minister, Arthur Cook, was the secretary. The amount raised was £115, much less than for the coronation of George's parents, and the programme was less ambitious. Several buildings were decorated with flags and bunting, special services were held in the churches, and in the afternoon there were sports in the park at Stansted Hall followed by the children's tea. Tickets for refreshments worth 4½d. each were provided for 1,084 adults. Each child was given a coronation mug with three new pennies, and in the evening there was dancing until nine o'clock.

The great events in the Fuller-Maitlands' lives were celebrated in similar fashion, establishing their social leadership of the parish as a local paradigm of the royal leadership of the country. The wedding of William Fuller-Maitland with Evelyn Gardner in 1881 has already been described, and was no doubt vividly remembered by the villagers for many years. The next great event was the coming of age in 1904 of the squire's son, William Alan Fuller-Maitland, who was a Lieutenant in the Coldstream Guards, though William Alan himself could not be there, being on guard duty at Buckingham Palace. There were sports and amusements for the children - about 600 of them marched from Lower Street to the Hall – and a garden party for those connected with the estate. At the call of a bugle the whole company assembled on the terrace, where Harford Green (inevitably) toasted Mr. and Mrs. Fuller-Maitland, and after Fuller-Maitland had replied, rejoicing, he said, in the friendly feelings that had been shown to him, there was dancing on the lawn. The party closed at 8 pm with the playing of the National Anthem and 'hearty cheers'. The village's gift to William was a lifesize portrait of himself.

An event that appealed most strongly to the ordinary villagers and the children was the May fair, the sale of horses and cattle and the pleasure fair on two days at the beginning of May. For this there was no support or patronage from the gentry. On the contrary, fairs were regarded as occasions of disorder and licentiousness, and the Fairs Act of 1871 was based on the premise that they were 'unnecessary', 'the cause of grievous immorality' and 'very injurious' to the local inhabitants. On petition from the local community the Home Secretary could abolish a fair, and throughout the country there were moves to drum up the required signatures. Several of the fairs around Stansted were abolished, notably at Bishop's Stortford in 1873.

There was a similar movement to get rid of the rumbustious harvest celebrations, or horkies as they were known locally, and to have them replaced by the more sober and decorous harvest festivals controlled by the churches. The horky at Stortford was suppressed, and in 1861 the *Observer* noted that horkies were largely a thing of the past and expressed relief that in these enlightened times the streets of the town were no longer infested by intoxicated labourers demanding gratuities from the tradesmen.[19]

Though the Stansted fair continued the sale of horses and cattle declined. Trade was described as 'moderate' in 1895, and in 1905 only 50 head of cattle and a few horses were offered for sale. Proceedings were described as 'very quiet' and at some point this part of the fair was discontinued. The pleasure fair, however, still flourished. It seems that it was once held in Lower Street, and that it was later moved to a meadow behind the Bell. Its centrepiece was Thurston's 'steam circus', and it drew in many visitors from neighbouring villages. There was still rowdiness at times. In May 1890, when the watchmaker, Ticker Francis, was woken at 1 am on a Saturday morning by the sound of laughing and talking, he thought the sound might come from some men passing by 'who had become elated on account of the fair'. (In fact he was mistaken, since they had broken into his house where they helped themselves to the sloe and rhubarb wine in his cellar.)[20] In 1894 a man accused of being drunk and disorderly tried to excuse himself on the ground that it was 'fair night'.[21]

Many years later a man giving his initials as BWL, in an account of his schooldays from 1896 to 1906, relived what it was like when the fair came to the village:

> Well, we are all getting excited now as tomorrow is the first of May, and Thurston's fair is already here in the Bell Field at Cambridge Road - swings, roundabouts and side shows. The chimney sweeps will be going around the village on a wagon, singing and accompanied by tambourines, and of course black faces.[22] Are you coming to the Recreation Ground after school this morning as it's May Day, and all the cattle will be there for sale, and all sorts of things that are used on the farms. I'll see you there, and after school tonight I am going to the fair in the Bell Field. I wish they had the fair in Lower Street as they used to years ago. They tell me they had stalls all along the street....

1. The main sources for the Institution are the Green Papers in ERO, T/P 68/18, and articles in the *CC* and the *HEO*. Unless stated otherwise quotations are from the papers in T/P 68/18.
2. The papers of the Central Hall Company are in Irving Sanders's collection. There are more papers in ERO, D/Z 41//1, and also, mainly posters, in ERO, T/P 68/20.
3. *HEO*, 29 November 1879, letter from 'a Sufferer and Sympathiser'.
4. *CC*, 9 February 1855.
5. *CC*, 21 March 1856.
6. *HEO*, 28 April 1866.
7. *HEO*, 11 December 1875.
8. *HEO*, 7 and 14 March 1863.
9. *HEO*, 22 February 1878.
10. Seyyid was a native of Algiers, had been converted to Christianity, and was now studying at Cambridge for a medical degree. His illustrations of Arab Life were a way of financing his education.
11. *HEO*, 28 March 1868.
12. *HEO*, 11 March 1876.
13. *HEO*, 4, 11 and 18 February and 4 March 1882.
14. *HEO*, 28 April 1906.
15. *HEO*, 26 April 1884.
16. *HEO*, 7 April 1888.
17. The show was reported in the *HEO* each year. For the rules, see ERO, T/P 68/16/1-2.
18. *SMPM*, May, 1937.
19. *HEO*, 31 August 1861.
20. *HEO*, 10 May 1890.
21. *HEO*, 19 May 1894.
22. Sweeps in London had one day's holiday a year, the first of May, which they celebrated by parading through the streets. It seems that the sweeps in this part of Essex had the same custom.

31: SPORT

Stansted's men of property enjoyed their hunting and shooting, as they had done for many generations. When one of the larger houses was put on the market to be leased or sold the proximity of two local hunts, the Essex and the Puckeridge, was sometimes advertised as an attraction,[1] and it was held to be an advantage for some of the meets that those who wanted to hunt could come up on an early train from London and go back on a late train.[2]

The leading huntsmen in the area were the Goslings at Farnham, where Robert Gosling became Master of the Puckeridge Hounds in 1875. Several farmers in Stansted took part, and two of the Spencers were elected to the managing committee in 1876, together with Robert Fuller-Maitland, the squire's younger brother. For the farmers it was perhaps a way of social advancement and they would have taken pride and pleasure in attending the hunt balls with their families and rubbing shoulders with the gentry. But hunting was pursued with a passion that easily gave rise to conflict, and Gosling ran into a storm of acrimonious opposition.

When he had bought the hounds from his predecessor he had moved them close to his home at Farnham. This was some way from the centre of the hunting country so that some outlying parts were hunted less than before, and when the hounds did go there they came back at an early hour because of the long return hack in front of them. This gave rise to great dissatisfaction and in 1885 the dissidents set up a new pack which they called the Puckeridge while Gosling hunted the original Puckeridge hounds which he called 'Mr. Gosling's'. This went on until 1890 when Gosling finally resigned.[3]

The Stansted farmers, being close to Farnham, had probably been among Gosling's supporters, and both they and Robert's sons and grandsons continued to take part in the hunt. Susan Spencer-Smith, whose father, a tenant farmer, was a huntsman, spoke to us in breathless admiration of the magnificent sight of the hunt setting out, with five of the Goslings' sons in their red coats. It was part of the local tenancy agreements that the tenants were not allowed to shoot foxes, and after WW1, again according to Susan Spencer-Smith, one of the Goslings' tenants shot a fox and life was made so uncomfortable for him that he left the area.

The main centre for shooting, however, was the Stansted Hall estate, where the pheasant-filled woods and copses enabled the Fuller-Maitlands to entertain their neighbours and friends in much the same way as the mediaeval lords of the manor had entertained their neighbours and friends to hunting parties in their park. Shooting was an important social activity, whether on informal visits to and from other landowners or on grand occasions, 'big days', when a distinguished party of guests would be invited, and it added greatly to the Fuller-Maitlands' prestige that they were able to entertain in this way, especially if the beaters could put up a large number of birds.[4]

A good gamekeeper was highly valued. When John Wilkins went as gamekeeper to the first William Fuller-Maitland in 1843 his main reason, according to his father, was that his master at that time was 'a great fox-preserver' and hunted a good deal, 'and John would prefer to live with a gentleman who preserves pheasants and not foxes'.[5] As Wilkins himself later explained, his first priority in Stansted was to provide pheasants for his master and his guests to shoot: he did not kill foxes – that would have given him a bad name with the hunt[6] - but he had to make sure that they did not kill many birds.[7]

Shooting parties, both at Stansted Hall and his other estates in the neighbourhood, were also important for the second William Fuller-Maitland, and the following account in the local paper conveys the great social prestige which they conferred:

> *Stansted Hall. William Fuller Maitland Esq. MP and the Hon. Mrs. W. Fuller Maitland have been entertaining a distinguished party of guests during the present week. The company staying at the Hall were the Earl of Onslow, the Earl and Countess of Ellesmere, Lord Wald[e]grave, Sir Henry and Lady Selwin-Ibbetson, Colonel Gardner and Miss Fuller Maitland. Shooting took place on Tuesday at Birchanger, at Rowney (Debden) on Wednesday, Durrell's (Stansted) on Thursday, and again at Debden today, Friday.... All greatly enjoyed the excellent sport in the well-stocked preserves of their genial and generous entertainer.[8]*

A week later five of the same guests enjoyed 'a good day's sport' at Stansted Hall and 'bagged 735 head'.

The Blyths also enjoyed shooting. In 1895, under the heading of a 'good bag' at Stansted, it was reported that Henry Blyth, Sir James's brother, had brought down 700 pheasants at Alsa Wood and at Elmdon.[9] His nephew Audley was also a good shot, but the pheasants of Essex were not exciting enough for him, and at the end of 1907 or the beginning of 1908 he went out to British East Africa on a safari with his wife, the glamorous Effie, whom he had married in 1903. The circumstances are not clear, but it seems that Effie fell in love with the man leading the safari, John Patterson, and that Audley, sick with fever and despair, committed suicide by shooting himself through the head. There were rumours, however, that he was killed by Effie, and after burying him she and Patterson did nothing to allay the suspicions against them by continuing the safari, sharing the same tent, and giving the impression to local officials that they were 'on very friendly terms' and would soon be married.[10]

Robert Fuller-Maitland, William's youngest son, was also drawn by hunting in British East Africa, where he settled in 1910. Two years later he was crushed to death by an elephant near Lake Baringo.

Only the wealthy could afford to play polo, which in Stansted was almost exclusively the sport of the social set centred on the families of the Gilbeys, the Blyths and the Golds. The Stansted Polo Club was started in 1892, and played about ten or so matches each year against teams such as Hurlingham, Fetcham, Gaynes Park and Ranelagh. Its most successful year was 1896, when it won nine of its 11 matches. The sport was popular enough for the local tailors, Tissiman's, to advertise and sell polo breeches, but the club came to an end in 1903.

The latter part of the nineteenth century was a time when sport became more organised and when organised sport became more popular. In Stansted a Lawn Tennis Club was opened in 1890 with four courts and 'a large number of members'. Only a few minutes' walk from the station, it provided 'a great boon to the district'.[11] In 1902 a nine-hole golf course was opened on rising ground close to the railway station, part of it being Castle Hills. Philip Gold was the club secretary, and by 1903 it had about 130 members, 30 of them being women.[12] A bowls club in Green's meadow was started in or around 1909, and when, in 1912, it moved to its present site behind the Post Office, it had about 60 members. It was well patronised: William Fuller-Maitland was the President, and among the Vice-Presidents was Sir Walter Gilbey, who owned the new site and leased it out for a nominal rent.[13]

But the two sports that attracted the most interest and support were football and cricket. Football began to become popular in the 1870s, and clubs were formed in Saffron Walden in 1872 and in Bishop's Stortford in 1874. In Stansted games were arranged for children on school outings or in village celebrations, but it was late 1890 or early 1891 before a properly organised football club was established. Its first game, played on 'the Cricket Field' in February 1891, resulted in a 5-2 defeat by Saffron Walden Town.[14]

None of the leading families took part as players. They were supportive, but their support was limited. The 'gentleman' who was most closely involved in these early years was Irvine Rowell, a Cambridge blue for cricket, who was the treasurer in 1899, and who will appear more prominently below in the account of Stansted's cricketers. Concerts were held occasionally to raise funds, but without any great success.[15] In 1897 the captain was George Luckey, who was listed as a general labourer in the 1891 census, and the secretary and

74. Stansted's football team, 1897.

treasurer was Frederick Coombs, who was listed as a journeyman. H. Spalding, the captain in 1899, was probably the same as the Harold Spalding who appeared in the census as a harness maker. The secretary was C.A. Tadman, a photographer and a parish councillor, who would have been too old to play. When cricketers were listed in the press their initials were usually given: footballers were listed without initials.

In or around 1896 the club was reconstituted as the Stansted Rovers Football Club. At its second annual meeting in September 1897 it was reported that of 14 matches played, 4 had been won, 9 lost, and 1 drawn.[16] By that time it was playing its games in Green's Meadow, and in 1907 there was a real improvement in the organisation of the game when six clubs joined together to form the Stansted District League – Stansted Rovers, Sawbridgeworth, Dunmow, Harlow, Saffron Walden Star and Saffron Walden YMCA – and in 1908 the club decided to compete for the Essex Junior Cup as well. Like all football clubs, the team's fortunes varied from year to year. It was well managed – for a time its secretary, then its treasurer, was Frank Dearch, the headteacher of the National School[17] - but its style of play did not always win approval. In 1898, when playing Chantry Villa at Bishop's Stortford, the Rovers kept the score down to 1-0 against them by 'playing three or four men in the mouth of the goal'.[18] And in a critical league game at home against Bishop's Stortford in 1913 'All attempts at combination [i.e. passing] by Stortford were quickly nonplussed by the vigorous tactics of the homesters', so much so that the second half was judged to be 'entirely unworthy of the name of football'. There were a lot of 'hard knocks'. One player had to have stitches over his eye, and the referee 'had occasion to suspend the game on two occasions'. But for the Rovers it was all worthwhile, for the final result was 3-0 and they went on to win the League for the first time in their history.

When the cricket club was founded is uncertain. Two printed sets of rules survive, both headed Stansted Park Cricket Club. One (in Green's papers) refers to the club being established in 1864, while the other (in Irving Sanders's collection) gives the date as 1860. Irving points out, however, that the game was played regularly in Stansted many years before that.

The first definite reference I have found to cricket in Stansted is in the *Chelmsford Chronicle* for 12 July 1844, and it records a match played at Stansted against Newport. In a close-run game Stansted won by 42 and 64 against 50 and 42. Occasional reports of matches at Stansted appeared in the years that followed. In 1845 it was reported that a field in Stansted Park had recently been set out as a cricket ground, no doubt because of the Fuller-Maitlands' enthusiasm for the game, after which the club was known as Stansted Park; and in a match against Dunmow Albion 'the first rate round-arm bowling of Mr. Sadler, only 17, was the theme of universal commendation'. By 1846 the club could be referred to as an 'established' club, and in 1856 the exploits of the young doctor, Samuel Welch, were celebrated – he was to appear many years later in the records as the club's oldest member and supporter.

For several years matches were played in Hargrave Park, and in 1881 the central part of the Recreation Ground was taken up, trenched and relaid for the use of the club. It was not ideal: cattle and horses were grazed there, though they were taken off on match days, and in 1885, through the much applauded generosity of the squire, a new ground was made available at Burton End. Six years later a pavilion was built at a cost of between £50 and £60, and entertainments were held to raise the money.

The game changed considerably over the years. Old Samuel Welch, who in 1890 was the only living member of the original Stansted Park Club, often regaled club members with his reminiscences,[19] and Harry Chester, who chaired the annual meeting in 1891 in Fuller-Maitland's absence, reminded his audience of the time when players were dressed in a 'Sunday-go-to-meeting' hat and braces, when there were only four balls to the over, and when bowling was under-arm. Only 'the worthy doctor' would have seen a match 50 years ago, when grounds were much poorer and the ball had the mastery over the bat.[20] Team scores seldom exceeded 100.[21]

Cricketers, unlike footballers, were often referred to as gentlemen, and cricket, 'the noble game', held a special place in the country's conception of itself and was seen as the national sport. The cricketing elite at Stansted went along with this. In 1885 Fuller-Maitland described it as 'the game of all games',[22] and at the annual meeting in 1890 Harry Chester, proposing 'Success to the Club', declared that the game was becoming more and more popular with the British people:

> Wherever the British flag floated could be found stumps, bats, and balls, and the perspiring Briton indulging in the game. It was a matter of common knowledge that cricket called forth all the qualities which Britons so admired. Cricket gave one a very healthy form of recreation at a low price, brought all classes together in friendly rivalry, and did much to encourage that kindly feeling which all genuine cricketers felt for one another.[23]

Cricket was approved of as a healthy, sober, well-conducted pastime, very different from some of the more 'cruel and brutalising sports' such as cock-fighting, which it was said to have replaced.[24] To ensure that proper standards were maintained one of the club's rules in 1864 was 'any person using bad language on the Ground to be liable to be expelled'. (In the 1860 rules the punishment had been a fine of two pence – evidently not a sufficient deterrent.)

In Stansted the glorification of cricket reached new heights at a complimentary dinner at the Working Men's Club in November 1894. A West Essex League had been formed, Guy Gilbey, Sir Walter's son, had donated a bowl to be presented to the winner, and in the first season Stansted Park had come out top. As well as the players and committee members, representatives from all the clubs in the League were invited. Since cricket was being extolled as a great formative influence and training ground for the English national character there were also representatives from the church and the armed forces. The Earl of Warwick, the League's President, was not able to be there but sent a message of support and congratulation, and William Fuller-Maitland took the chair as the club's President.

The hall was decorated for the occasion by plants supplied by the Pulteneys and Sir James Blyth, and toasts, interspersed with songs, were proposed to the Queen, the Prince and Princess of Wales and the royal family, the clergy of all denominations, the armed forces, the West Essex Cricket League, the donor of the bowl Guy Gilbey, and Fuller-Maitland as the President of Stansted Park. The responses to the toast to the clergy were given by the vicars from Birchanger and Ugley (George Valentine of Stansted was not there). A strong and healthy cricket club, said Cam from Birchanger, was 'a valuable auxiliary ... to the clergyman's work', 'one of the best means to counteract the worst influences' which were likely to prove a temptation when there was little else to do. General Boulton, replying to the toast to the armed forces, trotted out the old cliché that the battles of England had been won on the playing grounds of Eton, which he took to mean the playing grounds of the kingdom as a whole. No better training, he said, could be provided for those entering the armed services: all manly sports were beneficial, but cricket above all 'brought out the proper qualities of boys' and taught virtues such as obedience and the advantages of combined action.[25] There was another celebratory dinner in the following year when Stansted won the bowl for a second time.

75. Stansted's cricket team. Undated, but the earliest photo of the team that we have. It is tempting to think that the elderly gentleman on the left, posing with his bat, is Samuel Welch.

But how far did cricket really 'bring all classes together'? Certainly much more than other sports. William Fuller-Maitland, the great bowler, took part only occasionally, and in one of these matches, the game against Berden in May 1885, the *Observer* deferentially commented that it was 'really gratifying to state that the worthy squire, through whose kindness the club possesses such an admirable ground, took part in the match'[26] - and it was rare for the Golds, Gilbeys and Blyths to play, or the Pulteneys. The Greens, I suspect, were not noted for their sporting prowess, though Harford Green once proposed a toast at a league dinner. But Harry Chester and several of the farmers played, notably some of the Spencers and the younger Henry Trigg, who captained the team for several years, while Samuel Welch, 'the worthy doctor', was one of the club's mainstays. Irvine Rowell, who was elected as captain in 1899 and was the club's outstanding player for several years, was a Cambridge Blue and had played with Ranjitsinhji.[27] Most of the other players were of the middling sort, with the occasional labourer as well. In one team in 1890, for example, it has been possible to identify two brickmakers, a schoolmaster, a police constable, a shoemaker, two labourers, a gardener and a butcher.[28] Herbert Gayford, an auctioneer and estate agent, was captain for several years and Henry Douglas, a schoolmaster, and Frank

Bedlow, a wheelwright, were two of the team's most successful bowlers. In 1913 the curate, G.W.F. Howard, headed the batting averages.[29]

Members of the leading families occasionally raised teams for special invitation matches, sometimes playing Stansted Park, sometimes teams raised by other 'gentlemen'. But they strongly supported the village club, sitting as committee members, providing funds, and not only arranging for entertainments to raise money but also taking part in them. Some of Stansted's larger companies, such as Green and Marsh and the Mica Manufacturing Company, also held the occasional match, and there were less serious encounters, such as the annual match between married and single, and Ragamuffins versus Tag, Rag and Bobtail. In 1883 there was a match between two individual players, Francis and Middleditch.[30]

The vigour of Stansted's cultural life was impressive, but there were many villagers, perhaps most, for whom churches, literary institutions, musical societies and sports clubs held out little or no attraction or else were beyond their limited means. Many took their leisure and pleasure in the warmth and good company of the public houses of the village. And there were some who did not succumb to the pressures of social control, who were out of sympathy with the ethos of respectability and good works, and who resorted to crime, especially poaching, which was partly a protest against the stark inequalities of life. The 'dark village' persisted: towards the end of the century the 'rough element', as the local press referred to it, thrust itself more and more onto the scene.

1 See, e.g. *CC*, 28 March 1851 and 8 February 1856, and *HEO*, 1 October 1870. See also *HEO*, 11 September 1875: Fairfield Villa was advertised as a hunting box to let, within easy distance of the meets of the Hertfordshire and Essex Foxhounds.
2 *HEO*, 11 September 1875.
3 For this account, see E.F. Gosling, Robert's grandson, 'Four Brothers', n.d. Typescript made available to me by Toby and Frances Lyons.
4 Wilkins (1976: 158 and 191).
5 Wilkins (1976: 194).
6 Wilkins (1976: 431).
7 Wilkins (1976: 286).
8 *HEO*, 29 November 1884.
9 *HEO*, 23 November 1885.
10 The story is well told by Patrick Streeter (2004).
11 *HEO* 19 April 1890, 10 May 1890 and 14 January 1899.
12 *VCH vol. ii* (1907: 592). See also *HEO*, 4 October 1902, 3 January 1903.
13 *HEO*, 8 June 1912.
14 *HEO*, 14 February 1891. Peter Brown, in an article in *The Link* in 1988, identified the cricket field as part of the playing fields of what was then the Mountfitchet School.
15 *HEO*, 25 March 1893 and 21 April 1900.
16 *HEO*, 25 September 1897.
17 *HEO*, 16 March 1912.
18 *HEO*, 15 January 1898.
19 *HEO*, 31 May 1890.
20 *HEO*, 9 May 1891.
21 In a match at Birchanger in 1911, when Birchanger scored 16 and 26 and Stansted 40 and 5 for 1 wicket, it was reported that 'The state of the ground helped the bowlers considerably': *HEO* 23 September 1911. The proliferation of byes in many matches was another consequence of uneven pitches. In a match in 1845 Dunmow Albion scored 59 and 51, of which 26 and 16 were byes, while Stansted scored 82 and 32 for 1, of which 20 and 3 were byes.
22 *HEO*, 21 March 1885.
23 *HEO*, 31 May 1890.
24 *HEO*, 20 April 1867.
25 *HEO*, 10 November 1894.
26 *HEO*, 6 June 1885.
27 See his obituary, *HEO*, 23 December 1916.
28 *HEO*, 2 August 1890.
29 *HEO*, 1 November 1913.
30 *HEO*, 16 June 1883.

32: CRIME

The gentry prided themselves on bringing the classes together in cricket, but for many labourers and others it was their confrontations in the Petty Sessions with magistrates and landowners that brought them into the closest contact with the village authorities and that embroiled them in the sharpest manifestations of class conflict. In everyday life this clash was mediated through dealings with policemen and gamekeepers.

At first the Petty Sessions were held in Saffron Walden, but the distance to be travelled was so great that in 1897 it was agreed that an additional court should be set up in Stansted, manned by local JPs, and cases arising in Stansted and the villages around were then heard in the Central Hall. William Fuller-Maitland often chaired these sessions, and he was supported by his younger brother, Robert, and by several other JPs such as Harry Chester, Harford Green and Charles Gold. There had been a police presence in the village since the 1850s, and by 1897 there were two policemen there, a sergeant and a constable. Several of the big landowners, including the Fuller-Maitlands and the Goslings, had their own gamekeeper, the best known being John Wilkins, whose reminiscences were published in 1892. The gentry were very conscious of the debt that they owed to these men, both policemen and gamekeepers, who, often at great risk to themselves, manned the frontiers against attacks on property rights and made the village safe for their enjoyment.

The accused who appeared before the bench were for the most part labourers, and the most common offences for which they were tried were being drunk and disorderly, assault, poaching in all its various forms, theft and the occasional burglary.

The motives for crime were of course many and various. Some offences, such as assault or refusing to leave a public house, were often fuelled by drink, and poverty inevitably played a part, as in 1866 when a mother stole half a peck of peas from a field in order to feed her nine children – her appetite, she said, was 'very precarious at times'[1] - or in 1890, when two labourers stole water cress at Wicken because they wanted to make a little money – one of them said he had been out of work for a long time and thought he could sell a few.[2] Food figured in several cases. In 1869 George Peachey stole some turnips from William Spencer's farm to go with his Christmas dinner,[3] and in 1877 Ann Godfrey pleaded guilty to the charge of stealing 13 Savoy cabbages from George Little's allotment.[4] On the night of 3 October 1863 Clement Fletcher broke into the house of William White, a retired farmer, turned the whole place upside down, but took nothing but a damson pie which he had found in the pantry. He ate the crust and said, when caught, that if they fetched the fruit he would eat that as well, as he was very hungry.[5] Alfred Phillips commented that it was 'a period of poverty and want, when a turnip taken from the field, when unseen, meant survival'.[6]

Two poachers claimed that they were driven by poverty, but this was unusual.[7] No doubt men who trespassed in search of game were pleased to enjoy a good meal or to get a bit of extra cash by selling their game on, but for many poachers it was not so much a crime as a sport. Wilkins says that poachers often told him 'that they mostly take the game for the excitement, rather than on account of pecuniary benefit. It is a very common tale – public-houses first and devilment afterwards'[8] - and recounts how in one case he heard the poachers laughing as they chased their game. The same delight is celebrated in the words of the well known song, *The Lincolnshire Poacher:*

When I was bound apprentice in famous Lincolnshire
Full well I served my master for nigh on seven years
Till I took up to poaching as you shall quickly hear
Oh, 'tis my delight on a shiny night in the season of the year.

Many poachers believed that they had as much right as the landowners to the wild animals of the countryside – to the hares and rabbits, partridges and pheasants. They were usually young men, they often went out in small groups or gangs, and many of them were serial offenders. The two poachers who pleaded poverty, George Carter, 23, and George Powell, 22, were both labourers, and there were four previous convictions against Carter and ten against Powell. They were not untypical. In March 1890 ten men were accused of trespassing in search of game, aged between 16 and 23, all were found guilty except one and all had previous convictions. One of them, Henry Gray, had 21.

In his memoirs John Wilkins presented himself as a paragon of courtesy and respect in his dealings with poachers. They knew he spoke the truth, he said, that he did not exaggerate the case against them, and that he was not vindictive. So they were more inclined to plead guilty and did not challenge his evidence as a witness. He enjoyed such good relations with some of the men he caught that, to the amazement of his master, the first William Fuller-Maitland, he would walk back with the convicted men from Saffron Walden to Stansted evidently on the best of terms. He was invariably 'civil' with them, he explained to Fuller-Maitland, though he agreed with the squire that he would not take 'any of their nonsense'.[9]

But conflict, very fierce conflict, was built into the relationship between gamekeeper and poacher. It could hardly have been otherwise when, having caught them, the gamekeeper would confiscate any game the poachers had taken and any guns they carried, shoot their dogs on the spot and then testify against them in court. *The Lincolnshire Poacher* says it again:

As me and my companions was setting out a snare
'Twas then we spied the gamekeeper, for him we didn't care,
For we can wrestle and fight, my boys, and jump from anywhere
Oh, 'tis my delight on a shiny night in the season of the year.

One night in 1850 Wilkins and two assistants, Joslin and Hutley, came across a gang of six poachers setting nets to catch hares. In the fight that followed Wilkins was thrown to the ground and was kicked so often and so hard that his arm was broken as he tried to ward off the blows. Some of the gang wanted to finish him off, but he was saved by the intervention of one of them, a former gamekeeper, who was well known to him, and he was left bleeding and helpless in a ditch. Eventually he was able to climb out and staggered back to the village. One of the gang turned Queen's evidence and was not punished, but the man who had saved him was given six months' hard labour, another was given twelve months, and the other three, the worst offenders, were sentenced to be transported for seven years.[10]

In 1886 five boys, all of them from Stansted, attacked George Wilkinson, another gamekeeper, when he suspected they were poaching and tried to stop them, but this was only a minor affray.[11] In 1901 Arthur Haggerwood assaulted a gamekeeper employed by one of the Blyths and flung him to the ground.[12]

Such fights were part of a general pattern. In 1870, for example, a gamekeeper was shot at Widdington, in 1880 one of Lord Braybrooke's gamekeepers was killed at Audley End, in 1883 there was a serious attack on Walter Gilbey's gamekeeper in Elsenham, and in 1894 there was an assault on a gamekeeper in Manuden.[13]

The frequency of reports in the local press suggests that there was a substantial increase in poaching offences towards the end of the nineteenth century. More serious was an increase in disturbances caused by what the press called 'the rough element' in the village, mainly young labourers. An important factor in their behaviour seems to have been a reaction against respectability, and in particular against the strict sexual morality of the church, a reaction that was expressed by molesting people on their way to or from church – blocking the footpaths, forcing people into the road and making unwanted advances to young servant girls.

The first occasion on which I have found this reported was Christmas Day, 1865, when James Turner, a labourer, was charged with obstructing the footpath together with a number of other young men.[14] Two years later, in March 1868, William Prior and Nathaniel Palmer, labourers, were convicted of obstructing the footpath as people were leaving church. Police Constable Law said he had cautioned them about this before, but they had taken no notice. 'Complaints had frequently been made respecting it, and persons had to go off the pathway to pass them, while very unbecoming remarks were often made.' They were fined 7s. each with 1s. costs or in default 14 days.[15]

In 1877, under the heading of 'A Sunday amusement in Stansted', the *Observer* reported the case of Walter Judd, who took Emma Lacey by the arm as she was walking with a fellow servant to church, twisted her round two or three times and tried to kiss her. She struck him with her umbrella and broke free. 'Police-constable Brighten said great complaints had been made of this sort of Sunday amusement. A lot of young fellows got together and frequently molested young women on their way to church', and the Chairman of the magistrates said it was 'abominable that these cases were so frequently occurring'. The defendant was fined £1 with 16s. costs or one month in prison.[16] In 1880 a gang of seven boys, aged between 12 and 16, attacked George Prior as he was walking along the Elsenham road with a young woman, striking him with a stick and stoning him. 'The bench were informed that defendants were part of a gang who kept up a continual round of ill behaviour on the Sunday about Stansted, spending the day in a most disgraceful way.' The three ringleaders were each fined 5s.6d. and the others 4s.6d.[17] At a public vestry on 21 March 1890 it was resolved that a complaint should be sent to the Chief Constable about the lack of police protection afforded to the village and the behaviour of the lads generally, especially on Sundays. In 1891, however, there was another case of a group of young men forcing young women to step into the street if they wanted to get by.[18]

Stansted was not the only village where this happened. In 1880, for example, a group of youths in Birchanger disrupted the church service by sitting behind three girls, taking their umbrellas, using such bad language that the girls could not repeat it in court and generally making a nuisance of themselves: one of them scrambled over the pews and sat down on a girl's lap. 'The Rev. F. Rowden said he had had occasion more than once to speak to every one of the defendants because of their behaviour in church and he was constantly receiving complaints of their molesting people on their way to church.'[19]

There was the usual hooliganism after the public houses were closed on Saturday night, and when several young labourers were drunk and disorderly and threatening to fight it was often difficult and dangerous for the police to keep order. In 1891, under the heading 'Stansted: the rough element', the *Observer* reported a case of several young men being drunk and disorderly, one of them taking off his coat to fight and all of them using 'very bad language'. They were found guilty, and three of them had previous convictions.[20]

The police were threatened as they performed their duties, and in some cases these threats were carried out. The worst incident occurred in 1897. About 11 pm on a Saturday night the senior police officer stationed in Stansted, Sergeant Kemp, 'a highly respectable and efficient officer', was sent for to eject some men from the King's Arms. He got the men into the street, whereupon he was attacked by 'a mob of roughs' who 'knocked him down and kicked him brutally in the side and head'. Police Constable Britten, who was on duty at the nearby railway station, ran to Kemp's assistance. Kemp tried to rise and was felled again, but Britten then drew his truncheon and managed to disperse the crowd. Shortly afterwards two of the men returned carrying palings in their hands and knocked Kemp to the ground again. In the fight that followed the policemen managed to arrest one of the two men, George Wright, while the other, Thomas Harrington, got away but was arrested later.

Kemp was unable to attend the early stages of the trial, being confined to bed. He was still suffering from slight concussion and was 'terribly knocked about' with a large cut across the cheek and bruises all over the body. Britten gave evidence with a black eye, bruises about his head and arm, and a dent in the metal plate in his helmet. The case was too serious for the Petty Sessions and was referred to the Quarter Sessions, where the accused were sentenced to four months' hard labour.[21] There was a surprising sequel to this: 'In consequence of assaults on PC Kemp ... the Chief Constable has thought it advisable for that officer to carry a revolver'.[22] There is no evidence that he ever used it, but perhaps it acted as a deterrent.

Again what happened in Stansted was part of a wider pattern. Only a week before the attack on Kemp there had been a similar incident in Bishop's Stortford. When the police had tried to stop people 'loafing about' in the street there was a 'disgraceful riot' and the police were 'roughly handled'.[23] A few weeks later some labourers in Ugley threatened to deal with a policeman there as they had dealt with the policemen in Stansted.

There were very few cases of domestic violence, probably because the police did not regard it as appropriate to intervene. Of the cases that did come to court the most striking was Alice Watson's accusation that her husband John was threatening to kill her. When he was simply bound over to keep the peace Alice and her mother cried out 'This is not justice, there is no justice here'.[24]

Less disturbing were the various statutory offences that became more numerous as life became more regulated. There were many traffic offences – driving a wagon without reins, dangerous driving (or 'furious driving' as it was sometimes called), driving when drunk and even driving when asleep. Gypsies were punished for allowing their horses to stray onto the highway. There were several cases of cruelty to animals, the prosecutors being officers of the RSPCA. It was an offence to keep a dog without a licence, and for a time dogs had to be muzzled.

There were no murders in Stansted, the nearest being an attempted murder when a burglar was disturbed by a servant girl and fired a gun at her but missed.[25] Perhaps the most colourful case was that against Arthur Wiffen, a corn dealer and brewer, who was accused of fraud. He had been living above his means, buying horses which never won a race and littering his house with empty champagne bottles.[26] He had played cricket for Stansted Park, and as a performer had been enthusiastically applauded and encored at the entertainments in the Central Hall: 'Give Me a Man of Honest Heart' he sang, and 'The Fine Old English Gentleman'. He was gaoled for a time, but the prosecutions were dropped when he was declared a bankrupt.

Over the years there were several cases in the area of 'rough music', when villagers took justice into their own hands and put neighbours to shame by banging outside their homes on pots and pans, kettles and the like. In Stansted this practice took an unusual turn in what the *Chelmsford Chronicle* described as a case of 'horrible depravity' in 1836. James Banks, a labourer, aged 22, was charged with the capital offence of assaulting Amelia Cass, a girl of 11, and with a similar assault on two other young girls, Charlotte Godfrey and Emma Cuffley, though in their case it was not a capital charge that was pressed, i.e. a charge that might lead to the death penalty, but an ordinary misdemeanour. In the Assizes at Chelmsford a 'gross case' of assault on Amelia Cass was proved, but the jury was not satisfied that a capital charge had been substantiated. The case of assault on Charlotte Godfrey was also proved, but the case involving Emma Cuffley was dropped. The judge, in passing sentence, said that no one could have heard the case without feeling horror and disgust. There was too much reason to believe that Banks had been in the practice of corrupting persons of tender years to gratify his brutal appetite. He therefore imposed the severest sentence allowed for misdemeanour, two years' hard labour, and hoped that it would make Banks reflect with horror upon his offence and resolve never to do the like again.[27]

The prosecutors and their witnesses set off from Chelmsford to go home at about half past five. By nine they had reached Dunmow, and they then went on to Takeley. There they were met by a crowd of about 30 men (perhaps there were some women among them too, but none were named) who were incensed, not because James Banks had assaulted three young girls, as we might have expected, but because a capital charge had been made against him, and they now set up a great din, 'rough music', with sticks, kettles, frying-pans and horns. The prosecutors and witnesses, feeling threatened, took refuge in the house of a magistrate at Takeley, where the servants let them in and then let them out the back way. By this time it was 11 o'clock, and they were able to make their way home to Stansted without any further trouble.

A charge of riot was brought against eight of the men, who were represented in court by Dowling, the same lawyer who had defended Stansted's agricultural labourers in the so-called riot of 1834, and the central issue was the same: had the 'rioters' behaved in a way that was calculated to excite terror and alarm? The answer in this case was no, and the eight men were acquitted.[28]

1. *HEO*, 4 August 1866.
2. *HEO*, 24 May 1890.
3. *HEO*, 8 January 1870.
4. *HEO*, 3 March 1877.
5. *HEO*, 10 October 1863.
6. Alfred Phillips, 'Our Family', 1984, p. 5.
7. *HEO*, 27 January 1894.
8. Wilkins (1892: 212-3).
9. Wilkins (1892: 362-7).
10. *CC*, 6 December 1850 and 7 March 1851; *Lloyd's Weekly Newspaper*, 8 December 1850; Wilkins (1892: 229-48, 256-8).
11. *HEO*, 17 April 1886.
12. *HEO*, 5 January 1901.
13. *HEO*, 12 November 1870, 16 October 1880, 10 February 1883 and 10 February 1894.
14. *HEO*, 13 January 1866.
15. *HEO*, 21 July 1868.
16. *HEO*, 7 March 1868.
17. *HEO*, 28 August 1880.
18. *HEO*, 14 March 1891.
19. *HEO*, 2 October 1880.
20. *HEO*, 28 March 1891.
21. *HEO*, 23 January 1897 and 20 February 1897.
22. *HEO*, 20 February 1897.
23. *HEO*, 16 January 1897.
24. *HEO*, 25 November 1876.
25. *HEO*, 10 October 1863.
26. *HEO*, 4 December 1875.
27. *CC*, 8 April and 8 and 15 July 1836.
28. *CC*, 28 October 1836.

PART V
MODERN TIMES

33: THE FIRST WORLD WAR

'The 1914-18 War changed everything.' So wrote Alfred Phillips in his recollections as an old man: he was just a boy at the time, living in the house that is still called Montville, just off Chapel Hill.[1]

In one way Stansted was changed in the same way as every other village in the country: many of its men left to go to the war. The impact was devastating. The population of the village at the outbreak of hostilities was about 2,400. According to the Roll of Honour in St. John's Church more than 400 men served in the war, about one in three of the male population, and according to the war memorial 54 were killed. Many others were wounded.[2] Every class of society was affected, from the squire at Stansted Hall to the humblest labourers in their cottages. After the war, unveiling the war memorial, General Pulteney congratulated the village 'for the great part they had taken in the European War. He was astonished to see the number of men, in proportion to the population, who had fallen in that great cause.'[3]

But Stansted was changed in another way as well: to quote Alfred Phillips again, it 'became a huge military transit camp …. The whole village was full of soldiers', some of them in military encampments but many of them billeted in the villagers' homes.[4] The population of the village was doubled, and the whole tenor of village life was changed.

In August 1914 Britain was the only major European power not to have introduced conscription: its army was entirely voluntary. There were three branches:
- the regular army, with former soldiers making up the National Reserve;
- the Territorial Force, popularly known as the Terriers, which was set up in 1908 following the reorganisation of the former militias and other volunteer units; these were part-timers who trained at weekends or in the evening; and
- the Special Reserve, men who had been trained for six months and then for three to four weeks every year.

All three branches were liable to being called up in the event of a general mobilisation.

Compared with the armies of Germany and France the British Army was tiny – just 250,000 regular soldiers, about half of them posted abroad. The BEF, the British Expeditionary Force that was sent immediately across the Channel, was made up of only 130,000 men, organised into seven divisions. The Germans mobilised 1,850,000 men in 87 divisions and the French 1,650,000 in 62 divisions.

The authorities were desperate for more men, but they were not yet ready to impose conscription and called instead for volunteers aged between 19 and 35. The recruitment campaign was headed by Lord Kitchener, the Secretary of State for War, who pointed from posters throughout the land declaring 'Your country needs YOU'. By mid-September some 500,000 men had volunteered, but another 500,000 were then needed. The crisis became more and more pressing, but still conscription was resisted. Towards the end of 1915 the scheme devised by Lord Derby called for volunteers, who could either be enlisted at once or be placed on a reserve list divided into 46 categories according to age, 23 categories for single men and 23 for married men, to be called up as needed, the single and youngest first. The lower age limit was lowered to 18 and the upper limit was raised to 40. In all 350,000 volunteered under the Derby Scheme, which fell far short of what was needed, especially in view of the heavy casualties being suffered. The voluntary principle was now played out. Under the Military Service Act of January 1916 conscription for single men was introduced and in May was extended to married men. By the time of the armistice in November 1918 the British Army consisted of 56 divisions.

At the beginning there was great enthusiasm for the war. Few had any idea of the horrors to come, and there were some who expected the fighting to be over by Christmas. There were 'patriotic meetings' in Stortford, with patriotic songs, flags and decorations. The newspapers thrilled their readers with stories of British victories and shocked them with tales of German atrocities. Stansted, like many other villages, was swept by rumours of foreign spies and agents operating secretly to weaken the war effort, firing on troop trains and poisoning horses, and at a public meeting in the first week of the war a suggestion that 50 parishioners should become special constables to help the police was 'greeted by a long round of applause'.[5]

There were several Stansted men who were regular soldiers and who crossed the Channel at once with the BEF to Belgium. Others who were in the National Reserve, the Territorials or the Special Reserve were called up without delay. Almost immediately, it was noted, five of the Stansted Rovers football team were enlisted.[6]

But more were needed. On Tuesday 1 September a public meeting to obtain recruits for

76. Volunteers being collected in Lower Street by cars supplied by Dr. Haynes, Mr. Bannehr and others on Wednesday, 2 September 1914, to be taken to Saffron Walden.

Lord Kitchener's new army was held in the Assembly Room of the Stansted Men's Working Club. The report in the *Observer* captured both the solemnity and the excitement of the occasion:

> *There were upwards of 200 present.... Mr. Charles Gold was in the chair, supported by the vicar, the Rev. A.M. Winter, Mr. W.J. Bannehr[7] and others.*
>
> *The Chairman explained that the meeting had been called by the Committee of the Working Men's Club to consider what steps could be taken to help in obtaining recruits for the Army in view of the crisis. That great soldier, Lord Kitchener, had appealed for more men, and it was for every town and village throughout the kingdom to loyally respond to the call.*
>
> *Mr. Gawthorp (the club secretary) quoted the words of Sir Robert Nicholl, that it was 'a just and righteous war' and that Great Britain had taken the line she had done to uphold the neutrality of Belgium ... and also for our own preservation. There were several young men belonging to Stansted fighting at the front, and others belonging to the Territorials had been called up and he hoped that the young men would loyally respond to the call to arms.*

As a result of the meeting 17 recruits gave in their names and on the very next morning they were conveyed in cars lent by Dr. Haynes and others to Saffron Walden where they enlisted for the period of the war. They were given 'a very hearty send-off'.[8]

On the following Sunday, 6 September, 20 men came forward at a recruiting meeting on the Recreation Ground, and after that another 6, making a total of 43.

It soon became sickeningly clear that this was no jaunt in the French countryside and the prospect of an early peace soon receded. Quickly, all too quickly, reports of the first casualties reached the village. These were the men who had been regular soldiers at the outbreak of war and were therefore part of the BEF, and the first of Stansted's casualties was the squire's eldest son, William Fuller-Maitland, a captain in the Coldstream Guards, who died of wounds received in the battle of the Aisne on 19 September 1914. On 1 October Alfred Wootten, also of the Coldstream Guards, died of wounds received in the same battle. That was just the beginning of the carnage. As well as those killed or wounded there were those who were taken prisoners of war, those who went missing, and those who came back shattered from shell shock or were sent back medically unfit. Most died in France, some at Gallipoli or in German East Africa, and some at sea, since they had enlisted as sailors. Some families suffered multiple tragedies, such as the Luckeys, who lost three sons while a fourth was so severely wounded that he was discharged as unfit for military service. The youngest to die was Albert Patmore, who had barely turned 16. The oldest, Henry Levey, was 50. There was no slackening in the horror as the war went on: the worst month for Stansted was August 1918, when five of its soldiers were killed. There were also those who were awarded medals for gallantry, the Military Cross or the Distinguished Conduct Medal.

A striking feature of the casualty lists is the number of men who had emigrated before the war to Australia (8), New Zealand (1) or Canada (1) and who had enlisted with their colonial regiments, fighting in France or in Gallipoli and in some cases taking their leave with the families in Stansted they had left behind. There must have been many other such men who took part in the fighting but were not injured or killed.[9]

For those at home it was the waiting for letters and telegrams from the front that imposed the greatest anxiety and strain. They were relieved when they received a letter from a father, husband, son or brother, assuring them that he was still alive and well and thanking them for the provisions they had sent. But, as the toll mounted, many must have lived in dread of a very different communication, of a telegram announcing that he had been killed or wounded, or gone missing, or been captured by the enemy, though this last was often mingled with relief. In some cases the news of death came first in the form of a letter written by a comrade in the same regiment, and only later was it officially confirmed.[10]

The families at home were left in no doubt about the horrors of trench warfare. Letters home were surprisingly frank, such as the following from Walter Spalding, a Territorial writing in May 1915 to his parents in Silver Street:

> We have been in action during the last few days and under the most awful shell fire since I have been out here. It was simply hell on earth, and I wonder I am alive to tell the tale, and I can only thank God for bringing me safely through it. I will just explain if the censor will let it pass. The Irish Guards, our dear old mates, were to attack and the object was, I think, a farm which the Germans were holding. No. 1 Company of the 1st Herts were the first to support the Guards and as we moved up we came up under shell fire ... and heavy shrapnel. Well, we began to lose our men, but we got up to the first German trench, then our officer who deserves a V.C. shouted, 'Come on, No. 1 Company, over the parapet', and over we went, with German maxims firing upon us, and started to advance across the open country losing men as we advanced. Part of my company got within 50 yards of the farm but had to retire, as we had not enough support to take it. All night and next day we held the trenches, shells continually dropping, and when we were relieved at night our battalion had lost rather heavily. Of two brothers in my section one was wounded and the other killed. Well, anyhow, it shows that although only 'Terriers' [Territorials] we are not afraid to do our bit.[11]

The *Observer* was brutally frank. As early as 10 October 1914 it carried a report from the Rev. James Molloy, apparently an American, who wrote that 'the greatest slaughter in the world's history is going on behind that censorship curtain in France. When the world learns of the price that has been paid it will be staggered – sick at heart.' In spite of official disapproval the Christmas truce was fully reported in the *Observer* in letters sent home by soldiers from Bishop's Stortford and Thaxted. And no matter what the censors did or did not do, there was nothing to stop the soldiers on leave from speaking freely.

In spite of all this the people of Stansted remained fully committed to the war, at least in their public utterances. Walter Spalding ended his letter by saying that while it would be sad news for the Hertfordshire people when the casualties came to be known, 'they will have the satisfaction of knowing that they died doing their duty for King and country, and it is far better that, than stay at home and let the Germans reach England'. In January 1915 Arthur Law, a farm labourer from Burton End, was so keen to join the forces that he added four years to his age, saying he was 19 when in fact he was 15: when this was discovered he was discharged.[12] Later in the same year a military funeral was held in Stansted for Charles Patmore, who had been severely wounded by a shell in the trenches, brought home and admitted to hospital, but died from his injuries on 23 December. The inscriptions on the floral tributes were profoundly expressive of the pride taken in him by his family and friends - 'In Loving Memory of Our Dear Brother, who gave his life bravely for his King and Country', and 'In Memory of Charles Patmore, Another Son of Britain Gone to Join the Throng of those who have done their duty, heroes all'. There was also a wreath from the Fuller-Maitlands for whom he had worked as a gardener.[13] At a tea which she gave at Stansted House for about a hundred mothers and wives of Stansted's soldiers, Lady Jackson boasted that she had seven sons and sons-in-law in the forces, which was one more than the best family record among her guests.[14]

Not every man was liable to call-up under conscription. Men in 'starred' occupations might be exempt from service, including most agricultural workers, but they had to get exemption certificates from their local military tribunal. There were four grounds of exemption - that it was expedient in the national interest that the man should be engaged in other work; that serious hardship because of his business obligations or family commitments would result from his being called up; ill health or infirmity; and conscientious objection to combatant service.

The six-man Stansted tribunal, which covered the whole of the Stansted Rural District, was chaired by Walter Gold. The labour representative on the tribunal was Walter Prior of Stansted, who 'was a bell-ringer and a Friendly Society man and was in touch with the working classes'.[15] Another member of the Tribunal was Cunliffe Gosling from Farnham. As well as the six members Harry Chester of Stansted attended the tribunal as the military representative, and there was also an agricultural representative. The farmers found themselves pulled in both directions – they were under pressure not only to increase production but also to release as many workers as possible.

Tribunal hearings were reported in the press. In the case of conscientious objectors no details were given of names and places, but we can be sure that some of them came from Stansted, if only because of its Quaker community. Few applicants were exempted completely: it was more common for them to be ordered into non-combatant service.

For men who were engaged in other work it was normally the employer who made the application, and exemptions were often given for six months and then had to be renewed. In these cases the names of the places were published but not the names of the individuals involved. So we are told of a 'titled lady' in Stansted who applied for exemption for her married gardener and after close questioning was refused. Applications by a farmer for a cowman and a horsekeeper were also dismissed. A firm of builders which had only one bricklayer left, a married man aged 40 whose work included the repair of farm buildings, obtained an exemption for six months. A baker, a woman, who employed only one man, who was single and 18 years old, was granted three months.[16]

On the home front great efforts were made to support the troops. Lady Jackson set up a working party which met every Wednesday afternoon at the Friends Meeting House. In the course of 1916 it made 4,059 garments, most of them for hospitals, while mufflers, socks and mittens were sent to the soldiers and sailors from Stansted.[17] Money was raised in several ways, such as whist drives, auctions and tennis tournaments. Contributions were made to War Loans, and in 1916 a War Savings Association with about 100 members was

33: THE FIRST WORLD WAR

formed. Eggs for the wounded were collected under the National Egg Collection, and at the height of this activity, in eight weeks in the summer of 1916, 1,548 eggs were sent off.[18] Parcels were sent to prisoners of war.

Towards the end of the war, because of the activities of German submarines, food stocks began to run low and strenuous endeavours were made to increase production. Farmers were encouraged to turn their grassland into arable land, and also to grow potatoes. Forty-seven new allotments were established on land provided by Fuller-Maitland in Alley Field,[19] and every week the *Observer* carried tips for allotment holders and poultry keepers. People were encouraged to keep pigs and also to catch rabbits. In 1918, under a scheme promoted by the Ministry of Food and organised through the schools, over 47 hundredweight of blackberries were collected and delivered to the jam factory at Elsenham.[20] Also in 1918, in response to a plea from the National Salvage Council, fruit stones and nut shells were collected and sent to the Gas Works in Southend.[21] Although it was not made known at the time, when fired the stones and shells produced a high quality charcoal which could be used as a filter in gas masks.

By the end of the war rationing had been introduced for many items, such as sugar, butter, margarine and meat. Hoarding was forbidden, and prices were set for bread, meat, milk and coal. Even wages were fixed. Economy in the use of food was encouraged, and in May 1917 King George issued a Proclamation calling on his subjects to sign a pledge to do their best to save food and in particular to abstain 'from all unnecessary consumption of grain'.

In the absence of so many men from the farms women were called on to fill the gaps. By January 1917 1,800 women were being employed in agriculture in Essex, and in June 1918 the Women's Land Army, which had been formed in 1915, held a recruiting rally at

77. The parish fire engine. At the beginning of WW1 a second hand Shand Mason manual engine was delivered to Stansted. It replaced the existing appliance which had been made in 1822. Because so many horses were required in the war the engine often had to be drawn manually. It was taken out of service in 1927.

Stortford with banners such as 'England Must be Fed. Join the Land Army and Hold the Home Front'. Many women workers from farms in the neighbourhood took part 'with their hoes and other farm implements', and before the year was out at least two young women from Stansted had joined.[22]

There was provision for children of 12 and above being exempted from school for farm labour, and one child in Stansted is known to have taken advantage of this.[23] German prisoners of war were also employed. There was a camp at Bishop's Stortford in Chantry Road, where the local girls gave the prisoners cigarettes, which so infuriated the Town Council that it closed the footpath that went by the camp.

Another important support for the war was the work of the Stansted Remount Depot under Gerald Gold. Large numbers of horses were bought from neighbouring farmers, broken in and sent to France. The headquarters were in Elsenham, but much of the work was done at farms and buildings made available by Lord Blyth.[24] Many women were employed as well as men.

Because so many men were away in France it was impossible to get the Fire Brigade up to strength, and because of the shortage of horses the firemen had to pull the engine themselves. Meanwhile some of the older men worked as Special Constables, helping the police and taking on duties similar to those of air raid wardens in WW2, for which they were equipped with armlets, badges, truncheons, whistles and lanterns.

There were in fact no air raids on Stansted, but news came through of attacks on Braintree, Coggeshall and Colchester, and also on towns on the Essex coast, and there was a constant need for vigilance. The Parish Council was exercised about lights in the village after dark. At first the street lamps were kept on until eleven, but then a virtual blackout was imposed and several people, among them Lord Blyth, were taken to court for having their lights showing. It was still unlawful, however, to drive a vehicle without a lamp. Charles Whybrow, who was driving a coster's barrow at 11 pm without a light, said that he had told his boy to blow it out because he had seen a Zeppelin 'like a big cigar' in the sky. He was fined 5s. all the same.[25] But there were some genuine sightings of Zeppelins and two or three British planes crashed at Burton End.[26]

The other great change wrought by the war was the designation of Stansted as a military transit camp, and Alfred Phillips's account of this is so vivid and informative that it is worth quoting at length:

> *Stansted became a huge military transit camp. Pump Field was rapidly built over with rows and rows of stables for the Artillery, with all concrete floors and link roads – sections for guns and limbers, administration blocks, huts and guard rooms, with sentries at all approaches, which did not deter us boys from entering through holes in the hedge.*
>
> *The horses, guns, limbers and wagons were everywhere, constantly coming and going. Half-trained horses were continually tearing down Chapel Hill, in a long stream, often unable to hold back and brake at the bottom of the hill, causing a pile up ....*
>
> *The whole village was full of soldiers. The Alley Field and Brewery Field areas were covered with Bell tents for the Infantry who could not be*

accommodated in billets. The village was divided into sections for this purpose and a billeting officer visited every house in his section to assess the number of soldiers who could be accommodated. It was based on the floor area in each house, and it was compulsory to accept them. Our house "Montville" was assessed to billet six men, sleeping side by side in the front room, the other rooms for our own family. The men were provided with a mattress and two blankets each and expected to sleep on the floor in the allotted space. They had all their military equipment with them, stacked in the hall, packs, webbing, bandoliers of ammunition, trenching tools, greatcoats, rifles, groundsheets. Some had long, heavy swords, all packed in the passage ....

Our zone was first occupied by the 5th Lincoln Regiment, and later we were rezoned to have men from the 6th Lincolns. This caused great confusion. The men of the 5th liked their billet and refused to move out. For a time we had a blockade, until a day when the 5th were out on parade and the 6th moved in. So when the 5th came back we had both; eleven men all told. They had nowhere else to go. Mother Alice coped and harmony was restored. To the men it was home from home as far as was possible, and the men respected it.

All the time, day after day, week in, week out, foot soldiers were incessantly marching – four abreast – along the Cambridge Road to the embarkation ports. Each section of men interposed with a horse-drawn wagon, whose duty it was to pick up the men who fell out from exhaustion, having been pushed to the side of the road .... Every so often a field kitchen would come along, a great boiler on wheels, and a few supporting provision wagons, to feed the troops on the march.

Mother Alice was a splendid cook. The soldiers ate in, bringing their rations and supplies twice weekly. Each group took a sack to the quartermaster's stores and returned with it full. Huge 4lb. loaves of bread, quantities of potatoes, large lumps of meat, all manner of vegetables and sundries, such as margarine, lard, sugar, salt and condiments. Some had 'Bully Beef' (corned beef) or tins of condensed milk, fruit, tins of jam, etc. The quartermaster's stores were next door at St. John's Cottage, just over the wall, and many surplus items came over the wall such as, I remember, a large 7lb. tin of pepper. We also proved to be a dumping ground for cabbage leaves, damaged or dirty bread, carrots etc. for the chickens and rabbits. These, when converted into table poultry, eggs and rabbit pie were luxuries generally unobtainable for soldiers. The rabbit run covered a large part of the back yard, there were dozens of them.

The Army paid the household 6d. a night for each soldier billeted on them, and a small additional sum for cooking and preparing the rations. The food issued to the men was more than adequate for us all. We wanted nothing. We used discarded army blankets for our beds, after a good boiling in the copper .... True, it was difficult getting round the house while we had eleven men and ourselves. The hall, scullery and every available space was packed with equipment. To us it was a great source of enjoyment. We handled the rifles, bayonets. etc. and spent much of our out of school time with the soldiers around and in the Alley Fields tents.

78. Soldiers billeted in the village posing here with Mrs. Dixon and her family in Woodfields.

This, of course, was very much a child's view. For the youngsters it was all great fun. But for their parents it was very hard work. Jessie Berry, who was born in 1910, remembered how much she and her sister enjoyed having the soldiers in their house at 11 Recreation Ground. It was only a small house, she said, three up and three down, but sometimes they had as many as four soldiers at a time. Having to look after so many people wore her mother out and she died of tuberculosis in 1918. The soldiers who stayed with the Phillips were well behaved and respected the property, but that was not always the case. The soldiers billeted at Hole Farm, where Susan Spencer-Smith's father was the tenant, did a lot of damage to the oak panelling in the drawing room. It was common practice for those who were well off to move out, rather than to stay and have to share their home with soldiers. St. John's Cottage, which became the quartermaster's stores, had been the home of two women, and rather than having soldiers billeted on them they had given up the house and gone to live elsewhere. The billeting officers also seem to have made sure that the men allocated to the wealthier parishioners were officers and not just ordinary privates.[27] The Central Hall too was occupied and so at times were the Council and Church Schools. The parish room over the Working Men's Club became a recreation room for the soldiers, and concerts were held there on occasion. Inevitably the men got involved in village life. Some made friends with the local people, and sent back news when they went to the front. One at least married a local girl. Some were convicted of poaching, some of getting drunk and disorderly.

There were some in the village who tried to carry on as normal. In March 1916, looking ahead to the new season, Mr. Tissiman, the chairman of the bowling club, said he hoped that the club would flourish – 'for although the war is still on I do not see why old fogeys like myself should not amuse ourselves with a game of bowls instead of always thinking and talking about the war'.[28] And the Parish Council went on with its old worries about watering the village roads to keep down the dust, harvesting the mangolds at the sewage farm and the provision of dustbins – a muted counterpoint to the horrors of war.

I shall leave the last word with Walter Spalding. He had been in France since November 1914 with the Hertfordshire Regiment and had been involved in some of the fiercest fighting of the war. Writing to his parents in April 1918 after some particularly heavy engagements he judged that the last two weeks had been

> *the worst of all the time I have spent in this country. For 14 days we never had a roof over us, all our boots and clothes on. We have just gone back on rest and to refit etc. Poor old boys! They fought hard but they were hopelessly outnumbered, but Fritz paid a terrible price for his advance and I think his chance of victory is now over. It was heartrending to see the poor old civilians flying from their homes, taking what they could, carts, wheelbarrows and perambulators. Poor old men and grey-headed women trying to shove great loads in among the traffic. Farmers with their cattle which of course did not want to be driven from home. Young mothers with babies in their arms. I could have cried to think I should ever have witnessed such a thing, and I thought of England and thanked God that so far our homeland has been spared the worst horrors of war. When they grouse in England they ought to try and realise that they have a lot to be thankful for. Many of my mates I shall not see again, but I think now more than ever if only the Germans can be finally crushed and this sort of thing made impossible in future they will not have died in vain.*[29]

The news of the Armistice on 11 November 1918 was the occasion for a great outpouring of joy and relief. Houses were decorated with flags, services of thanksgiving were held in the various churches, and a celebration bonfire was lit on the Recreation Ground, topped with an effigy of the Kaiser, so huge that it burned for three days. In July 1919 a welcome dinner was given to nine officers and more than 150 men in the Assembly Room at the Working Men's Club.

In July 1920 the roll of honour was unveiled at St. Mary's and the war memorial at St. John's. The addresses at both were given by General Sir William Pulteney, who as a young man had spent some time with his family at Hargrave House. Otherwise known as Putty, he was described by one subordinate as 'the most completely ignorant general I served during the war', and,

79. Bentfield Hucks. Pioneer aviator. He died of pneumonia in 1918.

according to a damning entry in the Oxford DNB, 'Obtuse and underqualified, he made costly mistakes and may be considered one of the war's 'donkeys' and 'butchers and bunglers'. But the people of Stansted were pleased to welcome him back.

One of the victims of the flu epidemic of 1918/19 was Captain Bentfield Charles Hucks. His father, Bill Hucks, was the company engineer at Camden with W & A Gilbey, and he was born in 1884 in the Cottage at Bentfield End, which belonged to Henry Gilbey – hence the name Bentfield. He had trained as an engineer and was a well known pilot, being the first Englishman to loop the loop, and when war broke out he was given a commission in the Royal Flying Corps and was said to have done much valuable work on active service. He died in November 1918 of pneumonia following influenza. A plaque in memory of Bentfield Hucks was unveiled in the Day Centre at Stansted in 2014.

1   Ralph Phillips's papers, Alfred Phillips, 'Our family'.
2   The memorial in St. Mary's also refers to 54, though it lists only 51 names. The figures are problematic: how does one decide whether a man belonged to Stansted? It seems that the main criterion was the place of residence when the man enlisted, but there were some on the lists who were born in Stansted and had moved away. Those who lived in that part of Birchanger which was incorporated into Stansted in 1987 are recorded on the Birchanger memorial. Glyn Warwick, in his excellent study of the men who took part in the war, *They Sleep in Heroes' Graves*, covers both those who lived in the village and those who were born there and moved away.
3   Warwick (2008: 228).
4   Ralph Phillips's Papers, Alfred Phillips, 'Our family'.
5   Warwick (2008: 5).
6   Warwick (2008: 20).
7   Bannehr was a lawyer who held office in the Working Men's Club.
8   *HEO*, 5 September 1914.
9   Warwick (2008: 61, 70, 94, 96, 97, 100, 117, 125, 140, 163). See also *HEO*, 17 March 1917 and 1 March 1919.
10 Warwick (2008: 90).
11 *HEO*, 29 May 1915.
12 Warwick (2008: 30).
13 *HEO*, 25 December 1915.
14 *HEO*, 12 August 1915.
15 *HEO*, 12 February 1916.
16 For these cases, see *HEO*, 1 September 1917, 12 January 1918 and 13 July 1918.
17 *HEO*, 13 January 1917.
18 *HEO*, 5 August 1916.
19 *HEO*, 16 March 1918.
20 *HEO*, 23 November 1918.
21 *HEO*, 13 July 1918.
22 *HEO*, 15 June and 7 September 1918.
23 *HEO*, 15 May 1915.
24 *HEO*, 15 June 1918; Warwick (2008: 17).
25 *HEO*, 19 June 1915.
26 SMLHS, Interview with John Speller, November 1988, pp. 3, 7.
27 *HEO*, 8 May 1915.
28 *HEO*, 4 March 1916.
29 *HEO*, 20 April 1918.

34: BETWEEN THE WARS: THE DECLINE OF THE GENTRY, POLITICS AND ECONOMIC DEPRESSION

After the political excitements of 'radical Stansted', the intellectual demands of the Literary Institution and the lively entertainments at the Central Hall and the Working Men's Club, life in post-war Stansted was relatively subdued. The bold confidence of Edwardian England had been shattered. Scores of families had been stricken by the loss of husbands, sons and brothers, and the flu epidemic also took its toll.

The leading families had not been spared. William Fuller-Maitland had already lost his youngest son, Robert, in East Africa. The eldest, William, had been killed in the battle of the Aisne, and the only son who survived, Richard, an artist, had been wounded on the Somme and had taken no more part in the war. The squire's only daughter, Lydia, who had trained as a doctor, was no longer living in the village. His first wife, Evelyn, had died in 1902, and in 1911 he had married a much younger woman, Frances Walford. He was now away from the parish for months at a time, and for that reason he resigned in 1919 as chairman of the Parish Council, a post he had held for 25 years. Two years later he left the parish. He retained the lordship of the manor, though with the abolition of copyhold tenure in 1922 there was no longer any need for the manorial courts to meet, and Richard and Lydia retained strong links with the parish, paying for the restoration of the Lancaster chapel at St. Mary's in 1952. Lydia was buried and commemorated there in 1962.

The estate was put up for sale. A notice in April 1921 announced the coming auction in the summer of an 'important freehold sporting, residential and agricultural property of about 5,400 acres, known as the Stansted Hall estate'. It included Stansted Hall itself, an 'attractive modern mansion, exceptionally well built and containing Six Handsome Reception Rooms, 30 Bed and Dressing Rooms, Three Bathrooms, and Offices. Stabling and Garage Accommodation, etc.' Stansted House was also being put up for sale, together with '30 good arable farms, three nurseries, several residences, and small holdings, numerous cottages and Accommodation Land'. There were also 'Ground Rents and Business Premises' and about 200 acres of woodland. An 'important feature of the Estate' was its excellent shooting.[1]

In fact the auction was never held, and in September 1922 Fuller-Maitland entered into a contract for the sale of the estate to Albert Ball, a remarkable man who had begun life as a plumber, made a fortune as an estate agent and a general dealer in land and properties, and served as Lord Mayor of Nottingham. Stansted Hall was merely one of several properties that he acquired. It seems that the whole estate was sold to Ball, but he then gave the farm tenants the option of purchasing their holdings, an offer which most of them took up, while he himself retained only Stansted Hall and the immediately surrounding park and farmland.[2] In February 1923, however, just five months after agreeing to buy the estate, he sold the Hall and the wooded park of about 400 acres to J. Arthur Findlay.[3] Why

80. Arthur Findlay.

81. Gertrude Findlay as Red Cross Commandant.

he bought and then sold so quickly we can only speculate. Perhaps, with his experience as a dealer in land, he saw the possibility of making a profit on the two transactions.

Meanwhile Fuller-Maitland had put up his furniture and effects for auction in 1182 lots, ranging from lawn mowers and a tennis net to Chippendale and Hepplewhite chairs, and including a billiard table, a Broadwood grand piano and a library of 4,500 volumes.[4] To the Working Men's Club he gave '21 masks of big game shot on the Blue Nile or in British East Africa'. In what must have been a bizarre display they were hung, some in the hall and others in the reading room, the bar, the billiard room and the assembly room.[5]

The break-up of the Stansted Hall estate revolutionised landholding in the eastern part of the parish. Since the time of the de Veres it had been largely in the hands of a single owner. With the sale of most of the farms to sitting tenants and the rest to outsiders, a great concentration of power and influence ceased to exist. On the western side of the parish, however, the Goslings, still based in Farnham, retained their ownership of Bentfield Bury manor.

Although Arthur Findlay bought the Hall in 1923, it was February 1925 before he and his family were able to move there. Born in Glasgow in 1883, he worked for a firm of ship-owners, ship-brokers and insurance brokers, and became a leading stockbroker and a Freeman of the City of Glasgow. More important for Stansted, he was a convinced and active spiritualist, gave lectures and wrote several books on spiritualism, and would eventually, in 1964, give Stansted Hall to the Spiritualists' National Union.

Findlay played a full part in the public life of the district. He became a JP, sitting on the Bench at Quarter Sessions in Chelmsford; he was a member of the Board of Management for both the Bishop's Stortford and Saffron Walden Hospitals; he was elected as a member of the Stansted RDC and then served as its chairman until it was superseded in 1934 by the Saffron Walden RDC; and he joined the Executive Committee of the Saffron Walden Conservative Association, where he was one of those who selected Rab Butler as the Parliamentary candidate for the constituency in 1929.[6] He and his wife Gertrude threw open their gardens for school treats and for fetes in aid of various charities. Whenever subscriptions were called for they were usually the most generous givers, but Arthur took no part in the Parish Council, and, not being the lord of the manor, he was never regarded as the leading man in the parish in the same way as Fuller-Maitland.

Some of those who enjoyed the Findlays' hospitality had reservations about Arthur. He has been described to us as 'rather abrupt in his manner' and 'he rather enjoyed shocking people and manipulating them', but he could also be 'very kind' and was 'often quite talkative and witty'. By contrast Gertrude Findlay was 'sweet-natured and gentle', 'a generous, warm-hearted woman' who was 'much loved in Stansted and did a lot for the village'. She was heavily involved in the Church of England and several charities, paid for renovating the pews in St. Mary's, and helped to modernise the Fuller Almshouses.[7]

The new plutocracy was also not as strong as before. The great company of W & A Gilbey, while continuing to prosper, was losing its dominance in the wine and spirits trade. Sir Walter at Elsenham Hall, the grand old patriarch of the company, had died in 1914, and the prodigious outpouring of energy and initiative by the founders of the firm was not matched in the next generation.

Lord Blyth, pushy and networking to the end, died in 1925, and a year later his splendid house at Blythwood was destroyed by a fire which was apparently caused by an electrical fault. A new house was built close to the site and the second Lord Blyth, a quieter man than his father, lived there for a few years before leaving the district.[8] Although he and other members of the family were still occasional benefactors – in 1935 he gave the windmill to the parish – they were no longer a strong presence in the village. In 1934 the new house was taken over by the Gillons, who, like the Blyths before them, made the gardens available for various functions.

The Golds, however, were still the centre of an extensive social and kinship network, so much so that one informant has told us that 'Social life in Stansted in the 1930s revolved around the numerous members of the Gold family'.[9] When Sir Charles Gold died at the age of 87 in 1924 his home, the Limes (then still part of Birchanger), was inherited by his daughter, Amy, who had married her cousin, Sydney Gold. Walter Gold, one of Sir Charles' sons, whose first wife was a Gilbey, lived at the Hawthorns, a house he had had built for himself in 1904; Charles Gold, another son of Sir Charles, who was also married to a Gilbey, took up residence at the Ravens in 1917; and another son, Sir Archie Gold, lived with his wife at Croft House. Members of the family still played important roles in village life and were heavily involved in charitable work. In 1920, when the Central Hall Company could no longer remain solvent and the hall had fallen into a 'rather decrepit' state, Charles Gold bought it for £1150 and retained it as a social centre on behalf of the parish.[10] Ten years later it was sold to the Parochial Church Council.

At Hargrave House the Alders maintained a high social profile, but a few years after the death of Arthur Alder in 1930 the estate was broken up and sold. This was turned to Stansted's advantage, for in 1935 the Park was purchased by the Stansted Sports Association, which had been formed in 1933, and became a new sports centre for the village, the Hargrave Park Sports Ground, providing facilities for various sports, but mainly grounds for cricket and football. No new occupier could be found for the house, and eventually it was purchased by the Mary MacArthur Trust as a holiday home for women of the working classes who needed a rest in the country 'away from the drudgery of their everyday lives'. The home was opened by Queen Mary on 5 April 1939, an occasion long remembered by those who witnessed it. The village was gaily decorated, a banner of welcome was hung over the road, and hundreds of schoolchildren and adults lined the route waving Union Jacks. But what made the occasion memorable was a violent thunderstorm shortly before the Queen arrived. The rain fell in torrents and the onlookers were drenched. The Queen, they said afterwards, did not even look out of the car window.[11]

Among the other eminent families from the pre-war period Sir Thomas Jackson had died in 1915 and, together with one of his sons, Claud Stewart, who had been killed in the war, was commemorated in a stained glass window in St. Mary's. Newcomers, however, included Lord and Lady Henry FitzGerald at Stansted House. In our interviews with some of the older parishioners we were told that the FitzGeralds were 'right at the top of the social scale',[12] no doubt because of Lord Henry's descent from the Duke of Leinster, but they played little part in the public life of the village.

A more active newcomer was Major Edmund Cawkell of Bentfield Hall, who, as a nephew of Edmund Rochford and a director of the company, was generally regarded as the owner of Rochford's Nurseries in Stansted. Margery Baker placed him on the same social level as the Golds, and he was associated in one way or another with a wide range of village institutions. He was chairman of the local branch of the British Legion (he had been wounded in the war himself), a magistrate, president of the bowling club, the football club and the Junior Imperial League, captain of the fire brigade, secretary of the local Scouts, an active Conservative, a district councillor and a county councillor after Harry Chester had stood down. He was widely respected as a fair and considerate employer.

Green's Stores was still the major emporium in the village, advertising itself as '*The Stores of the District*', but there were no longer any Greens in Stansted, no Joshua to promote good causes, no Joseph to collect materials for future parish historians.

The Chesters at Broome End, who, like the Fuller-Maitlands and the Jacksons, had lost a son in the war, continued to play a major part in village affairs. Harry Chester was a JP and represented the Stansted Division on the Essex County Council for many years. He enjoyed cross party support and was elected unopposed. In the constituency politics of the Conservative Party he was probably the most influential man in the parish, though on one important issue he was not able to guide his party in the direction he wanted. Throughout the war Saffron Walden had been represented by Cecil Beck, a Liberal, and in the election of 1918 Beck stood as the candidate for the Conservative/Liberal Coalition that had led the country through the conflict. The prospective Conservative candidate, Captain Proby, whose father had briefly represented the constituency in 1910, announced that he would not be standing since he took the view that it would be unpatriotic to oppose a Coalition candidate. Chester condemned Proby's action as illogical and ridiculous,[13] but the election was fought with no Conservative candidate in the fray. For the first time, however, there was a Labour candidate, J.J. Mallon, and for the first time women aged 30 and over with the required property qualifications could vote. The result was an easy victory for Beck, with 10,628 votes against Mallon's 4,531.

In the next election, in 1922, the Conservative candidate, William Foot Mitchell, came top of the poll, and again in 1923 and 1924. In 1929 Foot Mitchell gave way to Rab Butler, who remained as Saffron Walden's MP until 1965. During this long period of Conservative control the Labour Party came to replace the Liberals as the main opposition, but there was never any serious possibility of a Labour victory in the constituency except in the Labour landslide of 1945, when Butler scraped home against Stanley Wilson with a majority of 1,158 votes.

Throughout the inter-war period there was nothing distinctive about Stansted's politics. With the exception of some of the Golds, all the gentry were now Conservative – the Findlays, the Cawkells and the Chesters, for example – and the local branch of the Women's Conservative Association, which appears to have replaced the Primrose League, was well supported: at a meeting in 1934 at Broome End, the Chesters' home, Rab Butler congratulated it on having more than 300 members (some of them no doubt from the surrounding villages).[14] Another flourishing institution was the Junior Imperial League, the 'Imps', whose aims were to promote imperial unity and the Conservative and Unionist cause.

At election times the Labour Party campaigned vigorously in the parish, but trade union representation was weak and there was nothing to match the drive and excitement of the pre-war Liberal organisation. In its membership, policies and idealism, however, the constituency party represented a new departure. Unlike the Conservatives and Liberals, it was not led by the gentry. Its best known supporter, it is true, was the Countess of Warwick at Little Easton, Edward VII's 'Darling Daisy', and among the clergy there were the 'Red Vicar of Thaxted', Conrad Noel, his son-in-law and curate, Jack Putterill, and P.E.T. Widrington, vicar of Great Easton, who was the chairman of the Divisional Labour Party. But, as Stanley Wilson makes clear in his memoirs, 'Our campaign was led by middle-class ladies, mainly teachers', and Wilson himself, at the time of joining, was a milk roundsman in Saffron Walden. In Stansted Alfred Phillips, who was then working as an apprentice in a firm of electrical and mechanical engineers, was for a time the secretary of the branch. He had joined the party with his brother Alec. 'I do not know what influenced us at that time', he wrote later, 'other than we had a great sense of the injustice all around us. We were a small company of people with great ideals.' The branch president was Harold Walker, a London stationer, and Sid Hudgell, a local chimney sweep, was the treasurer. Another prominent Socialist family was Mr. and Mrs. Matthews, who, with their daughters, raised funds by organising entertainments, whist drives and folk dancing in the Labour Hall in Church Road, formerly an old coach-house. Alfred and Alec cycled long distances to Labour meetings in the constituency – hard going when the country roads were so deeply rutted. They went to the vicarage in Thaxted for political meetings there, and they came into contact with some of the leading men and women of the age, such as Ellen Wilkinson, Will Thorne, George Lansbury, Manny Shinwell and Jimmy Maxton. Sometimes, when meetings were held in Stansted, their father allowed them to invite the speakers home for tea or supper, and on one occasion their visitor was Clem Attlee.[15]

The General Strike of 1926 provoked a flurry of headlines in the *Herts and Essex Observer* similar to those at the start of WW1. The Trade Unions were the enemy, manipulated in some cases from Moscow. They were seeking to coerce the Government. As for 'the so-called Labour representatives in the House of Commons', thundered Foot Mitchell, the local MP, they were 'more or less Socialists'.[16] The people of Stansted were directly affected when the railwaymen employed by the London and North Eastern Railway (LNER) went on strike. The company responded by enlisting volunteers, and with help from them and some retired employees it was able to build up a workable service in the southern part of its operations.

It was a course of action that was fraught with danger. On Monday, 10 May, at about 1 pm a freight train was about to set off from Cambridge to London. The volunteer driver was told that the road was clear, and with this in mind he began his journey. At each station along the line there were one or two men at work, and they signalled the 'right away' - except at Stansted, where there was no one on duty. So the driver went through, and as he turned the bend approaching Bishop's Stortford he was horrified to see a passenger and milk train at the station ahead of him. He tried desperately to stop, but the weight of the freight wagons behind him pushed him forward and he crashed into the back of the train. The impact was so great that part of the station roof was brought down. One man was killed, Harry Burrell, who for many years had been Sir Walter Gilbey's agent at Elsenham Hall. Two others were injured.

At the inquest in Stortford the driver explained that if there had been a man at Stansted he would have known that there was a train at Stortford because it would have passed through shortly before, and the signal could have been given for the driver to stop. The LNER's representative lamely explained that there was no one at Stansted because 'there was only one man there and he had probably gone away for a meal'. The Coroner, who was clearly determined to implicate the strikers, said that no blame could be attached to the company or the voluntary workers. In these circumstances, i.e. the strike, accidents were bound to happen. It was a wonder that there were not more. Following his lead the jury gave a verdict of accidental death, with the rider that 'in their opinion under normal conditions the accident would not have occurred'. The men on duty were not to blame.[17]

Three months later Lieut-Col. A.H.L. Mount produced a report on the accident for the Ministry of Transport. For a service to be provided during a strike, he wrote, 'considerable risks' had to be taken and great care had to be exercised. Instead of which no clear instructions had been given to the traffic staff about keeping the allotted time interval between trains and the volunteer driver had exceeded the speed restrictions that were in operation. Though he had slowed down as he approached Bishop's Stortford 'the train probably approached, and would have run through, the station at double the rate prescribed'.[18] It was a very different conclusion from that of the inquest.

The *Observer* welcomed the end of the strike as if it were the end of a war, and the gentry at Stansted no doubt agreed. In his monthly letter to his parishioners the vicar, Arthur Turberville, had no compunction about expressing his views. The whole country, he wrote, was returning to normality with great thankfulness that the 'splendid courage and resourcefulness of the people' had overcome a 'serious menace'. The country's great social and industrial problem had been solved by the Christian spirit of the people, and as for the Prime Minister, Mr. Baldwin, 'He inspires confidence because we feel that he is entirely sincere and entirely to be trusted'.[19]

One of the most urgent priorities for the Labour Party was to increase the wages of agricultural labourers, but this was not the best time to press for it. The farmers had done well in the war, but the 1920s and 1930s were a period of deep depression. At a public meeting in Stansted in 1922, when the Labour candidate, Bill Cash, advocated an increase in wages a voice was heard from the audience, no doubt a farmer's: 'how do you propose to make farming pay?'[20]

Susan Spencer-Smith, who was born in 1921, was the daughter of a tenant farmer at Hole Farm and later, after her father died, a tenant farmer herself. The 1920s and 1930s, she told us, were a terrible time for farming:

> That's why we had to keep horses. We kept them at livery for people .... They paid us for grooming and exercising them and then, once or twice a week, they would come up and hunt. Rents were low, about 30s. an acre, I think. Corn fetched so little then. A lot of farmers went bust at that time. There were so many empty farms on the [Goslings'] Hassobury Estate that they offered them to tenants to live and farm for one year rent free.[21]

Susan's landlord, Colonel William Gosling, confirmed that 'we had to give notice to six to eight tenants in the 1930s because they could not pay the rent', but, like Susan, he could not remember any in Stansted.[22]

At that time farming was still mixed, and the almost total concentration on arable farming would come much later. But profound changes were taking place. Horse-drawn ploughs were being replaced by steam ploughs, and Pamplin Brothers, a company of steam plough contractors, to be replaced in 1935 by How and Salmons, had a branch at the bottom of Chapel Hill. George Andrews, who worked for the company for a short period from 1929, described how the firm owned 20 sets of steam engines, with two engines to each set, with all the ploughing and cultivating gear for each engine. Half of these were controlled from Stansted and provided ploughing and cultivating services to farmers throughout Essex and Hertfordshire.[23] Towards the end of the period combine harvesters began to be used. Another significant change was the abolition of tithes, after a long and hard fought campaign, in 1936.

The Great Depression hit Stansted badly. Aubrey Levey's father ran a building and undertaker's business, and there were 'a couple of farmers who went broke or who practically went broke, owing my father money, and there was one man I remember very well... and he had a house, and there was a lot of work done to it, and he ... bunked off to somewhere in central Europe, and my father on enquiry of course found that he not only owed him money but he owed money to grocers, chandlers, wine merchants, spirit merchants, tailors, you name it ....' So he had to lay men off. 'The labour force went down drastically', Aubrey said. 'When I joined the business in 1933 it was down to six .... Normally there were 20-25.'[24]

The Leveys' experience must have been shared by many others, but perhaps the greatest blow was the closing down in or around 1931 of the commutator manufacturers, Dyer and Young. Marjory Cowan remembered that a lot of Stansted people worked there, it was 'like a little factory', and about 50 were thrown out of work.[25]

Unemployment relief was paid out at 10s a week, but for many this was barely enough. A small and unusual insight into the prevalent hardship is provided, almost casually and incidentally, in a newspaper article by an anonymous resident of Bishop's Stortford who decided to walk to Stansted one Saturday evening in November 1929. As he made his way into the village he met one or two cyclists going home after the day's work, and then a man wheeling a loaded-up pram and, behind him, a woman who tried to sell him some lavender; then two men, one of whom begged and was turned away; two more men 'with appealing glances', a solo walker, and then another pair, one of whom tried to sell him some laces and asked him for a light. He surmised that most of these people were making their way to 'the large premises', which I think was a term for the workhouse in Bishop's Stortford.[26] Others were even more distressed: Alfred Sawyer, of Western House, who had lost a lot of money on the Stock Exchange, committed suicide in 1934 - though the death of his wife and disagreements with his housekeeper were factors too.[27]

Over the inter-war period as a whole, however, Stansted held its own. The population was roughly stable, showing a modest increase from 2,344 in 1911 to 2,488 in 1931. (There was no census in 1941.) *Kelly's Directory* for 1914 listed 82 private residents and 114 commercial entries. In 1937 these figures were 78 and 106. The commercial concerns became more varied. The old trades continued, and Green's Stores were still spoken of as selling everything from a pin to an elephant, though soon after WW1 they had to sell their furnishing department to the London and Stansted Furnishing Company. They also faced more competition: as early as 1925, not far from Green's, there was a Stansted branch of the Cambridge Co-operative Society. But there were now mechanics and engineers of many descriptions – motor mechanics, for example, and electrical engineers, agricultural, cycle and wireless engineers. Most people could still get everything they wanted without leaving the village. In fact many stores delivered goods both within Stansted and to several of the villages around – in 1937 Green's advertised that they had added to their transport fleet 'a specially designed motor van equipped as a "Travelling Shop de Luxe"'[28] - while some of the stores in Bishop's Stortford delivered to Stansted. Buses to Stortford started in 1927, when the Acme service began its operations, soon to be followed by the Great Eastern service. No doubt some trade was lost in this way, but not enough to undermine Stansted as a commercial centre.

In 1923 the church vestry noted that since several well-to-do families had left the village it was more difficult to raise funds,[29] and in the same year the Parish Council expressed its concern that, as in the villages around, the rateable value of the parish had gone down partly because several big houses were lying empty.[30] By comparison with other villages, however, Stansted was still well off, and when funds were needed for a particular project in 1927 the *Observer* commented that Stansted was 'a prosperous village' and expressed the hope that it would 'keep up its reputation for generosity'.[31] When, in 1987, we interviewed some of the older parishioners about this period we were struck by how much they appreciated the economic benefits the wealthier families brought to the village. The Chesters at Broome End, for example, employed a parlour maid, a kitchen maid, a scullery maid, two housemaids, a boy, a head gardener and two to three gardeners. The Alders at Hargrave House employed a butler/valet, two housemaids, two parlour maids, a cook and a kitchen maid inside the house, and outside a gardener, the head groomsman and four men working under him. Just as before WW1, there appears to have been little antagonism between the classes. The gentry, said May Jordan, were 'friends to all'.[32] Marjorie Cowan, talking of the 'older families', said 'I know a lot of people condemn them .... But they were extremely good to their employees.' And she spoke of help being given if wives or children were 'poorly'.[33] But there were those who took a different view. Hilda Seymour, who worked for Walter Gold and his family, was always very deferential and respectful in her relations with them, but one of her neighbours, Don Turner, commented tartly that 'Hilda was always one for the gentry', clearly implying that he was not.[34] Queenie Banks, though acknowledging that the Alders at Hargrave House were 'very good' to her father, who was their head groomsman, had to open the gate when the Alders returned to the house in their car, which made her feel 'most inferior'.[35]

There was always, it seems, a residuum of the unemployed or the under-employed. In the years immediately after WW1 many soldiers returning from the front found themselves out of work, and, as Jessie Berry observed, 'some of them bought stocks of cheap articles like matches and toys, which they sold from trays suspended from their necks'. She remembered 'men coming to the door selling shoe-laces and others singing in the street to earn a few coppers'.[36] In 1921, according to one of the parish councillors, there were 80 unemployed men in the parish.[37] Nora Allsopp said that 'in the 1930s and 40s there was a veritable army of odd job people in Stansted, who would come round to the house at a moment's notice to mend the roof or clean windows or see to plumbing or do a little sewing or ironing'.[38]

With the population roughly stable, there was no great demand for housing. From time to time the Parish Council noted with concern that there were houses that were occupied by more than one family,[39] but according to the 1931 census there were 675 houses occupied by 679 families, with an overall population of 2,488, giving an average of 3.7 persons for each house.[40] The Rural District Council (RDC), which was the responsible authority, provided a small number of Council houses. In 1920 it decided to build ten houses in Stansted, four at Bentfield End and six in the Elsenham Road, and it planned to rent them out at 10s. a week for most tenants, but at 6s. a week for agricultural labourers.[41] In 1932 it asked the parishes to state their housing requirements, and, while Berden, Farnham and Henham said they did not need any more houses, Elsenham asked for 6, Manuden for 10, Great Hallingbury for 10, Birchanger for 20 and Stansted for 24. It decided to go ahead with 2 for Elsenham, 6 for Manuden, 12 for Stansted and 20 for Birchanger.[42] In 1939 the Parish Council noted that the RDC had decided to build 20 houses on Stoney Common at the end of Park Road.[43] (In fact 12 were built in what is now Stoneyfield Drive.) Private developers also operated on a small scale.[44]

Living standards were improving, but slowly. In many houses the accommodation was confined, typically two up and two down, perhaps with a scullery at the back. Most families had cold water on tap in the house, and they could heat this up in a copper as required, but others did not have even that. The Bedlows in the Cambridge Road had a wash-house at the back of the house containing a pump, and they got their water from that until the house was put on the mains in the 1940s or 1950s. Joyce Patmore's family at Burton End had no water supply, and they had to collect two pails each day from Monks Farm nearby. 'If there was a very dry summer we had to manage on less, as the water was needed for the cattle. There were always two or three water butts, which collected rain water, so that was used for washing, cleaning etc.' Before WW2 'hardly anyone' had a bathroom, and the normal practice was to have a zinc bath in front of the fire. Flush toilets were common, but for some families there was no more than a bucket in a small shed at the end of the garden.

For most people electricity also came in after WW2. Before that they had gas, though even then when you went to bed it was easier to take a candle. Jessie Berry, who lived with her sister on the Recreation Ground, had electricity installed only in the early 1950s, and Vera Wyatt, in Sunnyside, used oil lamps until 1967.

As for heating, there were coal fires – coal was cheap - and the kitchen range. Everyone remembered black leading the range, and housewives took great pride in keeping the burnished steel parts of it bright and shiny. The hearth was hearth-stoned to clean it and then whitened.

Those who were better off were naturally better provided. Stansted Hall was centrally heated, and so was the Hawthorns, the house built by Walter Gold for himself and his family in 1904. Margery Baker, whose father was a stockbroker, moved into Birchalls in High Lane in 1935, and the house already had mains water, gas, electricity and a phone.

Radios came in during the 1920s and 1930s. Jessie Berry's father had a radio as early as 1926 that had a big loudspeaker indoors and a rickety aerial in the garden that was blown down every time there was a storm. In spite of the initial operating difficulties the radio, or wireless as it was commonly called, had the effect of widening parishioners' horizons.

For the well-to-do and for those who needed them for work cars and vans began to replace horses, carriages and carts. Progress was naturally variable: Green's used delivery vans after WW1, whereas Bunting's, the grocers in Lower Street, started to use a van only after WW2. For those who could not afford cars, and for many who could as well, bicycles were very popular. Long distances were covered. We have already seen Alec and Alfred Phillips cycling to Labour Party meetings throughout the Saffron Walden constituency. Hilda Seymour cycled back to her parents' home in Harlow every weekend, and on winter Saturdays Don Turner cycled to see the Arsenal play at Highbury.

At first the roads were poor, with the exception of the Cambridge Road. The main roads were the responsibility of the County Council, the lesser roads of the RDC. There were constant complaints about the dust, and constant requests to the County Council for more use of the water-cart. In 1919 the residents in Lower Street, near the Dog and Duck public house, sent a protest to the RDC and threatened to stop paying their rates: the gravel stones at this spot were 'a thousand times worse than the sea beach's … people complain of the stones cutting their boots to pieces, and cyclists complain of their tyres'.[45] The only solution was a tarred surface, as the RDC acknowledged, and by the end of the inter-war period nearly all the roads in the parish were tarred, even the winding and little used Pennington Lane, and this had been so satisfactory that it was decided that Lime Kiln Lane should also be tarred.[46]

One development anticipated on a smaller scale the arguments that were to surface again in the campaign against the extension of Stansted Airport. In 1928 the County Council wanted to widen and straighten part of the main road through the village, and the Parish Council passed a resolution protesting against 'the prospect of the trees and hedges along this beautiful road being torn down'. Three councillors, however, Tissiman (the chairman), Norman and Moule, voted against the resolution, Norman arguing that it would be wrong to 'hold up progress' and that although they did not want to see trees cut down 'wider roads were necessary. In these days people must be able to travel fast in order to get a living.'[47] The County Council responded that it had no immediate intention of implementing the scheme, but in the meantime no new buildings were to be erected in that area without its agreement.[48]

1. *EC*, 15 April 1921.
2. *EC*, 4 January 1924. See also *HEO*, 19 May 1923.
3. *HEO*, 10 February 1923; Findlay (1988: 269).
4. *HEO*, 23 September 1922.
5. *HEO*, 16 September 1922.
6. Findlay (1988: 272).
7. SMLHS, Interviews with Norah Allsopp, 21 November 1988, and Josephine Hill, whose husband was Arthur Findlay's cousin, 25 November 1988.
8. The new house has now been converted into three residences in Blythwood Gardens.
9. SMLHS, Interview with Mrs. Norah Allsopp and her daughter, Mrs. Charmian FitzHerbert, 21 November 1988.
10. ERO, D/Z 41/1.
11. *HEO*, 8 April 1939, 'Thousands Brave Thunderstorm To Cheer Her Majesty'.
12. SMLHS, 'Reminiscences of Miss Margery Baker', 1 February 1989.
13. *HEO*, 27 July 1918.
14. *EC*, July 20 1934.
15. See also *HEO*, 23 January 1926.
16. *HEO*, 6 November 1926.
17. *HEO*, 15 May 1926.
18. *HEO*, 18 August 1926.
19. *SMPM*, June 1926.
20. *HEO*, 4 November 1922.
21. SMLHS, Interview with Susan Spencer-Smith, 3 July 1987.
22. SMLHS, Interview with Col. William Gosling, 1993.
23. SMLHS, 'Stansted, Essex, 1929-1932', enclosure with letter to Ralph Phillips, 28 February 1989.
24. SMLHS, Interview with Aubrey Levey, 9 November 1987.
25. *EC*, 4 December 1931, and SMLHS, Interview with Marjory Cowan, 23 March 1988, p. 16.
26. *HEO*, 30 November 1929.
27. *EC*, 3 and 10 August 1934.
28. *The Link*, October 1981.
29. ERO, D/P 109/8/6, vestry minutes for 16 April 1923.
30. ERO, D/P 109/30/7, Minutes of Parish Council, 9 January 1923.
31. ERO, D/P 109/30/8, undated press cutting with Parish Council minutes for 13 September 1927.
32. SMLHS, May Jordan, undated 'Memories', c.1982.
33. SMLHS, Marjory Cowan, Interview, 23 March 1988, p. 16.
34. Personal conversation, c.1987.
35. SMLHS, Queenie Banks, Interview, 9 March 1988.
36. SMLHS, Reminiscences of Jessie Berry, 13 April 1987.
37. *HEO*, 11 October 1921.
38. SMLHS, Nora Allsopp, notes, 21 November 1988.
39. ERO, D/P 109/30/8, Parish Council minutes for 9 April, 14 May and 12 November 1929, 11 March and 15 October 1930.
40. In 1871 there were 438 houses, 16 of them unoccupied, for a population of 1988, an average of 4.5 persons per house: see Frank Reader, 'Stansted in the Last Century', *SMPM*, June 1941.
41. ERO, D/P 109/30/6, Parish Council minutes for 29 November 1919, and *HEO*, 10 April and 11 December 1920.
42. *HEO*, 11 March and 15 April 1932.
43. ERO, D/P 109/30/10, Parish Council minutes for 30 May 1939.
44. See, e.g., *HEO*, 18 October 1935.
45. *HEO*, 12 July 1919.
46. ERO, D/P 109/30/10, minutes of Parish Council, 31 May 1938.
47. ERO, D/P 109/30/8, minutes of Parish Council, 9 October 1928.
48. *HEO*, 12 February 1929.

35: BETWEEN THE WARS: LOCAL GOVERNMENT

On the whole the local authority framework erected by the Victorians proved to be effective and resilient. The main change came in 1934, when 10 of the 12 parishes of the Stansted Rural District Council were amalgamated with the Saffron Walden RDC, while the other two, Great and Little Hallingbury, were incorporated into the Dunmow RDC. The move was not welcomed in Stansted because so much travelling to Saffron Walden was entailed. The Parish Council continued in much the same way as before. The committees which it established indicated the continuing range of its main responsibilities – the Recreation Ground and footpaths; lighting; charities; sanitation; and the fire engine. It also appointed a representative on the District Assessment Committee for the assessment of rates and advisory representatives for the Church School and the Council School. It made representations and was consulted on matters that fell under the RDC and the County Council, such as roads and refuse collection, and there were many other issues for which it took responsibility or in which it became involved, such as allotments, the clock on the Central Hall, the maintenance of the fountain, the flooding of the brook in Lower Street, and the celebrations for King George V's silver jubilee. Edmund Cawkell, who represented Stansted on the County Council, commented that, while the Parish Council had little direct power, it had plenty of influence.[1]

After Fuller-Maitland's resignation the Council's chairmen included W.H.S. Tissiman, a tailor, Albert Ratcliff, a painter and decorator, and Reginald Vercoe, who ran a jeweller's shop in the village. Annual parish meetings were open to all ratepayers: some were well attended and some elections were vigorously contested, but at some there were only one or two members of the public present and there were only as many nominations as there were vacant seats.

Politics played little part locally. At the County level the Conservative Harry Chester was elected unopposed and then Edmund Cawkell, also a Conservative. At the RDC level the man who came top of the poll in at least three elections (1922, 1925 and 1928), Ernest Oliver, who lived at Mont House, was a leading Liberal activist.

One of the most troublesome problems that the Parish Council had to deal with was Harford Green's legacy, the Liernur sewage system. In 1919 the District Surveyor reported that it was breaking down: so many openings had been made to relieve blockages that the vacuum no longer worked. There was further trouble in 1931 for the same reason: 'We have expected this for a long time', said Luther Norman grimly. 'It never has been a vacuum system.'[2] Over time the five inch pipes were replaced by 12 inch pipes and the vacuum system was in effect replaced by a gravitational system. By 1938, at last, the new system was said to be working well.[3]

Another problematic area was street lighting, which was provided by the Bishop's Stortford Gas Company. Stansted was one of the best-lighted parishes for miles around. Every year the Annual Parish Meeting set aside a sum to pay the company, but in 1921 the sum earmarked for lighting, £200, was not enough to match the tender put forward by the company. By 31 votes to 2 the Annual Meeting decided not to light the parish in the coming year. The company then indicated its intention to charge the parish 9s. 6d. per annum for each of its 60 lamp-posts, for which it had paid and which would now be standing idle. In the end the Council had to agree to this, but not before there had been an exchange of threats and counter-threats when the Council, worried about possible claims for damages, asked the company to paint the lamp-posts with luminous paint 'as a safeguard to pedestrians, and to prevent persons colliding with them'.[4] Not surprisingly the company refused. In the following year the Annual Meeting voted to spend £250, an increase of £50, and the matter was settled to everyone's satisfaction. For 15 years this arrangement worked well, but then, in 1937, the Council received two tenders, one from the gas company and one from the North-Met Electricity Company, and it decided to go over to electricity.

After the Blythwood fire the village fire brigade was reorganised. The old fire engine was replaced in 1927, and in the same year the Parish Council agreed to purchase land from Green's for £20 for the site of a new fire station on Chapel Hill. A local builder, Robinson's, agreed to build the new station for £133, the money was raised by public subscription, and in 1928 the new station was opened by Lady Blyth, who must have been still mindful of the conflagration at Blythwood. The brigade performed well under the captaincy of Edmund Cawkell. It was often called out to Bishop's Stortford and neighbouring villages as well as to Stansted, and the parish took great pride in its bravery and achievements. Appreciative speeches were made and long-service medals handed out at the brigade's annual dinners. In 1939, however, it was taken over by the RDC, and in 1941 by the National Fire Service. (In 1948 it was handed back to local control, this time the Essex County Council.)

In 1927 the overseers of the poor ceased to have any role, in 1930 the Board of Guardians was abolished, and the long history of the parish's involvement with the administration of the Poor Law came to an end.

The most contentious issue that faced the Parish Council during the inter-war period arose from the break-up of the Fuller-Maitlands' estate. There was an old road which led from the village to Burton End, going past the vicarage, St. Mary's Church and Stansted Hall. The first William Fuller-Maitland had wanted to divert traffic away from the Hall, and to this end he had the new Church Road built to the east at his own expense and in 1867 obtained a court order to close the old road. He had died before putting this into effect, and his son, the second William Fuller-Maitland, knowing nothing about this it was said, continued to allow traffic to the church to pass along the old road, though not to continue past the church to Burton End. In the meantime new arrivals in the village, Mr. and Mrs. Watson, bought the vicarage, which was renamed the Manor House, and when the estate was broken up they bought the old road from Fuller-Maitland. Now they wanted to activate the order obtained by the first William Fuller-Maitland and to close the old road to traffic, while allowing it to continue to be used as a footpath. In October 1923 it was reported to the Parish Council that Watson had built a gate across the road. In a letter to the Council from his solicitor in May 1924 it was explained that he was worried about the impact of passing funerals on his young family. At this stage he had no intention of locking the gate.

The Council was immediately up in arms. So was the Church Council, and so indeed was the whole parish. A right of way that had existed for nearly a thousand years was being curtailed. The villagers were determined that, as in the past, the road should be kept open for people travelling on horseback or by carriage or car to the church.

Almost a year passed, and the Watsons informed the Council, through their solicitors, that they were closing the old road to vehicular traffic. At a special meeting of the Council it was decided to refer the matter to the RDC, which had in the past repaired the road, even though it did not own it, and on 22 July this was supported at a heated Annual Parish Meeting by 111 votes to 0. When the RDC took no action, the Essex County Council was asked to take it over on the ground that the RDC was failing to carry out its duty. After a public inquiry at the Working Men's Club, however, attended by 50 villagers, the Local Government Committee of the County Council announced that it could not see its way to make any order to the District Council.

In the meantime, in September 1924, a 'mob' of 'hundreds' of people, organised it was said by Luther Norman, though he denied this, went up the old road early one morning and cut the gate down.[5] Mrs. Watson brought a legal action against Norman, asking for an order restraining him and his agents from entering her land, for damages for trespass and for costs. By this time it was clear that Norman could expect no financial support from any of the councils involved: people wanted to fight, he said ruefully, but they did not want to pay. More than that, Mrs. Watson had offered a compromise whereby she would allow a footpath to the church and an area near the church for the parking of cars and carriages, and the Parish Council had accepted this. Norman had no alternative but to accept defeat. Mrs. Watson withdrew her request for damages and costs, but insisted on the injunctions, which were granted.[6]

---

1 *HEO*, 15 March 1937.
2 *HEO*, 13 January 1931.
3 *HEO*, 29 November 1938.
4 *HEO*, 11 January 1921.
5 Cissy Brown, née Snelling, remembered being there as a girl of about nine years old: there were crowds of people, she said, and Luther Norman drove up in his car with his cutters. Information given by Peter Brown, Cissy's son, 21 May 2015.
6 The story can be traced in ERO, D/P 109/30/7, the minutes of the Parish Council, with the relevant cuttings from the *HEO*.

36: BETWEEN THE WARS: RELIGIOUS AND SOCIAL

The Anglican Church remained powerful and continued to be well supported by the gentry. Before the war seats had in effect been reserved for particular families. As Oakshott observed, 'There are seats that have been attached to certain houses from time immemorial'. But these seats were not paid for. 'Our custom is to invite *Subscriptions* to the Parish Church [i.e. St. Mary's], and then, in return, to allot certain seats or a seat, *if possible.*'[1] It seems that by the end of the war this system had largely come to an end: we have been told that there were seats near the choir for the Fuller-Maitlands and the Golds, but otherwise people could sit where they liked.

It was partly because of the pressures exerted by the gentry that attendances remained high: 'they were sticklers in this sense', said Marjory Cowan, 'they would sail into church … and cast their eyes along the pews and their employees had to be there. When people talk about the tremendous congregations in churches years ago, a lot of them were there because … they *had* to attend.'[2] The choir was well supported, especially after the arrival as vicar in 1915 of Ethelbert Goodchild, who loved church music and established a Choral Society with himself as conductor. The Sunday School too was well attended. But perhaps the main buttress of the church's influence was the Church School, where every day began with prayer, where the importance of religion was built into the curriculum, and where the vicar came so often that he was almost like a member of staff.

The war, however, added to the strain of having to keep two churches going and this led to at least two disputes which were given much damaging publicity in the local press. In order to ensure that services were conducted at the new church of St. John's the Pulteneys had left an endowment fund which provided a dedicated income of £45 each year, which was generous but fell short of what was needed for an assistant priest. Goodchild, according to Fuller-Maitland, took the money but did not take the services, and he made matters worse by suggesting that the granting of the endowment had been imposed on the Pulteneys as a condition for agreeing to the building of a new church. This infuriated Fuller-Maitland, who obtained a letter from Arthur Pulteney dismissing Goodchild's account as 'a complete travesty of the facts'. At the Easter Vestry in 1917 Fuller-Maitland said he was no longer willing to be the vicar's churchwarden, and refused when pressed to change his mind.[3]

82. Ethelbert Goodchild, vicar 1915-1920.

Then, at the Easter Vestry in 1918, a row began to brew up between Goodchild and Walter Gold, the people's churchwarden. Gold reported that over the past few years there had been 'a very large falling off' in church collections and subscriptions. In 1914 they had amounted to £569 and in 1915 £568, but in 1916 they had plummeted to £390 and in 1917 to £378. Over a long series of meetings the vicar blamed Gold for this, at one point declaring that all he had done was to create deficits. In this he was supported by his own churchwarden, Harold Smith (the man who had supported George Valentine), who went even further, asking at the Easter Vestry in 1919 if Gold was working for the church or not and begging to differ when others said he was. Most if not all of the other members of the vestry supported Gold. He had worked hard for many years, it was said, and was trusted and respected throughout the village. He had been 'shabbily treated'. At a further meeting in 1919 it was agreed that Gold's accounts should be approved and that he should be accorded very hearty thanks for his services as the people's churchwarden. This was greeted with applause.

Gold was then appointed as people's warden for the coming year. But one of his supporters sounded a note of reproof and warning. They should now look to the future, he said. 'They did not want these continual bickerings at Stansted, but to make up their minds to work as amicably as possible. They had all had a "jumpy" time during the war, and now they wanted peace.' It was a sign of the continuing bitterness that two of the men nominated as sidesmen, Gawthorp the station-master and Vercoe the jeweller, refused to serve.

Later that year, in November, Gold resigned: after ten years, he said, a change in the wardenship was desirable.[4]

83. Arthur Turberville, vicar 1920-31.

Goodchild served as vicar for five years, until 1920, when he was replaced by Arthur Turberville, who wore a large, broad-brimmed circular hat, like an 'upturned soup bowl', said Aubrey Levey, and gave the impression of having been 'left over from the Victorian and Edwardian periods'.[5] He found the large, rambling old vicarage near St. Mary's inconvenient, and so he was given a smaller vicarage on the Recreation Ground. (The old vicarage, it will be remembered, was bought by the Watsons and renamed the Manor House.)

Turberville has been described to us as middle of the road in his beliefs and practice. His letters in the *Parish Magazine* suggest that he was more high church than low. He was very firm in his adherence to the teaching of the Church of England, but at the same time he repeatedly stressed the importance of avoiding bad feeling with those with whom one disagreed and there was no unpleasantness in his relations with the Nonconformists.

In 1931 there fell into his hands a tract written by Richard Ward, the vicar at Stansted during the Civil War, whose writings I have quoted at some length in the chapter dealing with that war. It was entitled *Analysis and explanation and application of the Solemn League and Covenant* and was published in 1643. The Covenant was the outcome of an agreement between the Scots Covenanters and the English Parliament whereby the Scots agreed not to invade England if Parliament abolished episcopacy and adopted a Presbyterian form of church government. Turberville still bristled with anger at the thought of it: Parliament at that time, he wrote, did not represent the people of England. It was 'the Government of a Clique by force of arms'. Ward, he wrote, was 'evidently a Puritan of extreme views and a Subscriber to the League and Covenant'. The idea that Parliament should control the church was anathema to him.

For Turberville this was not just history, but was charged with contemporary significance because of the recent dispute over the revised prayer book in which the House of Commons, to his fury, had rejected the church's proposals. Did those who approved of what Parliament had done 'really approve of Parliamentary Christianity?' Would he, Turberville, have approved of Parliament's decisions in the 1640s? Christmas Day, 1644, 'was ordered to be observed as *a fast!*' '"Why!" you might well say', he addressed his readers, '"That is very like Bolshevism!"'[6]

Turberville left in 1931, and in 1932 his place was taken by a blunt North countryman, John Barrow. It was during his time that the vicarage on the Recreation Ground was sold and a house was bought in St. John's Road which became the vicarage until the late 1970s. The best description of Barrow comes again from Aubrey Levey, whose father was on friendly terms with him. He was, said Aubrey, 'a very businesslike sort of man. He called a spade a spade, and if he thought a person wanted to be spoken to a bit sharply, well, he spoke to him a bit sharply. But the next time he met them everything would be back to just what it was before. People on the whole, they could see his faults … but nevertheless they thought that by and large they weren't doing too badly.'[7] Tom and Marion Johnson, who got to know Barrow after WW2, confirmed this impression. Marion described him as 'a tartar'. 'He was the boss. Definitely the boss. He said to me, the first week I was in church, "You'll take over the Sunday School tomorrow." On Saturday he said it to me. And I did.'[8] 'If he said jump', said Tom, 'you usually jumped.'[9]

84. John Barrow, vicar 1932-1954.

Largely because of the need to maintain two churches the finances of the parish were repeatedly under strain, and one of Barrow's most important initiatives was the introduction in 1926 of the Free Will Offering Scheme, under which parishioners undertook to give so much each week. While this did not completely overcome the church's difficulties it enabled it to keep its head above water.

Barrow was more high church than Turberville,[10] but like him he avoided any doctrinal disputes within the church and enjoyed friendly relations with the Nonconformists. In 1934, when the Congregationalists opened a new Lecture Room behind their church, Barrow was one of the speakers and made a short address of congratulation.[11]

Like Ethelbert Goodchild, he was keen on music – he was vice-chairman of the Royal School of Church Music - and he was well supported by Mrs. Godefroy, who was the organist at St. Mary's from 1901 to 1950, and by two excellent choirs which sometimes combined for special services and for performances of Bach's Passions and Stainer's Crucifixion at Easter.

85. Marian Annetta Godefroy, church organist 1901-1950.

Barrow was a strong and forceful presence. In 1935 he expressed his appreciation of the happy and united way in which his Church Council worked with him, and two years later Charles Gold praised him for being 'always full of vigour for the benefit of the parish'. In the same year there were 379 communicants at Easter, the largest number, it was said, for more than 30 years.

86. Arthur Davies, Congregational minister 1922-1927.

87. Sydney Pay, Congregational minister 1929-1935.

88. Illingworth Jagger, Congregational minister 1936-1939.

Meanwhile the Congregational Church, formerly the Independent Church, was holding its own, with morning and evening congregations of about 100 and a flourishing Sunday School in the afternoon. The arrival of a new Minister, Arthur Davies, in 1922 brought new energy to the church, and his sermons were a welcome change after Arthur Cook's long addresses. Davies moved on in 1927, however, and his place was taken by Sydney Pay (1929-1935) and then by Illingworth Jagger (1936-39). Both were judged to be successful ministers. Pay's most lasting legacy was the spacious Lecture Room which was built behind the church and opened in 1934. (The Sunday Schoolroom in Silver Street, which had begun life as Josiah Redford's Meeting House, was judged to be too far from the church and was eventually sold off to become a depository for a department store in Bishop's Stortford.) Pay had the advantage of being well supported by his musical wife, who conducted the church choir in a performance of the Messiah and brought a new standard of excellence to singing in the local schools. At the end of his ministry extensive repairs were carried out on the church and a new porch was added.

In 1987 we were able to interview William Bunting, then aged 90, who had come with his father to Stansted in 1912 and taken over the greengrocer's shop in Lower Street. He and his wife became church members in 1922, and he went on to become a deacon and a life elder. We asked him if there were any social distinctions between the Anglicans and the Congregationalists in the village, and he replied that most of the farmers were Anglicans and only two of them Congregationalists, one of them being his father-in-law, Mr. Harrett. All the deacons at the Congregational Church were 'in business'. He also said that there was no bad feeling between the two churches. There might have been a time when the Anglicans thought they were superior, but no longer.[12]

The temperance movement was strong, and among the Congregationalists it was headed by the Stansted Tent of the Independent Order of Rechabites, a friendly society that promoted teetotalism.

The Quakers continued to maintain a small but influential presence, but after the departures of the Greens they were no longer a major force in village affairs. George Andrews remembered an Adult School in the Cambridge Road, which he described as a Quaker establishment, which met every Tuesday evening for talks and discussions on 'literature, history and contemporary problems'. It was like a smaller version of the Literary Institution of the Victorian period, an exercise in self-improvement, and attendances were 'very good'. George himself spoke on William Morris and Christopher Columbus.[13]

The Primitive Methodists continued to make a very different appeal. Alfred Phillips, whom we have already encountered as secretary of the local branch of the Labour Party, gave the following account:

> *Sundays for me were a day apart. My parents were Primitive Methodists and worshipped at the Primitive Methodist chapel on the Cambridge Road. My father was also a local preacher and was "planned" to preach at one of the villages round about most Sundays. In the early days it meant walking long distances; Manuden, Pelham, Langley and so on. We went to chapel morning and evening, and Sunday school in the afternoon without fail. The services at chapel were "powerful", the congregation continually ejaculating "Hallelujah", "Praise the Lord", etc. A favourite hymn was "Work, for the Night is Coming, when Man Works No More". We were "teetotallers" and joined the "Band of Hope".[14]*

The church in the Cambridge Road was not well sited: it was on the edge of the village, and services were often disturbed by the noise of traffic. In 1929 the Chapel Committee entered into an agreement with the Society of Friends for the use of the Friends Meeting House on Chapel Hill, and in 1932 the old chapel was sold for £150 when the Primitive Methodists and the Wesleyans were reunited in the Methodist Church.[15]

The schools continued on the paths set out for them before WW1. There were still a few small independent schools, mainly for those children at the infant and junior stages whose parents thought that they could do better there than in the rough and tumble of the village schools. I asked Aubrey Levey, who with about ten other children was sent to a school run by the doctor's daughter, Miss Haynes, if it was regarded as a cut above the others. 'Scholastically, no', he said. 'Socially probably yes.' For the children of the gentry there were the public schools, but for most parishioners the only two schools that could be seriously considered were the Council School and the Church School. In 1924 the Parish Council proposed that the two schools should be amalgamated, but this was rejected by the managers of the Church School.[16] In 1932 the same proposal was made by the county authorities, and again it was rejected by the managers.[17] The Church School, it was said, was 'a sacred trust'.[18]

The Council School on Chapel Hill had replaced the British School, in effect the Nonconformist school, in 1912, when new buildings had been added for an infants school and a girls school. The Church School was still at Gall End, in Lower Street. In both the Church and the Council Schools girls and boys were taught together in the infants, and separately as juniors.

The school log books for this period are in the Essex Record Office and under the 100-year rule cannot be examined. We know, however, that in 1925 the Council School had 239 pupils, one master and seven mistresses, compared with the Church School, which had 128 pupils, two masters and three mistresses. So there was an overall average of 28 children per teacher, which was not thought to be too many.[19] In fact, in common with many other rural schools, the Church School was suffering from declining rolls. In 1916 there had been 207 scholars, and by 1922 this number had fallen to 150, by 1928 to 106, in 1931 to 86, and in 1938 to 73. The infants and the juniors were therefore amalgamated under one Head Teacher.[20]

After WW1 John Woolley continued as the Head Master of the Council School, and was highly regarded. Before the war he had been an active Liberal, and he was strongly attached to the Congregational Church. He had two daughters, both of whom became teachers. One left the village, but the other, Irene, became Head Mistress of the girls school, and was invariably spoken of with admiration and affection. Woolley's successor was Mr. Mitchell.

The Church School meanwhile was under the guidance of Frank Dearch, who was Head Master from 1907 to 1932, and who also helped with the running of the village football club as a highly efficient secretary and then treasurer. As Aubrey Levey remembered, he always wore brown leather gaiters up to his knee. Dearch was replaced in 1932 on a temporary basis by Mr. Enoch and, in 1934, Mr. Enoch by Mr. Pretty, who served until 1945. (Enoch returned in the 1940s as Head Master of the Council School.)

Children attended school until they were 14, but at 11 they could take an examination, and the few who did this and passed could go to Newport Grammar School for boys or to the Herts and Essex High School in Bishop's Stortford for girls. But they were very few: Tom Johnson, for example, was the only boy in his year at the Council School to go to Newport. Attendance was enforced by Mr. Diss, the attendance officer, who lived on Chapel Hill and covered all the schools in the area. He inspected the registers, and if any children were away without a reason being given he would go to their homes and find out why. Marjory Cowan remembered that if she felt that she wanted to stay at home her mother would say that there was nothing wrong with her and she must go to school 'because otherwise we shall have Mr. Diss knocking at the door!' There was informal control as well: 'Stansted was so small then even the shopkeepers could spot a truant, if they saw a child aimlessly around the village, and if it wasn't with its parent they'd know.'[21]

For the Council School as well as the Church School each day began with a religious assembly, and the curriculum was much as might have been expected – maths, English, geography, history and scripture, as well as nature study, painting, singing and country dancing, with woodwork for the boys and needlework and cooking for the girls. There was PE, or 'drill', but for the most part no organised games, if only because there were no playing fields, though both schools could use the Recreation Ground, and the boys played cricket, football and rounders in the playground and the girls played netball. There were no school dinners: children who lived nearby went home to eat while children from a distance brought in packed lunches.

Concerts were held to raise funds, and there was a regular arrangement for an annual concert to be held to finance the school treat. Marjory Cowan, who went to the Council School after WW1, remembered the excitement of the treat - getting through the lessons in the morning 'with tremendous impatience', bolting down her lunch, and then being taken with the rest of the school to the Castle Hills where they spent the afternoon playing games. Then they had tea, 'all sitting at trestle tables, with buttered buns and all the rest of it', and after that they were lined up in 'a long, long crocodile' and went up to the table where Reginald Vercoe, one of the school governors, would be standing 'in a little frock coat' and they would each be given an orange, a bun and a silver threepenny bit.[22]

As in the years before WW1 history was taught in such a way as to encourage patriotism. Vast tracts of the world map on the classroom walls were painted a bold red to proclaim the largest empire the world had ever known, and Empire Day was celebrated on 24 May. The Essex County Education Committee offered guidance on how it should be observed – teachers and pupils assembling together, raising the Union Jack, saluting the flag and singing 'The Flag of Britain', lectures on the Empire, 'the recitation of some poem illustrative of heroic duty and of self-sacrifice on behalf of the Nation', Rudyard Kipling's 'Lest We Forget', the National Anthem and the final salute. In the afternoon there was to be a half-holiday.[23] While the older villagers we interviewed had strong memories of Empire Day the full programme never seems to have been carried through, but the flag was hoisted, patriotic songs such as Rule Britannia were sung, and a half day holiday was enjoyed. Audrey Harvey and her sister had to write essays and won several medals between them for that.[24]

Inevitably the children's responses to their school experience varied widely. Several told us how much they enjoyed it, and this was sometimes linked with being taught by a popular teacher. But others were unhappy, and for boys this was often due to being caned. 'For me school was a misery', said Alfred Phillips, who was born in 1906 and went to the Council School. 'For every misdemeanour it was the cane. I was always late, as I had to do a newspaper round before school.'[25] It was the same at the Church School. 'Of course', said John Speller, 'we used to get the cane in those days … six of the best invariably by Mr. Dearch.' He did not cane the girls, but 'we also had a teacher called Miss Gailer from Manuden … and she was another one who could use the cane'.[26] Jessie Berry confirmed John Speller's account. Mr. Dearch, she said, was 'very strict': he 'caned a few boys every day'. And Miss Gayler was 'a proper little tartar': she often caned her girls and was thoroughly disliked.[27]

Mr. Enoch, who succeeded Mr. Dearch at the Church School on a temporary basis, was another teacher with a bad reputation, though in his case it was also associated with the way he conducted himself when, after several years away from the village, he returned in the 1940s as Head Teacher of the Council School. Enoch, we have been told, was 'brutal'. For his first spell at the Church School we have a fragment of documentary evidence – the punishment book issued by the Essex Education Committee dating from 1934 in which all cases of corporal punishment had to be recorded. Under the regulations recorded in the book only the Head Teacher could inflict corporal punishment on the boys and only an

Assistant Mistress on the girls. Each case of punishment had to be recorded in the book which had to be laid on the table at each meeting of the managers. Under no circumstances could any blow be given on the face or head.

In this book we can see Mr. Enoch at work in the last weeks of his headmastership at the Church School. Between 9 January and 16 February 1934 he recorded seven canings, more than one a week, all of them one or two strokes on the hand for talking or incessant talking, untidy work, copying, disobedience or being late. Then Mr. Pretty became Head Master, and in the rest of 1934 20 cases were recorded. In 1935 there were 22, in 1936 24, in 1937 12, in 1938 12, and in 1939 4. Again the punishment was usually one or two strokes on the hand, though in some cases three or four strokes were given, and in two cases of bullying and one case of lying and misbehaviour the offender was given four strokes on the buttocks.[28]

For sport the most important development has already been touched on – the acquisition of Hargrave Park by the Sports Association, which had been formed in 1933 under the chairmanship of Edmund Cawkell, and the great boost this gave to sport in Stansted. The money came from a few generous donations and a loan, leaving a debt of £120, and the annual subscription was fixed at 2s. 6d. At the same time a Jubilee Arch was erected with funds left over from the Jubilee celebrations. On 2 June 1935 the Hargrave Park Sports Ground was formally opened.

The football club benefited in particular. Although it had more than held its own, its pitch at Green's Meadow had been 'just rough mud'.[29] The new Hargrave pitch was a great improvement, and in 1939 a stand costing £200 was added, giving the ground a seating capacity of 150. It had the luxury of separate dressing rooms below with showers and electric lights.

The club responded well to these changes. It held its annual meeting in the summer to decide which leagues and cups it wanted to enter in the coming season, and made its applications accordingly on behalf of both the first team and the reserves. The governing bodies of the leagues and cups then decided at the beginning of each season which teams to accept. For Stansted the high point was the 1934/5 season, when five trophies were won – the East Herts League, the East Herts Challenge Cup, the Stansted and District Challenge Cup and the West Essex Border Charity Cup by the first team, and the Bishop's Stortford Charity Cup by the reserves. Supporters noted approvingly that the players were all 'Stansted boys'. Gates were good: 1,000 people watched the West Essex Border Charity Cup final. The club now had an excellent foundation for the progress which it made after WW2, and the popularity of the game was now so great that a second club was formed at Burton End.

The cricket team had been playing at Hargrave Park since 1921 – Sydney Alder, who lived at Hargrave House, was the club captain in 1922 - and in 1933, when the Hargrave Park estate was put up for sale, the club bought the cricket ground there for £205. These arrangements were then brought within the framework of the Stansted Sports Association. A reserve team had long been established and by 1936 the club had 60-70 members.

Some of the other sports established before WW1 continued to flourish – tennis, bowls and billiards – and the Puckeridge Hunt continued to hold a full programme, including the occasional meet at St. Mary's Church. The great shooting parties at Stansted Hall were now a thing of the past, but in the west of the parish the Goslings still kept a meticulous gamebook of all the pheasants and partridges they killed. They insisted on strips of rough land being maintained on either side of the hedges to provide cover for the birds, and it is to them that we owe the attractive windings of the Stort on Stansted's western boundary, since after WW2, unlike landowners upstream towards Manuden and downstream towards Stortford, they and their formidable agent, Major Durrack, again to provide cover for the birds, refused to straighten out the river on their land. Two of the pre-war sports that depended heavily on the gentry, however, polo and golf, were no longer played in the village.

Shortly before WW2 a Homing Society was active, and the flights of pigeons from distant parts of the country were carefully recorded together with their 'velocities'.

There were two local heroes. In 1926 H. C. Burton, whose parental home was Spencer House, played rugby for England against Wales at Cardiff, and according to Harry Viner was 'pulled up Chapel Hill in a car from Mayhews Garage'. (He played his rugby for Richmond, and before that had captained Bishop's Stortford.)[30] And in 1938 Jack Turner, a lightweight boxer from the village, fighting at Chelmsford, overcame an opponent from Braintree, 'attacking furiously from the first bell', and then, at Bury St Edmunds, knocked out his opponent.[31]

As well as the churches, the schools, the sporting clubs and the political parties, village life was enriched by a great array of social organisations. Some of them catered especially for women, and of these the most important was the Women's Institute. The first WIs had been founded during WW1, and in 1937 one of the speakers at Stansted, Mrs. Arthur Browne, claimed that the Institute 'had become the greatest organisation of women in the world in 21 years'. The aim was to improve conditions in country life,[32] and for the most part it was headed by women from the leading families – Madge Gold, Sir Charles's grand-daughter, held office for many years – and in the summer its monthly meetings were often held in the gardens of their splendid houses. Members engaged in a wide variety of activities, most of them relating to the roles which they were expected to play in a rural community – competitions for the best home-made biscuits, for example, for the best home-knitted jumper, and for the largest quantity of potatoes that could be grown from one potato. There were talks ranging from the practicalities of country life to the need for world peace. Country dancing and community singing were popular, and the Stansted choir won several competitions organised by the regional federation of WIs. Concerts and sales of work were held to raise funds for various charitable activities. Every year a party was held for the 'old folks' of Stansted, usually about 150 of them in the Central Hall, and after a 'sumptuous tea' fancy hats and crackers were handed out, there was community singing, and the men were given 'smokes' and the women chocolates and tea. At Christmas toys were collected for poor children in Limehouse, financed by the proceeds of an 'Olde English Fayre', and on one occasion mothers from Limehouse came to the village and were entertained and shown around.

There were at least four other women's organisations. The first was the Girls' Friendly Society, which was still very active along the lines established before WW1. The second was the Mothers' Union, which was linked with the Church of England. The third was peculiar to Stansted – the Women's Own, which was founded in November 1918 and was originally a group of women praying for their husbands at the front. After the war it became a Christian fellowship.[33] Each year it held what it called its 'Great Day', when a bazaar and a concert were held to raise funds for charity. It enjoyed good support: at its 20th birthday party in 1938 the Central Hall was said to be crowded.

The fourth organisation was the local branch of the Essex County Nursing Association, which aimed to provide a local nursing service. Its main method of raising money was to hold fetes in the gardens of the big houses in the village, such as Stansted Hall, Stansted House and Blythwood. At its annual meeting in April 1935 it was reported that its membership numbered 327 and that in the previous year its two nurses had made 3,916 visits.[34] They were housed in two cottages which were bought for them in 1937 for £950.

There were other organisations which looked mainly to the men of the village, and pre-eminent among these were the Working Men's Club and the British Legion, whose chairman was Edmund Cawkell. As well as its run-of-the-mill activities the biggest event of the Legion year was the Christmas and New Year Party which it held for the children of members and of war widows. Sometimes as many as 200 youngsters attended, not just from Stansted, but being brought in by car from the nearby villages as well. The Legion was always prominent on Armistice Day.

For the young there were the Scouts and the Guides, who regularly took part in church parades and were encouraged to see themselves as loyal subjects of the King. In 1935, for example, the Scouts were given the patriotic duty of preparing the line of bonfires for George V's Jubilee and in 1937 of selling Coronation programmes.

There were fetes and concerts for Dr. Barnardo's Homes, and on occasion Dr. Barnardo's Musical Boys sang to 'delighted audiences'. 'Buttercup Day' was organised by Gertrude Findlay for the Royal National Orthopaedic Hospital.

For the Anglican Church one of the most effective ways of raising funds was the church fete, held every summer, usually in the grounds of Blythwood House, and in 1927 this was linked with an extraordinary pageant, the Pageant of Saint Thomas Becket, organised by the Marquis d'Orsy, or, to give him his full name, Amand Edouard Ambroise Marie Lowis Etienne Phillipe d'Sant Andre Tournay, who was not a marquis at all, but Brother Ambrose Thomas, a failed Benedictine monk turned Anglican layman who had come to live at the nearby hamlet of Pledgdon Green. He designed pageant costumes and painted furniture 'in an extravagant baroque manner', and took a keen interest in folk-dancing and other religious and social activities organised by Conrad Noel, the Socialist vicar of Thaxted. He was especially well suited, or so he claimed, to organise the pageant, or to inspire it, as the vicar said, as its 'presiding genius', since his family were 'kinsfolk of the French royal house whom Becket took refuge with at the Chateau d'Orsy when he was compelled to fly to France', and he brought off a stunning success which drew praise in the national press, including the *Daily Mail*, whose reporter described the various scenes which he devised as 'wonderfully done in the most glowing colours' that caught 'the naïve beauty of the pictures in an eleventh century Missal'. The *Mail* drew special attention to

> the delightful scene representing the passage of Becket over the Channel to France: there was the little medieval boat and the Marquis himself in it as the Great Archbishop .... An attendant plied a small red oar and the half-moon

barque rocked back and forth, drawing cries of delight from the spectators. They say that ordinary people do not care for pieces of consummate art. At Stansted they do ....

The church benefited to the tune of £321 18s. 8d. There were other pageants, but not on the same scale as Thomas Becket.[35]

The occasion of the greatest ceremony in the village was George V's Silver Jubilee, which was celebrated in much the same way, though not on the same scale, as Queen Victoria's Golden Jubilee. 1935, wrote the vicar, John Barrow, would always be remembered as Silver Jubilee Year, 'one of the happiest and most wonderful years in the history of our country'.[36]

The main methods of raising money have already been mentioned – concerts, fetes, jumble sales, sales of work and dances. For fetes the music was sometimes provided by the Bishop's Stortford Band or the Essex Yeomanry Band, and for dances by groups such as the Syncopaters, the Harmonica Boys, The Tempo Band and Fred Rogers' Arcadia Dance Band. But by far the most common money-raiser was the whist drive, sometimes followed by a dance. 'Everlasting whist drives', Aubrey Levey complained,[37] and he is borne out by the pages of the local press. Whist drives were held to raise money for almost every organisation in the village, from the football club to the church parochial funds. Only the Nonconformist churches seem to have been exempt. A typical press report, supplied no doubt by a local informant, would record the number of tables in play, who presided over the occasion and handed out the prizes, who won the prizes and how much money was raised.

In the 1930s, however, a new and highly demanding enterprise was undertaken, the production of a musical comedy each year by the Stansted Amateur Operatic and Dramatic Society. This was put on at the Central Hall and ran for three to five evenings to packed and appreciative audiences. Donald Gold was the producer, Madge Gold was his assistant, and the singers were all local. Mrs. Godefroy, the church organist, was the musical director, and her piano playing was so good that it was possible to dispense with an orchestra. She was, it was said, 'a host in herself'.[38] In 1932 the Yeomen of the Guard was produced, in 1933 the Belle of Brittany, in 1934 The Rebel Maid and in 1935 Tom Jones. The Jolly Roger was chosen for 1936, but there was some disagreement over this and it was cancelled, whereupon the Golds resigned. Mr. E. T. Dodd became the new producer, and another musical was chosen, The Geisha. There were fears that it would not be possible to maintain the Golds' high standards, but the production was a great success.[39] In 1937 The Arcadians was also a success: this, said the Society's secretary pointedly, was because 'all had worked happily together'.[40] When The Quaker Girl was put on in 1938 it was regarded as the best show the Society had produced.[41]

There was, however, one major event that would no longer require any expenditure of money or effort, and that was the annual Horticultural Show which had so dominated the summers before WW1. It was discontinued soon after the war, and in 1934 or 1935 the Stansted and Birchanger Horticultural Society came to an end.[42].

To the delight of the children, however, the Stansted fair continued.

When we interviewed older inhabitants in the 1980s those whom we asked were unanimous that when they were children there was very little crime in the village, and this is borne out by the local papers. The changes from the Victorian and Edwardian period are striking. The 'rough element' which had caused so much trouble in the 1890s was no longer in evidence, and there were comparatively few cases of poaching, which had been endemic before the war.

Another great change was the proliferation of prosecutions for traffic offences. The police station was situated on the Cambridge Road, which provided an excellent vantage point for catching offenders. On a single day, 7 May 1924, no fewer than 13 drivers were caught returning from the Newmarket Races and exceeding the 10 mph speed limit. The gentry were caught as well as ordinary parishioners. Walter Gold was fined 14s. for driving an unlicensed motor caravan, and Joan Oliver was fined 30s. for causing an obstruction. Before WW1 most of the accused who appeared in the dock were local people: traffic offenders came from a much wider area.

In spite of this clamping down on what for the most part were petty infringements of the law, standards of driving were appalling. The statistics for deaths in Great British road accidents speak for themselves – 4,886 in 1926 rising to 7,305 in 1930, compared with 1,713 in 2013. As early as 1900 there were complaints that cars were not slowing down when approaching horses and that accidents occurred when the horses shied. Sir Walter Gilbey, who had been accustomed to driving around the district in a phaeton, never drove on the main Cambridge Road for fear of meeting a car.[43] During the inter-war period there were several accidents involving Stansted cyclists and motorists. The most revealing case was the accident which resulted in the death of Michael Spencer-Smith, a director of the Bank of England who lived at Norman House. Going north on the road to Newmarket on a misty morning in 1928 he approached a cross-roads at 30 mph, took no more precaution than a warning toot on his horn, and was killed in the ensuing collision with a car coming from one of the side roads. The jury returned a verdict of accidental death.[44]

WW1 had been hailed as the war to end war, and one of the most important initiatives for promoting peace was the League of Nations, which was supported throughout the country by the League of Nations Union. In Stansted the local branch of the Union was chaired by Arthur Findlay, who was backed by John Barrow, the vicar, by Sidney Pay, the Congregationalist minister, and by Pay's successor, Illingworth Jagger. The League was seen as a good cause, and supporting it was uncontroversial.

In his determination to preserve peace Sidney Pay went even further. In 1934, in a statement reminiscent of the resolution passed by the Oxford Union the previous year, 'that this house in no circumstances will fight for King and Country', nine local Congregational Ministers, Pay among them, declared that war was un-Christian, a denial of the sacredness of human personality, a negation of the spirit of human brotherhood and an irrational method of solving international disputes, and that they would refuse in the name of Christ actively to support its prosecution should they ever be called upon to do so.[45]

Ultimately, however, as one speaker to the Women's Institute reluctantly acknowledged, the League was a failure. Throughout the thirties the threat of war loomed ever larger, and the country began to get into a state of readiness. Stansted was directly affected. By 1937 there was an army camp in the grounds of Hargrave Park and the village was disrupted by manoeuvres involving, it was said, thousands of men,[46] and in 1938 an ARP (Air Raid Precautions) meeting was held in the Assembly Hall when the plans for the district were explained. A call for volunteers met with a ready response.[47] Leaflets were distributed on what to do in the event of an air raid, and shortly before war was declared gas masks were distributed. The country stood on the verge of a bloody conflict that would take the men of Stansted to fight many miles from their homes in many parts of the world.

1 *SMPM*, July 1905.
2 SMLHS, Interview with Marjory Cowan, 23 March 1988, p. 16.
3 *HEO*, 21 and 28 April 1917.
4 For this dispute, see *HEO*, 13 April 1918, 28 June 1919, and 15 November 1919.
5 SMLHS, Interview, 7 December, 1987.
6 *SMPM*, April 1931.
7 SMLHS, Interview, 7 December 1987.
8 SMLHS, Interview, 27 February 2014.
9 SMLHS, Interview, 24 June 2014.
10 Graham Leonard, who became his curate in 1950 (and later became a controversial Bishop of London) described Barrow's churchmanship as 'Prayer Book Catholic', i.e. he was an Anglo-Catholic who not only used the Book of Common Prayer but believed it to be the liturgy par excellence for Catholic worship: Peart-Binns (1988:14).
11 *EC*, 7 December 1934.
12 SMLHS, Interview, 11 March 1987.
13 SMLHS, Notes attached to letter to Ralph Phillips of 28 February 1989.
14 SMLHS, Alfred Phillips, notes, n.d.
15 Ralph Phillips, 'The Primitive Methodist Connexion. Stansted Mountfitchet', n.d.
16 *EC*, 3 October 1924.
17 *EC*, 30 September 1932.
18 *SMPM*, August 1930. See also *SMPM* February 1946.
19 ERO, D/P 109/30/7, minutes of Parish Council, 10 March 1925.
20 *SMPM*, August 1938.
21 SMLHS, Interview with Marjory Cowan, 23 March 1988, pp. 8-9.
22 SMLHS, Interview with Marjory Cowan, 23 March 1988, p. 14.
23 *HEO*, 5 May 1923.
24 SMLHS, Audrey Harvey, 'Childhood Memories', n.d.
25 SMLHS, Alfred Phillips, Notes, n.d., p. 1.
26 SMLHS, Interview with John Speller, November 1988, p. 3.
27 SMLHS, Reminiscences of Jessie Berry, 13 April 1987, p. 1.
28 This punishment book is now in the Essex Record Office and cannot be consulted under the 100-year rule, but I was able to see it before it was deposited there.
29 *HEO*, 1 January 1939.
30 *HEO*, 9 and 23 January 1926, *EC*, 15 January 1926.
31 *EC*, 22 and 29 October and 17 December 1937. His entries on the internet give him a record between 1937 and 1942 of 1 win and 3 losses, but are clearly incomplete.
32 *EC*, 10 December 1937.
33 SMLHS, Interview with Josephine Hill, 25 November 1988: Josephine was present at the first meeting, and when she was interviewed in 1988 the group was still meeting weekly.
34 *EC*, 12 April 1935.
35 *EC*, 17 June 1927, *SMPM*, July 1927. For the Marquis, see Julian Lytten, 'The Marquis d'Orsy: Aesthete, Eccentric and Enigma', *Saffron Walden Historical Journal*, New Series Vol. 12, No. 24, Autumn 2012, pp. 20-26. See also SMLHS, Interview with Margery Baker, 1 February 1989.
36 *SMPM*, January 1936.
37 SMLHS, Interview, 7 December 1987.
38 *EC*, 21 January 1938.
39 *EC*, 13 March 1936.
40 *EC*, 12 March 1937.
41 *EC*, 28 January 1938.
42 *EC*, 12 April 1935.
43 *EC*, 7 January 1938, quoting R. D. Blumenfeld's diary of 1900.
44 *EC*, 27 January and 16 March 1928.
45 *EC*, 12 January 1934.
46 *SMPM*, September 1937.
47 *EC*, 21 October 1938; *SMPM*, November 1938.

37: THE SECOND WORLD WAR[1]

Only 20 years divided the end of WW1 from the beginning of WW2, but for the fighting men it was a very different experience. Conscription was introduced at once: all men between 18 and 41 were liable to be called up, except, as in WWI, those engaged in vital industries or occupations and conscientious objectors. By 1942 all men between 18 and 51 were liable, and all unmarried women between 20 and 30 unless they were looking after a child. So there was no intensive recruitment campaign for volunteers, no WW2 equivalent of Kitchener's posters. People remembered, perhaps with embarrassment, the euphoria that had greeted the outbreak of WW1 – and they remembered what followed. This time there was no jubilation, no confident expectation that the war would be over quickly. The response was more sober and reflective.

In WW1 the British Expeditionary Force had crossed the Channel and had immediately been engaged in terrible fighting: Stansted's first casualty, William Fuller-Maitland, had been killed within weeks and others had quickly followed. In WW2 there was at first a lull, the so-called phoney war. The first Stansted casualty was Redvers Taylor, of the Royal Naval Reserve, who was drowned when his ship was sunk in November 1939, and it was November 1940 before the next man died, John Wren of the Royal Army Service Corps. In WW1 the BEF had been able to establish a footing and was never dislodged from France. In WW2 the British Army was routed and in May and June 1940 had to retreat to England from the beaches of Dunkirk. The soldiers of WW1 had been bogged down in a war of attrition, and the dominant experience had been trench warfare in France and Belgium. In WW2 armies were more mobile and the conflict was more widely flung. Stansted's fighting men were almost as likely to be in the Navy or the RAF as in the army.[2] George Ecclestone died as a prisoner of war (PoW) after being captured at El Alamein, his brother Tom in a bombing raid over Holland. Leslie Carter died as a PoW taken after the loss of Hong Kong, Charlie Johns as a PoW in Thailand. Bill Carter was killed in Italy and was buried in the Sangro River cemetery. Among those who survived Aubrey Levey served in West Africa, while young Peter Philpott, just 18, took part in the Normandy landings at Ver-sur-Mer, wading ashore on D-Day + 1, pushing his way through the corpses. The overall casualties in WW2, as recorded on the war memorial, were 17, compared with 54 for WW1. For WW1 the names of the fallen were in alphabetical order under rank. For WW2 the rank ordering disappeared.

On the home front, as in WW1, there was the anxious waiting for news from men who were abroad, or, if they were still stationed in this country, the waiting for them to come home on leave. Olive Bunting used to work for the Post Office as a young girl. Among her many duties she had to take down messages over the phone, write them out as telegrams and deliver them by bike around Stansted and the nearby villages. Sometimes she was literally the messenger of death and people dreaded to see her in case she brought bad news. There were also cards from PoWs, some of them in Japanese camps.

The experience on the home front was very different in other ways too. War was expected and preparations had been made in advance. After Neville Chamberlain's declaration of war on 3 September 1939 many people expected German air-raids at once. Gas masks had already been issued, and the villagers had been trained in their use. But the biggest immediate impact was the arrival of evacuee children from London.

In the country as a whole there were three waves of evacuation. First there was a mass evacuation at the beginning of the war. But when nothing happened, when the dreaded air-raids did not materialize, many of the evacuees were taken back home. Then, in 1940, came the Blitz, which set off the second wave of evacuation. Finally there was a third, smaller wave towards the end of the war in order to escape the V1 and the V2 rockets.

The first two waves, though not the third, are reflected in the school log books and in the memories of those villagers who lived through the war.[3] The Church School acted as a receiving station for Government evacuees. On 2 September 1939, the day before war was declared, the log book records that 'The School was used as a Receiving Station for Government Evacuees. 350 mothers and children arrived from Tottenham instead of 700 children as expected.' Throughout the following week the staff were 'busy doing the clerical work in connection with the billeting of the Evacuees', and when the school reopened on 13 September there were 157 children on the books, including 25 evacuees from Tottenham and 24 'private cases', i.e. children whose evacuation had been organised by family and friends rather than the Government. The phoney war resulted in a drift back to London, and by 2 January 1940 the number of children had gone down to 139. By 28 October 1940, during the Blitz, this number had gone up again to 161, of whom about a third were evacuees. On 22 September 1941 there were 175 children on the books, the highest number recorded, but by 17 April 1944 this number had gone down to 131.

At the Council School, for the Boys' Department, the log book gives a similar but less detailed account. On 13 September 1939 65 local children and 14 evacuees were present, and in the following month, in addition to 64 local children, there were '5 Government and 14 Private evacuees', a total of 83. On 7 October 1940, at the height of the Blitz, there were 106 names on the register, and by January 1941 108, including 40 evacuees. By 22 September 1941 the total had come down to 98, of whom 28 were evacuees, but then 18 more evacuees were admitted, raising the total of evacuees to 46 and the total of children as a whole to 116.

At nearby Bishop's Stortford arrangements had been made for the reception of a whole school of evacuees, the Clapton County Secondary School for Girls, who were taught at the Herts and Essex High School for Girls in Bishop's Stortford, which several girls from Stansted attended. This held classes for the evacuees in the morning, from 9 till 1, and for the local girls in the afternoon, from 1 to 5.

Margery Baker in Stansted was the billeting officer's clerk, and in 1989 she gave us her account of the arrangements made in the village:

The old Council offices in Lower Street were my headquarters, and here I interviewed the people who were willing to take in children from the East End of London and from Canvey Island. I also had to try to sort out the problems that were brought to me about children who had lice in their hair, or unwanted children's relations who insisted on staying with the host families against their wishes. Where possible brothers and sisters were billeted in the same house along with their mother. But most of the mothers just stayed long enough to get the children settled, and then returned to London.

And here are the memories of Jean McBride, who was eight when the war started and was attending the Council School on Chapel Hill:

The immediate change in the village was the influx of evacuees, most of whom returned to London within a few months, but who left a lasting impression because of their extreme poverty and lack of clothing, and the epidemic of fleas and lice that went through the school; most of these were young children .... The second arrival was in 1940, mostly mothers with babies and very young children who had been bombed out. They were allocated empty, mostly very run down properties, some in Lower Street and Bull Yard, but they stayed longer.

It is possible that the local people exaggerated the fleas and lice. At the Boys' Department in the Council School two examinations are recorded: on 13 November 1939 the nurse examined the children's heads and found 'all satisfactory', and on 5 January 1942 she reported once again that all was 'clear'.

Win Baxter, who as a 12 year old girl was an evacuee with the Phillips family, who were then living in Bishop's Stortford, also remembers the arrival of the second wave of evacuees. It was

the weekend when the Blitz started and the docks etc. were set alight. As we went to school on the Monday a train had just arrived and people were pouring out of the station. Obviously having endured two whole days and nights of intense bombing they had fled out of London. They all looked very dishevelled and frightened.

Doris Thistle, who lived in Woodfields, and who was 13 when the war broke out, gave us her account of her family's experience:

We had two evacuees from Bethnal Green, Betty and Gerald .... Betty I think was barely five, and Gerald was a year old. As always happened, the parents took them back when they thought the war was over. So they were taken home. Then the bombs started again, and by this time my grandmother was ill and my aunt was looking after her and my mother was helping, and my mother was asked if she would have the children back. Gerald was a little difficult to deal with. My mother had to get up during the nights with him. So my mother said she would have Betty but she couldn't have Gerald because she was doing other things, you see. So that was what they did. We did have Betty for some time, and she was a lovely little girl.

Gerald's trouble, in fact, was bed-wetting, a common problem among evacuees.

Doris's family looked after another evacuee, a dog called Bonny, an apricot poodle. Doris's aunt, who was living in Stansted, was asked to look after Bonny because a friend in London did not think it was fair to keep a dog in London during the war. So Doris's aunt kept Bonny throughout the war, and after the war too. This aspect of the conflict is often forgotten: in the first four days of the war, because of the evacuation, 400,000 pets were put down in Greater London alone, mainly cats, but many of them dogs. Then, when many evacuees returned home in the phoney war, there was no dog or cat to greet them.

Not all evacuation was organised by the Government. In many cases there were informal arrangements made by family and friends. Audrey Rodgers was a case in point. She was eight when war broke out and was living with her family in Colindale, in Middlesex. Her aunt, Rose Turner, her mother's sister, lived with her husband, Frank, in Bentfield End, where they ran a shop. Audrey's father, who was a keeper at the London Zoo, could not leave his job, and so she and her mother came and lived with the Turners. But her mother wanted her own house, and so from there they went to live in the Cambridge Road.

In 1940, however, they in their turn had evacuees billeted on them. This was in the second wave of evacuation.

> *We had a grandmother, two mums, and two children. They were evacuated on us. And mother and I slept under the kitchen table until the evacuees left.*

They did not stay long and as far as Audrey remembers they went back to London when the Blitz was over.

Inevitably there was a wide range of experience with evacuees. Derek and Barry Francis, who lived in Woodfields, had one refugee, an Italian boy, but they remember very little about him. They went to the Council School where they have no memories of evacuees at all. Nor does Jim Ward, who also went to the Council School. In many families, of course, there was no room for evacuees.

It was not only individuals and schools which were evacuated, but a few companies as well. Among them was the Southend Telephone Monitors Office which moved to Gorsefield, on Grove Hill, in July 1940. It was a company which dealt with all the telephone accounts in the Southend area, and Doris Thistle, when she left school, went to work as a messenger girl for them. Later she became a Temporary Clerical Assistant, and when the company moved back to Southend in 1944 she went with them. Another company that came to Stansted was ACWEECO, which made electrical insulation testers.

Bombs were a constant threat. Black-out precautions were rigidly enforced, and a warning siren was set up at the army camp in Hargrave Park (about which more below). In nearby Bishop's Stortford there were over 800 alarms in the course of the war.[4] At first raids were conducted during the day, but were switched to the night when the Luftwaffe began to suffer heavy losses. During the Blitz it was possible to look south at night and to see the red glow of the flames in the sky.

Travelling at night was difficult, for under the blackout regulations car sidelights were restricted to an aperture of one eighth of an inch, enough for persons on the road to see the car but no more. There were more problems if you were unsure of your way, because all the signposts were removed.

Margery Baker told us of her experiences as an ARP volunteer (Air Raid Precautions) and an ambulance driver:

> *Mr. Ralph Ball, the night-time Superintendent of the ARP service in Stansted, was ... based at the Council Offices [in Lower Street]. He received information by telephone concerning air-raids and other incidents and instructed his staff accordingly. I was on duty two nights a week from about 7 p.m. to 7 a.m at the Council Offices, where I and my colleagues got what sleep we could in the wash-house behind the building. There were lots of blankets and pillows available, and we slept higgledy-piggledy, six or seven of us, men and women, on piles of stretchers laid out on the floor. It was rather damp, but we had a fire going, and brewed endless pots of tea to keep our spirits up.*

37: THE SECOND WORLD WAR

When the warning siren was heard from the Fire Station, Mr. Ball would be told the nature of the emergency, and if casualties were expected I had to leap onto my bicycle and peddle through the streets made very dark by the blackout to Bentfield Place, where the ambulance was kept in charge of Mr. Gosling, who was head of the ARP and ambulance services in Stansted. This ambulance was a converted Chrysler with green canvas sides that swayed about terrifyingly when in motion. I never had to drive it at night, luckily, but I remember going one night to investigate a bomb that had been dropped at Manuden, and on another occasion I accompanied the Stansted firemen when they went to put out a fire at a cottage in Henham that had been started by an incendiary bomb.

There is some confusion about the exact number of bombs that fell on the village, but everyone is agreed that a few bombs did fall and that they did little damage. There were no casualties. The two bombs that almost everyone mentions are the bomb that fell on the Recreation Ground, leaving a large crater, and the bomb that fell at the same time in the alley, or 'twitchel', leading off from the Recreation Ground between the Sanderses' house and the Spaldings'. Hubert Sanders, the brother of Irving, the local historian, gives us the date – 12 October 1940. He was home on leave with his wife Kath:

We went in the house and Mother got the supper. We all sat round the table eating, drinking and chatting away, when all of a sudden Kath jumps up and dives behind an armchair. Then there was a terrific noise, the windows and blackout came flying across the room, glass and plaster with it. Father was drinking a cup of coffee at the time and all that was left was the handle in his hand. Mother got up and went to the kitchen. She called out "No wonder they are dropping bombs. Someone left the door open." We went and looked. The blast had blown it off, it was lying on the top of the cooker. We could hear water rushing somewhere. I grabbed my tin hat and went out to investigate.

I found the bomb had burst the water main. What a mess! The wall was down, bricks were lying about all over the place, and the neighbours' 6ft high fence had disappeared. The bomb crater was in the passage that was between the two houses, and the passage looked more like a fast flowing river now.

.... There was another bomb crater on the recreation ground, and we found out later another at Rochford Nurseries.

Many people went up to have a look at the damage that had been done, and Jim Ratcliff remembers going there as a boy to get shrapnel.

Others, like Hubert Sanders, remember the third bomb at Rochford Nurseries. Apart from destroying a few greenhouses, it did not do much damage. Others remember a bomb near Bentfield End, and Jim Ward adds the detail that it was on the land of George Rose. Again no one was hurt. There are reports also of a stick of bombs falling on the cutting on the railway siding, two bombs between West Road and Pesterford Bridge, and one falling by Alsa Lodge, leaving a large crater. A land mine fell in Burton End, in the area that is known as Turner's Spring, doing no damage but leaving a deep crater.

What did the most harm, however, was not a bomb at all, but a Mosquito aircraft which crashed into Bentfield Bury Farm on a test flight at 5.10 pm on 10 June 1942. According to the accident investigation report, now in the National Archives, two planes took part in the test, and afterwards one of them returned to base. The other was seen flying at high speed in a north to north-easterly direction, and then it turned and broke up with a big bang, but there was no fire. The pilot and his co-pilot were killed. The wreckage spread over two square miles, and because of the growing corn much of it was not immediately discovered. Examination of the wreckage revealed that the rear entry door had not been properly closed, and the Chief Inspector concluded that this was what had caused the accident. There were no casualties on the ground, but some farm buildings were destroyed.

There are also several accounts from people who saw the accident, and perhaps the most vivid is that by Gerald Snow of Bentfield Green in his autobiography. Gerald was with his mother, his Aunt Dora and his cousin Pamela. They had just come back from Saffron Walden, Aunt Dora had gone upstairs to lie down, and Pamela was outside in the garden.

> *I was indoors. Mother was getting the tea ready when an aeroplane came over, the engine spluttering. Suddenly it stopped, then there was just like a thunderclap. Pamela who came running from the garden said, 'the aeroplane, it has all broken up in the sky'. We knew it had crashed, looking out of the window and across the fields opposite there was a huge cloud of black smoke going up. Next there were crowds of people all saying there had been a plane crash, fire engines, ambulances and police were rushing down Plantation Hill. Everybody was running across the field opposite. My mother, Pamela and I went as well.*
>
> *Miss Trundle joined us, she had come up the road, she said that she had been outside talking to Violet her daughter-in-law, she said to Violet, 'Oh my God he's all in flames and has crashed on Mr. Tinney's farm [Bentfield Bury], now the farm is all alight'. When we arrived on the scene there were crowds of people and more coming. The aeroplane laid on the ground still burning. It had crashed right next to the thatched barn, which was alight and burning like an inferno. Someone told us they had seen two men brought out of the wrecked aeroplane and taken away on stretchers to an ambulance .... We heard after that both men had died in the crash. My mother said, 'listen to those poor pigs', they were in the thatched barn and squealing as if they had gone mad. The fire brigade was there but it lacked water. Just as the fire was going down the roof caved in and crashed down in a cloud of sparks and black smoke, then the fire took on a new lease of life and flames shot into the sky. Then we went home, there were still more people coming. We heard afterwards from people nearer the fire that some of the poor old pigs were running about terribly burnt and had to be shot to end their suffering. Mr. Tinney was cross as it had crashed on a field of young sugar beet and the people trampled all over it.[5]*

According to Jim Ratcliff another plane came down over Alsa Wood.

> *I was biking towards Elsenham and this plane exploded in the air and it fell over Alsa Wood. I got my bike and went across. Quite a few people were gathered there. The police were there. And we had to search this wood to find the bodies. Because we'd seen, or I'd seen, no parachute or anything. The plane*

exploded and when we did get into the wood we did find a body, buried up to his shoulders. The plane was British, a Mosquito, but the two people in the plane were Canadians.

Many people saw rockets flying across, the so-called buzz bombs or doodlebugs, and Jim Ward remembers that when the engine cut out he and his parents used to get under the table.

It was just as well that so few bombs fell on Stansted, since very few families had shelters, and such shelters as there were afforded little protection in most cases. The Ratcliffs were unusual in having a Morrison shelter. Most of our informants told us that when they heard the siren they simply went under the table. Jim Ward, however, had the benefit of a do-it-yourself shelter.

Yes, we had a shelter. It was on the green at Potash Cottages. Bert Gray built it. He was a very practical man. We dug a hole, then put railway sleepers over it, then galvanized iron on that, and then soil on top of that. I put in the electricity, you know, run off a battery. It had stairs going into it at a right angle. We used that a lot.

During the Blitz the raids were sometimes so intense that school had to be cancelled in the morning or its opening delayed. At first there were no shelters in any of the schools, and the children took refuge under their desks. On 26 August 1940 the Head Teacher at the Council School noted: 'Air raid alarm 3.15 p.m. Children sang songs from their positions under the desks.' And when the shelters were constructed – in 1940/41 it seems – they gave no assurance of safety. Jean McBride, a pupil at the Council School, having described how the school windows were 'stuck with Andrew's crosses of paper to reduce the risk of flying glass', records that

Two air raid shelters were built on the school field .... [They] were of brick and above ground. We practised the occasional air raid drill when they were first erected, and, perhaps once used them in real earnest during a raid, but most of the time they were unused.

Barry Francis says much the same:

It was a brick-built shelter, concrete flat roof, square building. Useless I would have thought because it wasn't underground, it was just a building on the field. ... we never used it. There were times when the siren went when we were at school, but I can't really remember going into the shelter.

The Church School was no better provided for. As Audrey Rodgers remembers,

We had an earthen shelter there .... You had to crawl into it. It wasn't underground. It wouldn't have stood an earthly if it had been hit. And at home there was nothing. Living opposite the army camp we didn't use to get up until we heard the claxon going from the camp. When the claxon went in the camp the enemy was within five miles of us. So we used to get up and go out into the garden. Did we have a shelter there? No, we just used to get up and go outside.

There was only one casualty on the home front: Winnie Johnson, aged 21, was working at the Hoffman Ball Bearing factory in Chelmsford when it was struck at one in the morning by a V2 rocket. Thirty-nine people were killed and 138 injured, 47 of them seriously.[6]

As well as providing information about evacuees and air raids the school log books take us through many of the practical impacts of living through the war. As early as November 1939 about three quarters of an acre of the field at the Council School was ploughed up for the spring planting of potatoes, and in October 1941 Class II gathered rose hips and about 20 lbs were despatched to 'the centre'. There are several references to fund raising and the associated winning of prizes. In January 1941, for example, 10s. was raised from the sale of cabbages and given to the Soldiers' Comfort Fund organised by the WI. In March 1941 £20 2s. 10d. was collected for War Weapons Week, and four of the girls won prizes for slogans. In March 1943 Police Constable Clark gave a talk on 'objects dropped from aeroplanes', and in March 1944 he showed various types of anti-personnel bombs to the scholars and warned them of the dangers of touching them. There is an interesting entry for 14 October 1946, after the war was over, about the admission of Thomas Klein, a Czech refugee, who had spent 12 years in a German concentration camp, and stayed in Stansted as 'a temporary measure to give him some background education and build up his confidence' before going on to America.

The schools' fundraising activities were just part of a constant round of activity to support the war effort. The WI was ideally placed to give help, throughout the war sending parcels of comforts for men in the services and clothing to the Merchant Navy, and making prodigious numbers of pots of jam and chutney and cans and bottles of fruit. In March 1940 its Entertainments Committee gave an Empire pageant play entitled 'Britain Awake', with one of its members taking the part of Britannia. The ladies of the leading families, however, were more drawn to the Stansted and District Red Cross. Gertrude Findlay was its president. It held a working party every Tuesday, and in November 1941 it was able to report that over the past year it had sent 3,000 garments to the three services and over 800 to the Central Hospital Supply Service, as well as making 700 pairs of curtains for soldiers' huts. Each week there was a penny a week collection for the Red Cross, which in Stansted produced about £20 a month. There were record collections on Poppy Days - £144 in 1942, for example - and, just as before the war, whist drives were popular.

Most of the goods made and the money raised went to the services or to the Merchant Navy, but in 1940 the Boy Scouts held a whist drive to raise money for Scouts in Finland, and there were more appeals to generosity when Russia entered the war. In December 1941, at a social evening organised by the British Legion, the auction of a live rabbit realised £4 1s. for aid to Russia, in January 1942 a whist drive organised by the Women's Section of the British Legion raised £14 17s., and at its annual meeting in 1943 the WI reported that 35 children's dresses had been knitted for Russia. In Bishop's Stortford the local Communist Party was quick to take advantage of the goodwill towards Russia. A Bishop's Stortford Anglo-Soviet Friendship Committee was formed, films were shown and lectures given (by Hewlett Johnson, the Red Dean of Canterbury, among others), money was raised for a Bishop's Stortford and District Ward in the Stalingrad hospital, and Volakalamsk was adopted as Stortford's sister town, There was nothing comparable in Stansted.

37: THE SECOND WORLD WAR

Large sums of money were in effect lent to Government through the purchase of War Bonds, Savings Bonds, Defence Bonds and Savings Certificates, and the people of Stansted made substantial contributions in the Wings for Victory campaign in 1943 and the Salute the Soldier campaign in 1944. Advertisements exhorted them to lend and not spend, and scrap metal was salvaged.

In 1942 a British restaurant was opened in Bentfield Hall, offering three-course meals for less than a shilling. For some time this was used by schoolchildren for their lunches, and it was very popular with the local soldiers.

In WW1 every suitable house had been appropriated for billeting soldiers. In WW2, except for a few WRACs (members of the Women's Royal Army Corps) there was no billeting of the military on local people, but Hargrave House and Park became a transit camp once more, and there were encampments on Pump Field and in a field off Church Road. There was also a Women's Land Army Hostel.

The clearest memories of Hargrave House are those of Gwen Saunders, who was then Gwen Morgan. In the summer of 1939 she had joined the Auxiliary Territorial Service (ATS), which 'was to help the men in every way we could'. She was just 18, and 'not being very wise I signed on the dotted line and didn't think any more about it. Why did I do it? Well, we were expecting war, and I think everybody was feeling very patriotic.' A week before the war began she was called up, and she and her colleagues 'got into the backs of lorries and drove to our secret destination, which was Stansted Mountfitchet. I'd never heard of it before. And when the convoy came through the East End of London people called out and they were in the streets throwing chocolate and sweets and all sorts of things into the backs of the lorries.' At Hargrave House 'we girls stayed in the house and the men stayed in tents in the park' until buildings were erected. 'They were part-time Territorials, and they came from all over. They didn't stay a fixed length of time, but moved on to a war front. It was like a transit camp.' While in Stansted she met her husband, who was in a reserved occupation, working at Rochford's Nurseries.

> People in the village were very friendly and invited us into their homes ... there were dances, and we used to go to see the searchlight regiment. There were entertainments at the NAAFI at Hargrave House, and there were lots of activities at the Central Hall. The Central Hall was the centre of the village, it was the centre of everything.

Gwen married Reg Harbridge in April 1942, but she continued to live in Hargrave House until she had a baby and was discharged in 1944.[7]

The Central Hall was used as a canteen for the troops and the Land Girls. Tea, coffee and simple snacks were served and there were games such as darts. Gwen mentioned the shows at Hargrave House, and Doris Thistle and Jean McBride went to see Charlie Chester entertaining the troops there.

Audrey Rodgers remembers

> one of the old dears who was a member of the Blyth family ... she was enormously wealthy, her family came from Northumberland, and she used to come up and stand with boxes of cigarettes, tossing them up, and crates of beer, tossing them up into the troops' lorries as they were outside our house queuing up to get petrol.

37: THE SECOND WORLD WAR

Stansted Hall became a home for convalescent soldiers, where several of the local women were nurses and helpers. It was known as the Blue Boys' Home because the patients wore blue uniforms. As Audrey Rodgers remembers:

The Red Cross were very active up there. And the VAD, the Voluntary Aid Detachment. Even as Girl Guides we used to go up there and help get breakfast at the weekends.

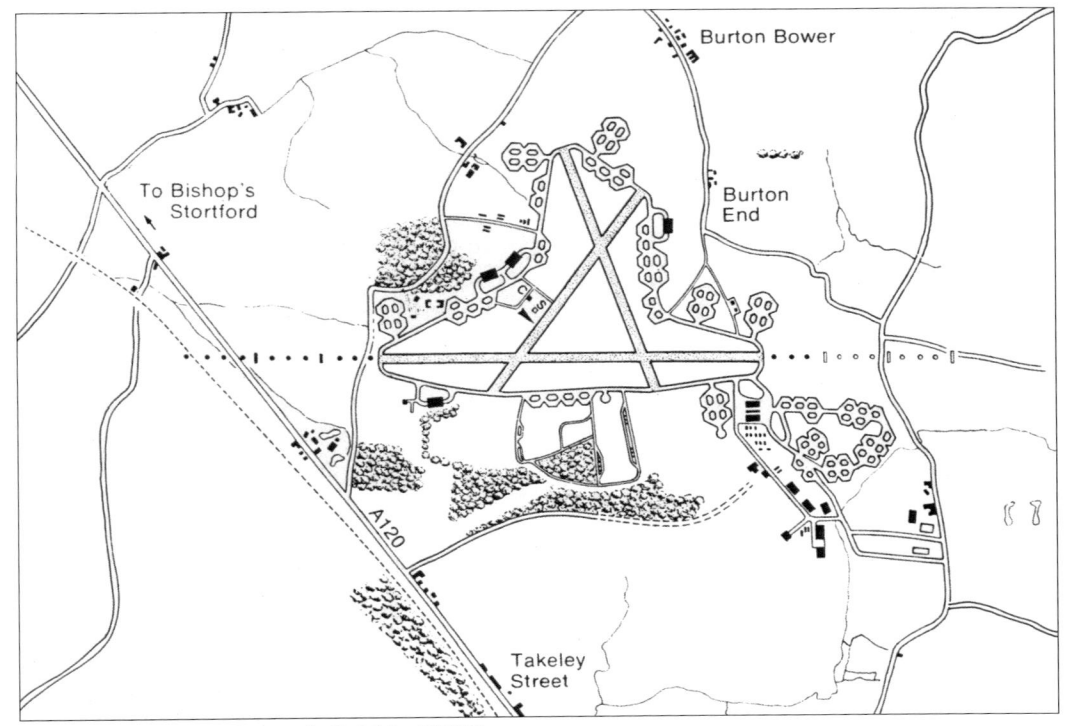

Map 8. The American airfield in WW2.

The most striking development in WW2, a development that was to have far-reaching consequences after the war, was the establishment of an airfield for the USA Air Force. This was part of a massive American commitment in East Anglia: there were more than 20 such airfields in Essex alone. The site was chosen in the spring of 1942, in July 1942 the work of construction began, and in August 1943 USAAF station 169 was opened. It was based on a triangular plan, with the main runway extending 6,000 feet in length and two subsidiary runways 4,200 feet each. At first it was under the Eighth Air Force Service Command, but was then transferred to the Ninth. For more than a year it was mainly concerned with aircraft maintenance and repair, and the first combat group, the 344th (Medium) Bomb Group, arrived in February 1944. Its Martin B-26 Marauders were normally a drab olive-green with grey underneath, but some of the pilots in the Group believed that stripping off the grey to reveal the shiny bare metal increased the speed at which they could fly, and so the Group became known as the Silver Streaks. Its first mission was on 6 March 1944, and it played

37: THE SECOND WORLD WAR

89. American airbase. 'Sad Sack', one of the Silver Streaks with its crew.

a major part in the bombing that supported the D-Day invasion. It went on mounting operations from Stansted until September, when it was moved to the continent closer to the battlefront. In all it flew over 140 missions from Stansted, dropped 7,739 tonnes of munitions, and lost 26 aircraft in action. After that period of intense activity Stansted again became a repair and maintenance base, and also for a time a rest and rehabilitation centre for returning American airmen. In August 1945 it was handed back to the RAF, and for a time it housed German PoWs. In December 1946 it was opened for civilian use.[8]

For more than two years the base was a bustling American township, complete with club and cinema, everything to make its occupants comfortable by American standards. Many of the airmen sought recreation in Bishop's Stortford, but some came to Stansted, and the villagers were profoundly affected, mixing with them socially, providing services, and counting their planes as they flew out and returned. The Americans' favourite pub was the Barley Mow on Chapel Hill.

Doris Thistle and her friends were asked to help out at their club:

> We were issued with a pass and taken to the club in a truck usually driven by 'Chuck'. Our duties included collecting the dirty crockery and doing mending jobs such as shortening trousers, sewing on buttons, etc. A friend of mine remembers going cycling with a friend and two Americans. The Americans provided lovely sandwiches and a fruit cake sent from America by a relative. Also they provided chewing gum for the children where she lodged.

Another consequence of the Americans' presence was the building of the railway sidings to the north of Stansted station to supply the airfield with oil. For many years they were known as the Yankee sidings.

Jim Ward remembers the Americans coming and building the runway.

They got sand from Wright's gravel pits. Wright was supposed to have become a millionaire because of that. And they had a huge concrete mixer up there, as big as a house. They said it was the longest runway in Europe. The villagers were invited up there when they had entertainments. I remember one entertainment with Bob Hope and Frances Langford. And they gave out the old doughnuts. We had a wonderful time. We walked up there in those days.

Was there much socialising with Americans? Doris Thistle thinks that went on mainly in Bishop's Stortford, where they had cinema shows.

I've always reckoned that we met mainly married Americans who didn't want to go into town. Somebody we were friendly with at Gorsefield, Mrs. Cheney, she befriended two American soldiers, and she used to invite us up there. They were Gene and Van. They were very nice guys, very nice. And really we knew them more than we knew any others. .... Did they give us any presents? Well, I don't remember that we ever got nylons!

I asked Derek and Barry Francis and Jim Ratcliff what they remembered of the American airmen.

BF *I remember the chewing gum! They gave you chewing gum, threw it out of the back of the lorries. If a convoy was coming through we were on the streets. And tobacco.*

JR *Cigarettes! I was smoking at the time. I was only 10 or 12 then. When they arrived they pitched their tents off Church Road. I used to work for W.H. Smith at the railway station at the time, and our bikes used to have two panniers. I used to take laundry from them down to my Mum and she used to wash it, and then I used to go back with it. Because they'd arrived, hadn't they, but their facilities were nothing. They'd only just got tents. So that was quite a handy thing for them really. And for me, because they used to give me two bob and all that! I was going there quite a time, and I had a mess kit as well and I used to sit with them and have breakfast with them.*

BF *What struck me with the Americans as a youngster was how healthy they looked. And they were always smart. They had gabardine. Our guys had woolly clothes. You can understand why relationships built up between the women and the blokes.*

DF *I remember when they had more permanent buildings, and if you were clever you could get into the cinema. They had films up there, and also shows. I remember seeing Bob Hope up there.*

JR *And Joe Louis was up there, at one stage.*

BF *It was like America. They had their own police. And the PX.*

JR *Which was like our NAAFI. It was incredible what they had.*

BF *Stuff you hadn't seen, let alone buy. I remember when they did depart, the stuff they left behind! Just incredible.... Record players, records. I think they*

left in a hurry. But there was so much stuff. Coffee urns and tea urns. Standing there. And no one was there. You could just walk through.
PS *So people helped themselves.*
BF *I guess they did.*
PS *Do you remember any black airmen?*
JR *They used to drive the lorries.*
BF *I remember fights at the dances at Central Hall. And when the American military came in to deal with their own they were absolutely vicious. Truncheons drawn and used. And I've seen people flattened and carried outside, and they'd have their truck there ready to take them back. Big fights, really big fights. And I'm not sure whether they weren't there the same time as the army.*
PS *So was there friction between British soldiers and the Americans?*
All *Oh yes.*
PS *And were the black Americans involved in the fights?*
BF *Yes, absolutely.*
PS *And were the fights sometimes racial?*
BF *Don't know. We were just on the outside. We weren't even allowed to go in. But I remember them coming outside fighting. It was frightening, absolutely frightening. Never seen anything like it before.*

Jim Ward says:

There was a lot of fighting. Trouble at dances at the Central Hall, and at the King's Arms. Trouble between the Americans themselves and trouble between them and the local boys. Homicide Hayden from Henham, he used to turn up and see a girl dancing with someone, and he'd say 'I'm going to dance with her', and the trouble started. I think one girl married an American. And they were around after the war too. Valerie Dellow married an American after the war.

Audrey Rodgers says that she can only think of one marriage now between an American and a Stansted woman. They went to America but came back, and they are both buried in St. Mary's churchyard.

Jean McBride's account is very frank.

The Americans came down into the village looking for entertainment and girls, both of which they found in the pubs, which did a fantastic trade. One place one did try to avoid after dark was St. John's Church Gardens, now called the Remembrance Gardens. One house nearby became notorious for its 'entertaining' and the overflow progressed naturally to more space and darkness over the road.

The village was affected in many other ways by the war. As in WW1, in the absence of men in the forces more women went out to work. Margery Baker was taken on as a delivery driver for Green's Stores, and there were land girls who worked on the farms. After the depression of the inter-war years the farmers flourished once again, and more acres were converted from pasture to arable. More people kept chickens and rabbits, and more allotments were allocated as people were encouraged to dig for victory. Rationing affected everyone, except the soldiers at Hargrave Park and of course the Americans. The Home Guard carried out its duties conscientiously, a pill box was built at Walpole Farm, and there were at least two anti-aircraft emplacements, one in Lower Street and the other in Park Road.

By comparison with WW1 the victory celebrations were restrained. On VE Day, Tuesday 8 May, flags were flown and the church bells were rung, five bonfires were lit and searchlights played above the village in a V for victory sign. In the evening there were the inevitable whist drives, one at the Mary MacArthur Home and the other at the British Restaurant, and also a dance in the Central Hall. According to the *Observer*, 'perhaps the most popular feature of all' was on the Wednesday afternoon when the schoolchildren marched with banners and flags to St. John's Church for a special service conducted by the vicar and the Congregational minister.[9] There were similar celebrations on VJ Day, 15 August – another whist drive and a dance, and this time a children's fancy dress parade, followed on the Sunday by a crowded service at St. Mary's, a full parade of servicemen and women at the sports ground, and a thanksgiving service at St. John's.[10] Over the next two years three welcome home dinners were given to 324 returning servicemen and women, and gifts and cards recording their service were given.[11]

1. Transcripts of the interviews quoted are kept by the Stansted Mountfitchet Local History Society.
2. Glyn Warwick gives 25 names – 14 soldiers, 8 airmen and 3 sailors. Also Winnie Johnson, a civilian killed in a bombing raid at Chelmsford.
3. The log books of the Church School and the Council School are now in the ERO. They are not open to the public but were briefly examined before being deposited with the ERO.
4. *HEO*, 5 May 1845, where the figure of 816 is given, and log book of Henry Devey, an ARP Warden in Bishop's Stortford, now with Tony Wellings.
5. For a further account see Tinney (2012: 64-66).
6. Warwick (2008: 262).
7. After Reg's death Gwen married again.
8. Graham Smith (1996: 235-243), Kosky (2000) and Winter (n.d.)
9. *HEO*, 12 May 1945. See also *SMPM*, June 1945.
10. *HEO*, 25 August 1945.
11. *SMPM*, June 1947.

EPILOGUE: STANSTED SINCE 1945

I acknowledged in the introduction that to bring this history of Stansted down to the present time on the same scale as in earlier chapters would make a long book very much longer, such had been the pace, the extent and the variety of change, and this epilogue should be regarded not so much as a continuation of previous chapters, but as a brief summary of what has happened since WW2, a summary that aims to provide a framework and perspective for what has gone before.

I once asked Irving Sanders what the main change had been in Stansted in his lifetime. He replied simply that the village had increased in size. In 1921, the year in which he was born, the population was 2,398. By 1991 it had more than doubled to 4,943, and today it is more than 7,000. Fields where Irving played as a boy have disappeared under housing, most of it private developments, but also a large Council estate, much of which has been sold off to its tenants. In 1987 the parish boundaries were extended to take in part of Birchanger, and again in 2012, when a new residential development, Forest Hall Park, was absorbed.

Stansted is still generally referred to as a village, but it is a very large village. Many of the older inhabitants tell us regretfully that in the past you could walk to the shops and almost everyone you met would be a friend or acquaintance. That is not so today. There is still a sense of community, but many parishioners are strangers to each other and pass each other by without greeting or acknowledgement.

The roads are increasingly congested with traffic, though the increase has not been uniform over time. Traffic along the Cambridge Road often slowed to a crawl or came to a halt before the pressure was relieved by the opening of the M11 from Birchanger to Stump Cross in 1979. The villages to the north were also relieved, and when a youthful Ken Clarke, then junior Transport Minister, opened the motorway the people of Newport raised a large banner – 'Thank heaven for the M11'. Stansted also rejoiced. But since then the traffic has built up again, and again congestion is common. The old roads in the centre of the parish, such as the Cambridge Road, Chapel Hill and Lower Street, are often clogged and disfigured by lines of parked cars.

This has not been the only degradation of the environment. Several of the older houses have been lost, and the Cambridge Road in particular has suffered from insensitive development.

With increasing mobility, and with increasing demand for a wider range of goods and services, Stansted has become less self-sufficient. Many people go regularly to Bishop's Stortford for their everyday needs, travelling by car or bus, and for special purchases they go to Cambridge or London. Many shops have disappeared, most of them small concerns, but among them the old establishment of Green's stores. In the 1960s the directors decided to sell out, and the premises were bought by Edgar Harman and Co., the Stansted estate agents. They split up the departments into separate shops and leased them out piecemeal. The centrepiece, the grocery and hardware store, was acquired by Caton's, but they stopped trading in 1982. After almost 300 years the business set up by John Day came to an end.

More recently, however, the process of decline has been halted, and even reversed, as the rise in population has made it commercially viable to open up more shops in the village. On the Cambridge Road a small Co-operative supermarket has been established for many years, and a second small supermarket, Tesco Express, has now been added.

Farming has been transformed. Many hedges have been uprooted. John Tinney tells us that at the beginning of WW2 there were 33 fields on Bentfield Bury Farm, where his father was the tenant, and that by 2012 this number had been reduced to 16. The aim of course was to increase production, and it resulted in a dramatic change in the landscape. At the close of WW2 farming was still mixed, with not just cereals but cattle, sheep, pigs and poultry. Now entire farms are devoted to arable farming, with the emphasis on wheat, barley and oilseed rape, and horses for ploughing have been replaced by tractors. Except for a few sheep at Hole Farm there is hardly a farm animal to be seen. Helped by grants from the European Union production has soared, and there is no longer any talk of depression. With increasing mechanisation fewer people are employed. At Bentfield Bury there were about 12 locally based farm workers at the beginning of WW2: now there are none.[1] Local women used to be employed for seasonal work. Now they are no longer needed, though at one of the farms that James Blyth used to own there is a large field given over to 'Pick Your Own'. Patterns of ownership however have not changed a great deal: the agribusinesses that have invaded so much of East Anglia have so far been kept at bay.

Most of Rochford's Nurseries closed in 1970, leaving a wasteland of derelict and vandalised greenhouses that has recently been cleared for the Forest Hall housing estate. With the exception of the Old Bell in that part of Birchanger which was incorporated into Stansted, the old coaching inns along the Cambridge Road have all ceased operating as public houses and hotels. From north to south, the Three Colts has closed and is in a state of abandoned neglect, the Bell has become a restaurant, and the Rose and Crown is now private housing. Against this there has been a proliferation of small businesses, with many people working from home, and in 2013 Stansted was named as the UK's fourth most internet-friendly town after Stratford-upon-Avon, Edinburgh and Richmond. According to Wikipedia, 'The Google eTown Awards recognise the top places where businesses are most actively embracing the web, and Stansted's high ranking reflects the increased use of the internet to spur economic growth'. In 1987 the railway was electrified: many people commute to either London or Cambridge, and for some Stansted is little more than a dormitory town. Mountfitchet Castle is now a lively tourist attraction, and close by is the House on the Hill Toy Museum.

The biggest local development has been Stansted Airport, which is now a major source of employment. Both the village and the airport may be described as falling within the M11 corridor, with the great economic engines of London in the south and Cambridge with its University and science park in the north.

Socially Stansted is much more egalitarian. The families which used to be referred to as the gentry have all departed or died out, or else are no longer referred to as gentry. In 1964 Arthur Findlay gave Stansted Hall to the Spiritualists' National Union and it became a spiritualist college. Lord and Lady FitzGerald died in the 1950s and Stansted House was pulled down in 1958. Hargrave House is now a care home, and so too is Broome End, once the home of Harry and Mildred Chester. On the other hand the Fuller Almshouses are now private homes.

There is still a great spate of social activity. The WI continues to flourish, and so do many other societies, such as the British Legion, the Workers' Educational Association, the University of the Third Age, the Social Club, the Gardening Club and the Local History Society. The Working Men's Club, now the Social Club, has been thrown open to women. After WW2 the Central Hall continued as the venue for various forms of entertainment and was known at different times as The Supreme Ballroom and Rocky's Disco – a far cry from the idealistic aspirations of the Stansted Literary Institution. It was converted into flats in 1987, when it was renamed 'The Old Court House'. There is still however plenty of accommodation for social and educational activities, such as the church hall, the lecture room behind the Congregational Church (now the Stansted Free Church) and the assembly room at the Social Club. The Day Centre for the elderly was opened in 1983 and a new health centre will shortly be opened in Lower Street. For business gatherings there are several suitable venues at Stansted Airport. It has to be said, though, that for most of their public entertainments the people of Stansted look elsewhere, to the cinemas at Bishop's Stortford and Saffron Walden for example, or even to the theatres and concert halls of London. Stansted is no longer renowned for its concerts and light operas.

The coronation and royal jubilees have been celebrated with street parties – for the coronation almost every home was decorated - and at the Festival of Britain in 1951 there was an impressive programme of events that would have delighted our Victorian forebears. The schools gave a joint concert, the WEA presented a thriller in the Central Hall, there was an organ recital at St. Mary's, a cricket match at Hargrave Park, a dance at the barn in Burton Bower, a grand camp fire and sing-song led by the Scouts on Castle Hill, a flower show at Stansted Hall, a Punch and Judy show, 'dancing on floodlit lawns', an exhibition to illustrate Stansted's history over the previous 100 years, and – the climax of it all – a pageant with 100 players in a 'Prologue and Seven Picturesque Episodes on "Stansted Mountfitchet", Life through the ages in an Essex Parish showing the first Baron Montfichet and other Lords of the Manor' and monarchs from Queen Elizabeth I to Queen Victoria. For this ambitious display parishioners donned period costumes and acted out the various parts. In the finale, as the programme recorded, it was 'fitting to gather together representatives of those engaged in a wide range of activities in Stansted Mountfitchet, some with banners, some in their uniforms, some in everyday garb, but all with a brave spirit of service to others in the English tradition which has remained unbroken from the early days of our island history to modern times'.[2]

In 2015, because Richard de Montfichet had been one of the 25 barons chosen to ensure that King John observed Magna Carta, the 800th anniversary of that document was celebrated with a 'medieval fayre', complete with jousting, a display of archery, a pig roast and Morris dancing, all in the gardens of Stansted Hall, and a colourful embroidery was made depicting Magna Carta and the history of the village.

The May fair is no longer held, but 1961 saw the beginning of the Stansted Carnival, hailed in the press as Stansted's 'biggest event of the year'. A Carnival Queen was chosen about a month in advance, and the Carnival itself consisted of a parade of floats and many supporting activities, such as fancy dress parades and tugs of war. The proceedings were opened by television personalities, such as Nicholas Parsons in 1971, or by individuals who were celebrated in other fields, such as the naturalist, Sir Peter Scott, in 1974. In 1972

90. St. Theresa's Roman Catholic Church.

the Carnival attracted 3,500 visitors. It was discontinued, however, in 2002 mainly because the costs of insuring the floats was so high.[3] An annual fete is held to support the windmill, which has been splendidly maintained by a dedicated team of volunteers. Its 200th anniversary was celebrated in 1987. Meanwhile sport has become increasingly popular. A second cricket club, Stansted Hall, was started in 1947 and a skatepark was opened in 2015. In 1984, in what must be the village's greatest sporting achievement, the football team beat Stamford 3-2 in the final of the FA Challenge Vase at Wembley.

Organised religion is much less of a force than before. The effort needed to maintain St. Mary's as well as St. John's finally proved to be too demanding, and in 1990 it was closed as a place of worship and made over to the Churches Conservation Trust. St. John's, however, which became the parish church, is still well attended. In 1997, in another economy measure, the vicar of Stansted became the rector of the united benefice of Stansted Mountfitchet with Birchanger and Farnham. Except in having the same rector, however, the three parishes are still independent of each other. The Congregational Church, which in 1972 combined at the national level with the Presbyterian Church to form the United Reformed Church, still meets on Chapel Hill. In 2006 it was joined by the Methodists, and it is now called the Stansted Free Church. A small band of Quakers still holds its meetings at the top of the hill, where a new Meeting House was opened in 1967. But perhaps the biggest change has been the establishment of a Roman Catholic Church, the church of St. Theresa, first, in 1958, in a converted house in Millside, and then, in 2003, in a new building in the Cambridge Road.

The schools meanwhile have undergone several transformations, some brought about by changes in educational policy, not least by Rab Butler's Education Act of 1944 and the later shift to comprehensive education, others by the demands of an increasing population. In 1948 the Church and Council Primary Schools at last joined together to form St. Mary's Church of England Foundation Primary School, which continued on the site of the Church School in Lower Street, while the Council School on Chapel Hill was taken over by the new Stansted County Secondary School. Boys and girls who passed the 11+ examination

38: EPILOGUE: STANSTED SINCE 1945

91. Forest Hall School, a photo taken in 2010 when it was still the Mountfitchet Mathematics and Computing College.

continued to go to Newport Grammar and the Herts and Essex High Schools respectively, and some pupils went on to the Cambridge Technical School.

In 1960 the Secondary School was moved into new premises in Forest Hall Road, and its premises on Chapel Hill were taken over by the Primary School, which later, in 1978, moved into new buildings in St. John's Road and in 2012 to its present premises in Forest Hall Park. In 1978 a second primary school was opened, the Bentfield Primary School.

Meanwhile the Secondary School in Forest Hall Road had 330 pupils, 18 class rooms and a science block. In 1984, however, the sixth form was removed leaving the school to cater for 11 to 16 year olds only. It was renamed the Mountfitchet Mathematics and Computing College for a few years and in 2013 was rebranded as Forest Hall School, a Secondary Comprehensive. It is now under the control and guidance of the Burnt Mill Academy Trust. Both primary and secondary schools take in many children from the surrounding villages as well as from Stansted itself.

In politics the greatest excitement came in 1945, when there was a landslide Labour victory in the country as a whole and Stanley Wilson, the Labour candidate, came within just over 1,000 votes of defeating Rab Butler in the Saffron Walden constituency. Since then Saffron Walden has become an increasingly safe Conservative seat, with majorities of well over 10,000 from 1977 onwards, and from 1974 to 2010 the Liberals (or, to be more precise, in 1974, 1977 and 1979 the Liberals, in 1983 the Social Democrats, and from 1992 onwards the Liberal Democrats) have again been the main party of opposition, forcing the Labour candidate into third place in every election. In 2015, however, second place was taken by UKIP, with the Labour Party third and the Liberal Democrats fourth.

At the county level control has for the most part been in Conservative hands, though there have been periods when no party was in complete control. At district level a new district of Uttlesford, named after the old Anglo-Saxon Hundred, was formed in 1973 by the merger of the Dunmow Rural District, the Saffron Walden Rural District and the borough of Saffron Walden. For the most part Uttlesford has been controlled by the Conservatives, but there has been one period in which there was no overall control, 1995-2003, and one period of Liberal Democrat control, 2003-2007.

At the Parish Council level lip-service was still paid to the principle that there should be no politics. But the realities were very different, as Irving Sanders, an independent, discovered to his cost in 1964. He had been chairman since 1960, but in 1964 the Conservatives commended 11 candidates for the 11 seats, and Irving, who was not one of the 11, was not elected. This gave rise to widespread anger and regret, even among the Conservatives, and two years later he was nominated as vice-chairman in his absence. In 1970, when the Conservatives again put forward a list of 11 candidates, Irving, though an independent, was one of them and was duly elected. In 1976 the Parish Council chose its first woman chairman, Rita Humphreys. From the 1980s onwards control of the Council has fluctuated between the Conservatives and the Liberal Democrats. The parish remains an important unit of local administration, continuing to exercise direct responsibility for street lighting, public footpaths and open spaces, bus shelters, the village hall, the cemetery, the Recreation Ground and playing facilities, and in other areas, particularly in planning, continuing to influence the district and county councils and to provide a channel of communication with them.

Stansted is still a vigorous and thriving community, with unemployment in the area running at less than 3%. In 2001, in a survey conducted by a Sunday newspaper, taking into account a wide range of factors, such as the quality of schools and the incidence of crime, the District of Uttlesford was voted as the best place to live in England. In the Halifax Quality of Life Survey in 2014 it was judged to be 'the most desirable rural area to live in'.

Hanging over the village's future, however, is the possible expansion of the airport. At present it may still be fairly described as 'The Airport in the Countryside', but if its growth is not checked, with all its attendant developments, it may dwarf and dominate the entire parish and indeed many parishes around, and that countryside may be irreparably blighted. So far expansion has been kept in check. There is still no second runway. But if a second runway is built the character of the area will change beyond all recognition.

Stansted's past, of course, has been a story of constant change and development. It has never been a quiet backwater. It has always been on the beaten track. As the title of this book implies, that has been one of its most important characteristics. But it has also been a story of continuity and community. The future too will be a story of change, but a massive extension of the airport, a doubling to the size of Heathrow, would be a change too fast and too far.

As long as the parish of Stansted Mountfitchet escapes the worst possibilities of expansion, of being absorbed in urbanisation, as long as it remains a unit of local government and a centre of social organisation, and as long as it continues to attract commitment and inspire affection, so long will it continue as a vibrant community rejoicing in the beauty of its surrounding countryside, proud of the richness of its long and varied history and confident that its future development will add more chapters to the story.

---

1 Tinney (2012: 47).
2 *Souvenir Programme: Festival of Britain,* 1951.
3 In 2002 the Queen's jubilee was celebrated, and there was no Carnival from that year onwards.

APPENDIX: STANSTED AIRPORT

There is one reason why the name of Stansted is widely known, and that is the airport, which in fact has taken in a large area of Takeley as well as of Stansted. It has a throughput on its single runway of about 23mppa (millions of passenger movements per annum) and has planning permission to go up to 35mppa. Its world-renowned terminal was designed by Norman Foster, and it is a major source of local employment.

In July 2015 the Airports Commission under the chairmanship of Sir Howard Davies issued its Final Report. It had been set up in September 2012, and its remit was to identify and recommend to the Government how the UK could maintain its status as a global aviation hub. It had three specific tasks:
    to recommend how to make best use of existing capacity,
    to decide whether there was a need for more capacity, and
    if it decided that more capacity was needed, to recommend where this should be.

In December 2013 the Commission published its Interim Report, in which it stated that one new runway would be needed by 2030 and that it should be at either Heathrow or Gatwick. A further runway, however, might be needed by 2050, in which case a second runway at Stansted might be one of the options. In its Final Report the Commission recommends an extra runway at Heathrow. It is now for the Government to respond.

It may be thought that there is no longer any serious possibility of a second runway at Stansted, at least for the immediate future. But there is no certainty that the Commission's recommendations will be accepted, and already the Manchester Airports Group (MAG), the owners of Stansted Airport, are pressing for the planning cap of 35mppa on the existing runway to be raised sooner rather than later. In the long term, if demand increases, they will no doubt be pressing for a second runway.

The history of aviation policy is a cautionary tale, and the account that is given below is based largely on evidence which I prepared as chairman of Stop Stansted Expansion (SSE) for the public inquiry which was due to be held into the application by BAA, the former owners, for planning permission to build a second runway.

In 1949 Stansted Airport, previously the American airbase in WW2, came under the control of the Ministry of Civil Aviation. There was very little traffic, but in 1963 an interdepartmental committee of Government officials recommended that Stansted, with two runways, should be London's third airport. In response to the ensuing outcry an independent inquiry was set up. It was conducted by Inspector G.D. Blake, and became known as the Chelmsford Inquiry. In his report, dated May 1966, Blake concluded:

> *It would be a calamity for the neighbourhood if a major airport were placed at Stansted. Such a decision could only be justified by national necessity. Necessity was not proved by evidence at this inquiry.*

One of the organisations that had given evidence to Blake was the North West Essex and East Herts Preservation Association (NWEEHPA), which had been set up in 1964 to fight the threat of major expansion. In the judgement of Peter Hall, NWEEHPA had produced 'an excellently reasoned technically competent counter-case. It was skilfully based not on opposition to the Stansted development *per se*, but on the need for a prior independent inquiry into a national airport policy, which was demonstrably lacking.'[1]

The Government had given clear undertakings that it would not overrule the Chelmsford Inquiry, but in its White Paper of 1967 it adhered to its decision to make Stansted London's third airport. Not only that, it also raised the possibility that in due course Stansted could become an airport with four runways. This provoked more opposition, and eventually, as NWEEHPA had advocated, a new independent inquiry was set up, the Roskill Commission, with the remit of finding the most suitable site for a four-runway airport.

The Roskill Commission lasted two and a half years, from May 1968 to December 1970. It examined 78 sites, and after seven months' work whittled this number down to a shortlist of four. Stansted was not one of them. Eight other sites were considered more suitable. The Commission recommended Cublington in Buckinghamshire, but one member, Colin Buchanan, recommended Maplin in the Thames Estuary. In his view 'It would be nothing less than an environmental disaster if the airport were to be built at any of the inland sites'.[2]

It was Maplin that the Conservative Government chose in 1971. This, however, was an expensive option, and it was mainly because of this, and because of the oil crisis of 1973-4, that it was abandoned by the incoming Labour Government. In the light of its revised forecasts of demand the Government decided that there was no need for the time being to select a third major airport in the South East, and in its White Paper of 1978 it announced what it described as a step by step approach. It ruled out Maplin. It accepted that local people had a right to expect that there should be limits on the development of airports, and it decided that this could best be achieved by limiting the number of terminals. It gave undertakings that there would be no more than four terminals at Heathrow and two at Gatwick, but it gave no assurances about Stansted. It saw no objection to permitting Stansted to handle 4mppa, but acknowledged that an increase to 16mppa would raise wider issues, including major changes in planning policies.

In effect, however, the Government had given the green light for further development at Stansted, and the British Airports Authority (as BAA was then known, before privatisation), which owned Stansted as well as Heathrow and Gatwick and had consistently advocated its development, applied for an increase to 15mppa.

This application was considered by Inspector Graham Eyre, who recommended that expansion to 15mppa should be allowed. Looking further ahead, as the Government had asked him to do, he indicated that in due course there should be no objection to expansion to 25mppa, which was then regarded as the full capacity of the existing runway. To accommodate these developments he recommended that the airport should be expanded from 366 hectares (904.4 acres) to 957.5 hectares (2,366 acres), an increase of 591.5 hectares (1,461.6 acres).

Eyre firmly rejected a second runway at Stansted. 'A major two runway airport with an ultimate capacity of up to 50 mppa should never be developed at Stansted,' he wrote, 'and whether such a project represents a commitment, a proposal, a probability or a mere possibility there is no justification for pursuing it'.[3] The terms in which he dismissed a two runway airport could hardly have been stronger. It would be an 'environmental catastrophe', he wrote, 'a major environmental and visual disaster'. He wrote feelingly of the attractiveness of the Essex countryside, and declared emphatically that 'such a monster cannot and must not be inflicted on this precious landscape'.[4] It would be 'an unprecedented and grotesque invasion of a large area of pleasant countryside'. It would be 'wholly unacceptable'.[5]

Many of those who made representations warned Eyre of the dangers of the step by step approach – that granting permission for 15mppa would lead inevitably to an application for 25mppa, and that this in turn would lead to an application for a second runway. In response to these representations Eyre was emphatic that planning permission for 15mppa should be granted only if the Government gave an unequivocal declaration of intention not to go beyond 25mppa and not to establish a second runway. In the absence of such an undertaking he would recommend 'unequivocally' that the application be refused.[6]

In their decision on the application the Secretaries of State for Environment and Transport declared their agreement with Eyre's view that

> *the environmental and other effects of expansion on Stansted beyond 25 mppa would be of a quite different order from the effects of the development currently proposed. They consider, on the evidence before them, that there is no case for the provision of a second main runway at Stansted, and wish to make it clear that they have no intention of pursuing such a course of action.*

In the White Paper of 1985, published at the same time, the Government again recorded its agreement with Eyre's recommendations. It gave its approval for development to 15mppa, with a review being conducted at 8mppa, but it accepted 'unreservedly' that there should be no development beyond the existing runway.

In the event the development from 8mppa to 15mppa took place with almost no public debate, and in 2003 Uttlesford District Council granted planning permission for further development at Stansted subject to upper limits of 25mppa and 241,000 air transport movements (ATMs).

In the meantime there had been a sharp increase in the demand for air travel because of the rise of the low cost airlines, notably Ryanair and EasyJet at Stansted, and in July 2002, shortly before the 25mppa planning permission was granted, the Government published its Consultation Document in which it put forward a series of options for the development of air travel in the South East. Among the options for Stansted were (in various configurations) the development of the existing runway to its maximum use, the building of a second runway, the building of a third runway, and the building of a fourth runway.

Remembering the Government's unequivocal declaration in 1985 that it had no intention of promoting a second runway, and faced with the possibility of being blighted by a four runway airport, twice the size of Heathrow, the reaction of the local community was one of profound shock and anger. Large protest meetings were held, and a new campaigning body was set up, Stop Stansted Expansion (SSE), which was formally a working group of NWEEHPA but in practice operated independently. Chaired by the much respected Norman Mead of Great Hallingbury, a veteran campaigner with NWEEHPA, and by myself when Norman retired in 2004, and serviced by a very able campaign manager in Carol Barbone, SSE was a powerful group in itself, able to call on experts in every field, and it worked in close association with local MPs and MEPs, local councils and, under the umbrella organisation of Airport Watch, other campaigning bodies such as those at Heathrow and Gatwick. Local support was overwhelming. In 2003 the Uttlesford District Council conducted a referendum on whether or not there should be any additional runways at Stansted. In a 69% turnout, more than for a general election, 89% voted against a second runway. SSE's membership ran into thousands. The inhabitants of Stansted were inevitably among the organisation's strongest supporters, though the village itself, lying at right angles to the runway, was not as badly overflown as many others.

In response to the Government's Consultation Paper SSE produced a powerful statement, *Stansted – the Case against Irresponsible Growth,* but to no avail. In its 2003 Air Transport White Paper Government came down in favour of the development of the existing runway to its full capacity and the building of a second runway as well. The unequivocal declaration of intent given by the Government in the 1985 White Paper, that there would be no second runway, was ignored. When challenged on this by his political opponents, the Secretary of State, Alistair Darling, made no attempt to argue against Eyre's judgement that a two-runway airport would be an environmental catastrophe but asserted that it had been overtaken by events. Because of the increase in demand for air travel it could be set aside. Because circumstances had changed, the Government's 'unequivocal declaration' fell away.

Legal proceedings, some successful, others unsuccessful, delayed the process, but in 2006 BAA submitted its application to increase the use of the existing runway, raising the number of Air Transport Movements (ATMs) from 241,000 to 264,000 and removing the limit on passenger movements entirely. Uttlesford District Council, the local planning authority, rejected this application, and BAA then appealed to the Secretary of State for Communities and Local Government who established a Public Inquiry under Inspector Alan Boyland. In the course of the Inquiry BAA modified its application, no longer applying to remove the limit on passenger movements entirely, but to increase the permitted limit from 25mppa to 'about 35mppa'. In October 2008, acting on Inspector Boyland's recommendation, the Secretaries of State for Transport and for Communities and Local Government determined that the upper limit for passenger movements at Stansted should be raised from 25mppa to 35mppa and that the number of ATMs allowed should be raised to 264,000. SSE's appeal against this decision was turned down by the High Court in March 2009.

Meanwhile in March 2008 BAA had submitted its application for a second runway at Stansted, and arrangements were set in train for another major public inquiry. At this point the Competition Commission ruled that it was improper, being restrictive of competition, for BAA to own both Heathrow and Stansted, a ruling which led to protracted legal proceedings, and successive Secretaries of State took the view that it would be inappropriate to go ahead with the public inquiry until the question of ownership had been settled. In May 2010, while the inquiry was still pending, the Labour Party lost the general election and one of the first statements made by the new Coalition Government was that there would be no more runways at Stansted and Heathrow, whereupon BAA withdrew its application for a second runway at Stansted and the inquiry was abandoned.

After eight years of campaigning SSE had won. For its supporters it was an occasion for celebration and congratulation. Or so it seemed. But at once the aviation industry mounted a campaign to overturn the Government's decision, and, falling back on the argument that it could not bind its successors, the Government opened up the issue once again and in September 2012 established the Airports Commission with the terms of reference referred to above.

It is a profound relief to most local residents that, like Inspector Blake, the Roskill Commission and Inspector Eyre, the Airports Commission has rejected the case for a second runway at Stansted, at least for the present generation. But the Government has still to make a decision on the Commission's recommendations and is subject to fierce political pressures. More than 50 years after NWEEHPA, its parent organisation, was founded, SSE is still campaigning.

1 Peter Hall (1981: 21).
2 Quoted in Peter Hall (1981: 37).
3 Eyre Report (1984), Chapter 50, 6.41.
4 Eyre Report (1984), Chapter 50, para 6.17.
5 Eyre Report (1984), Chapter 28, para 2.29.
6 Eyre Report (1984), Chapter 25, 12.12,13.

SOURCES

A - ARCHIVAL SOURCES

British Library
Egerton MSS 2647.
MSS EUR F 206/35,36,127. Correspondence of William and Charlotte Fuller-Maitland.

Dr. Williams's Library
New College MSS: L.52/4,5 series: correspondence relating to William Chaplin, R.E. May, Josiah Redford, Stansted, Stansted congregation and others.

Essex Record Office
A.F. Assize files.
Census records.
D/ABR, D/ABW, D/ACR. Wills.
D/ACA 48. Archdeaconry of Colchester Act books, including church courts.
D/AZ series. Extracts made by R.H. Browne from Archdeaconry of Colchester records.
D/CT 328A and 328B. Tithe commutation map and schedule for Stansted, 1843.
D/DBa/O18 series. Documents relating to the Civil War, 1643-4.
D/DGL M series. Bentfield Bury manor, 1649 onwards.
D/DKw 04. Poll book for 1679.
D/DTu 235. Persons executed in Essex 1767-1848.
D/DU 87/2,3. Instructions to constables of Thaxted, 6 and 23 June 1648.
D/DWv M series. Thremhall Priory, rentals, court rolls etc.
D/DWv T series. Documents relating to Thremhall Priory and manor of Thremhall Priory, 1200 onwards. See also transcription of D/DWv Tl/1 in T/Z 197/9.
D/NC 2 series. Independent (later Congregational, later United Reformed) Church.
D/P 109/1-9. Registers of baptisms, marriages and burials, 1558-1837.
D/P 109/3/1-4. Tithe records 1682-1818.
D/P 109/5/2. Miscellaneous receipts, 1718-1807.
D/P 109/7/1. Settlement of dispute between Edward Hubbard and parishioners, 1593.
D/P 109/8/1. Persons seeking relief, 1789-1790.
D/P 109/8/4-6. Vestry minutes, 1638-1971.
D/P 109/12/1-16. Overseers' Accounts, 1744-1814, 1919-1925.
D/P 109/13/1. Indemnity bonds and certificates, 1697-1782.
D/P 109/13/2. Removal orders from Stansted, 1702-1834.
D/P 109/13/3. Removal orders to Stansted, 1722-1857.
D/P 109/14/1. Indentures, 1684-1836.
D/P 109/14/2. Register of apprentices, 1813, 1836.
D/P 109/15/1. Bonds and orders, 1743-1813.
D/P 109/15/2. Warrants for apprehension, 1740-1743.
D/P 109/15/3. Examinations, 1743.
D/P 109/17. Instructions to churchwardens and overseers to pay militia men or their substitutes, 1793-1810.
D/P 109/18/4. Miscellaneous papers, 1740-1819.
D/P 109/19/2. Lists of paupers etc., 1849-62.
D/P 109/25/1. Legacy of Sir Thomas Myddelton, 1725/6.
D/P 109/28/6. Printed resolutions of inhabitants of Uttlesford etc. 1793.
D/P 109/30/7-12. Parish Council minutes, 1922-1960.
D/Z 41/1. Stansted Literary Institution, minute book, 1883-1920.
E/E 210/7/2. Log Book of Stansted Council School, Girls' and Infants' Department, 1937-1948.
E/E 210/7/3. Log Book of Practical Subjects Centre, Stansted, 1937-1947.
E/E 210/7/4. Log Book of Stansted Council School, Boys' Department, 1935-1948.
E/ML 307/1. Church School. Infants school log book, 1866-1904.
E/ML 308/1. Church School. Mixed school log book, 1863-1901.
L/L 1/2. Lieutenancy records. Quarterly returns 1811.
L/L 3/1-3. Volunteers from Essex Militia into regular army, 1809-1815.
L/R 5/1. Militia returns, 1809-1813.
L/R 6/2. Militia returns, 1815.
LIB/POL series. Poll books and registers of electors.

Q/CR 1/1. Abstract of overseers' returns, 1787.
Q/FAc 3/8,14,22. Men serving in militia: justices' certificates for payment, 1800-1815.
Q/RDc 36A. Enclosure award, 1847.
Q/RJ 1/2. Freeholders' book, 1759.
Q/RLv series. Records of licensed victuallers, 1769-1832.
Q/RPl series. Land Tax assessments.
Q/RTh series. Hearth Tax returns, 1662-1673.
Q/SBA series. Quarter Sessions papers, 1610-71.
Q/SBb 204. Quarter Sessions Bundle, 1755.
Q/SO 20. Quarter Sessions, Order Book, 1807-10.
Q/SR. Quarter Sessions rolls, especially, Q/SR 355 series (1652/3), 396 series (1663), 408 series (1666) and 449 series (1685/6).
T/A 42/1. Ship Money assessment 1636-7.
T/A 229/1. Humphrey Repton's Red Book of Stansted Hall, 1791.
T/A 418/175/25. Constables' presentments, Bentfield hamlet, 1672.
T/A 420/1. Compton census, 1676.
T/P 68. Green Papers.
T/P 181/10/19. Cuttle collection of newspaper cuttings relating to Stansted Mountfitchet.
T/Z 13/56. Janet Catchpole, 'The Cultural Development of Stansted Mountfitchet', n.d.
T/Z 597/1. J. Siegel, 'The Second Civil War. "Essex must not escape"'.

Friends House, London
L 14/47. Papers relating to Green's stores.
V 252 a. Instructions issued by Green and Marsh to their staff, n.d.

Hertfordshire Archives and Local Studies Centre, Hertford
D/ELw Z22/1-3, records of Sir Thomas Myddelton's funeral in Lawes-Wittewronge papers.

London Metropolitan Archives
Gibson Papers, Ms 9583/11.
Gibson Papers, Ms 9583/14,15.
Gibson Papers, Ms 25,751. Episcopal Visitation 1727.

National Archives
Calendar of Inquisitions Miscellaneous 1392-99, no. 14.
HO 129/1139. Religious census, 1851.
MH 12 series, Poor Law records of Bishop's Stortford Union, 1834 onwards.
WO 97/8/79. Records of individual soldiers in French Wars.
A search of the National Archives website using 'Stansted Mountfitchet' reveals a wide range of documents, such as wills, ordnance survey maps, manorial court rolls (mainly relating to Thremhall Priory and Bentfield Bury), census records, court cases, deeds, enclosure records and Quarter Sessions rolls. Most of these have been copied to the Essex Record Office, which is where I consulted them and where they appear in this list of sources.

National Library of Wales
Chirk Castle papers, including E.5602. Humphrey Jones to person unnamed, 3 September 1639.

Rothamsted Research
Anonymous: The Muses Oblation, n.d., c.1631.

Saffron Walden Library
Jack Sayers, 'The Arms and History of the Manor Lords of Stansted Mountfitchet in the County of Essex 1066-1922', n.d.

Saffron Walden Museum
On display, notice of ploughing match at Stansted, 1834.
Red tessellated floor, c.300 AD.

Stansted Mountfitchet Local History Society
Interview records from 1987 onwards.
'Gerald Snow of Bentfield Green. An autobiography', n.d.

B - PRIVATE PAPERS

Michael Day
Papers relating to the Days and the Greens.

Toby and Frances Lyons
E.F. Gosling, 'Four Brothers', n.d.
Documents and maps relating to the manor of Bentfield Bury.

Ralph Phillips
Alfred Phillips, 'Our family', 1984.
Ralph Phillips, 'The Primitive Methodist Connexion. Stansted Mountfitchet', n.d. (late 1990s).
Ralph Phillips and Peter Brown, 'The Recreation Ground, Stansted Mountfitchet', n.d.

Irving Sanders's Collection (ISC)
Now in the possession of Louise Barker, Lesley Lister and Tim Sanders. These papers have not been classified. They include 'The autobiography of a Quaker Antiquary 1854-1911 by Joseph J Green'.

Margaret Sylvester
'Rochford's Nurseries and the Stoney Common Community', n.d.

Tony Wellings
Log book of air raids kept in WW2 by Henry Devey.

C - NEWSPAPERS AND MAGAZINES
Single references are indicated in the footnotes.
Chelmsford Chronicle (1764-1884); *Essex County Chronicle* (1884-1920); *Essex Chronicle* (1920 -).
Essex Standard (1831-1900).
Herts and Essex Observer (1861 -).
The Link (Stansted's village magazine) from 1979 onwards.
Stansted Mountfitchet Parish Magazine (1901-1955: incomplete series in St. Mary's Church).

D - PRINTED BOOKS, ARTICLES, ETC.
Allen, D.H. (1974), *Essex Quarter Sessions Order Book 1652-1661*, Chelmsford: Essex County Council.

Andrews, C. Bruyn, ed. (1954), *The Torrington Diaries: a selection from the tours of the Hon. John Byng (later Fifth Viscount Torrington) between the years 1781 and 1794*, London: Eyre and Spottiswoode.

Anon. (1831), *Essex County Election. Report of the Speeches delivered at the hustings, and of the interesting proceedings during the contest of fifteen days, for the representation of the County of Essex, Commencing on Friday, the 6th of August, 1830, and terminating on Monday, the 23rd* ... Chelmsford: Meggy and Chalk.

Anon. (n.d.), *Joseph Joshua Green. A Life Sketch.*

Archer, Angela, ed. (1995), *A Village in Time: the history of Newport, Essex, by Bernard Nurse, Joy Pugh and Imogen Mollet,* Newport: Newport News.

Bannard, Henry E. (1936), 'Essex Committees in the Civil War', *Essex Review* XLV, pp. 101-5.

Barker, Gordon, and Sayers, Jack (1999), *A history of the village of Elsenham in the county of Essex,* Alan Duce and Company.

Bateman, John, 4th ed. (1883), *Great Landowners of Britain,* London: Harrison.

Bishop's Stortford and District Local History Society [1969] (1973), *Bishop's Stortford: a Short History,* Bishop's Stortford: Bishop's Stortford and District Local History Society.

Britton, John, and Brayley, Edward Wedlake (1803), *Beauties of England, Volume 5,* London: Vernon and Hood, Longman and Rees, etc.

Bromley, Henry (1873), *A Brief History of the Congregational Church, Clavering, Essex,* London: John Snow and Co.

Brooks, Howard, and Bedwin, Owen (1989), *Archaeology at the Airport. The Stansted Archaeological Project 1985-89,* Chelmsford: Essex County Council.

Brooks, Rob (2005), 'Two Medieval Deeds', article in Spring 2005 Newsletter of Friends of Historic Essex, pp. 11-12.

Brown, A.F.J. (1969), *Essex at Work 1700-1815,* Chelmsford: Essex Record Office.

Brown, A.F.J. (1990), *Meagre Harvest,* Chelmsford: Essex Record Office.

Brown, A.F.J. (1996), *Prosperity and Poverty. Rural Essex, 1700-1815,* Chelmsford: Essex Record Office.

Brownell, Elija Ellsworth, ed. (1957) [1937], *Topographical Dictionary of 2885 English Emigrants to New England 1620-1650, by Charles Edward Banks,* Baltimore: Genealogical Publishing Co.

Burke, Edmund (1801), *The Annual Register,* the 'Chronicle' section.

Byng, Cranmer (1952), 'Essex Prepares for Invasion', *Essex Review,* No. 242, April 1952, Vol. LXI.

Cadbury, Henry J., ed. (1943), 'John Farmer's First American Journey 1711-1714', reprinted from *Proceedings of the American Antiquarian Society for April 1943,* Worcester, Massachusetts: the Davis Press.

Chapman-Waller, William (1911), 'Inventories of Church Goods, 6 Edward VI', *TEAS* Vol. XI (New Series), p. 96.

Charity Commissioners, *Report* (n.d., 1830s).

Chisenhale-Marsh, U.B. (1922), 'Stansted Montfichet', *Essex Review,* Vol. XXXI, pp. 125-9.

Clare, John (1823-6), 'The Parish: a Satire'.

Cockburn, J.S. (1978), *Calendar of Assize Records, Essex Indictments, Elizabeth I,* London: HMSO.

Cockburn, J.S. (1982), *Calendar of Assize Records, Essex Indictments, James I,* London: HMSO.

Cole, G.D.H., and Postgate, Raymond (4th ed. 1949, reprinted as University paperback 1961), *The Common People: 1746-1946,* London: Methuen and Co. Ltd.

Cooper, Jacqueline (2005), *Bishop's Stortford: A History,* Chichester: Phillimore and Co. Ltd.

Cox, Thomas (vol. I, 1720), *Magna Britannia et Hibernia,* London: M. Nutt, J. Morphew etc.

Cruickshanks, Eveline, Handley, Stuart, and Hayton (2002), *The History of Parliament. The House of Commons 1690-1715,* published for the History of Parliament Trust by Cambridge University Press.

Dampier, William (1937) [1697], *A New Voyage round the World,* London: Adam and Charles Black.

Davids, T.W. (1863), *Annals of Evangelical Nonconformity in the County of Essex*, London: Jackson, Walford and Hodder.

SOURCES

Dictionary of National Biography, entry for Sir Thomas Myddleton or Middleton.

Dictionary of Welsh Biography Online.

Dobson (1982), 'Remembering the Peasants' Revolt, 1381-1981', pp. 1-20 in Liddell and Wood, edd., *Essex and the Great Revolt of 1381*, Chelmsford: Essex Record Office.

Dodd, A.H. (1961), 'Mr. Myddelton the Merchant of Tower Street', chapter IX, pp. 249-281 in Bindoff, Hurstfield and Williams, edd, *Elizabethan Government and Society*, London: Athlone Press, University of London.

Dodd, A.H. (1971), *Studies in Stuart Wales*, Cardiff: University of Wales Press.

Drury, John (2006), *Essex Workhouses*, Felsted: Farthings Publications.

Dugdale, Sir William (1817-1830) [1655-1673], *Monasticon Anglicanum*, Vol. VI, Part 1, London: Longman, Hurst, Rees, Orme and Brown.

Duke Henning, Basil, ed. (1983), *The History of Parliament. The House of Commons 1660-1690*, published for the History of Parliament Trust by Secker and Warburg.

Dymond, Robert (1882), 'The History of the Parish of St. Petrock's, Exeter', *Transactions of the Devon Association*, vol. 14, 1882.

Edwards, A.C. (1958), *A History of Essex with Maps and Pictures*, London: Darwen Finlayson Ltd.

Embleton, Paul (1998), *Images of England: Around Stansted Mountfitchet*, Stroud, Gloucestershire: Tempus Publishing Ltd.

Emmison, F.G. (1970), *Elizabethan Life: Disorder*, Chelmsford: Essex County Council.

Emmison, F.G. (1973), *Elizabethan Life: Morals & the Church Courts*, Chelmsford: Essex County Council.

Essex Congregational Remembrancer, 1827 onwards, Bocking.

Everett, Martyn (2007), *Saffron Walden and the English Civil War*, Saffron Walden: Ragged Robin Press.

Farries, Kenneth G. (1988), *Essex Windmills: Volume 5, A Review by Parishes S-Z*, London, Charles Skilton Ltd.

Festival of Britain: Souvenir Programme (1951).

Findlay, Arthur [1955] (1988), *Looking Back. The Autobiography of a Spiritualist*, London: Psychic Press Union.

Forster, Josiah (1829), *Selections from the letters and other papers of William Grover*, London: Harvey and Darton.

Fowler, R.C. (1906), 'Inventories of Essex Monasteries in 1536', *TEAS*, Vol. IX (New Series), pp. 280-92, 330-47.

Fowler, R.C. (1923) 'Essex Chapels', *TEAS*, Vol. XVI (New Series), pp. 104-21.

Fowler, R.C. (1923), 'Uttlesford Hundred, East and West', *TEAS*, Vol. XVI (New Series), pp. 183-6.

Framework Archaeology (principal authors Nicholas Cooke, Fraser Brown and Christopher Phillpotts) (2008), *From hunter gatherers to huntsmen. A history of the Stansted landscape*, Oxford and Salisbury: Framework Archaeology.

Freeman, Jane (1989), *A History of St. John's Church, Stansted Mountfitchet*.

The Friend (Philadelphia) vol. 28, 1926, p. 316, 'Biographical Sketches. John Farmer'.

Fry, Katharine (1888), *History of the Parishes of East and West Ham*, London: private publication, edited and revised by G Pagenstecher.

Fry, Katharine (1873a), 'Some Account of Robert Gernon and his Successors, the Barons Montfichet', *TEAS*, Vol. V (1st series), pp. 173-207.

Fry, Katharine (1873b), 'Some Account of Ralph Bainard and the Honor of Castle Baynard', *TEAS*, Vol. V (1st series), pp. 265-72.

Gibbons, Alfred (1891), *Ely Episcopal Records*, Lincoln, privately printed.

Gittings, Claire (1988) [1984], *Death, Burial and the Individual in Early Modern England*, London: Routledge.

Green, Joseph (1887), *Ye Hystorie of a Countrie Business att Stanstede in ye countie of Essexe, 1687-1887*: Ashford: H. D. & B. Headley, Invicta Printing Works. Also printed with another title page: *Two Hundred Years' History of a Country Business, 1697-1887. Joshua Green & Company, Stansted Montfichet, Essex.*

Gyford, Janet (1999), *Public Spirit: Dissent in Witham and Essex 1500-1700*, Witham: private publication.

Hall, Peter (1981) [1980], *Great Planning Disasters*, Harmondsworth: Penguin Books.

Hampson, Ethel Mary (1934), *Treatment of Poverty in Cambridgeshire, 1597-1834*, Cambridge: CUP Archive, 1934.

Hampson, Gillian (2011) [1983], www.historyofparliamentonline.org/volume/1660-1690

Harper, Charles G. (1904), *The Newmarket, Bury, Thetford, and Cromer Road*, London: Chapman and Hall.

SOURCES

Havis, Richard, and Brooks, Howard (2004), *Excavations at Stansted Airport 1986-91,* Chelmsford: Essex County Council, in conjunction with ALGAO East.

Holmes, Clive (1974), *The Eastern Association in the English civil war*, Cambridge: Cambridge University Press.

House of Commons papers, volume 41, Abstract of Education Returns 1833.

Hunt, William (1983), *The Puritan Moment. The Coming of Revolution in an English County,* Cambridge, Massachusetts and London, England: Harvard University Press.

Hunter, John (2003), *Field Systems in Essex*, Colchester: Essex Society for Archaeology and History, Occasional Papers, New Series, No. 1.

Journal of the Friends Historical Society, vol. 22, 1925, 'Anecdotes of Benjamin Lay', pp. 72 etc., London: The Friends' Bookshop.

Journal of the Friends Historical Society, vol. 23, Notes and Queries, pp. 60-2, London: The Friends' Bookshop.

Keay, John (1993) [1991], *The Honourable Company. A History of the English East India Company*, London: HarperCollinsPublishers.

Kelly's Directory.

Kemble, James (2001), *Prehistoric and Roman Essex,* Stroud: Tempus Publishing Inc.

Kidd, Jane (1997), *Gilbeys, Wine and Horses,* Cambridge: The Lutterworth Press.

King, H.W. (1869), 'Inventories of Church Goods 6th Edw. VI', *TEAS*, Vol. IV (First Series), pp. 197-215.

Kingston, Alfred (1897), *East Anglia and the Great Civil War*, London: Elliot Stock.

Kosky, Nathan (2000), *Stansted Airport*, Thrupp, Stroud, Gloucestershire: Sutton Publishing Ltd.

Laslett, Peter (1983), *The World We Have Lost – Further Explored*, London: Methuen.

Lloyd, J.E., Davies W.L. and Davies, M.B. (1959), *The Dictionary of Welsh Biography down to 1940,* London, under the auspices of the Honourable Society of Cymmrodorion.

Lytten, Julian (2012), 'The Marquis d'Orsy: Aesthete, Eccentric and Enigma', *Saffron Walden Historical Journal*, New Series Vol. 12, No. 24, Autumn 2012, pp. 20-26.

Macfarlane, Alan, ed. (1976), *The Diary of Ralph Josselin 1616-1683,* London: Oxford University Press for the British Academy.

Malcolmson, R.W. (1981), *Life and Labour in England 1700-1800,* London: Hutchinson.

Marshall, Dorothy (1926), *The English Poor in the Eighteenth Century*, London, George Routledge and Sons, Ltd.

Maud, F.H. (1957), *The Hockerill Highway: the story of the origin and growth of a stretch of the Norwich road,* Colchester: Benham and Co. Ltd.

Morant, Philip (1763-68), *History and Antiquities of the County of Essex*: London: T. Osborne, J. Whiston etc.

Morris, Derek (2002), *Mile End Old Town 1740-1780,* London: The East London History Society.

Morris, Richard (2007), *Essex's Excellency. The Election of two Knights of the Shire for the County of Essex at the General Election of August 1679,* Loughton: Loughton & District Historical Society.

Muilman, Peter ('a Gentleman') (1770), *New and Complete History of Essex*, Chelmsford: Lionel Hassall.

The National Trust (1995), *Chirk Castle, Clwyd,* London: National Trust Enterprises.

Newcourt, Richard (2 volumes: 1708 and 1710), *Repertorium Ecclesiasticum Parochiale Londinense: An Ecclesiastical Parochial History of the Diocese of London*, London: Benjamin Motte.

Oliver, G. and Jones, J.P. (1828) *Ecclesiastical Antiquities of Devon etc.*, Exeter: E. Woolmer, Gazette Office, Exeter.

Oxley, J.E. (1965), *The Reformation in Essex to the death of Mary,* Manchester: Manchester University Press.

Pearson, Daphne, *Edward de Vere (1550-1604): the crises and consequences of wardship* (2005), Aldershot: Ashgate Publishing Ltd.

Peart-Binns, *Graham Leonard, Bishop of London* (1988), London: Input Typesetting Ltd.

Peel, Albert, ed. (1915), *Seconde Parte of a Register,* Cambridge: Cambridge University Press.

Pevsner, Nikolaus (1965) [1954], *The Buildings of England: Essex,* Harmondsworth: Penguin Books Ltd.

Phillips, Ralph, (n.d.), *Stansted Station: a History*, NetWork South East.

Pigot's Directory of Essex (1832).

Poor Law Enquiry Commissioners (1834), *Report of H.M. Commissioners on Poor Law*, no. 44.

Post Office Guide 1874.

Probert, Colonel G. Carwardine (1930), 'Sir Francis Hubert and the Hubert Family of Stansted Montfichet Hall, Essex', *Essex Review,* XXXIX, pp. 124-8.

Rackham, Oliver (1986), *The History of the Countryside,* London and Melbourne: J.M. Dent & Sons.

SOURCES

Rackham, Oliver (1989), *The Last Forest: the Story of Hatfield Forest*, London: J.M. Dent & Sons.

Reader, Frank H. (1939, 1941-4), articles in the *SMPM*.

Round, J.H. (1923), 'Church goods', *TEAS*, Vol. XVI (New Series), p. 120.

Royal Commission on Historical Monuments (England) (1916), *An inventory of the historical monuments of Essex, north-west*, London: HMSO.

Rush, Joseph Arthur (1897), *Seats in Essex*. London: King, Sell and Railton.

Sanders, Lizzie, and Williamson, Gillian, edd. (2005), *Littlebury: a Parish History*, The Parish of Littlebury Millennium Society.

Sanders, Peter (1989), *The Simple Annals: the History of an Essex and East End Family*, Gloucester: Alan Sutton.

Sandford Family History website.

Sayers, Jack (1995), 'A Brief History of the Lords of the Manor of Stansted Mountfitchet in the County of Essex, 1066-1922': privately published.

Scarfe, Norman (1975) [1968], *A Shell Guide. Essex*, London: Faber & Faber.

Sedgwick, Romney R, online member biography of Thomas Heath in *The History of Parliament* [n.d.], The History of Parliament Trust.

Sharpe, J.A. (1983), *Crime in seventeenth-century England. A county study*, Cambridge: CUP.

Smith, Graham (1996), *Essex Airfields in the Second World War*, Newbury, Berkshire: Countryside Books.

Smith, Harold (n.d.), *The Ecclesiastical History of Essex Under the Long Parliament and Commonwealth*, Colchester: Benham and Co. Ltd.

Smith, Harold (1925), 'Notes and Queries', *Essex Review XXXIV*, p. 210.

Smith, Harold (1924), 'Some Essex Royalist Clergy – and Others', *Essex Review*, XXXIII, p. 86.

Smith, J.R. (1992), *Pilgrims and Adventurers: Essex (England) and the Making of the United States of America*, Chelmsford: Essex Record Office.

Smith, Ken (1998), *Essex under Arms: the early years to 1900*, Romford: Ian Henry Publications.

Sokoll, Thomas, ed. (2001), *Essex Pauper Letters 1731-1837*, published for the British Academy by the Oxford University Press.

Spufford, Margaret (1974), *Contrasting Communities: English Villagers in the Sixteenth and Seventeeth Centuries*, Cambridge: Cambridge University Press.

Stenton, Sir Frank (1960), 'Norman London', in Geoffrey Barraclough, ed., *Social Life in Early England*, London: Routledge and Kegan Paul.

Stephenson, David (1976), 'The Myddletons of Stansted Mountfitchet: A Seventeenth-Century Gentry Family', *Essex Archaeology and History*, Vol. 8, pp. 282-7.

Streeter, Patrick (2004), *Mad for Zion: a biography of Colonel J.H. Patterson*, Harlow: The Matching Press.

Thompson, Roger (1994), *Mobility and Migration. East Anglian Founders of New England, 1627-1640*, Massachusetts: University of Massachusetts Press.

Thrush, Andrew, and Ferris, John P. (2010), *The History of Parliament. The House of Commons 1604-1629*, published for the History of Parliament Trust by Cambridge University Press.

J. Timby, R. Brown, E. Biddulph, A. Hardy and A. Powell (2007), *A Slice of Rural Essex. Archaeological discoveries from the A120 between Stansted Airport and Braintree*, Oxford and Salisbury: Oxford Wessex Archaeology.

Tinney, John F. (2012), *Memories – The Reflections of Two Young Boys on a Family Farm 1939 to 1945*, 'produced by MFP'.

Tricker, Roy (1992), *A Brief Guide to Saint Mary's, Stansted Mountfitchet*, a typewritten document. Printed edition published in 1994.

Tuck, Anthony and others (2015), *The Victoria History of Essex: Newport*, The University of London.

Victoria County History of the County of Essex, vol. II (1907), edd. William Page and J Horace Round, London: Victoria County History.

Vincent, Nicholas (2004), 'Richard de Montfichet', *DNB*, Oxford.

Wace (2002), *Le Roman du Rou*, translated by Glyn S. Burgess with text of Anthony J. Holden and notes by Glyn S. Burgess and Elisabeth van Houts, St. Helier, Jersey: Société Jersiaise.

Ward, Jennifer C. (1983), *The Medieval Essex Community: The Lay Subsidy of 1327*, Chelmsford, Essex Record Office.

Ward, Richard (1641A), *The Pious Man's Practice in Parliament Time*, London: printed by T. Cotes for P. Cole, at the signe of the Glove and Lyon in Cornhill neere the Royall Exchange.

Ward, Richard (1641B), *The Principal Duty of Parliament men*, London.

Ward, Richard (1642A), *The anatomy of Warre, or Warre with the wofull fruits and effects thereof, laid out to the life*, London: John Dalham and Richard Lownds.

Ward, Richard (1642B), *The Vindication of the Parliament, and their Proceedings*, London.

Ward, Richard (1642C), *Jehoshaphats going forth to battell ...* London.

Ward, Richard (1643A), *The Character of the Warre, or the Miseries thereof*, London.

Ward, Richard (1643B), *The Explication and Application of the Sacred Vow and Covenant*, London: Richard Bishop for John Dallam. Reprinted 1737 as *The Explanation and Application of the Solemn League and Covenant*. Reprinted 2015 by Isha Books, New Delhi.

Warwick, Glyn (2008), *They Sleep in Heroes' Graves*, Stansted Mountfitchet: Warwick Publishing.

Waters, Robert Edmond Chester (1878), *Genealogical Memoirs of the Extinct Family of Chester of Chicheley*, vol. 1, London: Robson and Sons.

Webster, Tom (1997), *Godly Clergy in Early Stuart England, the Caroline Puritan Movement c.1620-1643*, Cambridge: Cambridge University Press.

Webster, Tom, and Shipps, Kenneth (2004), *The Diary of Samuel Rogers, 1634-37*, Church of England Record Society, No. 11, Woodbridge: Boydell.

White's Directory of Essex, 1848.

John Wilkins (1976) [1892], *The Autobiography of an English Gamekeeper*, ed. Arthur H. Byng and Stephen M. Stephens, Chesham: Sporting & Leisure Press.

Wilson, Stanley (1971), *The Mayor and the Matron*, High Wycombe: Precision Press.

Winkley, G.W.D. (n.d.), *Parish Church of St. Mary, Stansted Mountfitchet, History*, Ramsgate: Church Publishers.

Winter, Derek (n.d.), *Stansted: The War Years 1942-1945*, Stansted Airport Ltd.

Wood, R.G. (1982), 'Essex Manorial Records and the Revolt', pp. 67-98, in Liddell and Wood, *Essex and the Great Revolt of 1381*, Chelmsford: Essex Record Office.

Wright, Thomas (Vol. 2, 1836), *The History and Topography of the County of Essex*, London: George Virtue.

Young, Arthur (1807), Vol. 1, *General View of the Agriculture of the County of Essex* (Vol. 1, 1807, Vol. 2, 1813), Blackfriars: Richard Phillips.

E - THESIS

Binfield, J.C.G., 'Nonconformity in the Eastern Counties, 1849-1885, with reference to its social background' (Ph.D. Thesis, Cambridge, 1965).

F - LECTURES

Medlycott, Maria, lecture given to the Saffron Walden Town Library Association, 13 June 2012.

Streeter, Patrick, 'The Blyth family', lecture given to Stansted Mountfitchet Local History Society, 6 April 2000.

Thompson, Christopher, 'The Civil War in this area', lecture given to Stansted Mountfitchet Local History Society, 7 October 1999.

INDEX

Italics indicate that there is a relevant illustration on the page.

AA, 154
Abbot, Robert, 66-7, 68, 72
Acme, bus company, 270
Act of Toleration (1689), 74, 75, 94
Actresses Franchise League, 193
ACWEECO, 296
Agricultural Protection Society, 135fn.
Agriculture, see under Farms and Farming
Air Raid Precautions (ARP), 291, 296, 306fn.
Airport, viii, 3, 4, 5, 8, 9, 10, 13, 21, 22, 23, 24, 26, 27, 29fn., 272, 308, 309, 312, 313-7
Airport Watch, 316
Airports Commission, 313, 317
Aisne, Battle of the, 253, 263
Albemarle, Earl of, 35, 39
Alcock, John, Bishop of Ely, 43
Alders, 265, 270-1; Arthur, 265; Gilbert, 170, 191, 229; Sydney, 286
Alexandra, Queen, 232
Alfred, King, 154
Allen, John, 86, 87
Alley Field, 6, 149, 153, 256, 257, 258
Allotments, 243, 255, 256, 275, 305
Allsopp, Nora, 271
Allyn, Margaret, 50
Almshouses, 109fn., 137, 157. See also the Fuller Almshouses, 6, 142, *143*, 145, 265, 398.
Alsa Lodge, 297
Alsa Street, 5, 84
Alsa Wood, 10, 87, 236, 298-9
Ambiani, 28
America, 10, 51, 63, 75, 132, 133, 134, 146, 254, 300
American airbase, viii, 8, 10, 302-6 (*302* and *303*), 313
Amey, J., *231*
Amiens, Treaty of, 112
Amsterdam, 152
Anabaptists, 67
Andrews, George, 269, 283
Anti-Corn Law League, 131
Apprentices, 53, 109, 109fn., 215, 244, 267
Arch, Joseph, 132, 218
Archaeology, viii, 13, 21-9, 81. See also Framework Archaeology.
Archer, Richard, 149
Arkesden, 72, 73, 74, 81, 118
Armstrong, Robert, 160

Arnold, Matthew, 221
Arsenal football club, 272
Arson, 93, 124, 129-32, 135fn.
Arthur Findlay College, 4, *160*, 308. See also Stansted Hall.
Arthur, Prince, 137
Artists in Maitland collection, 159-60
Ashdon, 74
Ashley, Northants, 169
Assize Court, 93, 130, 247
Atkin, John, 179
Atkins *231*
Attlee, Clement, 267
Audley End, 111, 133, 140, 185fn., 245
Augustinians, 35
Ault Rev Ebenezer, 146-7
Aulus Plautius, 25
Australia, 10, 94, 117, 118, 133, 134, 141, 192, 253
Auxiliary Territorial Service (WW2), 301
Aylett, Richard, 97

BAA, 13, 313, 314-6
Bailey, Marie, 188
Baker, Margery, 266, 272, 294-5, 296-7, 305
Baldwin, Stanley, 268
Ball, Albert, 263-4
Ball, Edward, 225
Ball, John, 44
Ball, Ralph, 296-7
Banks, Eliza, 217
Banks, James, 247
Banks, Queenie, 271
Bannehr, W.J., 252, 253, 261fn.
Baptisms, 13, 81, 105, 197
Baptists, 200
Barbados, 75
Barbone, Carol, 315
Baringo, Lake, 236
Barley Mow, 6, 137, *138*, 139, 140, 303
Barrington family, 62, 65
Barrington, Sir Thomas, 65
Barrow, John, 280, 281, 282, 289, 290, 291fn.
Bass, H., *231*
Batho, Mr. of Elsenham, 61
Bathurst, Miss, 192
Baxter, Win, 295
Bayley, Catherine, 77
Baynard's castle, 34

Baynard, Ralph, 34
Beck, Cecil, 193, 266
Becket, Thomas, 35, 288-9
Bedlows, 271; Frank, *231*, 240-1
Bedwin, Owen, 23-4
Belgium, 252, 253, 293
Bell Inn, 6, *89*, 91, 92fn., 129, 149, 166, 224, 233, 308
Bentfield Bury farm and barn, *82*, 83, 119, 131, 297-8, 308
Bentfield End, 3-4, 129-30, 138, 151, 197, 220, 261, 271, 296, 297
Bentfield End Causeway, 118
Bentfield Gardens, 166
Bentfield Hall, 266, 301
Bentfield Hamlet, 75
Bentfield Mill Farm, 85
Bentfield Place, 297
Bentfield Place Farm, 131
Berden, 84, 127fn., 147, 240, 271
Berkshire, 117, 158, 161
Berry, Jessie, 259, 271, 272, 285
Berry, John, 86
Bible Society, 201, 202, 206, 225
Bicycles, 193-4, 229, 267, 269, 272, 297
Billiards, 184, 227, 286
Binfield, John, 199
Birchalls, High Lane, 272
Birchanger, 4, 5, 51, 61, 81, 84, 92fn., 94, 123, 127fn., 146, 147, 149, 166, 190, 229, 236, 239, 241fn., 245, 261fn., 265, 271, 289, 307, 308, 310
Bishop's Stortford, 3, 4, 5, 9, 10, 11, 14, 25, 40, 42, 61, 72, 74, 81, 82, 85, 89, 90, 99, 108, 111, 112, 123, 124, 125, 126, 127fn., 132-3, 139, 141, 146, 147, 148, 149, 151, 154, 155, 156fn., 166, 167, 174, 195, 197, 199, 200, 203, 207, 219, 223, 226, 227, 228, 233, 237, 238, 245-6, 252, 254, 256-7, 264, 268, 269-70, 276, 282, 284, 286, 287, 289, 294, 295, 296, 300, 304, 306fn., 307, 309, 310
Bishop's Stortford Band, 139, 289
Bishop's Stortford Gas Company, 151, 275-6
Black Death, 41, 42
Black's wife, 105
Blake, Inspector G.D., 313, 317fn.
Blitz, 294, 295, 296, 299
Bloemfontein, 188
Blyth, in Nottinghamshire, 36
Blyths, vii, 10, 11, 172, 209-10, 228, 229, 230, 231, 235, 236, 240, 245, 265, 301; Agnes, 169; Audley, 188-9, 236; 'Effie', 236; Eliza, *168*; Henry, 167, 181, 188, 236; James, 11, 149, 151, *152*, 166, 167, *168*, 169, 172, 181, 188, 189, 239, 240, 257, 265, 308; second Lady Blyth, 276; second Lord Blyth, 83, 265; Nora, 169; Ormond, 67, 140; Rupert, 188-9

Blythwood Dairy, 168
Blythwood Gardens, 273fn.
Blythwood House, *166*, 168, 188, 229, 265, 273fn., 276, 288
Bokkyngg, Robert de, 40
Bolebec, Hugh and Margery de, 39
Book of Common Prayer, 47, 61, 63, 72, 291fn.
Botha, Louis, 189
Boudicca, 25-6
Boulogne, 112
Boulton, General, 240
Bourne, John, 215, 217
Bowls, 237, 260, 286
Boxing, 287, 291fn.
Boyland, Inspector Alan, 316
Brace, Arthur, 135fn.
Bradford, Mr., 221
Bradford Street (now Lower Street), 84
Braintree, 69fn., 106, 126, 257, 287
Braughing, 24, 25, 123, 127fn.
Braybrooke, Lord, 181, 185fn, 245
Brecon and Breconshire, 4, 117, 158, 161, 162, 181, 183, 192
Breeks, Mrs., 188
Brent's charity, 108, 218
Brentwood, 41
Brett, John, 150
Brett, Thomas, 94
Brewer, Widow, 104
Brewers and brewing, 5, 6, 54-5, 86, 90, 107, 123, 151, 247
Brewery Field, 257
Brewis, George, 183-4
Bright, A., *231*
Brighten, Police Constable, 245
Brighton, 148
Bristol, 197
British Columbia, 134
British East Africa, 134, 236, 253, 263, 264
British and Foreign Bible Society, 206
British and Foreign School Society, 203, 213. See also Schools, British.
British Legion, 266, 288, 300, 309
British Medical Journal, 125
British Restaurant, 301, 306
Britten, Police Constable, 246
Bronze Age, 23, 28
Brooks, Howard, 23-4
Broome End, 6, 266, 267, 270, 308
Brown, Arthur, 104, 129, 132, 133
Brown, C.B., 151
Browne, Mrs. Arthur, 141, 287
Browne's charity, 108-9
Browne, Joan, 94
Browne, Thomas, 50

INDEX

Buchanan, Colin, 314
Buck, parish councillor, 153
Buck's gift, 108-9
Buenos Aires, 174
Bull Yard, 295
Buller, Redvers, 187
Bullinger, John, his wife, 105
Buntings, 272; Olive, 293; William, 282
Burghclere, Lord: see Gardner, Herbert.
Burgoyne, Montague, 177, 178
Burials register, 13-4, 82, 108
Burlington city, 75
Burnell, Robert, Bishop of Bath and Wells, 39. See also manor of Burnells.
Burnet, John and wife, 75, 86
Burre, Benedicto, 40
Burrell, Harry, 268
Burton Bower, 309
Burton End, 3-4, *8*, 22, 131, 134, 149, 219, 238-9, 254, 257, 271, 276, 286, 297
Burton, H.C., 287
Bury Lodge Farm, 208
Bury Lodge Lane, 26
Bus services, 270, 307
Butler, R.A., 264, 267, 310, 311
Buttalls, Gyles, 66
'BWL', 233
Byng, Arthur, 16
Byng, George, 10

Caister, J., *231*
Cakebread, Mary, 97
Calvinism, 51, 66, 157
Cam, Rev., 239-40
Cambridge, 3, 4, 9, 90, 91, 148, 149, 181, 268, 307
Cambridge Co-operative Society, 270, 308
Cambridge Road. See under Roads.
Cambridge Science Park, 308
Cambridge University, 50, 62, 66, 78, 99, 148, 204, 234fn., 237, 240, 308
Cambridgeshire, 31, 64, 225
Camulodunon/Camulodunum, 23-4, 25, 26
Canada, 124, 132, 133-4, 141, 174, 253
Cannan, Margaret, 49
Canning, George, 87
Canning, William, 223
Cannon, 'Sister', 74
Canton, 77
Cape Town, 188
Capital punishment, 94, 131, 247
Caratacus, 25
Carnival, 309, 312fn.
Caroe, William, 166, 169
Cars, 153, 154, *252*, 253, 266, 271, 272, 277, 287, 288, 290, 296, 307

Carter, Bill, 293
Carter, George, 244
Carter, Leslie, 293
Carter, Thomas, 112
Cary, John, 47
Cash, Bill, 269
Cass, Amelia, 247
Castelow, Thomas, 97
Castles. Baynard's, 34; Chirk, 54, 55, 59fn., 71; Denbigh, 53; Hedingham, 39, 43; Hertford, 36; Tower of London, 34; Montfichet's Tower, London, 33, 34, 35; Montfiquet, Normandy, 35; Stansted, 5, 6, 10, 22, 32, 33, *34*, 35, 37, 38fn., 77, 308
Castle Hills, 7, 22, 94, 184, 237, 285, 309
Caton's, 307
Catuvellauni, 23-5
Cavalier Government, 72
Cawkell, Major Edmund, 266, 267, 275, 276, 286, 288
Caygill, Joseph, 134, 138, 151, *230*, *231*
Census, 51 (1620 religious), 72 (1676, Compton census), 79 (1811), 81 (Compton, 1801, 1831), 85 (1831), 88 (1801, 1811), 92fn. (1811), 99 (1811), 121 (1841), 132 (1851), 149 (1851), 201-2 (1851 religious), 237 (1891), 238, 271 (1931)
Central Hall, 6, 134, *145*, 146, 150, 151, 152, 153, 160, 172, 173, 181, 182, 183, 184, 192, 193, 208, 225, 226, 227, 228, 243, 259, 263, 275, 287, 288, 289, 301, 305, 306, 309. See also Magistrates' court, the Supreme Ballroom, Rocky's Disco and the Old Court House.
Central Hall Company, 16, 224-5, 227, 265
Chamberlain, Neville, 293-4
Chantry Road, Bishop's Stortford, 257
Chapel of our Lady (wayside chapel), 3, 6, *43*, 47, 48, 52fn., 71, 91, 166
Chapel, the area, 3, 151
Chapel Hill, 4, 5, 6, *7*, *8*, 73, 74, 75, 137, 138, 145, 148, 153-4, 172, 195, 203, 206, 209, 213, 214, 221, 251, 257, 269, 276, 287, 283, 284, 287, 295, 303, 307, 310
Chaplin, Rev. William, 195-8
Chapman, John, 126
Chappell, Sergeant-Major, 190
Charities, 108-9, 142, 150, 157, 213, 217, 218, 264, 265, 275, 286, 287, 288. See also individual charities.
Charity Commissioners, 108
Charles I, King, 55, 59fn., 62-8
Charles II, King, 9, 67, 71, 72, 83, 89, 94
Chartism, 129
Chelmsford, 62, 68, 72, 78, 93, 118, 177-9, 247, 264, 287, 299, 306fn.
Chelmsford Chronicle, 14, 17fn., 224, 238, 247

Chelmsford, Diocese of, 211
Chelmsford Inquiry, 313, 314
Cheney, Mrs., 304
Cheshire, Royalist uprising (1659), 71
Cheshunt, 146, 229
Chester, Constable of, 35
Chester, Charlie, 301
Chesters, 266, 267, 270, 308; Harry, 151, 154, 182, 184-5, 239, 240, 243, 255, 266, 275; Mildred, 140, 142
Chickney, 72
Chieveley camp, Natal, 187
Chimney sweeps, 233, 234fn., 267
Chippenham, 158
Chisenhale-Marsh, Miss, 141
Churches and Chapels. Anglicans/Church of England, 49, 50, 61, 73-4, 99-100, 108-9, 134, 140, 150, 158, 171, 178, 179, 195-6, 199, 201-211 (including *205, 206, 209-10*), 213-5, 265, 279-82, 287, 288-9, 306, 310; Congregationalists/Independents, 6, 14, *73*, 74, 76fn., 94, 99, 102, 146, 155, 173, 178-9, 181, 195-*200*, 201-02, *203*, *204*, 206, 210, 213, 218, 221, 223, 232, 281, *282*, 283, 284, 290, 306, 309, 310; United Reformed Church, 310; Stansted Free Church, 193, *204*, 309, 310; Presbyterians, 63, 67, 69, 157, 280, 310; Primitive Methodists/Methodists, vii, 6, 132, 173, *201*, 202, 283, 310; Quakers/Friends, 15, 63, *74*, 75, 86, 87-9, 94, 99, 102, 171-3, 179, 201, 202, 203, 221, 225, 230, 255, 283, 289, 310; Roman Catholics, 48-51, 61, 62, 63, 67, 71-2, 205, 206, 207-8, 210, 291fn., *310*. See also Nonconformists and Protestants.
Church courts, 97-100, 105
Church Road, 5, 6, 142, 267, 276, 301, 304
Churches Conservation Trust, 309
Churchwardens, 11, 14, 48, 51, 62, 69fn., 79, 93, 97-9, 101-3, 108, 109fn., 113fn., 122, 175fn., 206, 207, 209, 211, 230, 279-80
Cinema, 228-9, 303, 304, 309
Clapham Sect, 204
Clare family, 34, 35
Clare, John, poet, 103
Clarence, Duke of, 207
Clark, Henry and Nancy, 134
Clark, Police Constable, 300
Clarke, Kenneth, 307
Clarke, W., *231*
Clarke, William, 129-30
Claudius, Roman Emperor, 25
Clavering, 4, 42, 59, 72, 81, 118, 135fn., 146, 147, 149, 203, 225
Clavering, Half Hundred of, 27, 31, 62, 81, 111, 147

Clavering and Uttlesford Classis, 67-8
Clayton, John, 197-8
Coal, 10, 107, 125, 142, 148, 219, 256, 272
Coalition Government, 316
Coates, Dr., 193
Coggeshall, 257
Coins, 14, 22, 25, 28, 159
Colchester, 22, 23-4, 25, 44, 68, 75, 177, 181, 257. See also Camulodunon.
Colchester, archdeaconry of, 97
Coldstream Guards, 148, 190, 232, 253
Colindale, 296
Collin, curate, 137
Collins, Goody, 104
Colne Priory, 51
Communism, 281, 300
Compton, Bishop, 73, 81
Conservatives, see Tories.
Constables, parish, 64, 68, 69fn., 75, 93, 95, 101
Conventicle Act (1664), 72-3
Conyers, John, 78, 80fn.
Cook, Arthur, *203*, 204, 232, 282
Cook, William, 126
Cooke's charity, 108
Cooke, Thomas, 50
Cooke, William, 50
Coombs, Frederick, 238
Copyhold tenure, 41, 93, 101, 177, 263
Corbys, 220
Corn Laws, 117, 129, 135fn.
Corner Thatch, 119
Cornwall, Alan Gardner, 204, 211fn.
Coronations, 229-30, 232, 288, 309
The Cottage, 166, 261
Cowan, Marjory, 269, 270-1, 279, 284, 285
Crabbe, George, 103
Crabbe, Thomas, 50
Crane, John, 104
Cricket, 97, 140, 149, 162, 169, 219, 229, 237, 238-41, *240*, 284, 286, 309
Crime, 93-5, 241, 242-8, 290, 312
Crimea, 167
Croasdaile, Henry, 78, 111
Croft House, 265
Cromwell, Oliver, 64, 68, 71
Crystal Palace, 148
Cublington, 314
Cuffley, Emma, 247
Cunobelin (Cymbeline), 25

D-Day, 303
Dampier, William, 77
Darling, Alistair, 316
Darloe, Mr., 61
Dawkins, William, 78

Day Centre, 309
Days, 92fn.; Elizabeth, 88; John, 75, 87, 88, 171, 307; John (Tayspill John), 87-8; Samuel, 87-8, 171; Samuel Tayspill, 88, 171-2, 203
Day, Joane, 59
Dartmoor, 174
De Veres, Earls of Oxford, 4, 13, 39, 42-3, 47, 51, 71, 91, 166, 264; Aubrey, 39; John (7th Earl), 43; John (12th Earl), 39; Maud, 41; Richard (11th Earl); 43; Robert (9th Earl), 43
De Wet, Christiaan, 189, 190
Dearch, Frank, 238, 283, 284, 285
Debden, 42, 81, 236
Debden Hall, 162
Dedham Conference, 61, 62
Delaware River, 75
Dellow, Valerie, 305
Derby, Lord, 252
Devey, Henry, 306fn.
Diss, Mr., 284
Dixon family, *259*
Dodd, E.T., 289
Dog and Duck public house, 272
Domesday Book, 13, 21, 27, 31-2, 33, 38fn, 81
Douglas, Henry, 134, 215, 216, 217, 218, 240; Mrs. Douglas, 215, 218; Miss Douglas, 174
Dowling, 119, 247
Down Farm, 5, 130
Downe, Mark, 65, 66-7
Dr. Barnardo's Homes, 288
Drake, Francis, 54
Drum and Fife Band, 228
Dublin, 167
Duke of Cambridge's Own (DCOs), 188, 189
Dunmow/Great Dunmow, 25, 29fn., 41, 42, 64, 67, 81, 106, 111, 135fn., 137, 161, 223, 225, 238, 241fn., 247
Dunmow Rural District Council, 275, 311
Durrack, Major, 287
Durrell's Wood, 5, 236
Dyer, A.H.S., 149, 156fn.
Dyer and Young, 156fn., 269

Earls Colne, 133
East India Company, 10, 54, 56, 77, 78
Eastern Association, 64, 65
Eastern Counties Railway Company, 147
Easton Lodge, 169
EasyJet, 315
Ecclestone, George, 293; Tom, 293
Edgar Harman and Co., 307
Edgehill, 64
Edinburgh, 167
Edridge, John and wife, 74
Education Act (1870), 214

Education Act (1902), 210, 214
Education Act (1944), 310
Edward, King (the Confessor), 31
Edward III, King, 40, 43
Edward VI, King, 47, 49, 50
Edward VII, King/Prince of Wales, 150, 167, *168*, 172, 218, 226, 230, 232, 267
Egypt, 112
Elections, Parliamentary, 10, 14, 62, 71-2, 77, 78, 85, 99, 171, 176-80, 181, 182-5, 189-90, 191, 192, 205, 266-7, 311, 316
Electricity, 146, 149, 168, 224, 228, 265, 267, 270, 272, 276, 286, 296, 299
Elizabeth I, Queen, 14, 48, 49, 50, 51, 61, 62, 101, 309
Elizabeth II, Queen, 309
Ellesmere, Earl and Countess of, 236
Ellis, Esther and Joshua, 157
Elmdon, 236
Elms Farm, 6, 156fn.
Elsenham, 4, 5, 40, 61, 64-5, 77, 78, 81, 94, 97, 123, 127fn., 135fn., 147, 154, 218, 245, 256, 257, 268, 298
Elsenham Hall, 77, 160, 166, 167, 218, 265, 268
Elsenham Road, 6, 254, 271
Ely, 148
Emigration abroad, 10, 51, 63, 69fn., 75, 82, 124, 132, 133-4, 253. See also America, Australia, Canada, New Zealand, South Africa.
Empire Day, 285
Enclosure, 13, 83, *85*, 92fn., 129
Enfield District Council, 149
English Church Union, 208
Enoch, 284, 285-6
Essex, see throughout.
Essex Chamber of Agriculture, 132
Essex Chronicle, 17fn., 130
Essex Congregational Remembrancer, 196
Essex County Council, 23, 150, 153, 154, 155, 174, 214, 221, 266, 276, 277, 285
Essex County Nursing Association, 288
Essex, Forest of, 32, 33, 35, 36
Essex, kingdom of, 27
Essex Record Office, 13, 14, 15, 214, 284
Essex Soldiers Relief Fund, Boer War, 188
Essex Testimony (1648), 68
Essex Yeomanry Band, 289
Eton, 78
Evacuees (WW2), 294-7, 300
Evangelical Academy, Hoxton, 196-7
Eve, Henry, 97
Evesham, Epiphanius, 57
Exclusionists, 71-2
Exeter, 67
Eyre, Inspector Graham, 314-5, 316, 317

INDEX

Fair, May fair, Stansted, 219, 231, 232, 233, 289, 309; other fairs, 219, 232-3
Fairs Act (1871), 232-3
Fairfax, Thomas, 68
Fairfield Villa, 241fn.
Farmer, John and Mary, 75
Farms, farmers and farming, 3, 5, 10, 21, 23, 26, 28, 32, 37, 40, 41, 42, 54, *82*, 83-7, 88, 89-90, 91, 101, 106, 108, 113, 117-21, 123, 124, 129, 130-3, 134, 135fn., 137, 138, 143, 148, 149, 151, 165, 167-8, 174-5, 177, 182, 208, 213, 215, 218-9, 230, 233, 235, 240, 243, 254, 255, 256-7, 259, 263-4, 268, 269, 271, 282, 297, 298, 305, 308
Farnham, 4, 5, 31, 40, 85, 92fn., 117, 127fn., 147, 157, 182, 188, 235, 255, 264, 271, 310
Felsted School, 78
Festival of Britain, 309
Finchingfield, 118
Findlays, 267; Arthur, 263, *264*, 265, 290, 308; Gertrude, *264*, 265, 288, 300
Finland, 300
Fire Brigade, 257, 266, 276, 298
Fire engine, 129, 131, *256*, 275, 276, 298
First Life Guards, 112
Fitz Walter, Robert, 35
FitzGerald, Lord and Lady Henry, 266, 308
Fletcher, Clement, 243
Florence, Italy, 158
Flower, Rev., 225
Fobbing, 41
Football, 193, *237*, 238, 239, 252, 265, 266, 284, 286, 289, 309
Forest Hall housing estate, 308
Forest Hall Park, 307
Forest Hall Road, 310
Foresters, Ancient Order of, 137, 138, *139*, 140
Foster, Norman, 313
Framework Archaeology, 23, 26, 27, 28, 41, 42, 58-9
Francis, 241
Francis, Barry, 296, 299, 304-5
Francis, Derek, 296, 304-5
Francis, J, *231*
Francis, 'Ticker', 233
Fred Rogers' Arcadia Dance Band, 289
Freelove, Markwell, 229, *230*
French, Mr., at Birchanger, 61
Freshwell, Hundred of, 111
Friendly Societies, 137, *138*, *139*, 140, 210, 255, 283. See also individual societies.
Friends, see Quakers
Friends School, Saffron Walden, 192
Frinton, 148
Frobisher, Martin, 53
Fuller Almshouses, see under Almshouses.

Fuller, William, 157-8
Fuller-Maitlands, vii, 4, 10, 15, 77, 79, 85, 117, 130, 134, 147, 157, 158, 209, 229, 232, 235, 238, 243, 255, 276, 279; Bethia, née Ellis, 142, 157, 158; Charlotte, 158, 160, 162fn.; Ebenezer, 117, 147, 157, *158*, 204, 213; Evelyn, née Gardner, 161-2, 163fn., 210, 218, 232, 236, 263; Frances, 263; Lydia, née Prescott, 158; Lydia, dtr of second William, 236, 263; Mary, 160; Richard, 263; Robert, brother of second William, 182 183, 235, 243; Robert, son of second William, 134, 236, 263; William, senior, 10-11, 16, 130, 160-1, 205, 213, 223, 225, 235, 244, 255, 276; William, junior, 131, 133, 134, 138, 142, 146, 148, 150, 151, 154-5, *161*, 162, 181-4, 191, 192, 206, 208-10, 218, 228, 229, 230, 232, 236, 237, 238, 239, 240, 243, 256, 263-4, 265, 275, 276, 279; William Alan, 190, 232, 253, 263, 293. See also Ebenezer and Mary Maitland.
Funerals, 37, 55-7, 77-8, 105, 108, 137, 138, 139, 143fn., 157, 210, 254, 276

Gaffee, Benjamin, 196
Gaffee, Mrs., 196
Gailer, Miss, 285
Gall End, 284
Gallipoli, 253
Gardening Club, 309
Gardner, Colonel Alan, 163fn., 169, 236; Lord Alan and Lady Julia, 161, 163fn.; Clarence, 163fn.; Herbert, 162, 163fn., 169, 181, *182*, 183-5, 191
Garth House, Builth Wells, 158, 161
Gas, 146, 150, 151, 256, 272, 275-6, 291, 194. See also Stansted Gas Company and Bishop's Stortford Gas Company.
Gatwick Airport, 9, 313, 314, 316
Gawthorp, 253, 280
Gayford, H.H., *231*, 240
General Strike, 267-8
Geology, 3
George II, King, 78
George IV, King, 177, 229-30
George V, King, 232, 256, 275, 288, 289
German East Africa, 253
German Prisoners of War, 257
Gernon, Robert, 4, 10, 31-2, 39
Gernon, Robert the younger, 32-3
Giffyn, James, 85
Gilbeys, vii, 10, 172, 227, 228, 236, 240, 265; Alfred, 145, 165, 167; Daniel, 166; Guy, 239; Henry, father of Walter Gilbey, 166-7; Henry Parry, 145, 149, 151, 152, *165,* 166, 167, 169, 173, 181, 184, 202, 206, 261; Tresham and his wife, *152*, 188; Walter, 138, 145, *165,* 166-7, *168*, 169, 181, 218, 226, 237, 239, 245, 265, 268
Gilbey, Widow, 106

332

W & A Gilbey, 165, 167, 172, 181, 202, 228, 261, 265
Gillons, 265
Girls' Friendly Society, 140-2, 225, 287
Gladstone, William, 162, 167, 181, 182, 183, 184, 187, 189
Glasgow, 264
Godefroy, Marian Annetta, *281*, 282
Godfrey, Ann, 243
Godfrey, Charlotte, 247
Golds, vii, 10, 172, 189, 209-10, 227, 229, 236, 240, 265, 266, 267, 270; Amy and Sydney, 265; Archie, 265; Sir Charles, *152*, 166, 167, *168, 169*, 181, 185, 187, 188, 189, 190, 191, 232, 243, 253, 265, 279; Charles, son of Sir Charles, 253, 265, 282; Donald, 289; Gerald, 188, 228, 257; Guy, 188-90; Henry, 167; Madge, 287, 289; Philip, 188-90, 237; Walter, *152*, 174, 255, 265, 271, 272, 279-80, 290
Golding, Catharina, 97-8
Golf, 7, 237, 287
Gomme, 'Brother', 137
Gonville and Caius College, Cambridge, 99
Gooday, G.O., 150
Goodchild, Ethelbert, *139*, 211, *279*, 279-80, 281
Goring, Lord, 68
Gorsefield, 296, 304
Goslings, vii, 4, 119, 131, 132, 157, 235, 243, 264, 269, 287; Mr., 297; Alfred, 188, 189; Cunliffe, 255; Robert, 182, 183, 188, 235; William, 85, 117; Colonel William, 269
Grant, Richard, 86, 98, 101, 113, 195, 204, 206
Grave, Valentine, 86
Gray, Bert, 299
Gray, Charles, 189, 190
Gray, Frances, 102
Gray, George, 151
Gray, Henry, 244
Great Chesterford, 25, 26, 29fn.
Great Depression, 269-70
Great Eastern, bus company, 270
Great Eastern Railway, 147, 149
Great Easton, 267
Great Hallingbury, 4, 24, 127fn., 209, 271, 275, 315
Great Hormead, 94
Great Rebuilding, 83
Great Sampford, 61, 73
Greens, 15, 170, 172, 202, 203, 209, 240, 283; Green and Marsh, 14, 149, 172, 230, 241; Elizabeth, Joseph's wife, 202; Elizabeth, Joshua's wife, 14, 202; Harford, 6, 146-7, 150, 151, *152*-3, 155, 157, 162, 166, 169, 170, 173-4, 192, 193, 206, 225, 227, 229, *230*, *231*, 232, 240, 243, 275; Henrietta, 173; Joseph Joshua, 10, 14, 15, 16, 21-22, 26, 88, 92fn., 94, 107, 145, 146, 151, 154, 158, 160, 161, 170, 171-2, 173, 181, 184, 202, 207, 221, 225, 228, 266; Joshua, 14, 15, 145, 146, 151, 161, *171*, 172, 181, 183, 202, 220, 223, 224, 225, 228, *230*, 266; Joshua Green and Company, 14, 149, 170
Green's meadow, 237, 238, 286
Greens Motor and Transport Company, 173
Green's Stores, 6, 146, *171*, 173, 174, 266, 270, 272, 276, 305, 307
Green, John, 94
Greenfields, 4
Griggs, 118, 121; Alf, 190; Hannah, 98; Stephen, 130, 131; William, 131
Grinlings, 227: Henry, 167
Grocers, Company of, 53, 55, 56, 57
Grosvenor, Victoria, 141
Grove Hill, 187, 296
Grover, William, 88, 171
Guides, 288, 302
Guy Fawkes, 219
Gypsies, 246-7
Gyver, Thomas, 47

Haddesley, Edwin, 94
Haggard, Rider, 129
Haggerwood, Arthur, 245
Hales, schoolmaster, 99
Hall, Peter, 314
Halls, Robert, 102
Hamme, 32, 33
Hampton Court, 68
Hanau, 152
Hankau, 173
Harbridge, Reg, 301
Hargrave House, 78, *165*, 166, 167, 170, 192, 229, 260, 265-6, 270, 271, 301, 308
Hargrave Park, 169, 339, 238, 265, 286, 291, 296, 301, 305-6, 309
Harlakenden, Roger, 51, 63
Harlow, 133, 223, 238, 272
Harmonica Boys, 289
Harrett, Mr., 282
Harrington, Thomas, 246
Harris, 'old', 105
Hartford, Connecticut, 63
Harvest Festivals and Horkies, 201, 231, 232-3
Harvey, Audrey, 285
Harvey, Sir Eliab, 71-2
Harwich, 72, 177, 181
Hassobury Estate, 132, 269
Hastings, 148
Hastings, Battle of, 32
Hatfield Broadoak, 62
Hatfield Forest, 36, 140
Havis, Richard, 23

Hawkins, John, 53
Hawthorns, 265, 272
Haynes, Miss, 283
Haynes, Dr. W.F., 138, 146, 151, 208-9, 252-3
Headland, John, 105
Heard, Thomas, 66
Heaths, 4, 10, 77-80, 93, 116; Bayley, son of Thomas, 78, 85, 95, 101; Bayley, brother of last William, 78-9, 111, 116, 157; Bridget, 78; Thomas of Mile End, purchaser of estate, 72, 77-8, 80fn.; Thomas, first William's uncle, 77; first William, Thomas's father, 77; last William, son of Bayley and Bridget, 78, 108, 111, 117
Heathrow Airport, 9, 312, 313, 314, 315, 316
Hedgerows, 13, 41, 83, 257, 272, 287, 308
Helham, Robert, 50
Hempstead, 61
Henham, 74, 118, 123, 127fn., 205, 271, 297, 305
Henry I, King, 32
Henry II, King, 33, 34-5
Henry III, King, 36
Henry V, King, 43
Henry VII, King, 39, 49
Henry VIII, King, 47, 49
Hertford, 35, 36, 112
Hertfordshire, 3, 11, 31, 33, 35, 61, 64, 99, 112, 123, 127fn., 146, 154, 157, 241fn., 254, 260, 269
Hertfordshire, proposed transfer to, 1, 153-5, 210
Hertfordshire Regiment, 260
Herts and Essex High School for Girls, 284, 294, 310
Herts and Essex Observer, 14, 22, 131, 132-3, 142, 145, 188, 201, 224, 267
Heydon, 54
Heylin, Rowland, 55
Hicks, 175, 221; Alfred, 203, *230*; Charles, 123, 131, 252, *230* (these references may be to more than one man); Edward, 129, 148, 179; Thomas, 181, *230, 231*
High Barcaple, Kirkudbright, 158
High Commission, 62
High Easter, 118
High Lane, 6, 272
High Sheriff of Essex, 78
Hill, Josephine, 291fn.
Hobart, Miles, 55
Hoby, Charles, 228
Hockerill, 9
Hockerill Highway Turnpike Trust, 89, 148
Hoffman Ball Bearing factory, 299
Hole Farm, 41, 83, 119, 131, 259, 269, 308
Holme-Eden, near Carlisle, 207
Home Guard (WW2), 306
Home Rule Party, 183
Home Secretary, 129, 131, 232
'Homicide Hayden', 305

Homing Society, 287
Honeywood, John Lamotte, 71-2
Hope, Bob, 304
Hopkins, Matthew, 94
Hops, 86
Houblons, 4
House of Commons, 59fn., 154, 155, 179, 225, 267, 281
Houses of Correction, 93 (Saffron Walden), 94 (Newport)
House on the Hill Toy Museum, 308
House of Lords, 169, 185, 191
Housing, 4, 91, 143, 145, 146, 148, 271, 273fn., 307, 308
How and Salmons, 269
Howard, G.W.F., 241
Howard, Lord, 111
Howsden, Arthur, 99
Hoxton, 142, 157, 196
Hubbard, Edward, 51, 99; Francis, 51, 63; Margaret (Harlakenden by marriage), 63
Hubbard's charity, 108
Hubbert, Richard, 71
Hucks, Bentfield, *260*, 261
Hucks, Bill, 261
Hudgell, Sid, 267
Huguenots, 55
Humphreys, Rita, 312
Humphries, Edward, 134
Hundreds, 27
Hunsdon, Herts, 112
Hunstanton, 148
Hunting, 21, 23, 33, 36, 43, 58-9, 188, 235-6, 241fn., 269, 286
Hussey, Stephen, 130-1, 132
Hutchens, J.J.K., 203
Hutley, 244
Hutley, William, 187-8

Iceni, 25-6
Ilger, John, 49
Illegitimate children, 94, 98, 102, 104, 163fn.
Imperial Yeomanry, 188
India, 204
Ingles, Bessie, 225
Inns, 10, 91, 308. See also individual inns.
Inquest, 126, 174, 268
Ireland, 49, 112, 141
Irish Home Rule, 162, 183-4
Iron Age, 23, *24*, 26, 28
Isandlhwana, 163fn.

Jacksons, 266; Claud Stewart, 265; Sir Thomas and Lady Jackson, 170, 255, 266
Jacobite uprising (1745), 78

INDEX

Jacosa, 37
Jagger, Illingworth, *282*, 290
Jamaica, 78
James I, King, 51, 54, 62
James II, King, 71-2
Jenewaie, Mr. at Manuden
Jocelyne, Emma, 126
Johannesburg, 189
John, King, 5, 7, 10, 35, 37, 38fn., 309
Johns, Charlie, 293
Johnson, Hewlett, 'Red Dean of Canterbury', 300
Johnson, Marion, 281; Tom, 281, 284
Johnson, Winnie, 299
Jolly, Mr., 193-4
Jones, John, 68
Jordan, *231*
Jordan, Mary, 124
Jordan, May, 270
Joslin, 244
Joslyn, Sir Thomas, 48, 52fn.
Joslyn, Thomas, 48, 52fn.
Jubilees, royal, 172, 229, *230*, *231*, 232, 275, 286, 288, 289, 309, 312fn.
Judd, Peter, his wife, 103
Judd, Walter, 245
Judson, Jonathan, 86
Julius Caesar, 25
Junior Imperial League, 266, 267
Justices of the Peace/magistrates, 11, 70, 92, 93, 95, 102, 108, 118, 121, 149, 158, 160, 174, 227, 243, 245, 247, 264, 266

Kaiser Wilhelm, 260
Keddie, John, 151, 188-9, 190
Keen, Goodman, 87
Keen, Harry, 104
Kelvedon, 133
Kemp, Sergeant, 246
Kent, 27, 41, 68
Kerry family, 218
Kimberley, 187
King, Mr., surgeon, 104
King's Arms, 83, 105, 130, 131, 223, 224, 246, 305
'King's Evil', 105
Kipling, Rudyard, 188
Kitchener, Herbert, 187, 189, 251, 253, 293, 294
Klein, Thomas, 300
Kruger, Paul, 187

Labour Party, 266-7, 269, 283, 311, 314, 316
Lacey, Emma, 245
Lacey, John de, 35
Ladysmith, 187
Laing's Nek, 187
Lamb, Mr. Sidney, 188

Lancaster Chapel, 39, 51, 58, 263
Lancaster, John and Annora de, 39, 40
Lancaster, Roger and Philippa de, 39, *40*
Lanes, 5, 6, 13, 83. See also individual lanes.
Langford, Frances, 304
Langham, Sir Stephen, 98
Langley, 283
Lansbury, George, 267
Laud, William, 62, 67
Laughlin, Richard, 51
Law, Arthur, 254
Law, Police Constable, 245
Lay Subsidy (1327), 40
Layman, Elizabeth, 98
League of Nations and League of Nations Union, 290
Leeds, Mary, 75; Thomas, 74, 75; William, Daniel and Thomas, sons of Thomas and Mary, 75
Leigh, John, 86
Leighs Priory, 62
Leonard, Graham, 291fn
Levellers, 67
Levey, Alice, 217
Levey, Aubrey, 269, 280, 281, 283, 284, 289, 293
Levey, Henry, 253
Levey, Thomas, 134
Levey, Tom, 220
Liberal Democrats, 311, 312
Liberal Unionists, 162, 183, 184
Liberals, 10, 15, 133, 145, 160, 161, 162, 164, 166, 169, 173, 174, 181-5, 187, 189, 190, 191, 192, 193, 203, 204, 227, 266, 267, 275, 284, 311
Liernur and Liernur Syndicate, 151, *152*, 275
Lighting, 151, 275-6, 312
Lime Kiln Lane, 5, 6, 22, 272
The Limes, 166, 265
Lincoln, Battle of, 35
Lincoln Regiment, 258
Lindley, 189
Lindon House, 109fn.
Linward, William and Mary, 98
Listed buildings, 13
Literacy, 99-100
Little, George., *231*, 243
Little, R.B., 150
Little Easton, 267
Little Hallingbury, 72, 85, 124, 127fn., 275
Little Sampford, 73
Littlebury, 38fn., 59, 94
Liverpool, 134, 206
Local Government Act (1888), 150
Local Government Act (1894), 150, 191
Local Government Board, 152, 153, 154, 155
Local Government (Boundaries) Act (1887), 154
Lockie, Mr. (preacher), 62. See also Gervase Lockey, 69fn.

INDEX

Loder, Charles, 188
Lollards, 44, 61
London, 3, 4, 9, 10, 13, 15, 26, 27, 33, 34, 35, 41, 51, 53, 54, 55, 56, 64, 67, 68, 71, 72, 75, 77, 78, 83, 85, 88, 89, 90, 91, 104, 105, 117, 124, 142, 147-8, 152, 156fn., 157, 161, 166, 167, 168, 189, 196, 197, 219, 225, 226, 228, 234fn., 235, 267, 268, 294-5, 296, 301, 307, 308, 309, 313, 314
London, Bishop of, 14, 42, 47, 62, 102, 291fn.
London, City of, 54, 55, 56, 57
London, Diocese of, 27, 97, 206
London, Lord Mayor of, 42, 53, 54-5, 148, 168 (and Lady Mayoress)
London Metropolitan Archives, 14
London and North Eastern Railway (LNER), 267-8
London and Stansted Furnishing Company, 270
Long, Eustace, 155, *203*, 204, 207, 232
Lord Lieutenant of Essex, 111; Deputy Lieutenant, 65
Lorraine, Robert, 188
Lostwithiel, 158
Louis VIII, King of France, 35
Lovell, *231*
Lower Street, 6, *7*, 84, *139*, 166, 202, 205, 213, 214, 215, 216, 232, 233, *252*, 272, 275, 282, 284, 294, 295, 296, 306, 307, 309, 310
Lower Woodfield area, 151
Luard, Canon Thomas, 139, 140, 173, 202, *205*, 206, 215-6, 217, 218, 223, 226, 228, 230
Luard, Jane, 12, 206, 215-6, 217, 218. See also Mrs. Luard's Boot Club, 142.
Luckeys, 253; George, 237
Lucking, Mr., of Takeley, 61
Luddington, 61
Luther, Martin, 43
Luther, John, 78
Lyly, John, 52fn.
Lytton, Lord, 227

Macaulay, Lord, 204
Mafeking, 187, 189
Magistrates, see under Justices of the Peace.
Magna Carta, 4-5, 35-36, 38fn., 154, 184, 309
Maidstone, 68
Maitland, Ebenezer and Mary, 157
Majuba, 187
Maldon, 177, 181
Mallon, J.J., 266
Malteby, John de, 44fn.
Manchester Airports Group (MAG), 313
Manchester, Earl of, 64
Mandubracius, 25
Manitoba, 134
Manning, Miss, 192
Manor House, 6, 276, 280

Manor house, 37, 47
Manors and manorial courts: 11, 13, 21, 27, 31, 33, 37, 38fn., 41, 42, 47, 86, 93, 101, 263, 265; Bentfield Bury, vii, 4, 13, 27, 31-2, 38fn., 39, 40, 42, 78, 117, 157, 182, 264; Burnells, 39; Elsenham Hall, 78; Great Dunmow, 42; Stansted/Stansted Hall, 4, 13, 27, 31-2, 39, 40, 42, 51, 62, 70, 86, 117, 157, 263; Thremhall Priory, 4, 13, 39, 40, 41, 42; Walden, 42; Warish Hall, Takeley, 41, 42; Wyrardisbury, 38fn.
Manuden, 4, 5, 31, 38fn., 40, 44, 61, 66, 74, 85, 92fn., 108, 123, 127fn., 129, 131, 132, 133fn., 147, 245, 271, 283, 285, 287, 297
Manuden Hall, 132
Mapleton, Roger, 48
Maplin, 314
Markewell, Richard, 86
Marquis d'Orsy, 288-9
Marriages, royal, 63, 218, 226, 230
Marsh, James, 14, 149, 151, 172, 181, 221, 223, 225, See also Green and Marsh.
Marshall, Dorothy, 103
Marshall, William, 48
Mary MacArthur Home 266, 306
Mary MacArthur Trust, 266
Mary Murray's School, 213
Mary I, Queen, 48, 50
Mary, wife of George V, Queen, 232, 266
Maryon, John, 109fn.
Matthews family, 267
Maxton, Jimmy, 267
May, Jeremiah, 65
May, Robert, 179, 197-9
Maynard, Lord William, 55, 56
Maynard, Mary (née Myddelton), 55, 66
Maynard, Sir John, 55, 56, 59fn., 66, 69
McBride, Jean, 295, 299, 301, 305
McKinney, Alexander, *206*
Mead, Norman, 315
Merchant Adventurers, 56
Merioneth, 68
Messing, 68
Metal detectorists, vii, 21, 28
Metropolitan police, 129
Meyer, Lady, 193
Mica Manufacturing Company, 146, 147, 149, 156fn., 241, 269
Middleditch, 241
Middlesex, 27, 31, 161, 296
Midwives, 89, 97, 105
Mildmay, Colonel Henry, 71-2
Mile End, 72, 77
Milford, Connecticut, 63
Military Service Act (1916), 252
Militia, 14, 69, 70, 93, 111-2, 113, 133, 251

336

Millais, John, 160
Mills: watermills, 5, 32; windmills, 6, *83*, 92fn., *159*, 265, 309
Millside, 310
Milton, John, blacksmith, 71
Mincing Lane, 53
Ministry of Civil Aviation, 313
Ministry of Food, 256
Minstrel Troupes, 227, 228
Mitchell, Mr., 284
Mitchell, William Foot, 266-7
Molloy, Rev. James, 254
Mont House, 275
Montfichets, 4, 10, 31-7, 39, 43, 47, 77, 309; Aveline de, 39; Gilbert de, 33, 34, 35; Richard de, the first,, 33, 35; Richard de, the second, 4, 7, *9*, 35-7, 39, 53, 154, 184, 309; William de, the first, 32-33, 34, 38; William de, the second, 33; William de, the third, 33
Montfichet's Tower in London, 33, 34, 35
Montfiquet, village in Normandy, 32, 35
Montreal, 134
Montville, 251, 258
Morant, Philip, 32, 33, 39, 47, 52fn., 71
Mordaunt, Edward, 48
Mothers' Union, 287
Moule, 272
Mount, Lieut-Col. A.H.L, 267
Much Hadham, 123, 127fn.
Mudge, Elizabeth, 97
Muilman, Peter, 59, 79, 89, 91
Mumford, Daniel, 112
Mumford, Jane, 126
Munchall, John, 196
Music, 15, 55, 99, 140, 141, 148, 149, 188, 190, 206, 219, 223, 226, 228, 239, 241, 244, 252, 264, 279, 281, 282, 285, 287, 288, 289, 299, 309
Myddeltons, 4, 10, 77, 79, 82, 83, 93; Anne, 55; Elizabeth, widow of John Olmestede, 55; Elizabeth, widow of Miles Hobart, 55; Henry, 55; Hester, wife of first Sir Thomas, 53, 55; Hester Salusbury, daughter of first Thomas, 55, 57-8, 61; Hugh, 54; Mary, 55; Peter, 56; Richard, father of first Thomas, 53; Richard, son of first Thomas, 55; Richard 56; Stephen, 72; the first Thomas at Stansted, 51, *53*-9, 61, 62, 63, 82; Thomas at Chirk Castle, 55, 61, 65, 66, 67, 68, 69, 71; second Thomas at Stansted, 71-2, 77, 82, 98, 101; third Thomas at Stansted, 72, 86; Timothy, 55, 61, 64-9, 71, 92fn., 93; William, 51
Mylburne, John, 65
NAAFI, 301
Napoleon, 112
Nash, Edward, 95, 104
National Agricultural Labourers Union (NALU), 132-3, 137, 218
National Egg Collection, 256
National Fire Service, 276
National Gallery, 11, 160
National Insurance Act (1911), 126-7, 140
National Salvage Council, 256
National Society for the Promotion of the Education of the Poor in the Principles of the Established Church, 213, 215
Navy, Merchant, 300
Navy, Royal, 111, 112, 293
Nelson, Horatio, 226
New Model Army, 65, 67
New River Company, 54
New Zealand, 192, 228, 253
Newfoundland, 141
Newman, Thomas, 149, 150, 208-9
Newmarket, 9, 10, 89, 148, 153. See also Newmarket Road under Roads.
Newport, 4, 65, 93, 95, 130, 147, 156fn., 193, 203, 238, 307
Newport Deanery, 73, 206
Newport Grammar School, 99, 284, 310
Newport House of Correction, 93, 95
Newspapers, 224
Nicholl, Sir Robert, 253
Nightingale, Sir Thomas, 65
Nockolds, J.O., 135fn.
Noel, Conrad, 267, 288
Nonconformists, 73, 81, 101, 150, 158, 199, 201-3, 206, 213, 214, 280, 281, 283, 289. See also Churches and Chapels.
Nooitgedacht, 189
Norman, C.A., 151
Norman, Luther, *152*, 153-4, *231*, 272, 275, 277
Norman House, 5, 290
Normandy, 34, 35, 293
Normans, 4, 7, 10, 21, 22, 27, 31-8
North-Met Electricity Company, 276
North West Essex and East Herts Preservation Association (NWEEHPA), 313-4, 315, 317
North West Territories, Canada, 134
Norton, Sir George, 48
Norwich, 9, 147-8
Nothage, John, 85
Nottingham, 263

Oakshott, George, 139, 140, 155, 209, *210*, 214, 279
Odd Fellows, 130
Okehampton, Devon, 174
Old Age Pension Act (1908), 126, 140
Old Bell, 6, 92fn., 308
Oliver, Ernest, 275; Oliver, Joan, 290
Olmested, John, 55
Onslow, Countess of, 163fn.

INDEX

Onslow, Earl of, 236
Onslow, Sir Richard, 72
Orange Free State, 187, 188
Orchards, 4, 86, 87, 107
Order of Ancient Shepherds, 137, *138,* 139, 140
Oswald, Rev., *152*
Oxford, 64, 148, 162, 290. See also de Veres, Earls of Oxford.
Oxford Street, London, 167

Pache, Letice, 49
Packer, Mr., 107
Palladium, 24, *25*
Palmer, Abraham, 104
Palmer, Nathaniel, 245
Palmer's charity, 108
Pamplin Brothers, 269
Pankhurst, Christabel, 193
Pantheon in Oxford Street, 167
Parish magazine, 14, 210, 211, 280
Parish Room, 228, 259
Park Place, Henley, 158
Park Road, 271, 306
Parker, George, 135fn.
Parker, Robert le, 40-1
Parkers, 42
Parnell, Charles, 183
Parris, William, 123, 130, 131, 135fn.
Parrott, John, hermit, 43
Parsons, Nicholas, 309
Patmore, Albert, 253
Patmore, Charles, 130
Patmore, Charles, 254-5
Patmore, Eliza, 220
Patmore, Ellen, 220
Patmore, George, 124
Patmore, Joyce, 271
Patterson, John, 236
Pay, Sydney, and Mrs. Pay, *282,* 290
Payne, Parnel, 95fn.
Peachey, George, 243
Peacock, John, and his wife, 104
Peasants' Revolt, 39, 41-2, 43, 44
Pease, Joseph, 190
Peck's gift, 108
'Pelham', 283
Pembroke, Earl of, 36
Peninsular War, 112
Pennington Lane, 5, 6, 272
Penny Readings, 160, 223, 225-6, 227
Perceval, Lord, 77
Pest house, 15, 104, 123, 127fn.
Pesterford Bridge, 297
Petty Sessions, 93, 126, 243, 246. See also Justices of the Peace.

Pevensey, 78
Philadelphia, 75
Phillips family, 259, 295; Alec, 267, 272; Alfred, 243, 251, 257, 267, 272, 283, 285; Alice, 258; Ralph, 80fn., 148
Phillips, Edridge, 119, 121-2
Phillips, Elizabeth, 119
Phillips, Mr., 107
Phillips, Richard, 105
Philpott, Peter, 293
Pimblett, William, 208, 209
Plague, 21, 28, 41, 82
Player, David, 149
Playz, Hugh de, 35, 39
Playz, Margaret de, 40
Playz, Philippa de, 39
Pledgdon, 40, 288
Poaching, 16, 117, 241, 243-5, 259, 290
Police, 15, 124, 126, 130, 131, 184, 194, 240, 243, 245, 246, 252, 257, 290, 298, 300, 304
Polo, 236, 287
Poole, James, 112
Poole, Robert, 195
Poorhouse, 104, 107, 127fn., 129
Poor Law Commissioners, 118, 121, 124, 125
Poor Law, New, 11, 108, 121, 123-7, 129, 140, 154, 276
Poor Law, Old, 11, 89, 94, 95, 102-7, 118, 123, 124
Poplar, 102
Population, 10, 11, 21, 23, 27, 28, 32, 33, 37, 38fn, 40, 41, *81,* 106, 117, 124, 132, 143, 147, 148, 149, 151, 156fn., 251, 270, 271, 273fn., 307, 310
Portland Square, 168
Portugal, 112, 169
Post Office, 145, 193, 225, 227, 237, 293
Potash Cottages, 92fn., 299
Potts, George, 149
Powell, George, 244
Power, Alfred, 124
Poyntz, Ferdinando, 53, 55
Prague, 152
Preston, 68
Pretoria, 189
Pretty, Mr., 284, 286
Primrose League, 184, 267
Prince of Wales: see Edward VII
Prior, W, *231*
Prior, Walter, 255. This may be the same man as the previous entry.
Prior, William, 245
Privy Council, 62
Proby (father and son), 266
Protestant Reformation Society, 207
Protestants, 48-50, 61, 66, 207, 210. See also Churches and Chapels.

Pulteneys, 169-70, 172, 182, 206, 226, 228, 229, 239, 240, 279; Arthur, 279; Emma, 169; Richard, 169; Lieutenant General Sir William, 169, 251, 260-1
Pump Field, 6, 257, 301
Punch, 130, 131
Puritans, 49, 50, 51, 54, 55-56, 61-7, 94, 207, 280-1
Putterill, Jack, 267

Quaker Act (1662), 74
Quarter Sessions, 14, 93-5, 112, 150, 246, 264
Quendon, 72, 74, 81

RAC, 154
Race relations, 305
Rackham, Oliver, 13
'Radical Stansted', 10, 162, 181-5, 191, 263
Radio, 272
Radwinter, 25, 64
Railway, vii, 4, 6, 9-10, 16, 129, 133, 145-9 (Including *147*), 151, 156fn., 167, 170, 219, 235, 246, 268, 297, 304, 308. See also Eastern Counties Railway Company, Great Eastern Railway and LNER.
Raleigh, Walter, 54
Ralphs, Miss, 191-2
Ramsey, William, 151
Ranjitsinhji, 240
Rarotonga, 203
Ratcliffs, 220; Albert, 275; Annie, 220; Harry, 220
Ratcliff, Jim, 297-9, 304-5
Ratcliffe, A., *231*
Rationing, WW1, 256; WW2, 305-6
Raven, George, 130
Raven, John, 130
Ravens, 265
Rayne, 133
Raynsford, Robert, 108
Reader, Frank, 14, 59fn., 69fn.
Rechabites, 283
Recreation Ground, 16, *159*, 160, 190, 233, 238, 253, 259, 260, 272, 275, 280, 281, 284, 297, 312
Red Cross, 264, 300, 302
Redford, Josiah, 195, 197-9, 282
Redvers-Buller, 187
Reform Act (1832), 179, 181, 224
Reform Act (1867), 181
Reform Act (1884), 181-2, 183
Reformation, 43, 44, 47-52
Reid, Widow, 105
Revolt of 1173-4, 34-5
Reynolds, I, *231*
Reynolds, John, vicar, 75, 86-7, 92fn., 98-9, 108
Reynolds, John, 97
Rich family, 62

Rich, Lord, 48
Rich, Robert, Earl of Warwick, 62, 64
Richard I, King, 35
Richard II, King, 41-2, 43
Richardson, J, *231*
Rickling, 74, 94
'Riot' in Stansted (1834), 108, 117-21, 129, 177, 247; food riots in 1795 in Saffron Walden, Thaxted, Dunmow and Bishop's Stortford, 111, 118
Roads, 272; Cambridge/Great Newmarket/Turnpike/A11/B1383, 4, 5, 6, *9,* 10, 71, 88, 89, 90-1, 101, 129, 148, 150, 151, 153, 154, 166, 195, 198, 201, 202, 203, 233, 240, 258, 271, 272, 283, 290, 296, 397, 308, 310; M11, 4, 5, 8, 10, 13, 308; Silver Street, 6, 109fn., 151-2, 169, 195, 200, 254, 282; Stane Street/B1256, 5, 9, 10, 13, 22, 25, 26-7, 35, 36. See also Alsa Street, Bentfield End Causeway, Bradford Street, Bury Lodge Lane, Chantry Road (Bishop's Stortford), Chapel Hill, Church Road, Elsenham Road, Forest Hall Road, High Lane, Lower Street, Oxford Street (London), Park Road, South Street (Bishop's Stortford), St. John's Road; West Road.
Road safety, 290
Roberts, Lord, 187, 188-9
Robertson, John, 105
Robinson, Sarah, 102
Rochester, Diocese of, 206
Rochford's Nurseries, 146, 147, 148, 149, 266, 297, 301, 308
Rocky's Disco, 309
Rodgers, Audrey, 295-6, 299, 301, 302, 305
Roger in the Hale, 41
Rogers, Daniel, 62; Richard, 50, 62; Samuel, 62
Rogues and vagabonds, 94-5, 126
Romans, 9, 13, 21-2, 24-8, 29fn.
Rome, 25, 35, 43
Rose and Crown, 6, *91,* 92fn., 137, 308
Rose, George, 297
Rosebery, Earl of, 162, 184
Roskill Commission, 314, 317
'Rough element', 227, 241, 245-6, 290
'Rough music', 247
Rowden, Rev. F., 246
Rowell, Irvine, 174, 237, 240
Rowley, Mr., 104
Royal Academy, 160
Royal Agricultural Society, 150, 167
Royal celebrations, 229-32
Royal Commission on Historical Monuments, 83, 162
Royal Commission on Tuberculosis, 11, 169
Royal Declaration of Indulgence (1672), 73
Royal National Orthopaedic Hospital, 288

INDEX

RSPCA, 247
Rugby, 287
Rule, 'Poor', 106
Rumbold, Edward, 62
Runnymede, 35, 38fn.
Rush, J.A., 157
Rush's charity, 108
Russia, 300
Ryanair, 315
Rydley, schoolmaster, 99

Sacroticus, 26
Saffron Walden and Saffron Walden constituency, 4, 9, 11, 28, 40, 42, 61, 63, 64, 67, 75, 81, 93, 105, 111-2, 113, *120*, 124, 126, 127fn., 133, 160, 162, 167, 169, 181, 182, 183, 184, 189, 191, 192, 193, 203, 223, 237, 238, 243, 244, 252, 253, 264, 266-7, 272, 275, 309, 310, 311
Saffron Walden Agricultural Society, *120*, 121
Saffron Walden Infantry, 112, 113
Saffron Walden Rural District Council, 264, 275, 311
Saggers, David, 134
Salisbury, Lord, 189
Saltonstall, Richard, 53
Salusbury, Henry, 55, 58; Hester, 55, *58*, 61
Sanders, 220, 297; Arthur, builder, 149; Arthur, grocer, 202; Guiver, 198; Hannah, 105; Hubert, 297; Irving, 14, 15, *16*, 307, 311-2; Jane, 104; John, 104, 105; Kath, 297
Sandford, Andrew, 63; Robert, 63; Thomas, 63; Zachariah, 63, 69fn.
Sapseed, George, 118-21
Sapseed, William, 112
Sarl (Searle?), widow, 104
Saunders, Gwen, 301
Savages, 83
Savell, George, 84; John senior, 84; John junior, 84
Savil/Savill, Widow, 104, 106
Savill, John, 119, 121
Saville, Mary, 105
Saville, William, 63
Savings Bonds (WW2), 301
Savings Certificates (WW2), 301
Sawbridgeworth, 4, 123, 127fn., 238
Sawell, John, 49-50
Sawyer, Alfred, 270
Saxons, 3, 21, 27-28, 29fn., 31, 83, 311
Says, Goody, 104
Scarfe, Norman, 58
Schooling, Samuel, and his wife, 103, 104
Schools and education generally, 10, 97, 99, 134, 142, 145, 149, 210, 213, 214, 223, 231, 233, 237, 240, 256, 257, 264, 266, 282, 283, 299, 301, 306, 309
Schools in Stansted: Adult school in Cambridge Road, 283; Anglican/National School/Church School/St. Mary's Church of England Foundation Primary, 6, 14, 99, 100, 134, 195, 201, 205, 213, 214-20, 227, 238, 259, 275, 279, 283-6, 294, 300, 310; Bentfield Primary, 6; British School/Independent/Council School, 6, 99, 100, 160, 195, 201, *204*, 213, 214, 218, 221, 259, 275, 283-6, 294, 295, 299, 300, 306fn., 310; Burnt Mill Academy Trust, 310; Forest Hall, 6, *311;* proposed free school, 51, 99; Mary Murray's, 213; school run by Mordaunt White and his wife, 99, 177, 213; Mountfitchet Mathematics and Computing College, 310, 311; Mountfitchet School, 241fn.; Night School for Boys, 217; private schools in Stansted and dame schools, 99, 214, 283; Sunday schools, 173, *200*, 201-2, 207, 218, 279, 281, 282, 283; Welsh's charity school for girls, 213
Schools outside Stansted: Ackworth, 15; Bishop's Stortford workhouse, 124; Cambridge Technical School, 310; Clapton County Secondary School for Girls, 294; Felsted, 78; Friends' School, Saffron Walden, 192; school for orphans in London, 157; public schools, 283; Sidcot, 15. See also under Bishop's Stortford Grammar School, Herts and Essex High School for Girls, Bishop's Stortford, and Newport Grammar School.
Scotland and Scots, 40, 63-4, 65, 68, 141, 157, 158, 160, 163fn., 167, 280
Scott, Peter, 309
Scouts, 141, 266, 288, 300, 309
Seamer, John, 106, 123, 127fn
Selwin-Ibbetson, Sir Henry and Lady, 236
Seymour, Hilda, 162, 271, 272
Seyyid Mustafa Ben-Yusuf, 226, 234fn.
Shakespeare, William, 25, 226
Shepherd, Ward, 102
Shepphard, Elizabeth, 102
Shinwell, Emmanuel, 267
Ship Money, 63, 64, 92fn.
Shire Horse Society, 167
Shooting, 235-6, 244, 263, 286-7
Shoreditch, 148
Shymplynge, Thomas de, 44fn.
Sibbly, Thomas, 48
Sign, village, 4, *9*, 11, fn.
Silk, 102, 106-7, 150
Skatepark, 309
Skynner, William, 49
Slate, 10, 148
Slaves/serfs, 32, 78, 177, 178, 179, 196
Smallpox, 94, 104, 105, 134, 220
Smart, Joseph, 215, 217
Smiths of Bentfield End, 220

340

Smith, Albert, 153
Smith, Harold, 209, 280
Smith, James, 149
Smith, Joseph, 95fn.
Smith, W.H., shop at railway station, 304
Smith, William, 87
Smuts, Jan, 189
Smyth, John, 50
Snow, Gerald, 298
Soame, Elizabeth, 65
Soap-boiling, 88, 92fn., 171
Social Democrats, 311
Soldiers Comfort Fund, 300
Solmes, Edward, 72
South Africa, 134, 141, 187-90
South African Republic, 187
South Street, Bishop's Stortford, 228
Southall, John, 51
Southend, 256
Southend Telephones Monitors Office, 296
Southern, Samuel, 66
Spain, 112
Spaldings, 297
Spalding, George, 150
Spalding, H., 238
Spalding, Walter, 254, 259
Special Constables, WW1, 257
Speller, John, 190, 285
Spencers, 175, 182, 235, 240
Spencer, Charles, 119, 121-2, 209, *230*
Charles Spencer and Sons, 149, 150
Spencer, Frank, 138
Spencer House, 287
Spencer, William, 151, *230*, 243
Spencer-Smith, Michael, 290
Spencer-Smith, Susan, 235, 259, 269
Spion Kop, 187
Spiritualism, 4, 264
Spiritualists' National Union, 264, 308. See also Arthur Findlay College.
Spooner, Catherine, 49; Simon, Prior of Thremhall Priory, 47, 49
Springfield gaol, 93
St. Albans, Abbey of, 38fn.
St. Albans, Bishop of, 209
St. Albans, Diocese of, 206
St. Gregory, 49
St. John's Church, 4, 6, 146, 166, 169, *170*, 206, 209, 251, 260, 306, 309-10
St. John's Church gardens, 305
St. John's College, Cambridge, 99
St. John's Cottage, 258, 259
St. John's Road, 281, 310
St. Mary, 49, 50
St. Mary's Church, 4, 5, 14, 21, 22, 35, *36*, *37*, 39, *40*, 43, 47, 48, 51, 54, *57,* 58, 66, 67, 75, 77, *79*, 98, 100, 105, 158, 161, 162, 173, 190, 193-4, 195, 201, 204-5, *205*, 206, 210, 228, 231, 260, 261fn., 263, 265, 266, 276, 279, 280, 281, 286, 305, 306, 309
St. Paul's Cathedral, 37
St. Theresa's Roman Catholic Church, *310*
Stammers, C.J., 134
Stansted Amateur Dramatic and Operatic Society, 289
Stansted Brook, 3, 5, 33, 151, 158, 275
Stansted and District Liberal Association, 173, 181, 227
Stansted and District Red Cross, 300
Stansted Gas Company, 151, 172, 202
Stansted Hall (built by Myddeltons), 22, 54, *57*, 71, 78, 79, 227, 258, 260; (built by the first William Fuller-Maitland), 4, 5, *8*, 35, 77, 140, 148, 149, *160*, 161, 162, 184, 229, 230, 231, 232, 235-6, 251, 263-4, 272, 276, 286, 288, 302, 308, 309
Stansted Hall, manor: see under Manors.
Stansted (and Birchanger) Horticultural and Cottage Garden Association, 225, 229, 289
Stansted House, 158, *159*, 160, 170, 255, 263, 266, 288, 308
Stansted Literary Institution, 11, 15, 16, 145, 172, 202, 223-7, 228, 229, 230, 241, 247, 263, 283, 309
Stansted Mountfitchet Local History Society, vii, viii, 14, 16, 306fn., 309
Stansted Mountfitchet, name, 3, 4
Stansted Parish Council, 15, 134, 150, 151, 153-5, 174, 175, 191-2, 238, 257, 260, 263, 265, 270, 271, 272-3, 275-7, 284, 294, 296, 311, 312
Stansted Park, 4, 5, 33, 36, 40-1, 42, 43, 58, 59, 79, 140, 147, 161, 230, 232, 235, 238, 263
Stansted Parochial Church Council, 265, 277
Stansted Project (archaeological), 23-6, 28
Stansted Remount Depot, WW1, 257
Stansted Rural District, 255, 271
Stansted Rural District Council, 150, 151, 152-3, 155, 174, 264, 266, 271-2, 275, 276, 277
Stansted Sports Association, 265, 286
Stansted String Band, 228
Stansted Water Company, 151, 174
Stansted Working Men's Club, *139*, 185, 188, 227, 228, 232, 239, 253, 259, 260, 263, 264, 277, 288, 309. See also Stansted Social Club, 6, 166, 309
Stansted Working Men's Liberal Association, 184, 227
Stanwood, Benjamin, and wife, 75
Star Chamber, 62
Statute of Labourers (1351), 41
Steeple Bumpstead, 118
Stephens, Stephen, 16
Stepney, 134
Stevens, Mr., 225, 226

INDEX

Stock, Mr., 105-6
Stock, Thomas, 84
Stockbridge, Richard, 84
Stocking Pelham, 127fn.
Stocking Wood, 87
Stockport, 124
Stocks, 94
Stone Age, 23, 28
Stone, Widow, 104
Stoney Common, 84, 148, 271
Stoneyfield Drive, 271
Stonnerde, John, 49
Stoolball, 97
Stop Stansted Expansion, 313-6, 317
Stort Navigation, 10, 89-90
Stort, River, 3, *5*, 23, 25, 28, *84, 85*, 287
Stratford, London, 148
Street, the area, 3-4, 151, 220
Strutt, Charles, 182, 183
Strutt, J.J., 121
Stump Cross, 307
Subsidy Rolls, 13, 40-1
Suetonius Paulinus, 25-6
Suffrage, women's, 174, 191-4; Suffragettes, 192-4; Suffragists, 192-4
Sugar, 53
Sunnyside, 272
Supreme Ballroom, 309
Surplice, 48, 51, 62, 66
Surveyors (parish), 101, 230
Swash, Laura, 131, 132
Swing Riots, 108, 117-9, 121, 129, 196
Sylvester, Ellen, Ena and Margaret, 142
Syncopaters, 289

Tadman, C.A., 238
Takeley, viii, 4, 5, 21, 29fn., 31, 40, 41, 42, 61, 64, 66, 69fn., 94, 247, 313
Taxation: under Normans, 31, 38fn.; under Protectorate, 68, 71; hearth tax, 14, 81, 82, 83, 92fn.; land tax, 14, 177; Lay Subsidy (1327), 40; poll tax, 41; Ship Money, 92; window tax, 86; on wine, 167
Taylor, Redvers, 293
Tayspill House, 22
Temperance and Temperance Society, 148, 172, 173, 174, 201, 202, 203, 204, 206, 218, 283
Tempo Band, 289
Tennis, 229, 236-7, 255, 264, 286
Tesco Express, 308
Thaxted, 40, 42, 64, 68, 69fn., 72, 81, 111, 254, 267, 288
Thirty-nine Articles, 61
Thistle, Doris, 295, 296, 301, 303, 304
Thorley, 99

Thorne, George, and wife, 75
Thorne, Will, 267
Thoroughgood, John and Margaret, 50, 62, 63
Three Colts, 6, 90, 91, 92fn., 308
Thremhall Priory, 5, 9, 10, 11, 35, 36, 38fn., 40-1, 42, 43, 47, 48, 49. See also Manor of Thremhall Priory.
Thurgood, Nicholas and Thomas, 63
Thurston's steam circus, 233
Tinney, John, 298, 308
Tissiman, William, 153-4, 236, 259-60, 272, 275
Tithes, 14, 74, 75, 86-8, 92fn., 173, 195, 201, 269
Togodumnus, 25
Tollemache, A.E., 209
Tories/Conservatives, 71-2, 78, 158, 162, 171, 176-9, 181-5, 189-90, 191-2, 205, 264, 266-7, 275, 310, 311-2, 314
Torriano, Josias, 179, 201-2, 204-5, 206, 213, 223
Tottenham, 294
Tower of London, 34
Townshend, Viscount, 87
Trafalgar, battle of, 112
Transportation of convicted criminals, 93-4, 95fn., 117, 118, 130, 131, 244
Transvaal, 187, 189
Triggs, 175; Henry (senior), 155, 182, 207, *230*; Henry (junior), *230*, 240
Trinovantes, 23-4, 26
Trouville, 152
Trundle, 298
Tudor House, 83
Tunbridge, E.E., 174, *231*
Turberville, Arthur, 67, 268, *280*, 281
Turner, Don, 271, 272
Turner, Frank, 296
Turner, Jack, 287, 291fn.
Turner, James, 245
Turner, Rose, 296
Turner's Spring, 297
Turnham Green, 64
Turnips, 83, 86, 87, 243
Turnival, 'old', 105
Tweefontein, 190
Tyrell, Colonel John, 178-9
Tyler, Ann, 197
Tyler, John, 197
Tyler, Robert, 196
Tyler, Wat, 42
Tyler, William, 112

Ugley, 4, 5, 31, 40, 61, 78, 81, 84, 85, 102, 108, 123, 127fn., 147, 153, 219, 239, 246
UKIP, 311
University of the Third Age, 309
Upgrove Hill, 158

Uttlesford District, 13, 311, 312
Uttlesford District Council, 315, 316
Uttlesford, Hundred of, 27, 31, 62, 111, 311

V1 and V2 rockets, 294, 299
Valentine, George, 206-9, *209*, 210, 232, 239, 280
Valentine, Mrs., 209
Valentine's Day, 217, 219
Vercoe, Reginald, 139, 275, 280, 285
Vereeniging, Peace of, 190
Verulamium (St. Albans), 26, 27
Vestry, 14, 77, 78, 88, 101-9, 150, 195, 201, 207-9, 213, 270, 279-80
Victoria County History, 98
Victoria, Queen, 137, 172, 187, 215, 230-1, 289, 309
Vincent, William, 68, 69fn.
Viner, Harry, 287
Virginia Company, 54, 77
Volunteers in Boer War, 187, 188; in Civil War, 64-5; in French wars, 111-2, 113; in WW1, 211, 251, *252*; in WW2, 291, 293, 296, 302

Wace, 32
Wakes Colne, 94
Waldegrave, Lord, 236
Walden, Benjamin, 56
Wales, 148
Walker, Harold, 267
Walker, James, 84
Walker, Mrs. J.E., 191
Wallbury, 24
Wallingford, 158
Walpole Farm, 6, 83, 306
Walsham, John, 123
Walsingham, Francis, 53, 54, 62
Walsingham, Joyce, 47
Waltham Cross, 229
Walthamstow, 156fn.
Want, Elizabeth, 95
War Bonds, 301
War Loans, 255
War memorial, *170*, 251, 260, 261fn., 293
War Savings Association, 255
War Weapons Week, 300
Wars: Boer War, 10, 185, 187-90, 203; Civil War 10, 61-9, 71, 72, 74, 162, 225, 280; Crimean War, 167; French Wars, 10, 88, 106, 111-3, 117, 118; WW1, 10, 169, 211, 235, 251-61, 263, 266, 267, 270, 271, 272, 283, 284, 285, 286, 287, 289, 290, 293, 301, 305, 306; WW2, 10, 83, 86, 271, 293-306, 308, 313
Ward, Charles, 124
Ward, Jim, 296, 297, 299, 304, 305
Ward, Richard, 66-7, 69fn., 280-1

Ware, Osborne, 104
Warner, Andrew, 63
Warner, 'Plum', 169
Warwick, 118
Warwick, Countess of, *168*, 267
Warwick, Earl of, *168*, 239
Warwick, Earl of (Robert Rich), 62, 64
Warwick, Glyn, 14, 16, 261fn., 306fn.
Warwick, Samuel, his wife, 103
Warwick's wife, 105
Water Lane, 92fn., 151
Watermills, see under Mills.
Watney, Jack, 190
Watsons, Mr. and Mrs., 276-7, 280
Watson, Alice, 246
Watson, John, 246
Watson, Justinian, 99
Watson, Thomas, 47
Watts?, *231*
Watts, E.T., *152*, 153
Waugh, Evelyn, 162
Weaver, Mrs. Baillie, 193
Welch, Alfred, 207-8
Welch, Colonel, 230
Welch, George, 105
Welch, George, son of first George, 105, 177
Welch, George, grandson of first George, 105, 123, 223, 224, 225
Welch, Samuel, 123, 238-9, *240*
Wellesley, William, 178-9
Wellington, Duke of, 112, 178
Welpston, Elizabeth, 49
West Bergholt, 132
West Indies, 141. See also Jamaica.
Western, Charles Callis, 177-9
Western Australia, 134
Western House, 270
Wethersfield, 50
Wheathampstead, 23
Whigs, 71, 72, 77, 78, 177-9
Whipping and whipping post, 94, 95
Whist drives, 289, 306
White Bear, 6, *90*, 91, 92fn., 111, 166
White, John, 199-200
White, Mordaunt and wife, 99, 177, 213
White, Widow, 104
White, William, 243
Whybrew, John, 105
Whybrow, Charles, 257
Wicken, 243
Widdington, 245
Widrington, P.E.T., 267
Wiffen, Arthur, 247
Wigan, Oscar, 188
Wilberforce, William, 204

343

Wilkins, J, Rev., 225
Wilkins, John, *16*, 134, 158, 235-6
Wilkinson, Ellen, 267
Wilkinson, George, 245
Wilkinson, John, 51, 61, 62
William I, King, the Conqueror, 10, 31-2, 34, 38fn.
William II, King (Rufus), 33
William III and Mary, King and Queen, 72, 74
Williams, Mrs. Ival, 141
Williams, Sarah, 104
Willingale Doe, 94
Willis, George, 118-21
Wills 14, 47, 48-50, 52fn., 55, 59fn., 63, 77-8, 83-5, 87, 97, 196
Wilson, Stanley, 267, 311
Wilson, Thomas, 196-8
Winchester, 38fn.
Winchester, Bishop of, 34
Winchmore Hill, 174
Windmills, see under Mills.
Winter, Augustus Manley, *210,* 211, 253
Wiseman, Cardinal, 205
Witchcraft, 94
Witham, 129
Wodehouse, Armine, 189, 190
Women's Conservative Association, 267
Women's Institute, 287, 290, 300, 308
Women's Land Army (WW1), 256-7, 301
Women's Own, 287-8
Women's Royal Army Corps, 301
Woodfield/Woodfields, 4, 151, 160, 220, 259, 295, 296
Woodford, 94

Woodforde, James, 89
Woodley, Matthew, 129, 135fn.
Woodley, Richard, 86
Woods, 87
Wool, 74, 86, 89, 102, 103, 106, 125, 229
Woolley, Irene, *221*, 284
Woolley, John, 221, *231*, 284
Wootten, Alfred, 253
Workers' Educational Association, 308, 309
Workhouse, Bishop's Stortford, 123-6, 127fn., 128, 270
Workhouse, Stansted, 106, *107*, 109fn., 123
Wren, John, 293
Wright, owner of gravel pits, 304
Wright, George, 246
Wright, Richard and his wife, 105
Wright, Thomas, 91
Wyatt, Vera, 272
Wybrow, Elizabeth, 106
Wybrow, Henry, 105
Wycliffe, John, 44
Wylley, Richard, 84

Yarmouth, 148
Yeomans, Harry, 134
York, 150
Yorkshire, 133, 148
Young (Dyer's partner), 149 156fn., 269

Zeppelins, 257